Studies on Interdisciplinary Economics and Business - Volume IV

Özer Özçelik (ed.)

Studies on Interdisciplinary Economics and Business – Volume IV

PETER LANG

Bibliographic Information published by the Deutsche Nationalbibliothek
The Deutsche Nationalbibliothek lists this publication in the Deutsche Nationalbibliografie; detailed bibliographic data is available online at http://dnb.d-nb.de.

Library of Congress Cataloging-in-Publication Data
A CIP catalog record for this book has been applied for at the Library of Congress.

ISBN 978-3-631-84933-0 (Print)
E-ISBN 978-3-631-86049-6 (E-PDF)
E-ISBN 978-3-631-86050-2 (EPUB)
10.3726/b19054

Peter Lang – Berlin · Bern · Bruxelles · New York · Oxford · Warszawa · Wien

This publication has been peer reviewed.

www.peterlang.com

Contents

List of Contributors

Ahmet İnkaya
Ph.D., Assist. Prof., Afyon Kocatepe University, Faculty of Economics and Administrative Sciences, Department of Economics, inkaya@aku.edu.tr, ORCID:0000-0002-9426-8193

Ahmet Yanık
Ph. D. Assoc. Prof., Recap Tayyip Erdoğan University, Faculty of Economics and Administrative Sciences, Department of Accounting Finance, ahmet.yanik@erdogan.edu.tr; ORCID:000-0002-7283-2557

Ali Kestane
Ph. D. Assist. Prof., Kilis 7 Aralık University, FEAS, Department of Business Administration, alikestane@kilis.edu.tr , ORCİD: 0000-0002-7049-0354

Armağan Türk
Ph.D., Assist. Prof., Bandırma Onyedi Eylül University Faculty of Economics and Administrative Sciences, Department of Economics, aturk@bandirma.edu.tr, ORCID: 0000-0002-6646-9333

Arzu Al
Ph.D. Assoc. Prof., Marmara University, Faculty of Political Sciences, Department of International Relations, arzu.al@marmara.edu.tr, ORCID: 0000-0002-3287-3661

Belkıs Özkara
Ph.D., Professor, Afyon Kocatepe University, Faculty of Economics and Administrative Sciences, Department of Business Administration, bozkara@gmail.com, ORCID. 0000-0002-4324-9741

Berna Ak Bingül
Ph.D., Assoc. Prof., Kırklareli University, Faculty of Applied Sciences, Department of Finance and Banking, berna.akbingul@klu.edu.tr, ORCID: 0000-0002-2813-2780

Berna Dombekci Ozcelik
Ph.D., Assist. Prof., Kırklareli University, Social Sciences Vocational School, Accounting Program, dombekci@klu.edu.tr, ORCID:0000-0003-1269-4014

Cemalettin Hatipoğlu
Ph.D., Assist. Prof., Bilecik Şeyh Edebali University, Faculty of Economics and Administrative Sciences, Department of Management Information Systems, cemalettin.hatipoglu@bileck.edu.tr, ORCİD ID:0000-0002-3129-9725

Ceren Ece Göcen
Ph.D. Candidate, Marmara University, Institute of Social Sciences, Department of International Relations, cegocen26@gmail.com, ORCID: 0000-0001-8626-5808

Emre Sezici
Ph.D., Associate Professor, Kütahya Dumlupınar University, Vocational School of Social Sciences, Department of Business Administration, emre.sezici@dpu.edu.tr, ORCID: 0000-0002-9652-6511

Emre Ünver
Ph.D., emremunver@hotmail.com, Department of Business, ORCID: 0000-0002-0390-8327.

Emrullah Mete
Ph.D., Assist. Prof., Giresun University, Gorele School of Applied Science, Logistics Management, mtemrullah@gmail.com, ORCID: 0000-0003-2240-9248

Ersin Nail Sağdıç
Ph.D., Assist. Prof., Kütahya Dumlupınar University, Faculty of Economics and Administrative Sciences, Department of Public Finance, ersinnailsagdic@dpu.edu.tr, ORCID: 0000-0002-4022-8515

Esra Balli
Ph.D., Assist. Prof., Erzincan Binali Yildirim University, Faculty of Economics and Administrative Sciences, Department of Economics, esra.balli@erzincan.edu.tr, ORCID: 0000-0001-6993-9268

Ezgi Demir
Ph.D., Research Assist., Piri Reis University, Faculty of Economics and Administrative Sciences, Department of Management Information Systems, dem_ezgi@hotmail.com, ORCID:0000-0002-7335-5094

Gülaçtı Şen
Ph.D., Assist. Prof., Istanbul Esenyurt Unıversity, Department of Civil Aviation Cabin Services, gulactisen@esenyurt.edu.tr, ORCID:0000-0003-4168-0586

Güner Tuncer
Ph.D., Assoc. Prof., Kütahya Dumlupınar University, Faculty of Economics and Administrative Sciences, Department of Public Finance, guner.tuncer@dpu.edu.tr, ORCID: 0000-0001-5579-9436

Hakan Güveli
Independent Accountant and Financial Advisor, smmmhakanguveli@gmail.com, ORCID: 0000-0003-3212-377X

Hasan Hakses
Ph.D., Lecturer, Selcuk University, Vocational School of Social Sciences, Department of Foreign Trade, hasanhakses@selcuk.edu.tr, ORCID: 0000-0002-7018-1340

Haydar Karadağ
Ph.D., Assist. Prof., Recep Tayyip Erdoğan University, Faculty of Economics and Administrative Sciences, Department of Economics, Rize, Turkey, ORCID: 0000-0003-2398-7314.

Hüseyin Çağatay Karabıyık
Ph.D., Assist. Prof., Ankara Medipol University, Faculty of Administrative and Social Sciences, Department of Business Administration, h.cagataykarabiyik@gmail.com, ORCID: 0000-0002-1898-5907.

Hüseyin Sevgi
Ph.D., Research Asisst., Kırklareli University, Faculty of Economics and Administrative Sciences, Department of Labour Economics and Industrial Relations, hsevgi@gmail.com, ORCID: 0000-0003-0295-0723

Leyla Erat
Research Assist., Hitit University, Faculty of Economics and Administrative Sciences, Department of International Trade and Logistics, leylaerat@hitit.edu.tr, ORCID: 0000-0002-7136-2493

Mahmut Nevfel Elgün
Ph.D., Assist. Prof., Necmettin Erbakan University, Faculty of Political Sciences, Department of Business Administration, melgun@erbakan.edu.tr, ORCID:0000-0002-8380-886X.

Mehmet Şengür
Ph.D. Assoc. Prof., Eskisehir Osmangazi University, Faculty of Economics and Administrative Sciences, Department of Economics, msengur@ogu.edu.tr, ORCID: 0000-0002-2173-9977.

Melike Torun
Ph.D., Research Assist., Istanbul University–Cerrahpaşa, Vocational School of Social Sciences, Department of Management and Organization, melike.torun@gmail.com, ORCID:0000-0003-4828-9379

Meral Balcı
Ph.D. Assoc. Prof., Marmara University, Faculty of Political Sciences, Department of International Relations, mbalci@marmara.edu.tr, ORCID: 0000-0003-3638-5339

Mihriban Cindiloğlu Demirer
Ph.D., Assoc. Prof., Hitit University, Faculty of Economics and Administrative Sciences, Department of International Trade and Logistics, mihribancindiloglu@hitit.edu.tr, ORCID: 0000-0002-3530-2215

Muammer Tekeoglu
Ph.D., Prof., Cukurova University, Faculty of Economics and Administrative Sciences, Department of Economics, toglu@cu.edu.tr, ORCID: 0000-0001-8270- 3858

Münevver Bayar
Ph.D., Social Security Institution, Manager, munevverbayar@hotmail.com, ORCID: 0000-0002-8077-2160

Nadide Aktaş
Research Assist., Kayseri University, Faculty of Applied Sciences, Department of International Trade And Logistics, nadideaktas@kayseri.edu.tr, ORCID: 0000-0002-0571-1974

Nihat Onur Aşikoğlu
Ph.D., Research Assistant, Afyon Kocatepe University, Faculty of Economics and Administrative Sciences, Department of Business Administration, noasikoglu@gmail.com, ORCID: 0000-0002-7153-7839

Niyazi Kurnaz
Ph. D. Prof., Kütahya Dumlupınar University, FEAS, Department of Business Administration, niyazi.kurnaz@dpu.edu.tr, ORCID: 0000-0001-7019-0119

Nuran Coşkun
Ph.D., Research Assist., Mersin University, Faculty of Economics and Administrative Sciences, Department of Economics, ncoskun@mersin.edu.tr, ORCID:0000-0002-7803-7968

Nuran Varışlı
Ph.D., Social Security Institution, Specialist, gulmennuran@hotmail.com, ORCID: 0000-0002-0657-756X

Oğuzhan Özçelik
Ph.D. Babaeski Vocational Sciences. Kırklareli University, oguzhanozcelik@klu.edu.tr, ORCID:0000-0001-6666-8976

Ömür Demirer
Ph.D., Assist. Prof., Hitit University, Faculty of Economics and Administrative Sciences, Department of International Trade and Logistics, omurdemirer@hitit.edu.tr, ORCID: 0000-0002-9502-9935

Özer Özçelik
Ph.D., Assoc. Prof., Kütahya Dumlupınar University, Faculty of Economics and Administrative Sciences, Department of Economics, ozer.ozcelik@dpu.edu.tr, ORCID: 0000-0001-9164-5020

Özgür Aydoğuş
Research Assist., Afyon Kocatepe University, Faculty of Economics and Administrative Sciences, Department of Economics, ozaydogus@aku.edu.tr, ORCID:0000-0002-9747-9390

Rengin Ak
Ph..D., Prof., Kırklareli University, Faculty of Economics and Administrative Sciences, Department of Economics, rengin.ak@klu.edu.tr, ORCID: 0000-0003-0364-9975

Resül Yazıcı
Ph.D., Assoc. Prof., Bilecik Seyh Edebali University, Faculty of Economics and Administrative Sciences, Department of Economics, resul.yazici@bilecik.edu.tr, ORCID: 0000-0002-7875-3331

Reyhan Leba
Ph.D., Assist. Prof., Bursa Uludag University, Faculty of Economics and Administrative Sciences, Department of Public Finance, reyhan@uludag.edu.tr, ORCID: 0000-0002-9992-9666

Salih Türedi
Ph.D., Assoc. Prof., Recep Tayyip Erdogan University, Faculty of Economics and Administrative Sciences, Department of Economics, salih.turedi@erdogan.edu.tr, ORCID: 0000-0001-6294-1007

Şebnem Ekeryilmaz
Ph.D., Assist. Prof., Bilecik Seyh Edebali University, Faculty of Economics and Administrative Sciences, Department of Public Finance, sebnem.ekeryilmaz@bilecik.edu.tr, ORCID: 0000-0001-6033-2574.

Selami Erdoğan
Ph.D., Assist. Prof., Kutahya Dumlupınar University, Faculty of Administrative and Economics Sciences, Department of Public Administration, selami.erdogan@dpu.edu.tr, ORCID: 0000-0002-2245-4105

Selçuk Yeke
Ph.D., Research Assist., Ardahan University, Faculty of Economics and Administrative Sciences, Department of Business Administration, selcukyeke@ardahan.edu.tr, ORCID: 0000-0002-1953-6222

Selim Tüzüntürk
Ph. D. Assoc. Prof., Bursa Uludağ University, Department of Econometrics, selimtuzunturk@uludag.edu.tr.

Semra Altingöz Zarpli
Ph.D., Assist.Prof., Bilecik Seyh Edebali University, Faculty of Economics and Administrative Sciences, Department of Public Finance, semra.altingoz@bilecik.edu.tr, ORCID: 0000-0003-4597-0193

Serkan Varsak
Ph.D., Assist. Prof., Bilecik Seyh Edebali University, Faculty of Economics and AdministrativeSciences,DepartmentofEconomics,serkan.varsak@bilecik.edu.tr, ORCID:0000-0002-5894-1490

Serkan Göksu
Ph.D., Lecturer, Afyon Kocatepe University, Voctional School of Dazkırı, sgoksu@aku.edu.tr, ORCID:0000-0003-3261-6769

Tufan Sarıtaş
Ph.D., Assist. Prof., Karamanoğlu Mehmetbey University, Faculty of Economics and Administrative Sciences, Department of Economics, tufansaritas@gmail.com, ORCID No: 0000-0003-1728-2377

Tunahan Hacıimamoğlu
Ph.D., Research Assist., Recep Tayyip Erdogan University, Faculty of Economics and Administrative Sciences, Department of Economics, tunahan.haciimamoglu@erdogan.edu.tr, ORCID: 0000-0003-1474-8506

Wilkista Lore Obiero
Eskisehir Osmangazi University, Institute of Social Sciences, Department of Economics, lwilkista@gmail.com, ORCID: 0000-0002-0498-3142.

Zehra Yeni
Ph.D., Independent Researcher, zehrayeni08@gmail.com, ORCID: 0000-0002-5790-9165

Foreword

Researchers from various universities and institutions provided support for the third volume of the book Interdisciplinary Economics and Business, the first volume of which was published in 2018, the second in 2019, and the third in 2020. Most of the studies in this volume consist of economics and business administration branches. Studies have been specifically made for Turkey and generally made in global scale.

All publishing rights of the published book chapters belong to the publisher, and the content responsibility of the published articles belong to the author. The opinions in the book chapters are the personal opinions of the authors; it is not an official opinion of any institution or organization.

I express my gratitude to the authors of the book chapters that contributed to the book 'Studies on Interdisciplinary Economics and Business – Volume IV' without losing their research spirit in spite of the Covid-19 epidemic, which is on the global agenda,

Assoc. Prof. Özer Özçelik
Kütahya/Türkiye

Armağan Türk, Berna Ak Bingül and Rengin Ak

Pandemic and Migration in the Context of Covid-19

1 Introduction

Although there are many reasons for people's migration within or between countries, economic reasons are dominant. However, migrations also cause epidemics to spread to other geographies. With the emergence and spread of the COVID-19 outbreak in March 2020, the epidemic went far beyond a global health crisis, affecting all aspects of life economically, socially, and psychologically. It has been impossible to measure both the epidemic's full effects and the continuation of secondary effects caused by the epidemic's consequences over the long term. The financial and health-related results of the COVID-19 outbreak further affected vulnerable and fragile groups such as migrants, principally forcibly displaced populations, and posed a significant threat. With the pandemic, global lockdowns and the economic slowdown have harmed immigrants' physical and mental health, damaged their financial position and subjected them to violence and abuse and a lack of protection. In this study, the dimensions of the migration phenomenon during pandemic periods and the pandemic's effects on migration in the context of COVID-19 are discussed in different aspects.

2 Migration Phenomenon and Causes

Throughout history, nomadic tribes wandered for new pastures for their livestock, and other places for hunting and fishing. After people started migrating, they searched for more fertile land and created new settlements. Today, migration still occurs all over the world. Migration is the movement of an individual or group who intend to leave one country and settle in another country permanently. Migration is also a phenomenon that can occur domestically. People depart from rural areas and move to big cities to seek better opportunities (Montiglio, 2020). In the post-Second World War era, migration was chiefly the result of the refugee movement following the war and from former colonies in Asia and Africa in the 1950s and 60s. Migration from these regions to former empire centres such as the United Kingdom and France thus increased. There were two factors that accelerated migration in the post-World War II period. The first is the beginning of refugee movements in the post-war period, and the second is the end of colonialism in Asia and Africa in the 1950s and 60s (Parry, 2007).

The definition of migration can differ depending on the different perspectives on migration. According to worldwide organizations, migration is an international movement of people to a destination country where the people are not native or citizens, and who wish to settle as permanent residents or naturalized citizens (Refugee Council, 2021). In another description, migration is expressed as the abandonment of a country or region individually or collectively, depending on any social order such as economic, political, military, or illness (Immigration Bureau, 2020). These definitions divide migration into two as domestic and foreign. Therefore, while discussing the reasons for migration, it is necessary to consider the reasons for internal migration and external migration (intercountry) separately. Often in the context of immigration, there are both push and pull factors. The push and pull factors of migration are shown in Table 1.

Push Factors		Pull Factors
Cruelty, Violence, War	→	Security and stability, Freedom
Low wages, Unemployment	→	High salaries, Job prospects
Crop failure and famine, Pollution, Natural disaster	→	Food availability, Better environment
Limited opportunities, Lack of service, Family separation	→	Reunification of families, Better quality of life, Availability of services

Tab. 1: Root Causes of Migration
Source: Justice for Immigrants, 2017.

Although the reasons for migration between countries and within a country are substantially similar, internal and external migration reasons are discussed under different headings in the literature. In this context, the reasons for internal and external migration can be listed as follows (Immigration Bureau, 2020).

Causes of internal migration: The shrinkage of lands and livelihood difficulties due to population increases in rural areas; soils becoming infertile due to the desert effect and erosion as a result of agricultural activities; decreased demand for labour due to the mechanization of agriculture; limited employment opportunities in regions with small populations; increasing job opportunities in cities due to Industry 4.0; and more education, health, and similar social opportunities being available in cities.

Causes of external migration: Migration due to war; insufficient financial opportunities; the fact that some countries accept immigration within cultural exchanges; natural disasters; religious, political, sociological and cultural reasons; and few opportunities offered by the home country.

In addition to these effects causing migration, a more specific reason is that long-lasting epidemics affect a large part of society. There have been severe epidemics affecting countries in every period of history. From the Antonine Plague of 165–180 AD to the COVID-19 outbreak that started in 2019, all outbreaks have caused people displacement somewhat.

3 Migration During Pandemic Times

Pandemic periods are situations where human life deviates from the regular order. These unexpected shocks change the habits of many people, and lead to the emergence of new ones. There are various effects of pandemics on societies. These are classified as social and economic effects in the literature. The suffering during pandemic periods have slightly pushed the importance of the analysis of the pandemics' social and economic impacts into the background. Although it is easy to calculate health expenditure during pandemic periods, it is very challenging to calculate the costs caused by job losses, suffering, changed living conditions, changed habits, changed settlements and many similar changes. In this process, where the human factor plays an important role, the pandemic's social and economic impact can be shown as in Figure 1.

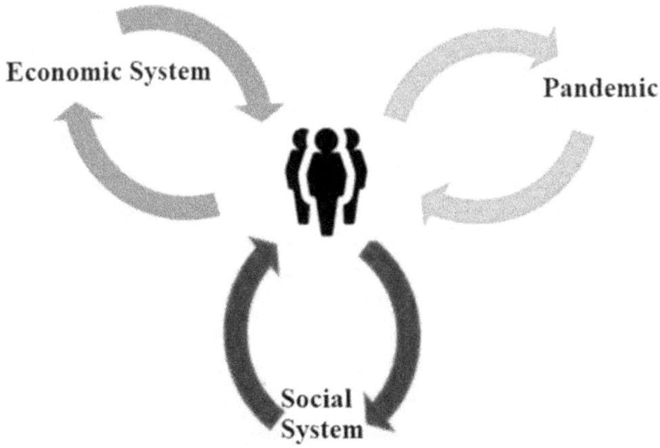

Fig. 1: *Interaction Process in Pandemics*
Source: Dignum et al., 2020

The migration phenomenon, a social and economic effect of pandemics, can occur in many different ways. Migration is seen simply as an escape from the pandemic. People tend to move away temporarily or permanently from places where there is a threat of disease, and this situation leads to a location change in employment. Employment movement is seen generally within a country, but in-country migration can be considerable. Furthermore, it has been observed that people show a tendency to relocate to new residential areas during and after pandemic periods. Another effect of migration reported in the literature is the dissemination of epidemics. In other words, migrations are a factor causing epidemic diseases to pass to different geographies.

When the literature is examined, besides the studies which show that the migration tendency increases during pandemic periods, many studies emphasize the measures taken by countries to prevent the spread of the disease by reducing migration. Also, some studies show that the epidemic diseases' effects are more intense in the regions where migrants live. Many epidemics emerged in the historical process and have been the subject of many studies. In the literature, many studies exist relating to epidemics cases. The studies dealing with the epidemics' economic and social effects with the migration dimension are summarized in Table.2.

Author	Date	Thesis	Author	Date	Thesis
Min Chen, Miao Li, Yixue Hao, Zhongchun Liu, Long Hu, Lin Wang	2020	Introduction of population migration to SEIAR for an effective response strategy with the COVID-19 pandemic	**P T Walker, T B Hallett, P J White, G P Garnett**	2015	Interpreting the decreases in HIV prevalence: The impact of spatial clustering and migration prevalence on the expected declines
Robert Peckham	2016	Pandemics in Asia in the post-1900 period	**Felicity Thomas**	2016	Migration and Health Handbook
David Baca-Carrasco, Jorge X. Velasco-Hernández	2016	Gender, Mosquitoes, and Outbreaks: Assessing Zika Disease Dynamics	**Hélène A. C. M. Voeten et al.**	2010	Strong Relationship between Internal Migration and HIV Prevalence in Urban Sub-Saharan Africa
Ibidun Fakoya et al.	2015	A systematic review of after-migration HIV acquisition in Europe among immigrants from countries with widespread HIV epidemics: Effective management methods of HIV prevention programs and policy	**Gui-Quan Sun, Quan-Xing Liu, Zhen Jin, Amit Chakraborty, Bai-Lian Li**	2010	The infection rate in spatial epidemics and the impact of migration on the destruction of the disease
Shangbin Cui, Meng Bai	2014	Mathematical analysis of population migration and its effects on the spread of epidemics.	**Carol S. Camlin et al.**	2010	Gender, Migration, and HIV in rural KwaZulu-Natal, South Africa
Catherine Cox, Hilary Marland	2013	Migration, Health and Ethnic Roots in the Modern World	**Klaus J. Bade**	2003	Migrations in European history
David Rees, Jill Murray, Gill Nelson, Pam Sonnenberg	2010	Epidemics of Silicosis, Tuberculosis and HIV Infection and Migration in South African Gold Miners	**Kevin D. Deane, Justin O. Parkhurst, Deborah Johnston**	2010	The connection among migration, mobility and HIV
Nazrul Islam Mondal, Hiroshi Takaku, Yasushi Ohkusa	2009	The impact of marriage age and immigration on HIV and AIDS; Epidemics in Japan	**Stephan Curtis**	2007	In the Sundsvall Region during the 1880s Epidemics Internal Migration, and Diphtheria Deaths of Children
Alice Mesnard, Paul Seabright	2008	Is It Possible To Avoid Outbreaks Through Migration? Quarantine Measures within the Scope of Asymmetric Information on Infection Risk	**Megan Coffee, Mark N. Lurie, Geoff P. Garnett**	2007	Modeling the impact of migration on the HIV epidemic in South Africa
Larry S. Liebovitch, Ira B. Schwartz	2004	Migration Induced Epidemics: Dynamics of Flux-Based Multipatch Models.	**M. Kirane, S. Kouachi**	1991	Asymptotic Behavior for a System that Identifies Epidemics by Spread and Amount of Infection
Daan Brummer	2002	Labor Migration and HIV/AIDS in South Africa	**William H. McNeill**	1984	Human Migration in a Historical Perspective

Tab. 2: Literature Studies Linking the Economic and Social Impacts of the Epidemics to the Migration Dimension

Source: It was created by the authors.

4 COVID-19 and Migration

The COVID-19 outbreak has made governments and people vulnerable, creating a widespread crisis. Although the virus has not discriminated in its global spread, some groups have been more affected than others. The epidemic has had severe and widespread implications for local and international migration models, while putting migrants, refugees, and displaced persons at high risk. People who are evacuated and displaced because of disasters face particular obstacles in conducting physical distance and other infection prevention measures. Inherently fragile ecosystems and livelihoods also place additional pressures on migrants who return to their home countries and locations (IOM, 2021-a). While border closures and increased controls make it difficult for migrants to continue their journey or return to their homes, immigrants who want to continue their travel face the risk of uncertainty, smuggling, and fraud (IMREF, 2020). In the context of COVID-19, the epidemic can be said to exacerbate both the vulnerability of immigrants and their inequalities, including gender and income inequalities (AEO, 2021). The effects of COVID-19 on migration have been examined in four dimensions: health, income inequality, gender-based violence and environmental impacts.

4.1 The Impact of COVID-19 on Migrants' Health Access and Inequality

During the COVID-19 outbreak, migrants, especially those working in low-wage jobs, are more affected by the spread of COVID-19 and are more vulnerable. According to statistics as of March 2021, the number of immigrants from the twenty countries with the highest number of COVID-19 cases accounts for one-third of the total immigrants in the world. In fourteen of these countries, the mentioned immigrants make up about 4% of the country's population. In nine of these fourteen countries, this rate approaches 10% (UN, 2020-a).

Difficult access to healthcare services, ignoring other health problems unrelated to COVID-19, and a deterioration in living and working conditions are the primary threats to the health of migrants. The lack and difficulty in accessing health services cause health inequalities (AEO, 2021). However, for some segments, the effects are more severe than others. The desperate situation of migrants is worsening, especially for the ones who are often assumed to be more vulnerable, such as children, older migrants, women, migrants with a disability or chronic illness, who are at risk of being arrested and becoming human trafficking victims (IMREF, 2020). These European Centre for Development Policy Management (ECDPM, 2020): For immigrants who are a vulnerable group, 'social distance' measures result in less vital support and less access to needs or services. Migrants are not in a position to follow health advice, such as hygiene, to prevent the spread of the epidemic, With the epidemic, immigrants lost their ability to cross borders and protect themselves, stopping resettlement opportunities due to pandemic, thus increasing disease risks. Exposure to increased psychological pressure on them leads to a loss of hope after years of uncertainty and procedures in compulsory residence camps and temporary settlements outside of Europe.

While pre-epidemic immigrants already have difficulty accessing health services, these arduous conditions worsened; with the emergence of COVID-19, priorities of implementing health policies changed negatively affecting immigrants' access to adequate information, treatment and services. Besides, it is suggested that, since the COVID-19 epidemic caused a widespread deterioration in health systems and reduced access to food, it also caused substantial increases in maternal and child mortality (Roberton et al., 2020: 906). The incidence of diseases such as tuberculosis and HIV will rise further because of the impact of adverse conditions in refugee camps.

During the pandemic period, another migration-related effect is that the pandemic affects migrant workers more. Low-skilled migrants working in crowded workplaces are affected severely by the COVID-19. Examples in Singapore and the Kingdom of Saudi Arabia show that the exposure of the immigrant population to the virus in these countries differs. According to Saudi Ministry of Health data, May 2020 statistics show that three-quarters of new COVID-19 cases have spread among immigrants coming into the country. More than 95% of cases confirmed in Singapore by 19 June 2020 were immigrants, and over 93% of total cases were related to immigrants' workplaces. In Singapore, statistics for March 2021 show that the number of new patients is decreasing. However, almost all of the new cases in the country are made up of immigrants (Migration Data Portal, 2021). Since international migrants are a very heterogeneous group, the impact on their health is also varied. Studies have found that the incidence rates among foreign workers and forcibly displaced people appear to be consistently higher than those who have changed countries for other reasons, when compared to nationals (Hintermeier et al., 2020: 3). Another result of the studies shows that immigrant infection and death risks in high-income countries are increased due to COVID-19 (Hayward et al., 2020: 3). Immigrants and their family members have trouble coping with the stress and anxiety associated with COVID-19, and reaching health services in the country's official language. Besides, troubled migrants and their families may hang back in accessing healthcare for fear of being expelled or being separated from their families (OECD, 2020).

Another interaction of immigrants with COVID-19 is seen in fighting the disease. Immigrants have contributed significantly to exterminating the epidemic. For example, according to international data in March 2021, among the twenty countries with the highest COVID-19 spread rate, at least seven countries (America, England, France, Spain, Italy, Germany and Czechia) employ a considerable number of foreign-born employees in the critical healthcare sector. For example, one-third of doctors and one-fifth of nurses in the UK are foreign-born (Lafortune et al., 2019: 11). Although international migration is seen as a problem for countries, the migration phenomenon has eliminated the qualified personnel shortage during the COVID-19 period. Approximately one-quarter of the healthcare personnel employed in the United States and the UK are foreign-educated people.

There is a link between migrant deaths and disappearances and the COVID-19 outbreak. The mobility restrictions brought about by the epidemic have not diminished the efforts of immigrants to improve their lives by escaping from the violence and poverty they have experienced; the immigrants continued to go on secret journeys. However, the restrictions on movement have made migrants' travel risky and uncertain, and have placed them in dangerous situations where no humanitarian aid or rescue is possible. According to IOM's data, approximately 4,000 people died during international migration between March 2020 and February 2021. This number does not include movement restrictions of migrant workers, deadlocks and deaths due to COVID-19 (Missing Migrant, 2021).

4.2 The Impact of COVID-19 on Immigrants' Income Inequality

Another issue related to COVID-19 and immigration concerns the income transfers of immigrants. The main source of income for 10% of the world's population is money sent by migrant workers. In this context, COVID-19 also affects the families and communities of migrant workers in their countries of origin. Lack of this kind of support for families and communities will impair economic progress by making it difficult to access basic needs such as health, nutrition and education. There was an estimated loss of more than $100 billion (US) in remittances due to COVID-19. This loss of income has caused more children to be forced into child labour worldwide. Globally, America, India, Russia, England, France, Italy and Germany rank among the top twenty countries with the highest number of COVID-19 cases. These countries are also the countries with the highest amount of remittances. Approximately 25% of global money transfers consist of such transfers (OECD, 2019). According to 2015 data, there are 11.5 million immigrant house-work workers worldwide, 8.5 million of whom are women. During the COVID-19 period, these people were unemployed due to closures, economic restrictions and health problems, and were stuck in countries where they lived in unsuitable conditions (ILO, 2015: 6). Other migration-related impacts seen during the COVID-19 process are trapped migrants and retrospective migration. In this process, the sudden border closures taken by countries in order to prevent the epidemic left many people suffering. During this period, many immigrants, including seasonal workers and students (on low incomes) had problems because they could not return to their home countries. As of July 2020, IOM estimates that at least 3 million people were left stranded because they could not return to their own countries (IOM, 2020: 9).

Due to having lost their jobs, and facing a higher infection risk, often in overcrowded living spaces, many immigrants returned to their home country, often through bilateral negotiations allowing the borders to be opened temporarily to bring back trapped migrants. Globally, among the returning immigrants, the highest number was Indians; over 4.7 million, returned to India as of 27 February 2021 (Indian Ministry of Civil Aviation 2021). Between 1 March 2020 and 25 February 2021, about 1 million undocumented Afghan immigrants returned from Iran and Pakistan. As of October 2020, about 150,000 Venezuelan immigrants and refugees have returned from other countries to Venezuela. According to IOM data, between April 2020 and February 2021, more than 50,000 migrants returned to Ethiopia, their country of origin, from neighboring African countries and the Kingdom of Saudi Arabia (IOM, 2021-b: 2).

Governments imposing restrictions on domestic and cross-border mobility to combat the spread of COVID-19 and reverse migration have brought different problems. When Western European countries evaluated the economic consequences of the measures they took at the height of the epidemic, they realized that the reverse migration of migrant workers from Eastern European countries caused massive labour shortages in primary economic sectors, including agriculture, construction, maintenance and services. However, Europe needed its immigrant employees. Despite the global unemployment rising to historical peaks with the pandemic, Italians, Spanish, Germans, Austrians and British did not wish to work in jobs left open after the immigrants left. While Italy foresees a shortage of 1 million workers in the agricultural sector, it is estimated that there will be a need for 200,000 seasonal workers in France, and about 400,000 in Germany and England. The seasonal worker problem in the agriculture sector has caused product spoilage and, consequently, food shortages. This situation has made Europe's most important food crisis inevitable (Ruxandra, 2020).

4.3 The Impact of COVID-19 on Gender-Based Discrimination of Immigrants

Women working in informal jobs and being on the poverty threshold feel the pandemic's economic and social effects intensely. Given that the COVID-19 outbreak affects women and men in different ways, taking gender into account to solve problems women's vulnerabilities at home and work should be addressed first (Linde and Gonzales Laya, 2020). As with the ebola epidemic, crises pose a severe threat to women's participation in economic activity, especially in the informal sectors. When gender inequality in livelihoods is coupled with epidemic and migration phenomenon, female migrant workers, especially those dealing with household and care work, can hardly support their families due to difficulties from unforeseen travel bans, which negatively impacts on their employment (GBVAoR, 2020). COVID-19 also increases the risk of increased sexual and gender-based violence against female workers during the migration process. In particular, women with irregular migrant status avoid reporting gender-based violence for fear of discrimination, arrest, or deportation. Past outbreaks have shown that women and girls, especially immigrant women and girls, are at high risk of gender-based violence, sexual abuse, and harassment. Like in the Ebola epidemic, violence increases during crises; human trafficking, child marriage, and sexual exploitation and abuse negatively impact immigrant women and girls, particularly given the vulnerable situation of women and children (UN, 2020-b).

Economic hardships and high gender-based violence during the epidemic period particularly affected migrant women. While COVID-19 weakens immigrant resilience by exacerbating existing gender inequality, the epidemic's gender-based impacts on migrants emerge in employment, security and access to services (AEO, 2021). ILO 2020 data shows that women's unemployment is higher than men's (ILO, 2020). The fact that female migrant workers work in low-paid and laborious jobs like healthcare and sanitation causes them to fight at the forefront of the COVID-19 outbreak, thus increasing their risk of exposure to the virus. Immigrant women face the risk of losing their livelihoods, being violated in their labour and human rights, and contracting the virus, besides which they face many forms of discrimination, such as gender-specific restrictions in migration policies, insecure work patterns, racism, and xenophobia (UN, 2020-b).

4.4 COVID-19 and the Environmental Impact of Migration

During the spread of the epidemic, countries tried to take measures by closing their borders to foreigners. These practices have led to a decrease in migration between countries. Immigration flow was the lowest in the history of migration flows to OECD countries in 2020 (OECD, 2020). Such a decrease in migration flow has also created demographic effects on countries that depend on migration for population growth. For example, estimates for 2020 show that the German population has not increased for the first time in the last decade due to a decrease in migration flow (German Federal Bureau of Statistics, 2021). In Australia, net migration is expected to be negative for 2020/2021 for the first time since 1945. As a result, the country's lowest population growth rate in a century is expected (Australian Population Center, 2020). Among 204 cities in China, Wuhan was among the top twenty cities by the immigrant entry, with 9.4% growth before the COVID-19 outbreak. In the post-epidemic period, migration to the region has decreased (Chen et al., 2020: 12). This data and many similar statistics show the impact of COVID-19 on migration.

Another significant effect of immigration is urbanization. It is estimated that about one in five international migrants lives in just twenty cities (Beijing, Hong Kong, Tokyo, Seoul, Shanghai, Singapore, Sydney in Asia, Berlin, Brussels, London, Paris, Vienna, Moscow, Madrid in Europe, Buenos Aires, Chicago, Los Angeles, New York, Toronto and Washington (USA) (IOM, 2015: 38). Studies show that the exposure rates to COVID-19 are higher in regions where foreign-born people live compared to other regions. COVID-19 also has reduced irregular border crossings and asylum applications compared to 2019 (European Commission, 2021). On the other hand, the twenty countries with the highest number of COVID-19 cases as of March 2021 hosted approximately 7 million refugees by the end of 2019. This number corresponds to about a third of the total refugees in the world. Today, 18.3 million of the 50.3 million immigrants are under the age of 15 and about 4 million over the age of sixty. These two groups are also vulnerable (IDMC, 2020: 69).

Another group affected by COVID-19 are foreign students. Globally, there were more than 5 million international students in higher education in 2017. Most of these students prefer Europe and North America. The countries that send the most students abroad are China, India, Germany, the Republic of Korea and Vietnam. One in four international students in the world come from China, India, or Germany. Both origin countries and destination countries' restrictions impacted international students, with the students losing their jobs due to restrictions and universities switching to online education and closing their campuses (UNESCO, 2020).

The SARS-CoV-2 virus that causes COVID-19 has affected everyone regardless of their nationality. When the epidemic flu preparedness plans were examined in twenty-one countries in the Asia-Pacific region in 2016, it was only at the borders of Thailand, Papua New Guinea and the Maldives that the health control measures extended to non-citizens (Wickramage et al., 2018: 252). The exclusion of migrants' access to healthcare rights within domestic law frameworks may adversely affect public health management by preventing early detection and treatment, thus increasing transmission risks (Zenner and Wickramage, 2020).

5 Conclusion

Throughout history humanity has struggled with many epidemics. Although MERS, EBOLA, and ZIKA, which are among the epidemic diseases experienced in the last century, have a regional character, the COVID-19 outbreak, having a global nature, has affected the entire world. Because the pandemic has not yet been brought under control, vaccination has not yet been completed and the epidemic produces different mutations, and the fight against the disease continues. However, while the epidemic proceeds, its economic, social, and psychological effects on livelihoods and vital resources will present long-term consequences. By acting alone, it will be difficult for countries to defeat the COVID-19 disease, which starts simply as a health crisis but extends beyond borders. Considering that we share the same future and fate, it is crucial to strive for common international solidarity against the pandemic's unfavourable effects.

Pandemics make the situation worse for immigrants who move for different reasons, and who live with many other people in overcrowded spaces, in unhuman conditions. The reasons are due to their financial difficulties and limited employment opportunities, poor access to health services, the poor conditions in the shelters, and being subject to gender-based violence, which increases their vulnerability. Considering the immigration movement's sociological and economic impact, it can be concluded that there is a need for international cooperation and the establishment of pandemic policies that include the protection of vulnerable and unprotected migrants. With a similar approach, migration issues should be discussed in the context of global problems, such as the environmental and global warming, and global solutions should be produced under an international cooperation framework.

References

AEO (2021). AEO-Migration-and-COVID-19-Redacted-Report-FINAL 2021 p:14 https://www.integrallc.com/wp-content/uploads/2021/02/AEO-Migration-and-COVID-19-Redacted-Report-FINAL-1.pdf (30.3.2021)

Australia Government Center for Population (2020). Population Statement, https://population.gov.au/publications/publications-population-statement.html (13.02.2021)

Baca-Carrasco, D. and Velasco-Hernández, J. (2016). Sex, Mosquitoes and Epidemics: An Evaluation of Zika Disease Dynamics, Bull Math Biol, 78:2228–2242.

Bade, K. J. (2003), Migration in European History, Blackwell Publishing, 1–402.

Brummer, D. (2002). Labour Migration and HIV/AIDS in Southern Africa, International Organisation for Migration, 1–26.

Camlin, C. S., Hosegood, V., Newell, M., McGrath, N., Barnighausen, T. and Snow, R. C. (2010). Gender, Migration and HIV in Rural KwaZulu-Natal, South Africa, PLoS One, 5(7):1–10.

Chen, H., Qian, W. and Wen, Q. (2020). The Impact of the COVID-19 Pandemic on Consumption: Learning from High Frequency Transaction Data, https://papers.ssrn.com/sol3/papers.cfm? abstract_id=3568574, 1–51.

Chen, M., Li, M., Hao, Y., Liu, Z., Hu, L. and Wang L. (2020). The Introduction of Population Migration to SEIAR for COVID-19 Epidemic Modeling with an Efficient Intervention Strategy, Information Fusion, 64:252–258.

Coffee, M., Lurieb, M. N. and Garnett, G. P. (2007). Modelling the Impact of Migration on the HIV Epidemic in South Africa, AIDS, 21(3):343–350.

Cox, C. and Marland, M. (2013). Migration, Health and Ethnicity in the Modern World, Palgrave Macmillan, 1–201.

Cui, S. and Bai, M. (2014). Mathematical Analysis of Population Migration and its Effects to Spread of Epidemics, Discrete and Continuous Dynamical Systems, 1–42.

Curtis, S. (2007). In-Migration and Diphtheria Mortality among Children in the Sundsvall Region During the Epidemics of the 1880s, Journal of the Hıstory of Medıcıne and Allıed Scıences, 63(1):23–64.

Deane, K. D., Parkhurst, J. O. and Johnston, D. (2010). Linking Migration, Mobility and HIV', Tropical Medicine and International Health, 15(12):1458–1463.

Dignum, F., Dignum, V., Davidsson, P., Ghorbani, A., Van der Hurk, M., Jensen, M., Kammler, C., Lorig, F., Gustavo Ludescher, L., Melchior, A., Mellema, R., Pastrav, C., Vanhee, L. and Verhagen, H. (2020), Analysing the Combined Health, Social and Economic Impacts of the Corovanvirus Pandemic Using Agent-Based Social Simulation, Minds and Machines, 30:177–194.

ECDPM (2020). Migration, Mobility and COVID-19 – Tale of Many Tales, https://ecdpm.org/talking-points/migration-mobility-covid-19-tale-of-many-tales/ (30.3.2021).

European Commission (2021). Migration Statistics Update: The Impact of COVID-19', European Commission – Press release, Brussel, 1–2.

Fakoya, I., Álvarez-del Arco, D., Woode-Owusu, M., Monge, S., Rivero-Montesdeoca, Y., Delpech,V., Rice, B., Noori, T., Pharris, A. J., Amato-Gauci, A., Del Amo, J. M. and Burns, F. (2015). A Systematic Review of Post-migration Acquisition of HIV Among Migrants from Countries with Generalised HIV Epidemics Living in Europe: Implications for Effectively Managing HIV Prevention Programmes and Policy, BMC Public Health 15, 561:1–14.

German Federal Bureau of Statistics (2021). No Population Growth Expected for 2020, https://www.destatis.de/EN/Press/2021/01/PE21_016_12411.html (13.02.2021)

GBVAoR (2020). The COVID-19 Outbreak and Gender: Key Advocacy Points from Asia and the Pacific

https://asiapacific.unwomen.org/en/digital-library/publications/2020/03/the-covid-19-outbreak-and-gender

Hayward, S. E., Deal, A., Cheng, C., Crawshaw, A. F., Orcutt, M., Vandrevala, T.F., Norredam, M., Carballo, M., Ciftci, Requena-Mendez, A., Greenaway, C., Carter, J., Knights, F., Mehrotra, A., Seedat, F., Bozorgmehr, K., Veizis, A., Campos-Matos, I., Wurie, F., Noori, T., McKee, M., Kumar, B. and Hargreaves, S. (2020). Clinical Outcomes and Risk Factors for COVID-19 Among Migrant Populations in High-income Countries: A Systematic Review, medRxiv, 1–92.

Hintermeier, M., Gencer, H., Kajikhina, K., Rohleder, S., Santos-Hövener, C., Talarek, M., Spallek, J. and Bozorgmehr, K. (2020). SARS-CoV-2 Among Migrants and Forcibly Displaced Populations: A Rapid Systematic Review, medRxiv, 1–26.

Immigration Bureau (2020). What is Immigration? https://gocmenburo.com/goc-nedir/ (18.11.20209).

Indian Ministry of Civil Aviation (2021), Covid-19 and VBM Information,

https://www.civilaviation.gov.in/ (13.02.2021)

IDMC (2020). Global Report On Internal Dısplacement, The Internal Displacement Monitoring Centre, April, 1–126.

ILO (2015). ILO Global Estimates on Migrant Workers, ILO Cataloguing in Publication Data, Geneva, 1–100.

ILO (2020). ILO Monitor: COVID-19 and the World of Work. Sixth Edition: Updates Estimates and Analysis. September 2020. p:15, https://www.ilo.org/wcmsp5/groups/public/@dgreports/@dcomm/documents/briefingnote/wcms_755910.pdf.

IMREF (2020). Exploring the Impact of COVID19 on the Vulnerabilities of Migrants on the Central Mediterranean Route, file:///C:/Users/90532/Desktop/Literatür/Göç-%20FULL-REPORT_IMREF-COVID-19-study-Part-2.pdf .(30.3.2021)

IOM (2015). World Migration Report 2015: Migrants and Cities: New Partnerships to Manage Mobility, International Organization for Migration, 1–202.

IOM (2020). COVID-19 Impact On Stranded Migrants, IOM UN Migration, 1–10.

IOM (2021-a). The COVID-19 Pandemic, Migration and the Environment, https://environmentalmigration.iom.int/covid-19-pandemic-migration-and-environment (13.02.2021).

IOM (2021-b). IOM Ethiopia, https://ethiopia.iom.int/sites/default/files/IOM%20Ethiopia%20-%20COVID-19%20Response%20Overview%20-%2025%20February%202021_0.pdf.

Justice for Immigrants (2017), Root Causes of Migration, https://justiceforimmigrants.org/what-we-are-working-on/immigration/root-causes-of-migration/ (13.02.2021).

Kirane, M. and Kouachi S. (1991. Asymptotıc Behavıour for a System Descrıbıng Epıdemıcs with Mıgratıon and Spatıal Spread of Infectıon, Internatıonal Centre for Theoretıcal Physıcs, 1–8.

Lafortune, G., Karolina, S. and Eric, V. (2019). Recent Trends in International Mobility of Doctors and Nurses, OECD, 11–35.

Liebovitch, L. S. and Schwartz, I. B. (2004). Migration Induced Epidemics: Dynamics of Flux-based Multipatch Models, Physics Letters, A 332:256–267.

Linde, A. and Gonzales Laya, A. (2020). What the COVID-19 Pandemic Tells Us About Gender Equality WEF, https://www.weforum.org/agenda/2020/05/what-the-covid-19-pandemic-tells-us-about-gender-equality/ (4.4.2021)

Mesnard, A. and Seabright, P. (2008). Escaping Epidemics Through Migration? Quarantine Measures under Asymmetric Information about Infection Risk, CEPR Discussion Papers, 1–20.

McNeill, W.H. (1984). Human Migration in Historical Perspective, Population and Development Review, 10(1):1–18.

Migration Data Portal (2021). Migration Data Relevant for the COVID-19 Pandemic, https://migrationdataportal.org/themes/migration-data-relevant-covid-19-pandemic (13.02.2021).

Missing Migrant (2021). Latest Global Figures, https://missingmigrants.iom.int/ (14.02.2020)

Montiglio, D. (2020). 14 Reasons Why People Emigrate, https://www.foreigner.bg/12-reasons-why-people-immigrate/ (21.01.2021).

Mondal, N. I., Takaku, H. and Ohkusa, Y. (2009). Impact of Age at Marriage and Migration on HIV and AIDS Epidemics in Japan, International Journal for Equity in Health, 2–10.

OECD (2019). OECD International Migration Outlook 2019, OECD, 1–409.

OECD (2020). OECD International Migration Outlook 2020.

Parry, S. (2007). Immigration, https://www.britannica.com/topic/immigration, Erişim tarihi (26.01.2021).

Peckham, R. (2016), Epidemics in Modern Asia, Cambridge Press, 1–355.

Rees, D., Murray, J., Nelson, G., and Sonnenberg, P. (2010). Oscillating Migration and the Epidemics of Silicosis, Tuberculosis, and HIV Infection in South African Gold Miners, Amerıcan Journal of Industrıal Medıcıne, 53:398–404.

Refugee Council (2021). The truth about asylum, https://www.refugeecouncil.org.uk/information/refugee-asylum-facts/the-truth-about-asylum/ (17.01.2021)

Roberton, T., Carter, E. D. and Chou, V. B. (2020). Early Estimates of the Indirect Effects of the COVID-19 Pandemic on Maternal and Child Mortality in Low-Income and Middle-Income Countries: A Modelling Study, The Lancet Global Health 8(7):E901–E908.

Ruxandra P. (2020), Europe's Essential Workers: Migration and Pandemic Politics in Central and Eastern Europe during COVID-19, https://onlinelibrary.wiley.com/doi/full/10.1002/epa2.1105

Sun,G., Liu, Q., Jin, Z., Chakraborty, A.and Li, B. (2010). Influence of Infection Rate and Migration on Extinction of Disease in Spatial Epidemics, Journal of Theoretical Biology, 264:95–103.

Thomas, F. (2016). Handbook of Migration and Health, Edward Elgar Publishing, 1–544.

UN (2020-a). International Migration, https://www.un.org/development/desa/pd/themes/international-migration (12.02.2021).

UN (2020-b).Women, Guidance Note: Addressing the Impact of the COVID-19 Pandemic on Women Migrant Workers. 2020. https://www.unwomen.org/-/media/headquarters/attachments/sections/ library/publications/2020/guidance-note-impacts-of-the-covid-19-pandemic-on-women-migrantworkers-en.pdf?la=enandvs=227)

UNESCO (2020). Sustaniable Development Goals,

http://data.uis.unesco.org/Index.aspx?DataSetCode=EDULIT_DS, (14.02.2021).

Voeten, H. A.C. M., Vissers, D. C. J., G. Simon, Z. Basia, White, R. G., de Vlas, S. J. and Habbema, J. D. F. (2010). Strong Association Between In-Migration and HIV Prevalence in Urban Sub-Saharan Africa, American Sexually Transmitted Diseases Association, 37 (4):240–243.

Wickramage, K. Gostin, L.O., Friedman, E., Prakongsai, P., Suphanchaimat, R., Hui,C., Duigan, P., Barragan, E. and Harper, D. R. (2018). Missing: Where Are the Migrants in Pandemic Influenza Preparedness Plans?, Health and Human Rights Journal, 20(1):251–258.

Walker, P. T., Hallett, T. B., White, P. J. and Garnett, G. P. (2015). Interpreting Declines in HIV Prevalence: Impact of Spatial Aggregation and Migration on Expected Declines in Prevalence, Sex Transm Infect, (Suppl II):42–48.

Zenner, D.and Wickramage K. (2020). National Preparedness and Response Plans for COVID-19 and Other Diseases: Why Migrants Should be Included", https://migrationdataportal.org/blog/national- preparedness-and-response-plans-covid-19-and-other-diseases-why-migrants-should-be (14.02.2021).

Ahmet İnkaya and Özgür Aydoğuş

Global Agriculture and Food Policies During the Covid-19 Process

1 Introduction

With the Covid-19 pandemic, there has never been a period in which the world went through such a crisis in terms of health, the economy and social life since the Second World War. Unlike other economic crises, this crisis has affected all countries and sectors. Shrinkages in supply and demand in economies have dug many sectors into a hole. The country lockdowns that occurred at the beginning of the pandemic and the accompanying panic environment first manifested themselves in the final food products. Consumers in many countries had difficulties accessing these products from time to time due to the empty market shelves as a result of panic purchases.

Although the agricultural sector is not the sector most affected by the crisis, it has been one of the most considered sectors due to its strategic importance. After the pandemic's announcement, countries closed their borders, and travel restrictions and quarantines triggered the economic crisis and recession fears. While the World Bank stated that one of the sectors that will be most affected by the pandemic would be the agriculture and food sector, the World Trade Organization (WTO) predicted that international trade would shrink between 13% and 32% (WTO, 2020).

2 Developments in Global Agriculture and Food Trade

When we look at the recent developments in global trade, after the recovery in 2017, trade tensions between the USA and China and the irregular Brexit process on the European side caused economic conditions to deteriorate and negatively affected the 2018–2019 period. However, available data for 2020 point to an 8% decrease in world trade. The sharpest decline in international trade during the Covid-19 pandemic was experienced in the 2nd quarter of 2020, and this decrease was more than 20% (Unctad, 2021, 5).

During the Covid-19 pandemic there were disruptions in agriculture and food products trade, and in other international trade sectors. These disruptions were caused by protective government policies and panic purchases that disrupted supply chains, changing consumption patterns, and the emergence of logistical barriers. States have tended to implement protectionist policies to maintain the supply of agricultural products in their own countries and reduce the population's income losses in this sector. With the reports of organizations such as the WTO, the Food and Agricultural Organization (FAO), the World Bank etc., which direct global economic policies, they continued to focus on food prices and poverty problems. At the same time, these organizations continued to make efforts for the sustainability of the production and trade structure to eliminate the adverse effects of globalization on agriculture and food production (Dogruel, 2020, 9)

GATT's purpose, which was established with an agreement signed by 23 countries in 1947 and entered into force in 1948, is to reduce import taxes, remove all barriers against international trade and terminate discriminatory practices in the trade. Its basic idea is to liberalize international trade by promoting liberalism in foreign trade by moving member countries away from protectionist policies to establish an international competition system. However, agricultural trade-in products could not be adequately negotiated with GATT. Cooperation for agricultural products trading has always been difficult, as the agricultural sector has strategic products. Therefore, until the 1980s agricultural trade remained out of GATT negotiations. After the Uruguay Round held in 1994, the legal basis of the WTO (World Trade Organization) was established in 1995, and it replaced the GATT in 1995, including the Uruguay Round agriculture convention.

The Uruguay Round is built on three basic principles regarding the agricultural sector and trade. These can be summarized as: entry to the market, export subsidies and domestic support. The WTO has become an organization that constitutes 98% of the world trade, has more than 160 member countries, and more than twenty countries want to participate (WTO, 2021). In the negotiations that continued with Seatle in 1999, Doha in 2001, Cancun in 2003 and Hongkong in 2005, agriculture was intensely discussed, and this issue came to a dead end. It is difficult to say that the expected targets have been achieved due to the countries' resistance and self-interested attitudes. However, the WTO tried to take binding measures to eliminate the problems experienced during the Covid-19 pandemic process.

The FAO is an organization that was established in 1943 to eliminate poverty and improve nutritional conditions, which became the specialized organization of the United Nations in 1946. The FAO, which has multiple effects on the fight against poverty, supports development projects for agriculture, forestry and fisheries and operates in more than 130 countries around the world, with more than 194 member states (FAO, 2021). It makes efforts to strengthen agricultural production, increase the availability of new technologies in agricultural production, and ensures the sustainability of agricultural product output. In this context, the FAO has increased the number of its projects related to reducing poverty and food insecurity, establishing its purposes during the Covid-19 process.

2.1 Protectionist Policies and Export Restrictions in Agriculture

Unlike other sectors, the agricultural sector is supported by special measures worldwide because it has strategic importance and involves different risks. Countries are to reduce foreign dependency on agriculture and food by ensuring self-sufficiency. In addition, the population employed in the agricultural sector is high, while the income of this population is relatively low. Except for developed countries, the rate of those employed in this sector represents a high percentage of total employment. For this reason, since the income losses experienced in this sector will affect a large part of the society, protectionist policies are applied. Apart from these, agricultural protectionism emerges as an important alternative policy tool in an unprecedented crisis like Covid-19.

After the World Wars, GATT was established to eliminate the negative effects of the protectionist trade policies adopted throughout the world. With the 1994 WTO Uruguay Round Agriculture Convention an important milestone in liberalizing trade in agricultural products worldwide was achieved. During the Covid-19 pandemic process it was understood that the WTO's efforts, which has been working toward international trade liberalization for about twenty-seven years, have been insufficient because the protectionist policies manifest themselves in different ways during crisis periods.

The Covid-19 pandemic has forced states to implement protectionist policies due to the closure of borders, the shrinkage in international trade and food supply security. One country's restrictions were responded to by other countries reprisals, and restrictions became common (Espitia et al., 2020:19–20). Countries such as Syria, which had a starving population, other countries with a significant depreciation in their currencies, and other countries that experienced a decline in commodity prices were more affected by this crisis (Food Security Information Network, 2020).

While the methods applied in classical protectionist policies are generally aimed at restricting the products coming from abroad and protecting domestic producers, these restrictions manifested themselves as supply restrictions during the Covid-19 pandemic. The main purpose here has been to secure domestic food supply (Kerr WA, 2020.228).

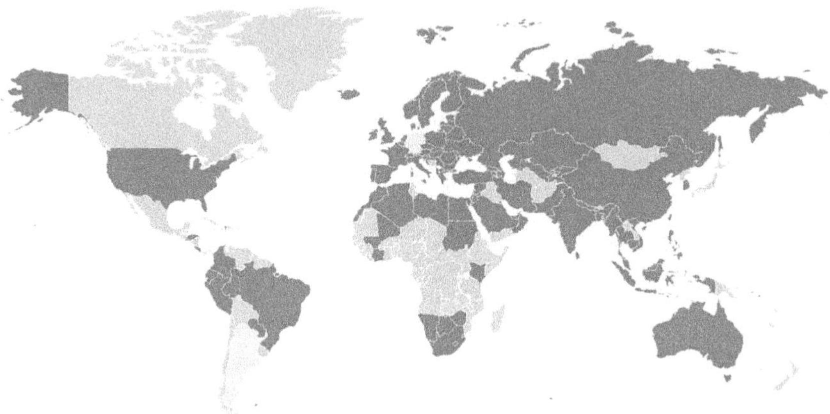

Fig. 1: *Covid-19 Temporary Export Measures*
Source: https://www.macmap.org/Covid-19 05.03.2021

Figure 1 shows the differences in restrictions imposed by countries on exports during the Covid-19 process. Countries shown in red represent ninety-eight countries that implemented restrictions and prohibitions on exports. The two countries shown in green represent countries that permitted freedom on exports. The other two countries, shown in orange, represent countries that implement both restrictions and release on exports. The remaining 137 countries have not taken any measures.

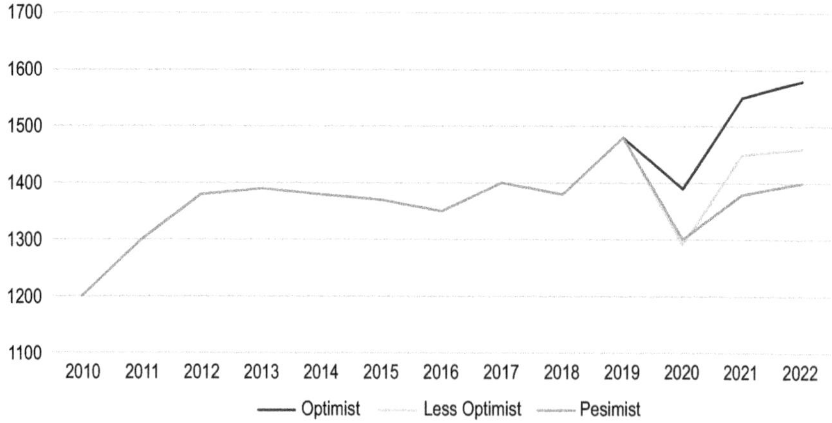

Fig. 2: *Global Agricultural Trade (USD Billion)*
Source: R.Sharma et al., 2006: 6

Figure 2 displays the statistics of agricultural trade volume in the world. While these figures show data until 2019, the data for 2020 and beyond include estimates. These estimates are offered in three different scenarios as optimistic, less optimistic and pessimistic. The optimistic scenario is shown with the blue line on the chart, estimating that the effect of the Covid-19 pandemic will be in 'V' shape. This means that after the collapse experienced in this crisis period, there will be a return to the old trend with a rapid recovery. According to the less optimistic scenario shown in yellow, the effect of the pandemic will be in 'U' shape. In other words, according to this scenario, the decrease in agricultural trade in the world due to the crisis will recover over a longer period. In the pessimistic scenario shown in red, an 'L' shaped development is estimated. Accordingly, the estimation that the decline in agricultural trade in the world will continue after the pandemic is dominant (R.Sharma et al., 2020: 6). In this environment, it is understood that countries will be more resistant to shocks such as Covid-19 in the future by keeping their production networks within their borders (Yazgan, 2020.158).

2.2 Developments in Agriculture and Food Prices

As a result of the panic decisions of countries, as well as individuals, the balances in the agricultural and food markets have deteriorated significantly. Fluctuations have been experienced in agriculture and food prices due to unpredictable increases in demand and distortions in the supply chain. These fluctuations manifest themselves during crisis periods. As can be seen in Figure 3, fluctuations and increases in the food price index can be observed in the crises between 2007–2008 and 2010–2011. Similar to these years, a price increase, which started in 2020 and continued in the first months of 2021, can be observed. It is estimated that these increases will continue in the following months of 2021, considering the fluctuations in the past crises (Hepburn et al., 2021: 3)

Fig. 3: *Food Price Index*
Source: FAO, Mountly Food Price Index

Although the increases in food prices due to panic purchases were observed in the first months of the pandemic, there were significant decreases in the prices of food and agricultural products during the first months of 2020 due to the decrease in total demand caused by the closure of restaurants and hotels throughout the world in the ensuing months (World Bank 2020). However, this situation has changed due to the reasons we have mentioned before; increases in food prices have started and, as of February 2021, the food price index is at its highest in the last seven years.

The agricultural product yield in 2020 was relatively high compared to other years. In fact, the production of agricultural products has been at record levels for many countries (USDA 2021). This high production level coincided with this crisis period when the pandemic prevented an excessive increase in food prices, contrary to the previous crisis periods.

3 Global Food Security

The meaning of the concept of food security, which is defined as 'the availability of sufficient, healthy, safe and nutritious food, physically and economically, to meet the nutritional needs and food priorities necessary for an active and healthy life of all people at all times' (FAO, 2001) can deepen in some periods. In today's world, where poverty and hunger problems persist, food security has become the focus of global threats during the Covid-19 pandemic, which has spanned more than a year.When we look at the concept of food security, we can see its four aspects in general. These are the availability of food, accessibility to food, quality and safety of food, and the first three aspects' stability (Keskin and Demirbas, 2012: 908). Regarding food security, which is the most important element of sustainable development, all countries try to support this with institutional arrangements while developing various strategies according to their conditions. They do this sometimes individually and sometimes through collaboration. The nature of international collaborations becomes evident in terms of food security, especially during crisis periods. Measures to be taken for countries experiencing difficulties in food security are vital. The prohibitions or quotas implemented on exports by some countries (with protectionist policies) at the beginning stage of Covid-19 demonstrate that food security and sustainable agricultural production may be interrupted on a global scale. In the face of such a situation, where the health crisis and financial crisis are experienced together, an inexperienced world has been severely affected by the pandemic, the like of which has never been seen before.

Although it is too early to measure the effects of the food crisis caused by the Covid-19 pandemic, the effects of food insecurity tend to rise beyond the estimates – as can be seen from the updated reports. According to the 2020 "The State of Food Security and Nutrition in The World 2020" Report published by FAO, the poverty problem increased even before the pandemic.. In 2019 approximately 690 million people, one in ten people in the world, were experiencing poverty problems. According to this report, it was estimated that the pandemic could lead 130 million people in the world into chronic poverty by the end of 2020 (FAO et.all., 2020).

Tab. 1: *Number of Food Insecure People in 2020 of International Food Security Assessment (IFSA) Regions*

	Updated 2020 Covid-19		**Pre-Covid-19 Estimate**	
	Number of Food-insecure (million)	**Share of the Population Food-insecure (%)**	**Number of Food-insecure (million)**	**Percentage of the Population Food-insecure (%)**
Asia	437.5	18.1	331.8	13.7
Latin America. and the Caribean	41.0	23.7	31.3	18.1
North Africa	10.7	5.5	8.2	4.2
Sub-Saharan Africa	431.5	41.2	389.6	37.2
Total for IFSA Countries	920.6	24.0	760.8	19.8

Source: Baquedano Et All 2021

The above table can be analysed to exemplify the effects of Covid-19. Since IFSA countries are the most problematic regions in the world in terms of food security, these countries are included in the table. Accordingly, while there were 760.8 million people who experienced food insecurity before Covid-19, according to updated 2020 data, this figure has increased to 920.6 million. According to the total population of IFSA countries, while those who experienced food insecurity amounted to 19.8% before Covid-19, this rate increased by 20 to 24% after Covid-19. In other words, one out of every four people living in these countries experiences food insecurity (Baquedano et al., 2021: 10).

The measures taken by the countries to control the crises disrupted the global food supply chains. Lockdowns caused by limitations and restrictions slowed down agricultural production, eroded livelihoods and prevented food transportation. Food loss and waste increase as producers struggled to get perishable vegetables and fruits to the market, and many people in urban centres had difficulty accessing fresh food.

In Turkey, which has a strategic position in rural development and food security, agricultural production's efficiency and sustainability are of great importance. The sustainability problem manifests itself significantly in our country, which has potential global climate change, drought and desertification to deal with. After the agricultural policies adopted through the structural adjustment programs that started in 2001 in Turkey, the ongoing supply-side agriculture problems have increased. Although food poverty is not in question for Turkey's small population, the insufficient supply, especially in animal food, causes food insecurity or nutritional deficiency problems. (Kıymaz and Şahinöz, 2011: 1)

4 Post-Covid-19

For the post-Covid-19 period, the experience gained during this pandemic has provided important lessons on both production under normal conditions and on how to act in a similar crisis. All processes, from the first producer to the end consumer, should be evaluated in different contexts. Production and production diversity should be made sustainable, and all supply chains should work effectively. It is understood that when agricultural and food products are released in an uncontrolled manner, production, agricultural employment, storage, logistics, financial resources and prices can be negatively affected. In this regard, these processes must be well planned, both nationally and globally, to protect against fluctuations.

Since the Covid-19 pandemic process is continuing all over the world, the accompanying uncertainties also continue. Although there is no panic environment (like at the beginning of the pandemic), the pandemic's risks regarding the processes we have mentioned above have not been eliminated.

After the pandemic, the effectiveness of international organizations on countries and their policies will determine the global production and trade of agricultural and food products. In this case, if the governments continue with restrictions, the breakages and problems in the supply chain will continue. On the contrary, if foreign trade restrictions are removed under the leadership of international institutions, trade volume and prices will be positively affected. This will also have positive consequences for countries suffering from food deprivation.

To ensure the sustainability of post-Covid-19 production in the agricultural sector, it is necessary to intensify the use of new technologies in this field, to remove the barriers to the mobility of the workforce, to increase agricultural production and diversity, and to provide capital support (Kumar et al., 2020: 838).

5 Conclusion

Although twelve years have passed, the effects of the economic collapse caused by the global financial crisis of 2008, to which the whole world was exposed, are still felt today. It can be predicted that the effects of the Covid-19 Crisis will continue over a long period. It will only be possible to measure and evaluate the effects of the Covid-19 crisis in the long term. Predictions about when we will come out of the pandemic process cannot be expected to be correct; therefore, unpredictability also increases the risks in a world of uncertainty. During this process, which is understood to remain on the agenda for a while, the markets' fragility may increase even more in the agricultural sector which, due to its nature, operates on the uncertainties. The solution to the global Covid-19 crisis should also be sought on a global scale.

A radical change in the food system can improve food security. There will probably be no problem in product supply for countries using advanced technologies in agriculture during the pandemic process. However, for countries that are labour-intensive and net importers of agricultural and food products, production disruptions during the pandemic period may continue.

Two potential alternatives appear after the pandemic. The first of these would be to develop methods that can continue free trade in similar crisis situations that may occur in the future, utilizing the experience gained during the pandemic. The other alternative would be to implement protectionist and self-sufficient agricultural policies. The results of the efforts of international institutions operating in this field, to direct their member countries to free trade, will be directly related to the decisions to be taken and the policies to be implemented by the countries independently.

References

Baquedano F., Zereyesus YA., Christensen C., and Valdes C. (2021). International Food Security Assessment, 2020–2030: Covid-19 Update, and Impacts on Food Insecurity, U.S. Department of Agriculture Economic Research Service Covid-19 Working Paper AP-087, P:1–33

Doğruel F. (2020). Küreselleşmenin Gölgesinde Türkiye'de Tarım, İktisat ve Toplum Dergisi, Yıl:10, Sayı 118, s:9–16

Espitia A., Rocha, N. and Ruta M. (2020). Covid-19 and Food Protectionism the Impact of the Pandemic and Export Restrictions on Wold Food Markets, World Bank Group Macroeconomics, Trade, and Investment Global Practice, Policy Research Working Paper 9253.

FAO, IFAD, UNICEF, WFP, and WHO. (2020). The State of Food Security and Nutrition in the World 2020, Transforming Food System for Affordable Healthy Diets. Rome FAO. https://doi .org/10.4060/ca9692en.

Food Security Information Network. (2020).Global Report on Food Crises: Joint Analysis for Better Decisions. https://docs.wfp.org/api/documents/WFP-0000114546/download/?_ga=2.18682361.1730104652.1592430424-175228185.1592430424 (accessed 17 June 2020).

Hepburn J., David L., Parent M. and Smaller C. (2021). Covid-19 and Food Export Restrictions: Comparing Today's Situation to the 2007/08 Price Spikes, International Institue for Sustainable Development (IISD).

Kerr WA. (2020). The Covid-19 Pandemic and Agriculture: Short and Long-Run Implications for International Trade Relations. Can J Agr Econ. 68:225–229. https://doi.org/10.1111/cjag.12230

Keskin B. and Demirbaş N. (2012). Gıda Güvencesi ve Hesaplama Yöntemleri Üzerine Bir Değerlendirme:Kısıtlar ve Öneriler, 10.Ulusal Tarım Ekonomisi Kongresi, 5–7 Eylül 2012, Konya.Ss.900–908.

Kıymaz T. and Şahinöz A. (2011). Dünya ve Türkiye – Gıda Güvencesi Durumu, Ekonomik Yaklaşım, Cilt.21, Sayı.76, ss.1–30.

Kumar A., Padhee AK. and Kumar S. (2020). How Indian Agriculture Should Change after Covid-19, Food Security 12, ss.837–840. https://doi.org/10.1007/s12571-020-01063-6

Sharma R., Shishodia A., Kamble S., Gunasekaran A. and Belhadi A. (2020). Agriculture Supply Chain Risks COVID-19: Mitigation Strategies and

Implications for the Practitioners, International Journal of Logistics: Research and Applications. DOI:10.1080/13675567.2020.1830049.

UNCTAD, United Nations Conference on Trade and Development. (2021). Key Statistics and Trends in International Trade 2020 – Trade Trends Under the Covid-19 Pandemic, United Nations Geneva, https://unctad.org/system/files/official-document/ditctab2020d4_en.pdf (22.03.2021)

USDA. (2021).World Agricultural Production, United States Department of Agriculture, Foreign Agricultural Service, Circular Series WAP 3–21, March 2021.

World Bank (2020) A Shock Like No Other: The Impact of Covid-19 on Commodity Markets, Commodity Markets Outlook / April 2020 Special Focus.

WTO, (2020). Trade statistics and outlook: Trade Set To Plunge As COVİD-19 Pandemic Upends Global Economy, https://www.wto.org/english/news_e/pres20_e/pr855_e.pdf

WTO, (2021). https://www.wto.org/english/thewto_e/thewto_e.htm (12.03.2021)

Yazgan ME. (2020).Koronavirüs Sonrası Dünyada Dış Ticareti Ne Bekliyor?, Salgın Ekonomisi,ss.141–162 324.ISBN:978-605-2294-37-6 Efil Yayınevi, Ankara.

Berna Dombekci Ozcelik

What Happened to the Profitability of Global Airline Companies during the COVID-19 Pandemic

1 Introduction

The global economy has been challenged several times by pandemics and diseases like the Severe Acute Respiratory Syndrome (SARS) outbreak in 2003, the avian influenza H5N1 in 2006, and the swine influenza H1N1 pandemic in 2009. Among these diseases, SARS was the most serious epidemic impacting airline traffic volumes. Overall in 2003, a loss of confidence and fears of the global spread impacted both business and leisure travel, resulting in Asia-Pacific airlines losing $6 billion (US) in revenue. However, monthly international passenger traffic returned to its pre-crisis level within nine months. On the other hand, 2005 and 2013 episodes of avian flu had a much softer and short-term impact, and air travel rebounded quickly as fears of global spread of virus eased. Air travel volumes began to recover after two months, and returned to pre-outbreak levels within six months (International Air Transport Association (IATA, 2020).

On 11 March 2020, a new pandemic named 2019-nCoV (COVID-19) was declared by the World Health Organization (WHO) (WHO, 2020a). This acute respiratory disease, due to a deadly virus, was first discovered in Wuhan, China in December 2019. By 31 March 2020 much of the world decided to go into lockdown as both death and infection numbers increased significantly (WHO, 2020b). The WHO (2021) reported 142 million confirmed cases of COVID-19, including 3 million deaths; the top ten countries for confirmed cases as of 21 April 2021 were the United States of America (US), India, Brazil, France, the Russian Federation, the United Kingdom (UK), Turkey, Italy, Spain and Germany. These countries closed their borders and imposed severe restrictions to avoid the spread of infection. The outcome of these measures was a contraction in their national economies. As a result, the aviation industry was severely affected by pandemic.

My study aims to analyse impact of pandemic on the profitability of international airline companies. The results are unique; the pandemic impact is assessed for each company. The organization of my paper is as follows: Section 2 underlines impact of COVID-19 on the aviation industry; Section 3 reviews literature; Section 4 shows research data; Section 5 analyses profitability ratios; and Section 6 includes concluding remarks.

2 Impact of COVID-19 on the Aviation Industry

As countries took measures to avoid the spread of infection, major airline companies withdrew almost all their domestic and international flights. As of 14 April 2020 EasyJet reduced its daily network traffic by -99%, IAG Airlines by -97%, Air-France-KLM by -96%, the Ryanair Group by -96% and the Lufthansa Group by -95%, respectively, compared to 2019. Thus, traffic between Europe and USA was diminished by 85% compared to 2019 (EUROCONTROL, 2020). The number of passengers decreased by 60% globally, from 4.5 billion in 2019 to 1.8 billion in 2020. The global capacity (available seat kilometers) was 57% lower year-on-year in December 2020. Revenue passenger kilometers dropped by 66% and the passenger load factor was recorded at 37% in April 2020, as opposed to 80% in April 2019 (International Civil Aviation Organization (ICAO), 2021). The numbers clearly reveal that COVID-19 had a significant impact on aviation industry operations. This impact is forecasted to translate in significant contraction in global trade and gross domestic product (GDP):

- An estimated contraction of -3.5 to -4.3% in world GDP in 2020, far worse than during the 2008 financial crisis, according to projections of IMF and World Bank (ICAO, 2021).
- A projected total economic loss of $22 trillion (US) between 2020 and 2025, according to IMF in the long run, which is compared to the Second World War (Turkish Airlines, 2020).
- A fall of global merchandise trade volume by 9.2% in 2020 compared to 2019.
- Approximately $48 billion (US) losses by airline companies in 2021 (IATA, 2021).

These inevitable contractions forced governments to impose fiscal and monetary stimulus packages so as to reach a strong recovery in 2021, and to protect the aviation industry. IATA declared that government supports given to airline companies reached $173 billion (US) in November 2020 (Turkish Airlines, 2020).

In 2021, the pandemic continued as the number of infected people continued to rise, due to the fact that countries were not able to vaccinate all of their citizens. For first week of April 2021, daily global flights were 65% lower compared to equivalent week in 2019. US airline passenger volumes were 41% below 2019 levels. Intra-Europe flights decreased by 67% compared to 2019 (EUROCONTROL, 2021). In Turkey, number of passengers dropped by 61% to 81.7 million passengers in 2020 (Directorate General of Civil Aviation, 2020).

3 Literature Review

Pandemics cause many problems for business activities; research provides evidence of this. The total impact of COVID-19 is being reviewed in detail by many authors of industry reports and articles.

Joo, Maskery, Berro, Rotz, Lee and Brown (2019) examined the economic impact of the Middle East Respiratory Syndrome (MERS) outbreak on tourism in 2015. Nhamo, Dube and Chikodzi (2020) studied the impact of COVID-19 on the aviation industry, adding weather and climate observations and employment. Suau-Sanchez, Voltes-Dorta and Cugueró-Escofet (2020) focused on the long-term impact of COVID-19. They postulated that, due to consolidations, a smaller industry would result. They underlined the importance of state aid, and they estimated a slower recovery in international flights due to teleworking and reduced disposable incomes. Gössling, Scott and Hall (2021) summarized estimated impacts of COVID-19 on tourism related industries. According to them, a more sustainable tourism strategy is needed ahead of the climate change challenge.

The aviation industry showed varying reactions to pandemics and diseases according to infection spread level. Albers and Rundshagen (2020) grouped European airlines' responses to COVID-19 into four categories: retrenchment, persevering, innovating and exit strategy. Retrenchment referred to significant costs and assets reduction, translating into fleet reduction, job cuts or reduced work. Persevering referred to protecting the status-quo through government aid and/or loans with favourable conditions or state guarantees. Innovating referred to strategic renewal meaning conversion of passenger aircraft to cargo transporters, entrance to new markets and setting new joint ventures. And, finally, some of them had to choose an exit strategy by discontinuing their operations.

Budd, Ison and Adrienne (2020) also proved evidence that every country – even every company – decided to undertake different measures, although they had to come together and take common measures to overcome global problems. They found consolidation and contraction to be short-term solutions. According to Dube, Nhamo and Chikodzi (2021), this pandemic proposed many opportunities for airline companies whose operations should have been more efficient and environmentally sustainable. This could be done by changing old and fuel-inefficient aircraft with new, narrow-bodied ones. They also advocated the adoption of sophisticated health and safety protocols to enhance their disaster risk reduction capabilities.

After discussing the impact of the pandemic and its possible outcomes, the recovery time from the pandemic gained importance for planning the future. Gudmundsson, Cattaneo and Redondi (2021) conducted a simulation model to predict recovery time for the aviation sector using past pandemics/crises. The model estimated passenger demand to recover in 2.4 years and air cargo in 2.2 years to pre-COVID-19 levels respectively. The model emphasized that the impact of pandemic will be temporary for an aviation industry subject to a structural transformation.

4 Research Data

The study used balance sheet and income statement data from thirty airline companies. The data covered the years between 2009 and 2020, and was obtained via Datastream. The financial data of 2009, belonging to Pegasus Airlines, IAG and Spirit Air, is missing due to data constraints. The airline companies were grouped on a country and/or region basis. The performance during two crises, the global financial crisis of 2009 and the pandemic crisis of 2020, was then compared. Average ratios between 2010 and 2019 were also calculated to find the average ratios in normal times. This comparison underlined how much the profitability ratios of the aviation industry deviated from normal times in 2020.

5 Profitability Ratios

The financial performance of airline companies was analysed with profitability ratios: the operating profit ratio; the Earnings before Interest, Taxes, Depreciation and Amortization (EBITDA) net profit ratio; and the return on total assets (ROA) (Brigham and Gapenski, 1996).

5.1 Operating Profit Ratio

The operating profit ratio is calculated as the operating profit divided by net sales. This ratio shows how many net sales are necessary to generate operating profits. Table 1 shows the operating profit of each company, and their average numbers.The average of all airline companies between 2010 and 2019 was calculated as 0.07. This means that every net sales of 100 TL generates an operating profit of 7 TL only. The average operating profit ratio in 2009 was 0.03; however, this ratio was recorded as -0.44 in 2020, pointing to a huge decrease. From a country and/or regional point of view, the average operating profit ratio of Turkish companies was -0.22 in 2020. This ratio for the UAE was 0.07, that is -23% lower compared to 2010–2019 average and 41% lower compared to 2009. This ratio was -0.55 in USA and -0.67 in Canada, respectively. An average operating profit ratio was recorded as 0.66 in Europe, -0.71 in Latin America and -0.21 in the Asia Pacific region, respectively. While the UAE has the highest operating profit ratio, the Latin America region had the lowest ratio in 2020. Unfortunately, in 2020 the total assets of airline companies in Latin America eroded by 20%, underlining the magnitude of their contraction, and their net sales decreased by 60%. Among the companies studied, positive operating ratios were only achieved by Air Arabia (0.07), China Airlines (0.02) and Korean Air (0.01), while minimum ratios belonged to Grupo Aeromexico (-1.38%), Norwegian Air (-1.20%) and Thai Airways (-0.82) in 2020.

Tab. 1: *Operating Profit and EBITDA Ratios of International Airline Companies by Country and/or Region*

		OPERATING PROFIT RATIO			EBITDA RATIO		
		FINANCIAL CRISIS	**COVID-19 CRISIS**		**FINANCIAL CRISIS**	**COVID-19 CRISIS**	
COUNTRY/ REGION	**COMPANY NAME**	**31.12.2009**	**31.12.2020**	**AVERAGE (2010–2019)**	**31.12.2009**	**31.12.2020**	**AVERAGE (2010–2019)**
TURKEY	Turkish Airlines	0.12	-0.08	0.05	0.17	0.17	0.17
	Pegasus Airlines		-0.35	0.07		0.15	0.13
UAE	Air Arabia	0.13	0.07	0.10	0.25	-0.03	0.21
EUROPE	Air France – KLM	-0.01	-0.42	0.003	0.03	-0.34	0.07
	Lufthansa	-0.05	-0.47	0.02	0.07	-0.26	0.11
	IAG	-0.06	-0.54	0.08	-0.002	-0.65	0.13
	Norwegian Air	0.07	-1.20	-0.01	0.11	-1.45	0.07
USA	Delta Airlines	0.003	-0.48	0.12	0.04	-0.58	0.15
	United Continental Holdings	0.01	-0.58	0.08	0.05	-0.35	0.12
	Alaska Air	0.07	-0.48	0.16	0.15	-0.37	0.21
	Hawaiian Holdings	0.09	-0.55	0.12	0.15	-0.61	0.14
	American Airlines	-0.01	-0.66	0.08	0.003	-0.44	0.09
	Southwest Airlines	0.08	-0.55	0.13	0.09	-0.30	0.17
	Spirit Air	0.16	-0.45	0.16	0.19	-0.12	0.18
	JetBlue Airways	0.08	-0.68	0.11	0.16	-0.40	0.17
CANADA	Air Canada	-0.03	-0.67	0.07	0.10	-0.41	0.11

Tab. 1: *Continued*

		OPERATING PROFIT RATIO			EBITDA RATIO		
		FINANCIAL CRISIS	COVID-19 CRISIS		FINANCIAL CRISIS	COVID-19 CRISIS	
COUNTRY/ REGION	**COMPANY NAME**	**31.12.2009**	**31.12.2020**	**AVERAGE (2010–2019)**	**31.12.2009**	**31.12.2020**	**AVERAGE (2010–2019)**
LATIN AMERICA	Copa Airlines	0.18	-0.58	0.17	0.27	-0.06	0.20
	LATAM Airlines	0.09	-0.57	0.03	0.21	-0.83	0.15
	Grupo Aeromexico	-0.05	-1.38	0.05	-0.03	-0.95	0.10
	Gol Linhas Aereas	0.07	-0.31	0.03	0.19	-0.49	0.05
ASIA PACIFIC	Aeroflot	0.08	-0.35	0.07	0.12	0.03	0.11
	Air China	0.03	-0.22	0.09	0.26	0.19	0.21
	Cathay Pacific Airways	0.02	-0.25	0.04	0.18	-0.08	0.13
	China Airlines	-0.01	0.02	0.03	0.09	0.29	0.15
	China Eastern Airlines	-0.08	-0.33	0.04	0.19	0.20	0.19
	China Southern Airlines	-0.05	-0.14	0.04	0.14	0.18	0.18
	EVA Airways	-0.02	-0.01	0.05	0.11	0.32	0.15
	Asiana Airlines	-0.06	-0.07	0.03	0.004	0.26	0.09
	Korean Air	0.02	0.01	0.05	0.14	0.20	0.16
	Thai Airways	0.09	-0.82	-0.004	0.22	-2.08	0.10
	AVERAGE	0.03	-0.44	0.07	0.13	-0.29	0.14
	MAXIMUM	0.18	0.07	0.17	0.27	0.32	0.21
	MINIMIUM	-0.08	-1.38	-0.01	-0.03	-2.08	0.05

Source: Datastream, 2021

5.2 Earnings before Interest, Tax, Depreciation and Amortization (EBITDA) Ratio

The EBITDA ratio is calculated as EBITDA divided by net sales. This ratio shows how many net sales are necessary to generate EBITDA earnings. Tab 1 shows the EBITDA of each company and their average numbers.The airline companies' average between 2010 and 2019 was calculated as 0.14. This means that every net sales of 100 TL generated EBITDA of 14 TL. The average EBITDA ratio in 2009 was 0.13; however, this ratio was recorded as -0.29 in 2020.

From a country and/or regional point of view, the Turkish companies' average EBITDA ratio was 0.16 in year 2020. This ratio was -0.03 for UAE, -0.41 for Canada and 0.40 for the USA, respectively. The average EBITDA ratio was recorded as -0.68 in Europe, 0.58 in Latin America and -0.05 in Asia Pacific region, respectively. While Turkey had the highest EBITDA ratio, Europe had the lowest ratio in 2020.

Among companies in 2020, the highest EBITDA ratios were achieved by EVA Airways (0.32), China Airlines (0.29) and Asiana Airlines (0.26), while lowest ratios belong to Thai Airways (-2.08), Norwegian Air (-1.45) and Grupo Aeromexico (-0.95).

5.3 Net Profit Ratio

Another profitability ratio is net profit ratio, which is calculated as net profit divided by net sales. This ratio shows how many net sales are necessary to generate net profits. Tab 2 shows the net profit of each company, and their average numbers.Between 2010 and 2019, all airline companies' averaged 0.04; that is, every net sale of 100 TL generated a net profit of 4 TL only. The average net profit ratio in 2009 was 0.03; however, this ratio was recorded at -0.62 in 2020.

From a country and/or regional point of view, the average net profit ratio of Turkish companies was -0.27 in 2020. This ratio was -0.10 in UAE, -0.47 in USA and -0.80 in Canada, respectively. The average net profit ratio was recorded as -1.14 in Europe, -1.08 in Latin America and -0.46 in the Asia Pacific region, respectively. While the UAE had the highest net profit ratio, Europe had the lowest in 2020.

In 2020 the highest net profit ratios were achieved by China Airlines (0), EVA Airlines (-0.04), Air Arabia (-0.10) and Asiana Airlines (-0.10), while the lowest ratios belonged to Thai Airways (-2.96), Norwegian Air (-2.53) and Grupo Aeromexico (-1.49).

Tab. 2: *Net Profit and ROA Ratios of International Airline Companies by Country and/or Region*

		NET PROFIT RATIO			RETURN ON TOTAL ASSETS		
		FINANCIAL CRISIS	COVID-19 CRISIS		FINANCIAL CRISIS	COVID-19 CRISIS	
COUNTRY/ REGION	**COMPANY NAME**	**31.12.2009**	**31.12.2020**	**AVERAGE (2010–2019)**	**31.12.2009**	**31.12.2020**	**AVERAGE (2010–2019)**
TURKEY	Turkish Airlines	0.08	-0.12	0.05	0.07	-0.03	0.03
	Pegasus Airlines		-0.41	0.04		-0.08	0.04
UAE	Air Arabia	0.23	-0.10	0.12	0.08	-0.02	0.04
EUROPE	Air France – KLM	-0.03	-0.64	-0.02	-0.03	-0.24	-0.02
	Lufthansa	-0.01	-0.49	0.04	-0.005	-0.18	0.04
	IAG	-0.06	-0.88	0.05		-0.22	0.04
	Norwegian Air	0.06	-2.53	-0.004	0.11	-0.35	-0.0002
USA	Delta Airlines	-0.04	-0.72	0.09	-0.03	-0.18	0.07
	United Continental Holdings	-0.04	-0.46	0.04	-0.03	-0.13	0.04
	Alaska Air	0.04	-0.37	0.09	0.02	-0.10	0.08
	Hawaiian Holdings	0.10	-0.60	0.06	0.12	-0.13	0.06
	American Airlines	-0.07	-0.51	0.02	-0.06	-0.15	0.02
	Southwest Airlines	0.01	-0.34	0.07	0.01	-0.10	0.06
	Spirit Air	0.12	-0.27	0.10		-0.06	0.11
	JetBlue Airways	0.02	-0.46	0.06	0.01	-0.11	0.04
CANADA	Air Canada	-0.002	-0.80	0.03	-0.002	-0.16	0.03

(*continued on next page*)

Tab. 2: *Continued*

		NET PROFIT RATIO			RETURN ON TOTAL ASSETS		
		FINANCIAL CRISIS	**COVID-19 CRISIS**		**FINANCIAL CRISIS**	**COVID-19 CRISIS**	
COUNTRY/ REGION	**COMPANY NAME**	**31.12.2009**	**31.12.2020**	**AVERAGE (2010–2019)**	**31.12.2009**	**31.12.2020**	**AVERAGE (2010–2019)**
LATIN AMERICA	Copa Airlines	0.19	-0.75	0.11	0.12	-0.15	0.07
	LATAM Airlines	0.07	-1.16	0.02	0.04	-0.27	0.01
	Grupo Aeromexico	-0.10	-1.49	0.02	-0.20	-0.49	0.04
	Gol Linhas Aereas	0.15	-0.94	-0.09	0.12	-0.43	-0.09
ASIA PACIFIC	Aeroflot	0.03	-0.39	0.03	0.03	-0.13	0.04
	Air China	0.10	-0.21	0.06	0.05	-0.05	0.03
	Cathay Pacific Airways	0.07	-0.47	0.04	0.04	-0.10	0.02
	China Airlines	-0.03	0.001	0.01	-0.02	0.0005	0.01
	China Eastern Airlines	0.004	-0.20	0.04	0.002	-0.04	0.03
	China Southern Airlines	0.01	-0.12	0.04	0.004	-0.03	0.02
	EVA Airways	-0.03	-0.04	0.03	-0.02	-0.01	0.02
	Asiana Airlines	-0.06	-0.10	-0.01	-0.04	-0.03	-0.005
	Korean Air	-0.01	-0.11	-0.01	-0.01	-0.03	-0.005
	Thai Airways	0.05	-2.96	-0.03	0.03	-0.63	-0.02
	AVERAGE	0.03	-0.62	0.04	0.02	-0.15	0.03
	MAXIMUM	0.23	0.001	0.12	0.12	0.0005	0.11
	MINIMIUM	-0.10	-2.96	-0.09	-0.20	-0.63	-0.09

Source: Datastream, 2021

5.4 Return on Total Assets (ROA) Ratio

The last profitability ratio is the return on total assets ratio, which is calculated as the net profit divided by average total assets. This ratio shows how much total investments generate net income. Tab 2 shows the return on total assets of each company and their average numbers.

The average of all airlines between 2010 and 2019 was calculated as 0.03. The average ROA in 2009 was 0.02; however, this ratio was recorded as -0.15 in 2020.

From a country and/or regional point of view, the Turkish companies' average return on assets (ROA) was -0.06 in 2020. This ratio was -0.02 in the UAE, -0.24 in Europe, -0.33 in Latin America and -0.11 in the Asia Pacific region, respectively. While the UAE had the highest ROA, Latin America had the lowest ratio in 2020. Among companies, the highest ROA ratios were achieved by China Airlines (0) and EVA Airlines (-0.01), while the lowest ratios belonged to Thai Airways (-0.63) and Groupo Aeromexico (-0.49) in 2020.

These massive negative operating EBITDA net profit ratios and ROAs provide evidence that the impact of pandemic was significant for the aviation industry. The success in vaccination and the reopening of the world's economies is crucial for the aviation industry's recovery.

6 Conclusion

Nations had to struggle with the global pandemic named COVID-19 in 2020. Every country imposed lockdowns and severe restrictions, which resulted in high levels of economic contraction. Service industries, mainly the aviation industry, were severely hit by the outbreak of the pandemic. In 2020, the total number of passengers declined by 60% on a global basis, from 4.5 billion in 2019 to 1.8 billion. Airline companies were faced with huge losses. IATA stated that government support given to airline companies reached $173 billion (US) in November 2020, in order to overcome these difficulties (Turkish Airlines, 2020). This study analysed the impact of the pandemic on the profitability of the biggest airline companies. The study data covered the financial data of thirty airline companies between 2008 and 2020.

The impact of the pandemic was analysed with operating profit, EBITDA and net profit ratios, and ROA. The average operating profit ratio in 2009 was 0.03; however, this ratio was -0.44 (2010–2019 average: 0.07) in 2020. The average EBITDA ratio in 2009 was 0.13; however, this ratio was recorded as -0.29 (2010–2019 average: 0.14) in 2020. The average net profit ratio in 2009 was 0.03; however, this ratio was calculated as -0.62 (2010–2019 average: 0.04) in 2020. The average ROA ratio in 2009 was 0.02; however, the 2010–2019 average was -0.15, compared with 0.03 in 2020. The results underline that airline companies recorded huge losses, and the impact of pandemic is incomparable when compared to previous pandemics and the 2009 financial crisis.

Infected cases and deaths continue to rise in 2021 due to a lack of widespread vaccinations. Consequently, this pandemic crisis forces researchers and experts to think about a future roadmap for sustainable growth. They suggest consolidations in the aviation industry, an increase in their liquidity, and a switch from old aircraft to fuel-efficient, narrow-bodied ones. In short, the industry should aim to prepare for climate change via sustainable tourism. They should also undertake new health and safety protocols to reduce their disaster risk. Although the impact of pandemic is severe, the recovery time is forecasted to last not more than three years. Meanwhile, the effects of the pandemic recession are estimated temporary for aviation industry if the industry undertake a structural transformation. The keys to recovery seem to be the vaccination of at least 60% of all humans and the reopening of economies.

References

Albers, S. and Rundshagen, V. (2020). European airlines' strategic responses to the COVID-19 pandemic (January-May, 2020), Journal of Air Transport Management, Volume 87.

Brigham, E, and Gapenski, L. (1996). International Financial Management, Dryden Press.

Budd, L., Ison, S. and Adrienne, N. (2020). European airline response to the COVID-19 pandemic – Contraction, consolidation and future considerations for airline business and management, Research in Transportation Business and Management, Volume 37, 100578.

Directorate General of Civil Aviation (2020). Annual Report 2020 (30.03.2021).

Dube, K., Nhamo, G. and Chikodzi, D. (2021). COVID-19 pandemic and prospects for recovery of the global aviation industry, Journal of Air Transport Management, Volume 92.

EUROCONTROL (2020). COVID19 Impact on European Air Traffic. EUROCONTROL Comprehensive Assessment. 14.04.2020. Available at: https://www.eurocontrol.int/sites/default/files/2020-04/covid19eurocontrolcomprehensive-air-traffic-assessment-14042020.pdf (05.04.2021).

EUROCONTROL (2021). COVID19 Impact on European Aviation. EUROCONTROL Comprehensive Assessment. Available at: https://www.eurocontrol.int/sites/default/files/2021-04/covid19eurocontrolcomprehensive-air-traffic-assessment-08042021.pdf (08.04.2021).

Gössling, S., Scott D. and Hall M.C. (2021). Pandemics, tourism and global change: A rapid assessment of COVID-19, Journal of Sustainable Tourism, Volume 29, Issue 1, 1–20.

Gudmundsson, S.V., Cattaneo, M. and Redondi, R. (2021). Forecasting temporal world recovery in air transport markets in the presence of large economic shocks: The case of COVID-19, Journal of Air Transport Management, Volume 91, 102007.

IATA (2020). What can we learn from past pandemic episodes? IATA. Available at: https://www.iata.org/en/iata-repository/publications/economic-reports/what-can-we-learn-from-past-pandemic-episodes/ (05.04.2020)

IATA (2021). IATA havayolları için 2021 zarar tahminini artırdı. Available at: https://www.bloomberght.com/iata-havayollari-icin-2021-zarar-tahminini-artirdi-2278911 (21.04.2021)

ICAO (2021). Feb 2021: Air Transport Monthly Monitor. 2021. Available at: https://www.icao.int/sustainability/Documents/MonthlyMonitor2021/Monthly_Monitor_February_2021.pdf (11.04.2021)

Joo, H., Maskery, B. A., Berro, A. D., Rotz, L. D., Lee, Y. K., and Brown, C. M. (2019). Economic impact of the 2015 MERS outbreak on the Republic of Korea's tourism-related industries. Health Security, Volume 17, Issue 2, 100–108.

Nhamo, G., Dube, K. and Chikodzi, D. (2020). COVID-19 and Implications for the Aviation Sector: A Global Perspective, Counting the Cost of COVID-19 on the Global Tourism Industry Book Chapter, Springer, September, pp 89–107.

Suau-Sanchez, P., Voltes-Dorta, A. and Cugueró-Escofet, N. (2020). An early assessment of the impact of COVID-19 on air transport: Just another crisis or the end of aviation as we know it?, Journal of Transport Geography, Volume 86, June, 102749.

Turkish Airlines (2020). 2020 Faaliyet Raporu, Available at: https://investor.turkishairlines.com/documents/yillikraporlar/thy_frat_2020_yillikrapor.pdf (05.04.2021).

WHO (2020a). Coronavirus disease 2019 (COVID-19) Situation Report – 51. World Health Organization. Available at: https://www.who.int/emergencies/diseases/novel-coronavirus 2019/situation-reports (30.03.2021).

WHO (2020b). Coronavirus disease 2019 (COVID-19) Situation Report – 72. World Health Organization. Available at: https://www.who.int/docs/default-source/coronaviruse/situation-reports/20200401-sitrep-72-covid-19.pdf?sfvrsn=3dd8971b_2 (02.04.2021).

WHO (2021). WHO Coronavirus Dashboard. Available at: https://covid19.who.int/ (21.04.2021).

Serkan Göksu and Özer Özçelik

Evaluation of Indicators Regarding Health Services: Example of Turkey and OECD Countries

1 Introduction

When the 1982 Constitution of the Republic of Turkey is examined Article 2, where 'Characteristics of the Republic' is defined, reads 'is a social law state', clearly stating that an understanding of social state is one of the essential qualities of the state. In addition to the said article, Article 5 of the 1982 Constitution, under the heading 'Main Objectives and Duties of the State', reads 'The main objectives and duties of the State are ..., to try to prepare the necessary conditions for the development of tangible and intangible existence of people'. Considered as a whole, together with Article 60, which states that everyone has the right to social security, and Article 61, which states that segments of society need to be specifically protected in terms of social security, as well as Articles 2 and 5, it can be said that the understanding of the social state, as laid down in the constitution, is the understanding that the state assumes the duty of improving the social status of people, providing them with a humane level of living, and providing them with social security (Republic of Turkey Constitution of 1982, Articles 2, 5, 60 and 61).

The social state is a state that observes and protects all kinds of tangible and intangible interests of everyone living within its political borders as well as its own citizens outside its political borders. In a governance model that employs a social state approach, the state acts for certain purposes and imposes certain obligations. These objectives include establishing social and income justice, standing by people who are right despite being weak, supporting citizens who are unable to meet their needs, and having social security under state guarantee. Taxes constitute the main item of income to be used by the state in the realization of these objectives. In addition, the state can generate income through fees, duties, goodwill, parafiscal revenues, seigniorage revenues, fines and tax penalties, property, initiative and privatization income, or by taking over the assets of its citizens who have no inheritors. Any tangible benefits the state obtains by winning wars directly (oil, natural gas, gold, precious mines, electricity, water, historical artifacts, real estates etc.) may also constitute the revenue of the state (Akdoğan, 2011: 117–9). 'Health' has been considered an important component of human capital since the 1990's, when human capital as well as physical capital began to be considered as one of the important dynamics of development. It requires the state to respond to the market through health expenditure in order to ensure justice in income distribution and to provide access to health services for people with insufficient income (Yalçın and Çakmak, 2016: 706). Health services spread positive externality to the whole society, starting from the persons receiving the service. It can be said that these externalities in the health sector are the reason for the state's response in this field (Stiglitz, 1988). While 'preventive health services' included in health services are expressed as fully public goods and services that no one can be deprived of, services offered in the field of health other than this can be specified as semi-public goods since they can be purchased and sold in the market (Şenatalar, 2003: 26). Health expenditure include expenditure for preventive health services to prevent losses through therapeutic activities related to regaining health. Economically, health expenditure lead to an increase in the welfare of individuals as well as labour productivity (Piabuo and Tieguhong, 2017: 7). This is because making the population healthier will enable the labour force to achieve a higher level of productivity and to generate higher income (Bayraktutan and Alancıoğlu, 2020: 2). Health indicators are one of the main components of both the human capital and the human development index (Akıncı and Tuncer, 2016: 49). Health expenditure made in this area generally cover the expenditure made for the protection and improvement of health. Especially due to the global pandemic experienced by countries in recent years, governments attach much more importance to health expenditure, and it can be said that this importance varies depending on the development level of the country. Although health services have increased both in quantity and in proportion in many developed and developing countries over the years, it can be said that the share allocated to health expenditure is higher in developed countries than it is in other countries. Increases in health expenditure are expected to have positive effects on people's quality of life and life span.

This study aims to examine the data on health indicators of Turkey and OECD countries, and to evaluate Turkey's position within the OECD. The study evaluates the effect of the developments in the health sector on health-related indicators, whose significance is increasingly felt due to the Covid-19 pandemic. The data used in the study was obtained from the Turkish Statistical Institute and OECD databases. In the next part of the study, the indicators related to health expenditure and health professionals are evaluated with the help of graphs, created specifically for Turkey as well as by comparison with other OECD countries. Then, the relationship between life expectancy at birth and infant mortality rates, which are health related indicators, and health expenditure per capita are analysed. Finally, the findings are evaluated and suggestions are made to policymakers.

2 Indicators Regarding Health Expenditure

In this part of the study, indicators related to health expenditure in Turkey are examined, and graphs and tables related to total health expenditure, health expenditure per capita, ratio of total health expenditure to gross domestic product, ratio of general government health expenditure to total health expenditure, and health investment expenditure are presented and interpreted comparatively with OECD countries.

Tab. 1: *Indicators Regarding Health Expenditure*

	Total health expenditure (Million TL)	Health expenditure per capita (TL)	Ratio of total health expenditure to gross domestic product (%)	Ratio of general government health expenditure to total health expenditure (%)	Health Investment Expenditure (%)
1999	4,985	79	4.7	61.1	199
2000	8,248	128	4.8	62.9	360
2001	12,396	190	5.1	68.1	310
2002	18,774	284	5.2	70.7	443
2003	24,279	363	5.2	71.9	603
2004	30,021	444	5.2	71.2	1 405
2005	35,359	517	5.2	67.8	2 067
2006	44,069	636	5.6	68.3	3 120
2007	50,904	726	5.8	67.8	4 409
2008	57,740	813	5.8	73.0	5 420
2009	57,911	804	5.8	81.0	2 616
2010	61,678	843	5.3	78.6	3 054
2011	68,607	924	4.9	79.6	3 236
2012	74,189	987	4.7	79.2	3 901
2013	84,390	1 108	4.7	78.5	4 688
2014	94 750	1 228	4.6	77.4	5 871
2015	104 568	1 337	4.5	78.5	7 782
2016	119 756	1 511	4.6	78.5	7 216
2017	140 647	1 751	4.5	78.0	9 666
2018	165 234	2 030	4.4	77.5	10 236
2019	201 031	2 434	4.7	78.0	13 357

Source: https://www.tuik.gov.tr/

Looking at the health expenditure figures per capita presented in Figure 1, they tended to increase continuously from 1999 to 2019, except for 2009. While an average health expense of TL 2,030 was made per capita in 2018, this figure increased by 20% to TL 2,434 in 2019. This increased rate in 2019 is well above the average increase trend.

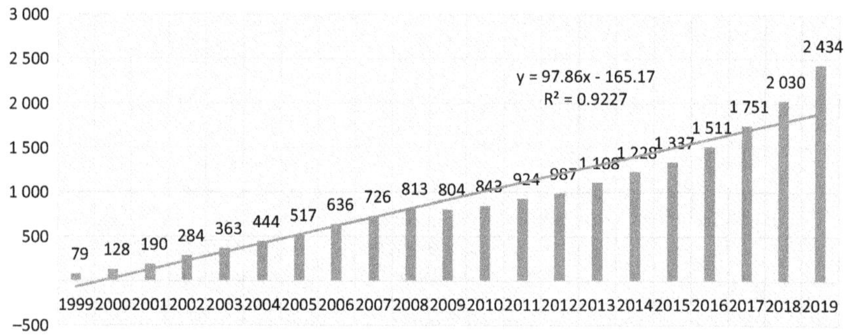

Fig. 1: *Health Expenditure Per Capita (TL) in Turkey*

In 2018, the ratio of total health expenditure to GDP was 4.4%. That is the lowest ratio since 1999; the same ratio was 4.7% in 2019.

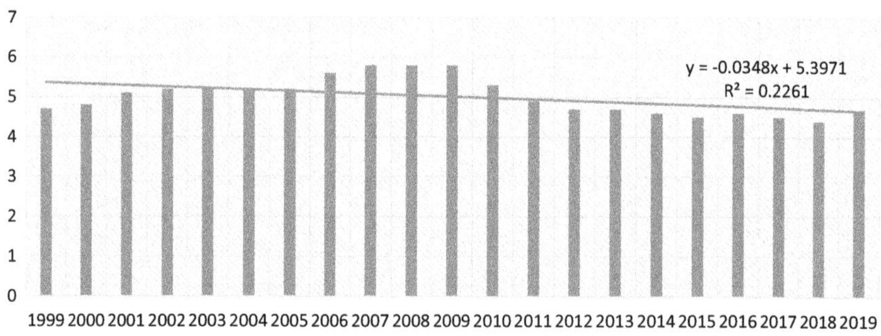

Fig. 2: *Ratio of Total Health Expenditure To Gross Domestic Product (%) in Turkey*

The total health expenditure made in 2019 increased by 21.7% compared to 2018 and reached approximately TL 201 billion. Approximately TL 157 billion of this figure is within the scope of general government expenditure, and approximately TL 44 billion was realized by the private sector. For 2019, while the share of general government health expenditure in total health expenditure was 78%, the share of private sector health expenditure was 22%. Compared to the previous year, general government health expenditure increased by 22.5% and private sector health expenditure increased by 18.8%. In addition to these figures, the share of health expenditure in the budget was 16.3% for 2019. Considering that this ratio was 11.3% in 2002, it can be said that health expenditure increased significantly.

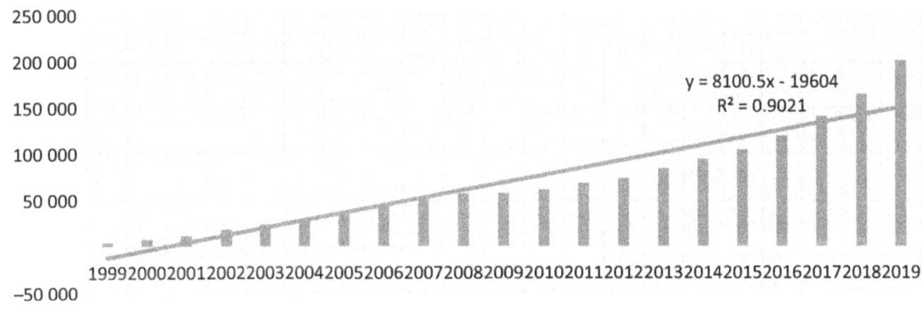

Fig. 3: *Total Health Expenditure (Million TL) in Turkey*

As can be seen in Figure 4, investments made within the scope of health expenditure in 2019 increased by 30.5% compared to 2018 and reached TL 13 billion 357 million. In Turkey, the reason for this increase in investment in recent years is because of hospital investments, whose advantage was greatly felt during the Covid-19 pandemic. On 19 March 2020 the Republic of Turkey Minister of Health, Fahrettin Koca, announced the current data on hospital bed capacities, which are increasingly becoming important during the pandemic in particular. According to that statement, the public and private sectors in Turkey have a total of 25,466 adult intensive care places, and there are on average 40 intensive care beds for every 100,000 people.

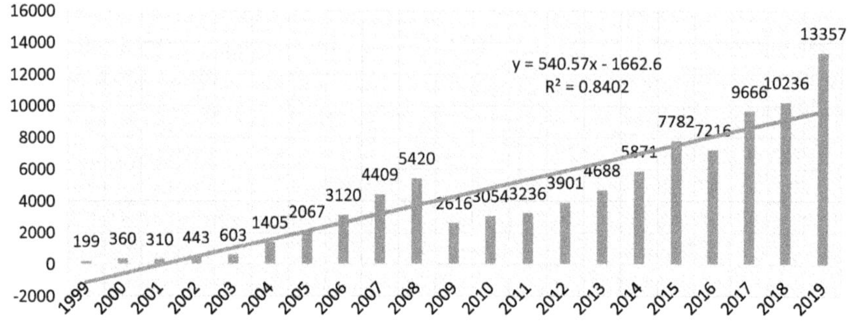

Fig. 4: *Health Investment in Turkey*

As can be seen in Figure 5, when the share of health expenditure of OECD countries in GDP was examined, they were on average 8.8% in 2018. This figure has remained more or less the same since 2013. The United States ranked by far the first among OECD countries with health expenditure corresponding to 16.9% of its GDP. Following them, countries such as Germany, France, Sweden, Japan and Canada spent approximately 11% on health services. Turkey, on the other hand, lies somewhere between China (5%) and India (3.6%), spending 4.2% of its GDP on health services (OECD indicators, 2019).

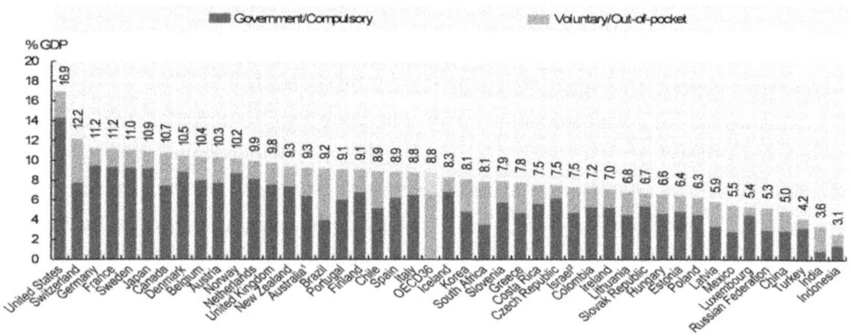

Fig. 5: *Health Expenditure As A Share of GDP, 2018 (or nearest year)*
Source: https://www.oecd-ilibrary.org/

According to the data on the financing of health expenditure presented in Figure 6; when we look at the OECD average, approximately three-quarters of health expenditure is covered through mandatory financing programs. Approximately 80% or more of health expenditure in Norway, Denmark, Sweden, Iceland and the United Kingdom are made up of central, regional or local government programs, while most of the rest are made up from out-of-pocket payments. In Germany, Japan, France, Luxembourg and the Netherlands, the dominant source of financing is compulsory health insurance, which account for about three-quarters of health expenditure. In Turkey, compulsory health insurance ranks first in the financing of health expenditure with a share of 56%, while it is below the OECD average in out-of-pocket health expenditure with a share of 17% (OECD indicators, 2019).

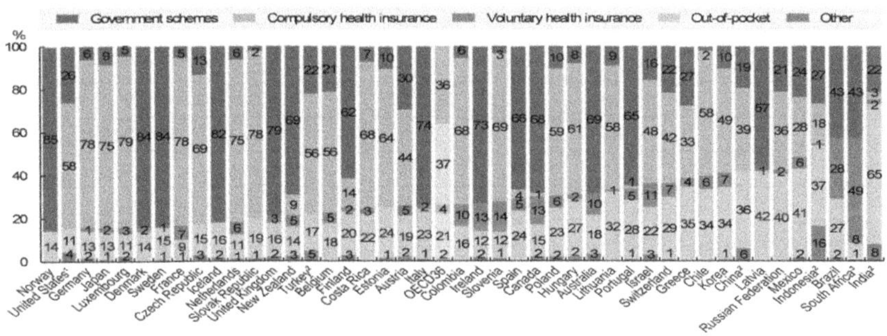

Fig. 6: *Health Expenditure By Type Of Financing, 2017 (or nearest year)*
Source: https://www.oecd-ilibrary.org/

3 Evaluation of Statistics on Health Personnel

In this section, the aim is to present the current view of the number of healthcare personnel in Turkey, graphs and tables regarding the number of physicians, number of people per physician, number of doctors and nurses per thousand people. These are presented and interpreted comparatively with OECD countries. Table 2 presents the number of people per healthcare personnel working in different fields in Turkey between 1951 and 2018. It can be said that any decrease in these ratios means faster access to health services.

Tab. 2: *Number of People Per Healthcare Personnel*

Years	Physicians	Dentists	Nurses	Other health personnel	Midwives	Pharmacists
1951	3,250	22,404	31 079	7,110	13,462	20,393
1955	3,371	24,903	15 644	6,075	11,923	18,994
1960	2,799	19,718	11 366	7,071	8,799	19,563
1965	2,859	16,123	6 783	6,661	7,179	17,588
1970	2,228	10,885	4 016	3,548	3,120	11,731
1975	1,843	7,932	2 703	3,632	3,085	5,716
1980	1,631	6,279	1 653	3,810	2,798	3,685
1985	1,381	6,057	1 630	4,780	2,797	4,336
1990	1,088	5,243	1 225	2,558	1,812	3,490
1995	862	5,100	930	1,740	1,511	3,130
2000	754	4,039	924	1,238	1,545	2,930
2001	725	4,052	897	1,229	1,562	2,945
2002	722	4,056	917	1,325	1,601	2,979
2003	711	3,786	902	1,170	1,613	3,003
2004	700	3,801	898	1,116	1,573	3,008
2005	683	3,794	881	1,110	1,582	3,026
2006	667	3,804	844	1,033	1,568	3,013
2007	651	3,661	746	889	1,496	2,944
2008	632	3,583	716	799	1,500	2,886
2009	612	3,524	690	776	1,470	2,879
2010	597	3,440	642	742	1,464	2,781
2011	593	3,542	598	674	1,440	2,864
2012	583	3,533	561	617	1,414	2,846
2013	573	3,439	549	582	1,435	2,838
2014	573	3,379	545	559	1,470	2,857
2015	557	3,171	515	540	1,483	2,860
2016	551	2,992	522	552	1,522	2,864
2017	539	2,898	486	520	1,504	2,834
2018	536	2,679	430	462	1,455	2,560

Source: https://www.tuik.gov.tr/

As can be seen in Figure 7, it is observed that the number of individuals per healthcare personnel decreased significantly in all branches without exception from 1951 to 2018. Of course, although this results in an increase in health expenditure, it means that it will be easier to access health services.

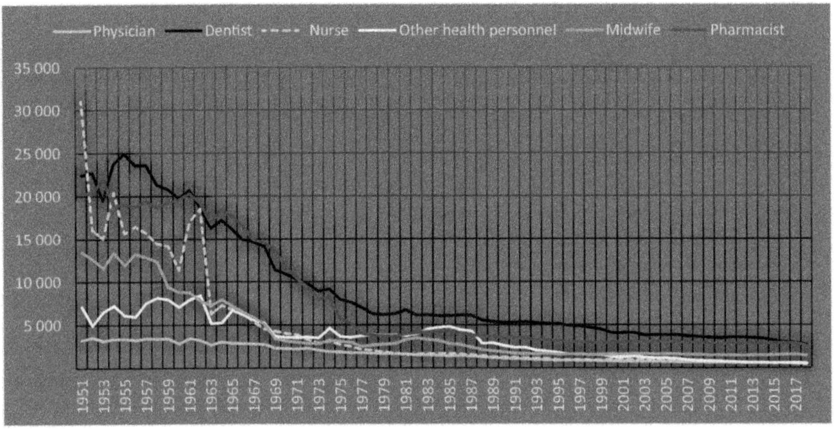

Fig. 7: *Number of Persons Per Health Care Professional*

When the graph showing the number of physicians in Figure 8 is examined, the number of physicians increased continuously from 2009 to 2018, and increased by 2% from 2018 to 2019. On the other hand, the most current data on health professionals was obtained from the answer provided by Republic of Turkey Minister of Health, Fahrettin Koca, in answer to a parliamentary question. According to these explanations, the total number of physicians in Turkey as of 1 January 2020 is 164,594, while the total number of nurses is 198,465. However, 61.4% of the doctors work within the organization of the Ministry of Health, 20.4% work at universities and the remaining 18.2% work in the private sector. The total number of dentists is 32,859.

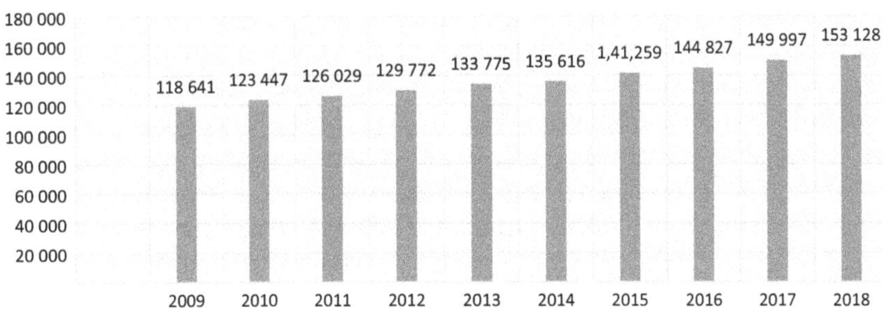

Fig. 8: *Number of Physicians*

According to the timeline graph showing the change in the number of patients per physician presented in Figure 9, the said number decreased continuously between 2009–2018, except for 2014. Considering that the population in Turkey constantly increased in those years, it can be said that the rate of increase in the number of physicians has increased more than the rate of population growth, and thus the number of patients per physician has been reduced. In addition, considering the reduction in the number of patients per physician together with the increase in population and the number of physicians in Turkey, it can be concluded that people can access health services faster.

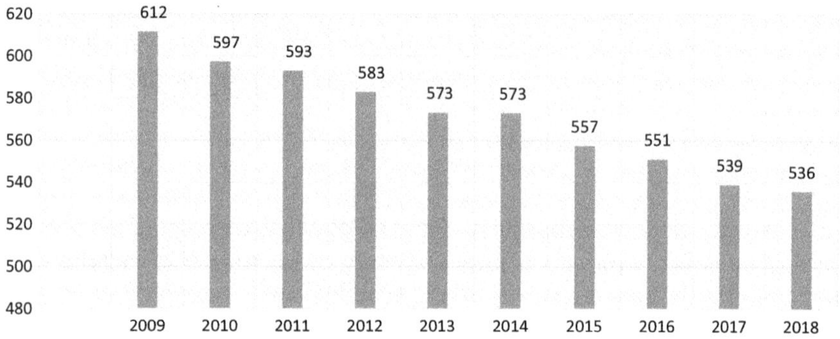

Fig. 9: *Number of Persons Per Physician*

Figure 11 shows comparatively the number of doctors per a thousand people related to OECD member countries and their key partners in 2000 and 2017. The number of physicians per thousand people in Turkey in 2017 was 1.9. Considering that the OECD average is 3.5 for the same year, it can be said that this ratio is insufficient for Turkey. With this figure, Turkey is the country with the lowest physician density among OECD countries. However, Turkey is better positioned than Brazil, South Africa, India and Indonesia, which are not only OECD members but also key partners. A striking result that can be obtained from the graph is that there is not even one doctor per a thousand people in South Africa, India and Indonesia, which are the last three countries in terms of physician density. It can be seen that, as of 2017, Greece has the highest physician density among OECD countries with 6.3.

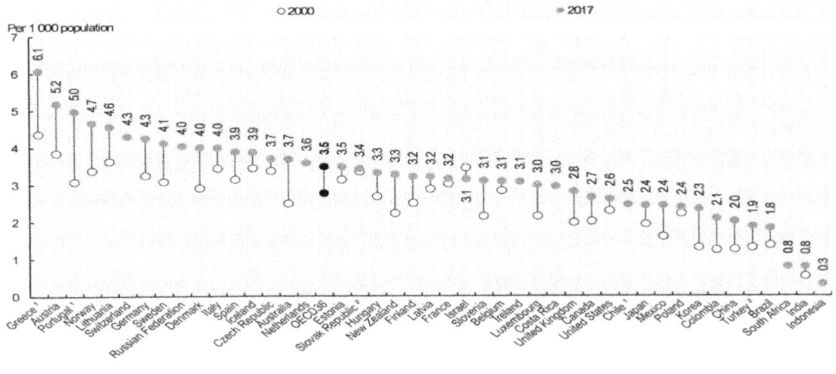

Fig. 11: *Practising Doctors Per 1,000 Population, 2000 and 2017 (or nearest year)*
Source: https://www.oecd-ilibrary.org/

Figure 12 shows comparatively the number of nurses per a thousand people related to OECD member countries and their key partners in 2000 and 2017. The number of nurses per thousand people in Turkey in 2017 was 2.1, which was an increase compared to 2000. Considering that the OECD average is 8.8, it can be said that this figure is behind the OECD average. Similar to the number of doctors, Turkey ranks last in the number of nurses per thousand people compared to OECD countries. The country with the highest ratio in this regard among OECD countries is Norway with 17.7.

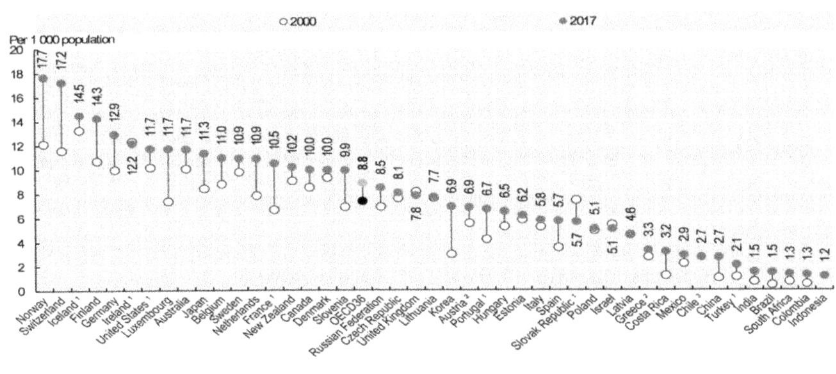

Fig. 12: *Practising Nurses Per 1,000 Population, 2000 and 2017 (or nearest year)*
Source: https://www.oecd-ilibrary.org/

4 Evaluation of Key Health Indicators

According to international health institutions, health-related indicators can be divided into three main groups: death, disease and fertility ratio. The increase in health expenditure per capita is expected to bring about positive changes in these health-related indicators. However, continuously increasing health expenditure does not mean that health indicators will continuously improve (Daştan and Çetinkaya, 2015: 123).

4.1 Life Expectancy at Birth

Average life expectancy can be considered as an indicator of the level of development of countries. Increasing people's life span has been one of the main goals of public authorities in many countries. It can be said that the life expectancy of developed countries at birth is quite high compared to developing countries. Figure 13, comparing life expectancy at birth between 1970 and 2017, shows certain increases in each country, while the increase in South Korea and Turkey is highly significant. As a result of this increase, South Korea exceeded the OECD average while Turkey neared the OECD average.

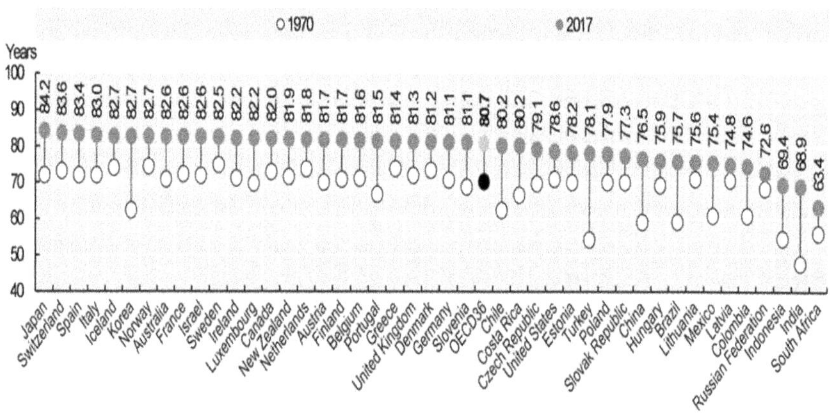

Fig. 13: *Life Expectancy at Birth, 1970 and 2017 (or nearest year)*
Source: https://www.oecd-ilibrary.org/

Figure 14 shows the relationship between life expectancy at birth and total health expenditure per capita in US dollars for 2019, or the nearest year for 37 OECD member countries. There is a positive correlation between these two variables. Japan (84.2) and Switzerland (83.8), which have a Bismarck health system model, are the countries with the highest life expectancy among OECD countries, while Latvia (74.9), Mexico (75) and Lithuania (75.8) are the countries with the lowest scores in this regard. Although a close examination of Figure 14 reveals that the increase in health expenditure per capita increases life expectancy, such increases can be said to be diminishing. Because, although the US has the highest health expenditure per capita with $11,071, it has the same average life expectancy as Turkey, which has an average health expenditure of $1,337 per capita. Turkey is better positioned in this regard than Colombia and Mexico.

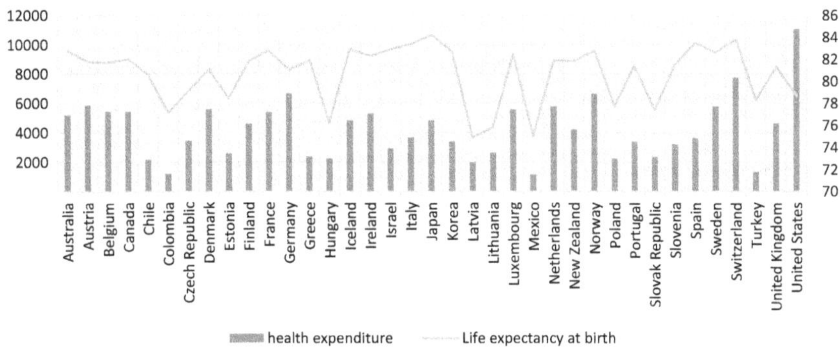

Fig. 14: *The Relationship Between Total Health Expenditure Per Capita in Dollars and Life Expectancy at Birth*

4.2 Infant Mortality Rates

Figure 15 shows the relationship between infant mortality rates per hundred thousand live births and total health expenditure per capita in US dollars. There is a negative correlation between these two variables. It is seen that infant mortality rates are the highest in Colombia, Mexico and Turkey, where health expenditure per capita is low. Colombia has the highest mortality rate with 16.8 per hundred thousand live births. Iceland, Slovenia (1.7) and Japan (1.9) have the lowest infant mortality rates.

Reducing infant mortality rates requires determined political will, robust strategies and adequate resources. The more dramatic aspect of these deaths is that they are mostly caused by preventable factors. Countries and global organizations need to do more work to improve infant survival rates.

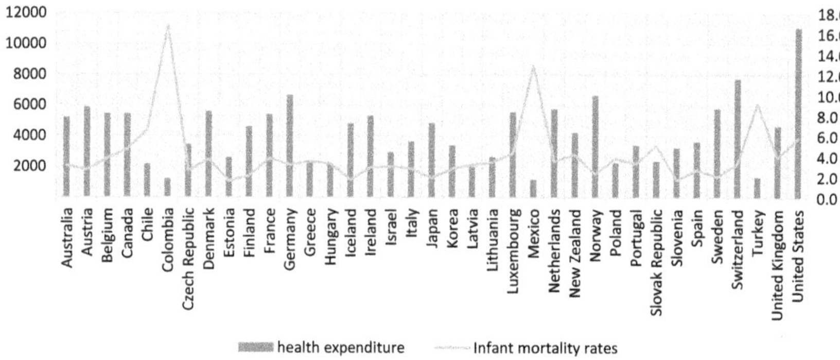

Fig. 15: *The Relationship Between Infant Mortality Rates Per A Hundred Thousand Live Births and Total Health Expenditure Per Capita in Dollars*

5 Conclusion

This study aims to examine the most current data on health indicators of Turkey and OECD countries and to evaluate Turkey's position within the OECD. According to the results obtained from the study, Turkey, where the social state approach is dominant, was found to be the country with the lowest scores among OECD countries in its GDP share of health expenditure, and the number of physicians and nurses per thousand people in 2018. In terms of average health expenditure per capita in dollars for 2019, Turkey is better positioned than Colombia and Mexico among 37 OECD countries. It has been concluded that an increase in health expenditure per capita increases average life expectancy, but this increase is diminishing, and that it reduces infant mortality rates. In addition, Turkey, which has come a long way in terms of life expectancy at birth, has unfortunately not shown the same success in infant mortality rates. Although there have been improvements in the health indicator over the years, Turkey is well behind the OECD average in many areas of data. In order for Turkey to improve its indicators regarding health services, it should allocate more of its budget to healthcare and increase the number of healthcare personnel without compromising quality.

References

Akdoğan, A. (2011). Kamu Maliyesi, Gözden Geçirilmiş ve Genişletilmiş 14. Baskı, Gazi Kitabevi Tic. Ltd. Şti., Ankara.

Akıncı, A. and Tuncer, G. (2016). Türkiye'de Sağlık Harcamaları ile Ekonomik Büyüme Arasındaki İlişki. Sayıştay Dergisi, 102, 47–61.

Bayraktutan, Y. ve Alancıoğlu, E. (2020). Sağlık Harcamaları-İktisadi Büyüme İlişkisi: Seçilmiş Oecd Ülkeleri İçin Panel Bootstrap Granger Nedensellik Analizi. Uşak Üniversitesi Sosyal Bilimler Dergisi, 13 (2), 1–12.

Daştan, İ. ve Çetinkaya, V. (2015). OECD Ülkeleri ve Türkiye'nin Sağlık Sistemleri, Sağlık Harcamaları ve Sağlık Göstergeleri Karşılaştırması. SGD-Sosyal Güvenlik Dergisi, 5 (1), 104–134.

OECD (2019). Health at a glance. OECD Indicators, https://doi.org/10.1787/4dd50c09-en, Access Date: 31.03.2021.

Piabuo, S. M. ve Tieguhong, J. C. (2017). Health Expenditure and Economic Growth: A Review of The Literature and An Analysis Between the Economic Community for Central African States (CEMAC) and Selected African Countries. Health. Economics Review, 7 (23), 1–13.

Statistics of Health Expenditure. 2019. Turkish Statistical Institute Newsletter, Issue: 33659 Link: https://data.tuik.gov.tr/Bulten/Index?p=Saglik-Harcamalari-Istatistikleri-2019-33659, Access Date: 31.03.2021.

Stiglitz, J. (1988). Economics of the Public Sector, W.W. NortonandCompany, Second Edition.

Şenatalar, B. (2003). Sağlık Ekonomisine Genel Bir Bakış. Cumhuriyet Üniversitesi Tıp Fakültesi Dergisi 25 (4), Özel Eki.

Republic of Turkey Constitution of 1982. (1982, October 20). Official Gazette (Issue: 17844). Link: https://www.tbmm.gov.tr/anayasa/anayasa_2018.pdf, Access Date: 31.03.2021.

Yalçın, A. Z. ve Çakmak, F. (2016). Türkiye'de Kamu Sağlık Harcamalarının İnsani Gelişim Üzerindeki Etkisi. Atatürk Üniversitesi İktisadi ve İdari Bilimler Dergisi, 30(4), 705–723.

Tufan Sarıtaş

The Effect of Calorie Consumption on Economic Growth: The Case of Sub-Saharan Countries

1 Introduction

With the development known as the 'Green Revolution' since the mid-20th century, scientists have succeeded in producing plant species that have higher yields and are more resistant to various diseases and harmful species. Plus, with this development, grain production increased by approximately 2.6 times worldwide in the period 1950–1984. This great increase in food production helped to reduce the hunger problem, especially in underdeveloped regions of the world. However, despite all of these positive developments, the problem of malnutrition in the world is still not fully resolved. Although the problem of malnutrition in the African continent has been brought to the agenda by many non-governmental organizations, scientists, politicians, economists and activists, it continues to be a problem that needs to be solved urgently as an affront to humanity. Many obstacles such as the difficulty of access to clean water, civil wars and the prevalence of AIDS and other diseases in the continent are shown to be the source of malnutrition in African countries. It is also noted that inadequate food consumption in less developed countries has a negative effect on economic performance. In this context, a permanent solution to the problem of insufficient food availability can give the economies of underdeveloped countries a more stable outlook, and may prevent the recurrence of this problem, especially in the long run. In this study, the possible relationship between calorie consumption and economic growth is discussed in the context of Sub-Sahara countries, and empirically evaluated.

2 Literature Summary

Correa and Cummins (1970) argue that malnutrition may adversely affect economic growth in poor countries. In this study, the effect of calorie consumption on labour productivity and thus economic growth was investigated by considering the period 1950–1962 in eighteen countries. "In the findings they obtained; they observed that in 9 nine Latin American countries, calorie consumption affected economic growth."On the other hand, in the model in which they considered nine developed countries, they found that the effect of calorie consumption on growth has a very small value. They also argue that calorie consumption may have a greater impact on economic growth in very poor countries than in Latin American countries.

Behrman and Deolaliker (1987), in their study on rural South India, argued that an increase in income will not lead to a significant increase in calorie consumption. In addition, the study emphasizes that even if income increases, a flat calorie-income curve emerges as there is a tendency to prefer calorie-free foods in very poor households. In their study Wimberley and Bello (1992) investigated the effects of foreign investments, exports and economic growth on food consumption in fifty-nine third world countries for the period 1967–1985. In the findings obtained it has been observed that lowering the level of dependency on exports increases food consumption and foreign investment dependency has a negative effect on food consumption. It is also stated that economic growth mediates a very small effect on food consumption. Behrman et al. (1997), in their study of rural Pakistan, observed that the income-calorie consumption relationship is largely dependent on the stage of production, the shape of the income, the liquidity of the assets, and the duration of the income.

Dawson and Tiffin (1998) investigated the relationship between calorie consumption, per capita income and food prices in India for the period 1961–1992. In their findings they found that economic growth, represented by per capita income, increased calorie consumption. Also, the study emphasizes that calorie consumption cannot be increased significantly with food subsidies. Abdulai and Aubert (2004) examined the relationship between calorie consumption, household expenditure and food prices in Tanzania for the period 1998–1999. They found that there is a positive relationship between household expenditure and calorie consumption. Besides, they also observed that there was a negative relationship between food prices and calorie consumption. Further, the study emphasizes that an increase in income can eliminate insufficient calorie consumption, and that food subsidies to very poor households can play an important role in increasing calorie consumption. Dawson and Sanjuan (2011) examined the relationship between income and calorie consumption in forty-one developing countries for the period of 1970–2013. In their discoveries; they observed that there is a bidirectional causality relationship between income and calorie consumption. The study emphasizes that increases in income can alleviate malnutrition to a limited extent, and that increases in calorie consumption can also increase income by providing more work effort.

Schneider et al. (2011) found that population growth increased total food production in their simulation study of different country groups. It is also emphasized that changes in income have a high impact on the level of food consumption. Smith (2015) deals with the gradual increase in malnutrition and low calorie consumption despite the economic growth in India since the mid-1980s. In the study, it has been argued that the tendency of people to consume outside the home is increasing, but the data collected is insufficient. Accordingly, it is stated that an erroneous observation has emerged; despite the economic growth in India, increasing levels of malnutrition have occurred.

Marques et al. (2018) examined the relationship between economic growth, sustainable development and food consumption in seventy-seven countries, divided according to different income groups for the period 1995–2013. According to findings obtained, economic growth increases the level of meat consumption in poor countries. However, as a country gets richer, this effect seems to begin to fade. It is also understood that a decrease in meat consumption in poor countries has a negative effect on economic growth. Additionally, it has been observed that the decrease in meat consumption in emerging economies has a positive effect on sustainable development.

3 Data and Method

In this study, thirty-one Sub-Saharan countries – including Benin, Botswana, Burkina Faso, Cameroon, Central African Republic, Chad, Congo, Cote d'lvoire, Gabon, Gambia, Ghana, Guinea, Guinea-Bissau, Kenya, Madagascar, Malawi, Mali, Mauritania, Mauritus, Mozambique, Namibia, Niger, Nigeria, Rwanda, Senegal, Sierra Leone, South Africa, Tanzania, Togo, Uganda and Zimbabwe – the effect of daily calorie consumption per capita on economic growth for the period of 1993–2017 was investigated by panel data analysis. The series used in panel data analysis is shown in Table 1.

Tab. 1: *Data and Sources*

Variable Code	Variable Name	Source
GDP	GDP (constant 2010 US$)	World Bank
CAL	Daily calorific supply kilocalories per person per day	United Nations Food and Agricultural Organization (FAO)
EXP	Exports of goods and services (% of GDP)	World Bank
POP	Population, total	World Bank

Logarithmic transformation was applied to all series used in the study. Summary statistical information and correlation matrix regarding the series are shown in Table 2.

Tab. 2: *Descriptive Statistics and Correlation Matrix*

Seri	**Mean**	**Min.**	**Max.**	**Std. Dev.**	**Obs.**
GDP	22.985	20.245	26.864	1.291	775
CAL	7.757	7.410	8.055	0.129	775
EXP	3.227	1.639	4.508	0.524	775
POP	16.005	13.845	19.067	1.174	775
	GDP	CAL	EXP	POP	
GDP	1				
CAL	0.39	1			
EXP	0.19	0.32	1		
POP	0.71	0.03	-0.34	1	

In this study, two different models are established on which the GDP series representing growth is dependent. In Model 1, the effect of the CAL series, representing the daily calorie consumption per person, on the GDP series representing growth was investigated. Although the same relationship is investigated in Model 2, EXP series representing export and POP series representing population are included in Model 2 as independent variables. The econometric forms for the models are as follows:

$$GDP_{it} = \beta_0 + \beta_1 CAL + \varepsilon_{it} \qquad \text{(Model 1)}$$

$$GDP_{it} = \beta_0 + \beta_1 CAL + \beta_2 EXP + \beta_3 POP + \varepsilon_{it} \qquad \text{(Model 2)}$$

Panel data analysis was used in this study. In order to determine the appropriate panel data model, the existence of unit and time effects in the models were investigated by using the F test (Moulton and Randolf, 1989). If the probability value of the F test for unit effects is statistically significant at the 5% level, the H0 hypothesis, which states that there are no unit effects, is rejected and the H1 hypothesis, which states that there are unit effects, is accepted. Conversely, if the probability value of the F test for unit effects is statistically insignificant at the level of 5%, the H0 hypothesis stating that there are no unit effects is accepted and the H1 hypothesis, which states that there are unit effects, is rejected.

The same is followed in determining the time effect. If the probability value of the F test for time effects is statistically significant at the level of 5%, the H0 hypothesis stating that there are no time effects is rejected and the H1 hypothesis, which states that there are unit effects, is accepted. Conversely, if the probability value of the F test for time effects is statistically insignificant at the level of 5%, the H0 hypothesis stating that there are no time effects is accepted and the H1 hypothesis, which states that there are time effects, is rejected.

The Hausman test (Hausman, 1978) was used for estimating the fixed and random effects in the models. If the probability value of the Hausman test is statistically significant at the 5% level, the H0 hypothesis, which states that there are fixed effects, is accepted and the H1 hypothesis, which states that there are random effects, is rejected. Conversely, if the probability value of the test is statistically insignificant at the level of 5%, the H0 hypothesis stating that there are fixed effects is rejected and the H1 hypothesis expressing that there are random effects is accepted. In addition, the 'Generalized Least Squares Method' (Kiefer, 1980), which can be used in both fixed-effect and random-effect models, was used as a panel data analysis method in the study. This method can make consistent predictions in models even under heteroscedasticity and autocorrelation problems.

4 Analyse Results

Table 3 shows the F test results for the models. According to the findings obtained, it can be seen that the F test probability value of Model 1 and Model 2 is statistically significant at the 5% level for unit effects. Therefore, the H0 hypothesis, which states that there are no unit effects, is rejected and the H1 hypothesis, which states that there are unit effects, is accepted. Therefore, it is understood that there are unit effects in Models 1 and 2.

On the other hand, it can be seen in Table 3 that the F test probability value of Model 1 and Model 2 is statistically significant at the 5% level for time effects. Thus, the H0 hypothesis, which states that there are no time effects, is accepted and the H1 hypothesis, which states that there are time effects, is rejected. Particularly, it is understood that there are no time effects in Model 1 and Model 2. For this reason, panel data models with one-way unit effect should be preferred in the estimation of Model 1 and Model 2. Consequently, the Generalized Least Squares Method, one of the panel data models with one-way unit effect, was preferred in the study.

Tab. 3: *F Test Results*

Effects	Models	
	Model 1	**Model 2**
Unit	674.14 (0.000)	602.90 (0.000)
Time	0.43 (0.993)	0.48 (0.983)
Suitable Model	One-Way Unit Effects Model	One-Way Unit Effects Model

Note: *Values in parantheses are probility values, others are coefficients.*

Table 4 shows the findings of Model 1 and Model 2 estimated using the Generalized Least Squares Method. It is seen that the probability value of Hausman test belonging to Model 1 is not significant at the 5% significance level. Therefore, the H0 hypothesis stating that fixed effects are valid for Model 1 is rejected and the H1 hypothesis stating that the random effects are valid is accepted. For that reason, the one-way random effects model was used for the prediction of Model 1, and the findings are reported in Table 4. In the findings of Model 1, it can be observed that the CAL series, which expresses the daily calorie consumption per person, positively affects the GDP series, which represents economic growth at a 1% significance level with a coefficient of 4.052. So according to Model 1, as daily calorie consumption per person increases, economic growth increases.

Tab. 4: Estimation Results (Generalized Least Squares)

Depended Variable: GDP	**Model 1**	**Model 2**
CAL	4.052 (0.000)*	0.744 (0.000)*
EXP	-	0.119 (0.000)*
POP	-	1.391 (0.000)*
C	-8.052 (0.000)*	-5.437 (0.000)*
Number of Obs	775	775
Number of Country	31	31
R^2	0.55	0.86
Hausman Test Stat. (Prob.)	0.01 (0.943)*	94.95 (0.000)*
Method	Rassal Effect	Fixed Effect
Suitable Model	One-Way Unit Effects Model	One-Way Unit Effects Model

***Note:** Values in parantheses are probility values, others are coefficients.

It can be seen that the Hausman test probability value of Model 2 in Table 4 is significant at the 5% significance level – inasmuch as the H0 hypothesis stating that fixed effects are valid for Model 2 is accepted, and the H1 hypothesis stating that random effects are valid is rejected. For this reason, the one-way fixed effects model was used for the estimation of Model 2, and the findings are also reported in Table 4. In the data of Model 2, with the coefficient of 0.744 of the CAL series, which expresses the daily calorie consumption per person, it can be observed that the EXP series representing exports, with a 0.119 coefficient and POP series representing population with a 1.391 coefficient, positively affects the GDP series representing economic growth at the 1% significance level. So according to Model 2, aside from the effects of exports and population, as calorie consumption increases, so does economic growth.

5 Conclusion

In this study, the effect of calorie consumption on economic growth for the period 1993–2017 in thirty-one Sub-Saharan countries was investigated by panel data analysis. In the study, two different models were established on which the GDP series representing growth depends. In Model 1, the effect of CAL series representing calorie consumption on the GDP series representing growth was investigated. Although the same relationship was investigated in Model 2, the EXP series representing exports and the POP series representing population were included in Model 2 as independent variables.

In the findings of Model 1 it can be observed that the CAL series, which expresses the daily calorie consumption per person, positively affects the GDP series, which represents economic growth, at a 1% significance level with a coefficient of 4.052. Elsewhere in the findings of Model 2, with a coefficient of 0.744 of the CAL series, which expresses the daily calorie consumption per person, it can be observed that the EXP series representing exports, with a 0.119 coefficient and the POP series representing population with 1.391 coefficient positively affect GDP series, representing economic growth at a 1% significance level. Thereby, in both models, it can be concluded that as calorie consumption increases, so does economic growth. This finding empirically supports the assessment put forward by Correa and Cummins (1970) in their studies that calorie consumption in poor countries can affect economic growth. As a result, in underdeveloped countries, especially in Sub-Sahara, calorie consumption should be taken into account as one of the determinants of economic growth, and individuals should be guaranteed sufficient calories by way interventionist policies. In this way, the economic performance of the less developed countries in the African continent can be increased and an important contribution can be made to the solution of the insufficient food consumption problem.

References

Abdulai, A. and Aubert, D. (2004). Nonparametric and Parametric Analysis of Calorie Consumption in Tanzania. Food Policy, 29(2), 113–129.

Behrman, J. R. and Deolalikar, A. B. (1987). Will Developing Country Nutrition Improve with Income? A Case Study for Rural India. Journal of Political Economy, 95(3), 492–507.

Behrman, J. R., Foster, A. D. and Rosenzweig, M. R. (1997). The Dynamics of Agricultural Production And The Calorie-Income Relationship: Evidence from Pakistan. Journal of Econometrics, 77(1), 187–207.

Correa, H. and Cummins, G. (1970). Contribution of Nutrition to Economic Growth. The American Journal of Clinical Nutrition, 23(2), 560–565.

Dawson, P. J. and Sanjuan, A. I. (2011). Calorie Consumption and Income: Panel Cointegration and Causality Evidence in Developing Countries. Applied Economics Letters, 18(15), 1455–1461.

Dawson, P. J. and Tiffin, R. (1998). Estimating the Demand for Calories. American Journal of Agricultural Economics, 80, 474–481.

Hausman, J. (1978). Specification Test in Econometrics. Econometrica, 46(6), 1251–1271.

Kiefer, N. M. (1980). Estimation of Fixed Effect Models for Time Series of Cross Sections with Arbitrary Intertemporal Covariance. Journal of Econometrics, 14, 195–202.

Marques, A. C., Fuinhas, J. A. and Pais, A. F. (2018). Economic Growth, Sustainable Development and Food Consumption: Evidence Across Different Income Groups of Countries. Journal of Cleaner Production, 196, 245–258.

Moulton B. R. and Randolf W. C. (1989). Alternative Tests of the Error Components Model. Econometrica, 57, 685–693.

Schneider, U. A., Havlik, P., Schmid, E., Valin, H., Mosnier, A., Obersteiner, M., Böttcher, H., Skalsky, R., Balkovic, J., Sauer, T. and Fritz, S. (2011). Impacts of Population Growth, Economic Development, and Technical Change on Global Food Production and Consumption. Agricultural Systems, 104(2), 204–215.

Smith, L. C. (2015). The Great Indian Calorie Debate: Explaining Rising Undernourishment During India's Rapid Economic Growth. Food Policy, 50, 53–67.

Wimberley, D. W. and Bello, R. (1992). Effects of Foreign Investment, Exports, and Economic Growth on Third World Food Consumption. Social Forces, 70(4), 895–921.

Güner Tuncer and Ersin Nail Sağdıç

The Nexus between Income Distribution and Economic Growth in Turkey

1 Introduction

The basic functions of public finance management are to promote efficiency in resource allocation, justice in income distribution and stability in the economy. Ensuring stability in the economy also includes achieving economic growth and development. What is the relationship between economic growth and income distribution in an economy? Kuznets (1955) tries to explain this relationship by asking whether inequality in income distribution increases or decreases with the economic growth of a country?

According to Kuznets, injustice in income distribution first increases in the early stages of economic development and decreases after a certain income level is reached (Özçelik, 2021). Kuznets's research question was first modeled by Robinson (1976). This model focuses on the movements of individuals from agriculture to industry, and the size of the economy is initially constituted by the agricultural/rural sector. This sector is characterized by low per capita income and relatively little inequality. The industrial/urban sector begins on a small scale, has higher per capita income and a relatively high degree of inequality. Economic development, in part, concerns people's mobility from agriculture to industry. Mobile individuals meet with a rise in per capita income, and this change increases the overall degree of inequality in the economy. The initial dominant effect in the industrial/urban sectors is the expansion in the size of a small and relatively rich group of individuals. At the early stages of development, the relation between the level of per capita production and the dimension of inequality is thus positive. As the size of the agricultural sector diminishes, the dominant effect of the continued mobility on inequality is that more poor agricultural workers can join the relatively rich industrial sector (Barro, 1999). Many workers who begin at the bottom rung of the industrial sector tend to move up more quickly than those who began as the richer workers within the sector. The decreasing size of the labour force in the agricultural sector also tends to raise relative wages. In the next phases of development, there is a negative relationship between the level of per capita product and the extent of inequality. Thus, inequality first rises and later falls as the economy becomes more developed.

The relationship between the Gini coefficient as an indicator of inequality and the level of per capita production is described by an inverted-U curve, the Kuznets curve.

Kuznets' inverted-U hypothesis has been discussed by many researchers, and there are several studies that are specific to Turkey. Tokatlıoğlu and Atan (2007) identify Kuznets curve for the regions of Turkey classified as at the NUTS-2 level. Dişbudak and Süslü (2009) find that income distribution in Turkey for the period 1963–1998 follows a course contrary to Kuznet's prediction. Günaydın and Çetin (2015) show, by using cointegration analysis, that Kuznets' inverted-U relationship is valid in the long run for the period 1960–2006. Using the autoregressive distributed lag (ARDL) model for the period of 1980–2012, Ak and Altıntaş (2016) find that for Turkey, the curve demonstrates a U-shaped rather than an inverted U-shaped relationship. The results of several studies in Turkey support the validity of Kuznets inverted-curve hypothesis (Akıncı and Akıncı, 2016; Akalin et al., 2018; Abdioğlu et al., 2019; Limanlı, 2020). However, some studies support the U-shaped relationship (Öztürk and Oktar, 2017). For example, Akıncı and Akıncı (2016) support the Kuznets inverted-U hypothesis in Turkey for 1960–2014. Moreover, Çütcü et al. (2020) identify the long-run relationship between economic development and income distribution, but no causal relationship between them. Takım et al. (2020) also find a negative relationship between economic growth and income distribution in the short run, but a positive relationship in the long run.

The aim of this paper is to analyse the nexus between income distribution and economic growth in Turkey. For this purpose, Kuznets' inverted U-curve hypothesis is investigated in this study.

2 Data and Method

The Gini coefficient and GDP per capita (US dollar) data from the Turkish Statistical Institute is derived at the level of NUTS 2 for Turkey for the period 2014–2019. SPSS 23 is used for analyses, and scatter plots and regression curve estimations with quadratic equations are applied. The dependent variable is the Gini coefficient, and the independent variable is GDP per capita (US dollar).

Tab. 1: *Model Summary and Parameter Estimates*

Year	Model Summary					Parameter Estimates		
	R Square	**F**	**df1**	**df2**	**Sig.**	**Constant**	**b1**	**b2**
2014	0.004	0.05	2	23	0.95	0.375	-1.91E-06	7.02E-11
2015	0.009	0.11	2	23	0.896	0.376	-2.51E-06	1.32E-10
2016	0.071	0.87	2	23	0.431	0.372	-2.07E-06	1.72E-10
2017	0.377	6.95	2	23	**0.004**	0.377	-6.99E-06	5.39E-10
2018	0.208	3.01	2	23	**0.069**	0.375	-4.36E-06	4.11E-10
2019	0.16	2.2	2	23	0.134	0.4	-1.27E-05	8.27E-10
Mean	0.138	1.85	2	23	0.18	0.378	-4.50E-06	3.03E-10

According to the model summary and parameter estimates set out in Table 1, the results for 2017 and 2018 are only significant at the 10% level for the period 2014–2019. Since the b1 coefficient is negative and the b2 coefficient is positive, the relationship between the Gini coefficient and GDP per capita is negative initially and becomes positive thereafter. This result shows that the relationship depicted by Kuznets' curve does not exhibit an inverted U-shape for Turkey. Although the periods of 2014, 2015, 2016, 2019, and the mean of 2014–2019 are not significant, the b1 and b2 coefficients of these periods may imply a U shape for the Kuznets curve. Visualized scatter plots and quadratic regression curves according to the parameter estimates are shown in Figure 1 below.

For the 2017 and 2018 periods, the relationship is statistically significant, and the curves clearly take the U-shape. Although the relationship in the other years and the average for the relevant period is not statistically significant, the U shape is again observed.

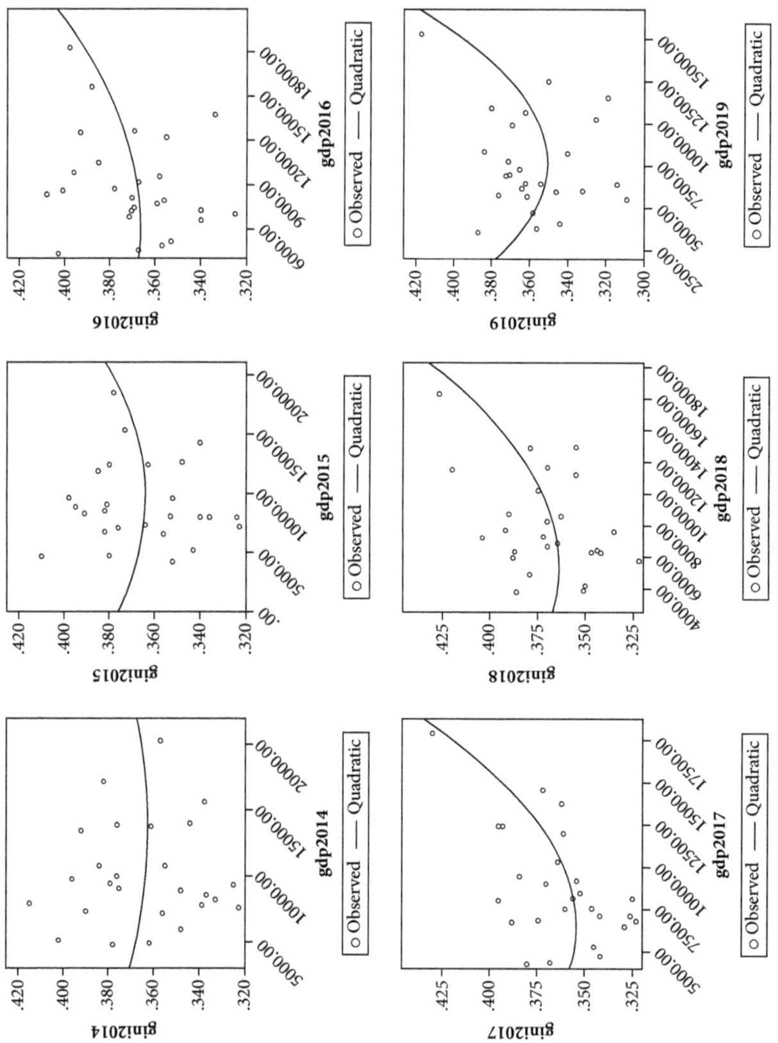

Fig. 1: *Scatter Plots and Quadratic Regression Curves*

3 Conclusion

Kuznets's (1955) hypothesis of the relation between income inequality and economic growth focuses on the mobility of individuals between the agricultural/rural and industrial/urban sectors. While some studies discuss this relationship in terms of intersectoral transition, recent studies focus on whether Kuznets' inverted U-curve is empirically supported. Our paper focuses on Kuznets' inverted U-curve without intersectoral transition. We select the period 2014–2019 for our analysis and based on regional data (NUTS2 level). If the analysis results are generally interpreted, the Kuznets curve is U-shaped for the 2014–2019 period in Turkey.

According to the World Bank (2021) data, GDP per capita growth (as an annual percentage) are as follows: 2014 (3.1), 2015 (4.3), 2016 (1.6), 2017 (5.8), 2018 (1.4), 2019 (−0.4), with an average (2.6). The Gini indices are as follows: 2014 (41.2), 2015 (42.9), 2016 (41.9), 2017 (41.4), 2018 (41.8), 2019 (41.9), with an average (41.8). Turkey's economic growth during the period 2014–2019 did not make a notable impact on the Gini index. Although macroeconomic efficiency has been realized with economic growth, there has been no improvement in ensuring a fair income distribution. This also emphasizes the efficiency-justice conflict in the Turkish economy.

When we consider this basic assessment for the country as a whole, together with the results of our analysis, the achievements in economic growth for Turkey as a developing economy are not reflected at the meso-level in a fair distribution of income. Economic growth is no doubt not the only determinant of income inequality. Further studies on the determinants of income inequality at the regional level may demonstrate why income inequality does not decrease despite the development of Turkey's economy. Thus, practical economic policies are needed to ensure justice in income distribution.

References

Abdioğlu, Z., Yamak, N., and Yamak, R. (2019). Türkiye'de Gelir Eşitsizliği ve Ekonomik Gelişme Arasındaki Uzun Dönem İlişkisi. MAKÜ İİBFD, 6(3), 721–735.

Ak, M. Z., and Altıntaş, N. (2016). Kuznets'in Ters U Eğrisi Bağlamında Türkiye'de Gelir Eşitsizliği ve Ekonomik Büyüme İlişkisi: 1986–2012. Maliye Araştırmaları Dergisi, 2(3), 93–102.

Akalin, G., Özbek, R. İ., and Çifçi, İ. (2018). Türkiye'de Gelir Dağılımı ve Ekonomik Büyüme Arasındaki İlişki: ARDL Sınır Testi Yaklaşımı. Kastamonu Üniversitesi İktisadi ve İdari Bilimler Fakültesi Dergisi, 20(4), 59–76.

Akıncı, G. Y., and Akıncı, M. (2016). Ters-U Hipotezi Bağlamında Ekonomik Büyüme, Finansal Kalkınma ve Gelir Eşitsizliği Mekanizmaları Üzerine. Finans Politik and Ekonomik Yorumlar, 53(622), 61–77.

Barro, R. J. (1999). Inequality, Growth, and Investment. NBER Working Paper No. 7038: National Bureau of Economic Research.

Çütcü, İ., Atay, G., and Akkurt, A. (2020). Kalkınma-Gelir Dağılımı İlişkisi: Türkiye Ekonomisi Üzerine Yapısal Kırılmalı Ekonometrik Analiz. Bartın Üniversitesi İktisadi ve İdari Bilimler Fakültesi Dergisi, 11(22), 448–466.

Dişbudak, C., and Süslü, B. (2009). Kalkınma ve Bireysel Gelir Dağılımı: Kuznets Hipotezi Türkiye İçin Geçerli Mi? Akdeniz İ.İ.B.F. Dergisi(18), 146–466.

Günaydın, D., and Çetin, M. (2015). The Impact of Economic Growth and Trade Openness on Income Inequality: An Emprical Analysis for Turkish Economy. IIB International Refereed Academic Social Sciences Journal, 6(20), 58–82.

Kuznets, S. (1955). Economic Growth and Income Inequality. The American Economic Review, 45(1), 1–28.

Limanlı, Ö. (2020). Kuznets'in Ters-U Hipotezi: Türkiye Özelinde Kısa Bir Tartışma. İktisadi İdari ve Siyasal Araştırmalar Dergisi, 5(12), 156–167.

Özçelik, Ö. (2021). Çevre ve Ekonomik Büyüme. Çevre Bilimleri (s. 171–201). içinde Ed.Abdullah Yılmaz, Eskişehir: Anadolu Üniversitesi.

Öztürk, E., and Oktar, S. (2017). Kalkınma Gelir Eşitsizliği İlişkisi: Türkiye Örneği. Akademik Hassasiyetler, 4(8), 101–123.

Robinson, S. (1976). A Note on the U Hypothesis Relating Income Inequality and Economic Development. The American Economic Review, 66(3), 437–440.

Takım, A., Ersungur, Ş. M., Dikmen, A. T., and Aksu, L. E. (2020). Türkiye'de Ekonomik Büyüme ile Gelir Dağılımı Arasındaki İlişki. Atatürk Üniversitesi İktisadi ve İdari Bilimler Dergisi, 34(1), 234–248.

Tokatlıoğlu, İ., and Atan, M. (2007). Türkiye'de Bölgelerarası Gelişmişlik Düzeyi ve Gelir Dağılımı Eşitsizliği: Kuznets Eğrisi Geçerli Mi? Ekonomik Yaklaşım, 18(65), 25–58.

World Bank. (2021, April 23). World Bank Open Data. available at: https://data.worldbank.org/

Emrullah Mete

Economic Complexity and Economic Growth Relationship

1 Introduction

Today, when economic globalization has become more intense, it has become very difficult for countries to gain a competitive edge through comparative advantage. It is important for countries to provide product diversity together with R&D investments and technological development in order to make their economic growth sustainable. In addition to product diversity, revealing and exporting highly value-added products puts countries one step ahead in terms of economic growth.

A significant part of the literature in the field of growth is related to the sources of growth or, in other words, the factors affecting growth. While classical factors such as physical capital, the workforce, natural resources and technology were considered the main sources of growth until the 1990s, studies began to be conducted thereafter arguing that some new factors are also among sources of growth. These factors, also referred to as indirect sources of growth, include factors that directly affect resources such as macroeconomic stability, institutions and commercial and financial openness. In this context, the structure of a country's production and export can also be considered an indirect source of growth (Çeştepe and Çağlar, 2017: 993). Nowadays, differences in the ability of countries to develop their production and turn to complex goods enable them to be one step ahead in terms of economic growth.

The concept of 'complex', which can mean scientifically qualified, unique, sophisticated and containing diversity, refers in economic terms to the knowledge and ability provided by the output generated in an economy as well as the combination of them (Türkcan, 2019: 600). Therefore, the more knowledge, ability and a combination thereof a product reflects, the more complex a product is deemed to be. The more complex a product is, the more added value it creates and the more high-value-added products the country producing that product is enabled to export.

Hidalgo and Hausmann (2009), who stated that the economic growth and development of a country is related to the level of development in the export complexity, developed an index showing the level of economic complexity of countries using the inter-country trade data. This index, called the Economic Complexity Index (ECI), is a concept that reflects the economic growth and welfare level of countries (Doyar and Yaman, 2020: 42). In addition, since production and exports are the most important instruments for countries to achieve competitiveness, economic growth and development, economic complexity is a concept that is also interested in the export composition of countries (Stojkoski et al. 2016: 2).

Hausmann and Hildalgo et al. (2011) established a model that compares trade data between countries in order to measure the economic complexity of the countries with the index they developed. In the model, the productive complexity of the country is indirectly measured based on the analysis of the export basket of a particular country. The economic complexity index was created by means of accessing comprehensive data of numerous products and countries, starting from 1963. According to this model, the economic complexity of a country depends on meeting two basic conditions: the first is that the products in the export basket are not widely available in the basket of other countries, and the second is that there is diversity in the products (Boğa, 2019: 362). The more diverse and unconventional products a country produces, the more competitive it is expected to be in high value-added products in export markets. Accordingly, the ECI index, which is calculated according to the diversity, mediocrity and quality coefficients of the products, analyses the output of countries in detail and measures the potential of growth and opening up to new industries (Yıldırım, 2018: 1).

The concept of economic complexity refers to the diversity of useful knowledge in an economy and the collective use of such diverse knowledge. There are many stages that need to be coordinated in the production of even the simplest goods. Hausmann et al. (2011) state that this coordination depends on many interrelated factors such as the design, marketing, financing, technology, quality, the human capital factor required and ensuring trade of the product, and that these factors constitute *the set of abilities* of the countries. As such, economic complexity is also referred to as the ability of a country's economy to accommodate and combine efficient knowledge, and this expression is an approach that fully combines the indicators used by theories that explain economic growth dynamics. As a matter of fact, regarding the question of what the factors are that provide the dynamics of economic growth, the answer of the classics is soil and labour, the answer of the neoclassics is capital and technology, and the answer of new growth theories is human capital (Sokcevic and Stokovac, 2011: 8). The economic complexity approach contains a set of abilities that covers all of these, and even more (Uçar et al. 2019: 139).

The ECI, which demonstrates the export composition of a country, states that if a product is produced by many countries, that product is ordinary and unqualified. Therefore, the ECI value of the countries exporting such products is low. On the other hand, the ECI value of the countries exporting high value-added products is greater. As a result, quality rather than quantity is important to attain a high ECI value.

ASEAN was established by Indonesia, Malaysia, the Philippines, Singapore and Thailand with the signing of the Bangkok Declaration on August 8, 1967. In the following period, the Kingdom of Brunei, Vietnam, Laos Democratic People's Republic, Burma (Myanmar), Cambodia and Turkey became members of the association.

The Association of Southeast Asian Nations (ASEAN), which became a more effective organization after the end of the Cold War, has come to the fore as a leading integration movement in terms of trade, economy and security in recent years. The organization, which is strongly integrated into the global economy, has managed to achieve higher growth rates than the world average. Another remarkable point is that ASEAN showed growth while the world economy shrank in the 2008 global economic crisis. There are a total of four ASEAN member countries, namely Indonesia, the Philippines, Malaysia and Thailand, which are considered to be higher performing market economies compared to other developing countries as they meet certain criteria such as market size, market growth rate, commercial infrastructure and economic freedom. Especially in 2010 and thereafter, the increase of the share of high-tech product exports in the exports of the member countries of the association was discussed in this study for evaluating the relationship between the ECI and economic growth.

2 Literature

While the issue of economic complexity has been trying to explain the dynamics of the real world as a theory that has been developing since the 2000s, it has also been a very interesting topic in economic literature, especially in recent years. The first study on the subject was conducted by Hidalgo and Hausmann (2009). Hidalgo and Hausmann (2009) concluded that there is a strong relationship between economic complexity and economic growth. In the study conducted by Hausmann et al. (2014), 128 countries were evaluated for the 1978–2008 period. When the ECI value was included in the model as the value of interaction with GDP, it was concluded that it had a negative effect. In other words, the impact of ECI on economic growth decreases as the income level of the country increases. Özgüzer and Binatlı (2015) did not find any relationship between economic complexity and economic growth in the regression model in which it included all countries in the study, where European Union countries in the period of 1995–2010 were examined. Later on in the analysis, they examined the countries in two groups. According to the regression results, they considered countries with an average complexity index above (-0.22) and countries below (-0.68); the ECI increases economic growth in countries above (-0.22). However, in countries with a value below (-0.68), the relationship was found to be negative; that is, the ECI reduced economic growth. Hausmann et al. (2016) concluded that there is a positive and strong relationship between ECI and economic growth in the study they conducted on Panama. Stojkoski and Kocarev (2017) evaluated sixteen southeastern and central European countries for the period 1995–2013 in their study, where the ECI positively affected economic growth. Zhu and Li (2017) examined 126 countries for the period 1995–2010 in their study and concluded that economic complexity and human capital positively affected economic growth in both the short and the long term. Çeştepe and Çağlar (2017) examined eighty-six countries by dividing the 1982–2012 period into six periods of five years each, and it was revealed that the ECI variable positively affected per capita national income growth. It was found that, for countries with a nominal national income per capita of less than $20,395 (US), the increase in the ECI value increased the growth rate, and this effect decreased as the country's national income per capita increased. Gala et al. (2018) concluded that countries with a high ECI have more potential of convergence with developed countries than countries with low ECI, in the study covering the period 1979–2011 for 147 countries using the ECI value as a variable of interaction with GDP. Uçar et al. (2019) examined the G8 countries during the 1992–2016 period and found that there was a causality from per capita income and exports to the ECI. In a study by Boğa (2019), evaluating thirteen transition economy countries in the 1995–2017 period, it was found that the effect of economic complexity on economic growth was positive and quite strong in the first group of countries with a GDP per capita of more than 10,000 dollars, and there was no statistically significant relationship in the second group of countries with a GDP per capita of less than 10,000 dollars. Türkcan (2019) examined Turkey for the 1995–2017 period and found that economic growth positively affected the ECI, but the ECI had no effect on economic growth. Yıldız and Yıldız (2019) examined the ten newly industrialized countries in the 1970–2016 period and found that there was a one-way causality from economic complexity to economic growth for Mexico, Malaysia and South Africa, and a two-way causality relationship for China. Throughout the panel, a one-way causality relationship was found from economic complexity to economic growth only. Şeker (2019) examined the 1989–2017 period for Turkey and found a long-term relationship between the ECI and high-tech product exports, domestic patent applications and fixed capital investments. Şahin and Durmuş (2020) examined the ten newly industrialized countries in the 1990–2017 period and found that there was a causality relationship from direct foreign capital investment to the ECI in China and Mexico. It was observed that there was a causality relationship from domestic patent applications to economic complexity in the Philippines. No causality relationship was found from gross fixed capital investments to economic complexity. It has been observed that there is a causality relationship from financial development to the ECI in Turkey and Mexico.

3 Methodology

Panel causality analysis was used in the study examining the relationship between economic complexity and economic growth. In the study examining the data of eight ASEAN member countries for the period 1994–2018, real gross domestic product per capita and ECI data were used as variables. The ECI data, which is an indicator of economic complexity, was obtained from the Atlas Media database, while the product data was obtained from the World Bank database. The Dumitrescu and Hurlin (2012) causality test was used as the method in the study. As stated by Dumitrescu and Hurlin (2012), a causality relationship that is valid for one country in terms of any economic phenomenon is likely to be valid for other countries as well. Therefore, the causality relationship can be tested more effectively with more observations in the panel data frame. In this context, the model used in the analysis was established as follows.

$$\text{lgdppc}_{it} = \beta_0 + \beta_1 eci_{it} + \varepsilon_{it} \qquad (1)$$

In the model, t means time, i refers to units, β refers to slope parameter and ε refers to error. In the analysis, first the cross-sectional dependence of the series will be determined using the Breusch Pagan and Pesaran tests. The Pesaran CADF unit root test, which considers cross-sectional dependence, will be applied to test whether the series are stationary at the same level. The Dumitrescu and Hurlin (2012) causality test, which takes into account the cross-sectional dependence, will be applied after the homogeneity test.

The Lagrange Multiplier (LM) test, which is the pioneering cross-sectional dependence test developed by Breusch-Pagan (1980), is as follows:

$$LM = T\sum_{i=1}^{N-1}\sum_{j=i+1}^{N}\hat{p}_{ij}^{2} \sim X^{2}_{N(N-1)/2} \tag{2}$$

If both time and cross-sectional dimensions are large, it is possible to investigate whether there is cross-sectional dependence using the Cross-Section Dependence (CD_{LM}) test developed by Pesaran (2004) .

$$CD_{LM} = \left(\frac{1}{N(N-1)}\right)^{1/2}\sum_{i=1}^{N-1}\sum_{j=i+1}^{N-1}\left(T\hat{p}_{ij}^{2}-1\right) \sim N(0,1) \tag{3}$$

The Pesaran (2004) CD test statistics was developed as a more general test considering that the CD_{LM} test may cause distortions in dimension in case of large N and small T. The CD test is as follows:

$$CD = \left(\frac{2T}{N(N-1)}\right)\sum_{i=1}^{N-1}\sum_{j=i+1}^{N-1}\left(\hat{p}_{ij}-1\right) \sim N(0,1) \tag{4}$$

Even when the Pesaran (2004) CD test yielded inconsistent results, the Adjusted LM (LM_{adj}) test was developed thereafter, since it yielded consistent results (Pesaran et al. 2008: 105). For this reason, the LM_{adj} test was performed in the study to test whether there is cross-sectional dependence. The LM_{adj} test statistic is as follows (Pesaran et al. 2008:108):

$$LM_{adj} = \sqrt{\left(\frac{2}{N(N-1)}\right)}\sum_{i=1}^{N-1}\sum_{j=i+1}^{N}\left[\hat{p}_{ij}^{2}\left(\frac{(T-k)\hat{p}_{ij}^{2}-\mu_{Tij}}{\vartheta_{Tij}}\right)\right] \sim N(0,1) \tag{5}$$

Pesaran (2007) conducted Monte Carlo simulations where they found Pesaran CADF unit root test was applicable in both N>T and N<T situations. The Pesaran CADF unit root test t value is found as below.

$$t_{1}(N,T) = \frac{\Delta Y_{i}'\bar{M}_{w}Y_{i-1}}{\hat{\sigma}\left(Y_{i-1}'\bar{M}_{w}Y_{i-1}\right)^{1/2}} \tag{6}$$

Finally, the delta test calculation developed by Pesaran and Yamagata (2008) for the homogeneity test was performed as below.

$$\hat{\Delta} = \sqrt{N}\frac{N^{-1}\bar{S}-k}{\sqrt{2k}} \tag{7}$$

$$\hat{\Delta}_{adj} = \sqrt{N}\frac{N^{-1}\bar{S}-E(\tilde{Z}_{it})}{\sqrt{Var(\tilde{Z}_{1t})}} \tag{8}$$

The Dumitrescu and Hurlin panel causality analysis can be applied after testing the cross-sectional dependence, stationarity and homogeneity of the series. Dumitrescu and Hurlin (2012) developed a test that explained the panel causality relationship, revealed different statistics for N>T and T>N situations and was suitable for both unbalanced panels and series with cross-sectional dependence. The calculation of the Wald statistic, found by dividing the averages of each cross-sectional unit by itself, is provided in the following equation.

$$W_{N,T}^{Hnc} = \frac{1}{N}\sum_{i=1}^{N} W_{i,T} \tag{9}$$

The ($Z_{N,T}^{HNC}$) statistic with asymptomatic distribution is used in case of N<T while the (Z_{N}^{HNC}) statistic with semi-asymptomatic distribution is used in case of T<N.

$$Z_{N}^{HNC} = \frac{\sqrt{N\left[W_{N,T}^{HNC} - N^{-1}\sum_{i=1}^{N} E(W_{i,T})\right]}}{\sqrt{N^{-1}\sum_{i=1}^{N} Var(W_{i,T})}} \tag{10}$$

$$Z_{N,T}^{HNC} = \sqrt{\frac{N}{2K}}\left(W_{N,T}^{HNC} - K\right) \tag{11}$$

4 Empirical Results

In the analysis, real gross domestic product per capita (gdppc) and economic complexity index (eci) data were used as variables. The results of the cross-sectional dependence and homogeneity tests related to the variables are given in Table 1.

Tab. 1: *Horizontal Cross-Sectional Dependence and Homogeneity Test Results*

Test	**Statistics**	**p-value**
Breusch and Pagan (1980) LM	233.2	0.0000*
Pesaran et al. (2008) LM_{adj}	75.34	0.0000*
Pesaran (2004) LM_{CD}	14.28	0.0000*
Test	**Statistics**	**p-value**
$\hat{\Delta}$	4.317	0.000*
$\hat{\Delta}_{adj}$	4.615	0.000*

* Shows 1% significance level.

According to the cross-sectional dependence and homogeneity test results, it is understood that the variables include cross-sectional dependence and have heterogeneous slope parameters. The Pesaran CADF unit root test results, determined according to homogeneity and cross-sectional dependence, are given in Table 2.

Tab. 2: *Pesaran CADF Unit Root Test Results*

	Level	**Difference**
Lgdppc	-1.565	-2.638*
Leci	-1.684	-3.300*

* Shows 1% significance level.

According to the results in Table 2, neither variables were stationary at the level and they both became stationary when their first differences were taken. The results regarding Dumitrescu and Hurlin panel causality analysis, which are suitable for the conditions requiring existence of horizontal cross-sectional dependence and heterogenous variables, are given in Table 3.

Tab. 3: *Dumitrescu and Hurlin Panel Causality Analysis Results*

	W-Stat	**Z-bar Stat**	**Prob.**
gdppc eci	17.5838	1.2384	0.2156
ecigdppc	4.9049	-0.8320	0.4054

According to the Dumitrescu and Hurlin panel causality test results in Table 3, no causality relationship was found from the increase in per capita product rate to economic complexity, and from economic complexity to the increase in per capita product rate.

5 Conclusion

The determinants of economic growth remain the oldest and most important topic in economic literature. The impact of the activities carried out by countries to increase competitiveness is very important for economic growth. Especially the concepts of human capital, technological development, R&D activities and high value-added product exports, which come to the forefront with internal growth theories, have been on the agenda of all countries for about half a century. Developed in 2009, the economic complexity index aims to measure the relationship between the export composition of countries and their economic growth. Measuring the knowledge, technology and the degree of added value contained in countries' export products, the index states that high index scores will increase competitiveness and thus economic growth will occur. In this regard, the relationship between economic complexity and economic growth was examined for ASEAN countries in the study. The Dumitrescu and Hurlin panel causality analysis was applied in the study, where no two-way causality was found between economic complexity and economic growth. When the result obtained is evaluated within the scope of the literature of the subject, it can be explained by saying that the level of complexity cannot positively affect economic growth without exceeding a certain level. It is also important that economic complexity is related to the level of development of countries, and that economic complexity has no significant impact on economic growth in countries with relatively low levels of development. ASEAN also includes important countries that achieved rapid economic growth, such as Singapore, Malaysia and Thailand, which are among the newly industrialized countries. These countries have both achieved rapid economic growth and have a significant level of high technology products in their export basket. In contrast, Laos, Cambodia and Vietnam are countries that continue their economic development. Although these countries have gained significant momentum in terms of high-tech products in recent years, it can be said that there is negative effect on the country group due to their low index value as of the period of the study. Overall, in order for countries to realize their economic growth in today's world, they need to increase their R&D activities and thus provide technological development and export high value-added products as a reflection of this. Today, when knowledge creates a comparative advantage, human capital is also important for the use, sharing and coordination of knowledge.

References

Boğa, S. (2019). Ekonomik Karmaşıklık Seviyesinin Ekonomik Büyüme Üzerine Etkisi: Geçiş Ülkeleri İçin Bir Panel Zaman Serisi Analizi. Akademik Hassasiyetler, 6(12): 357–386.

Breusch, T. ve Pagan, A. (1980). The Lagrange Multiplier Test and Its Applications to Model Specification in Econometrics. Review of Economic Studies. 47(1), 239–253.

Çeştepe, H. ve Çağlar, O. (2017). Ürün Sofistikasyonu ve Ekonomik Büyüme İlişkisi: Panel Veri Analizi. Uluslararası Yönetim İktisat ve İşletme Dergisi, ICMEB17 Özel Sayısı, 992–1000.

Dumitrescu, E. I. ve Hurlin, C. (2012). Testing for Granger Non-Causality in Heterogeneous Panels. Economic Modelling, 29(4), 1450–1460.

Doyar, B. V. ve Yaman, H. (2020). Ekonomik Karmaşıklık Endeksi, Gelir ve Yüksek Teknoloji İhracatı Arasındaki Karşılıklı İlişkilerin Analizi: Türkiye Örneği. Pearson Journal of Social Sciences-Humanities, 8, 41–52.

Gala, P., Rocha, I. ve Magacho, G. (2018). The Sructuralist Revenge: Economic Complexity as an Important Dimension to Evaluate Growth and Development, Brazilian Journal of Political Economy, 38(2), 219–236.

Hausmann, R., Cunningham, B., Matovu, J. M., Osire, R. ve Wyett, K. (2014). How Should Uganda Grow?. Harvard Kennedy School Faculty Research Working Paper Series, Working paper no. 235.

Hausmann, R., Hidalgo, C. A., Bustos, S., Coscia, M., Chung, S., Jimenez, J., Simões, A. ve Yildirim, M. A. (2011). The Atlas of Economics Complexity-Mapping Paths to Prosperity. Hollis: Puritan Press.

Hausmann, R., Morales, J. R., and Santos, M. (2016). Economic complexity in Panama: Assessing opportunities for productive diversification. Harvard University, John F. Kennedy School of Government.

Hidalgo, C. A. ve Hausmann, R. (2009). The Building Blocks of Economic Complexity. Proceedings of the National Academy of Sciences. 106(26), 10570–10575.

Özgüzer, G. E. ve Binatlı, A. O. (2016). Economic Convergence in the EU: A Complexity Approach. Eastern European Economics. 54(2), 93–108.

Pesaran, M. H. (2004). General diagnostic tests for cross section dependence in panels. CWPE, No: 0435.

Pesaran, M. H. (2007). A Simple Panel Unit Root Test in the Presence of Cross Sectional Dependence. Journal of Applied Econometrics, 22(2), 265–312.

Pesaran, M. H. ve Yamagata, T. (2008). Testing slope homogeneity in large panels. Journal of Econometrics, 142, 50–93.

Pesaran, M. H., Ullah, A. and Yamagata, T. (2008). A bias-adjusted LM test of error crosssection independence. Economic Journal, 11(1), 105–127.

Sokcevıc, S. ve Stokovac D. (2011). Macroeconomic Stability and the Economic Growth in European Transition Countries, The Economic Geography of Globalization, Piotr Pachura, IntechOpen, DOI: 10.5772/21511. Erişim tarihi: 23.03.2021

Stojkoski V, Utkovski Z ve Kocarev L. (2016). The Impact of Services on Economic Complexity: Service Sophistication as Route for Economic Growth. PLoS One, 11(8): e0161633.

Stojkoski, V. ve Kocarev, L. (2017). The Relationship Between Growth and Economic Complexity: Evidence From Southeastern and Central Europe MPRA Paper No. 77837.

Şahin, D. ve Durmuş, S. (2020). Yeni Sanayileşen Ülkelerde Ekonomik Kompleksite Düzeyinin Belirleyicileri. Ordu Üniversitesi Sosyal Bilimler Enstitüsü Sosyal Bilimler Araştırmaları Dergisi, 10(2), 334–351.

Şeker, A. (2019). Teknolojik Gelişme ve Yüksek Teknoloji İhracatının Ekonomik Karmaşıklık Endeksi Üzerindeki Etkisi: Türkiye Örneği. Yönetim ve Ekonomi: Celal Bayar Üniversitesi İktisadi ve İdari Bilimler Fakültesi Dergisi, 26(2), 377–395.

Türkcan, B. (2019). Türkiye İçin Ekonomik Karmaşıklık Endeksi ve Büyüme Arasındaki İçsel İlişki: Bir Eşanlı Denklem Sistemi Analizi. ICOAEF VI, 16–17 Kasım 2019, Balıkesir, Türkiye.

Uçar, M., Soyyiğit, S. ve Nişancı, M. (2019). Ülkelerin İktisadi Gelişmişlik ve Ekonomik Karmaşıklık Düzeyleri Arasındaki İlişki: G8 Ülkeleri Örneği. Cumhuriyet Üniversitesi İktisadi ve İdari Bilimler Dergisi, 20(1), 138–148.

Yıldırım, M.A. (2018). Kompleksite ve Urun Uzayi Metodolojisiyle Türkiye. Koç University-TÜSİAD Economic Research Forum Working Papers 1806.

Yıldız, B. ve Akbulut Yıldız, G. (2019). Ekonomik Karmaşıklık ile Ekonomik Büyüme Arasındaki İlişki: Panel Bootstrap Granger Nedensellik Analizi. Uluslararası Yönetim İktisat ve İşletme Dergisi, 15(2), 329–340.

Zhu, S. ve Li, R. (2017). Economic Complexity, Human Capital and Economic Growth: Empirical Research Based On Cross-Country Panel Data. Applied Economics, 49(38), 3815–3828.

Nuran Coşkun

Impact of R&D and Export Intensity on Profit: Evidence from Manufacturing Sectors in Turkey

1 Introduction

In recent years, with the advent of large plant and firm level data sets, the role of R&D (research and development) expenditure and export performance on profit has become popular and crucial for firm level profitability. The most important resource for creating comparative advantage for firms is R&D and innovation. Although there are many studies in the literature that studies the relationship between innovation, R&D expenditure, export performance and profitability, they didn't take into account endogeneity problem of the estimation. They investigated the relationship between innovation, R&D expenditure, export performance and profitability together in a model without considering the endogeneity problem. Furthermore, a large number of studies have considered the causality relationship to be one-way. It may be the reason for bias estimates and information pollution in the literature. The causal relationship between R&D expenditure, export intensity and profitability can be bi-directional, as in stated at the theoretical literature, and it can cause the endogeneity problem. To overcome this issue, the System GMM estimator, which is proposed by Blundell and Bond (1998) and Arellano and Bover (1995), was used in this study.

The aim of this study is to analyse the impact of export intensity and R&D expenditure on profitability of manufacturing sectors, taking into account the size of the firm. Therefore, the data is clustered into three scales (small, medium and large enterprises: SE, ME, LE). Analyses were made for twenty-two manufacturing industries with annual data between 2009–2019 for SEs and MEs, and thirteen for LEs. Export intensity is used for export performance, which is the percentage of exports in total sales. Returns on assets (ROA), returns on equity (ROE) and returns on sales (ROS) are calculated from the sectoral balance sheet, which was obtained from Central Bank of the Republic of the Turkey. The results revealed that the impact of R&D expenditure on profit is statistically significant, but is negative for SE, and exports are not statistically significant for ROA and ROE. Export intensity is statistically significant for ROS with a negative sign. The impact of R&D expenditure on profit is statistically significant for

MEs and with a positive sign as expected for all profit indicators (ROS, ROA and ROE). Export intensity is statistically significant for MEs and it has a positive sign for ROA and ROE, but it has a negative sign for ROS. The impact of R&D expenditure on profit (ROS) is statistically significant for LE and have positive coefficient just for ROS. The impact of export intensity on profit (ROE) is statistically significant for LE and have positive coefficient.

This study was planned as follows: After the introduction, the literature can be found in section 2. This has two sub-sections. The first sub-section covers theoretical literature and the second sub-section contains empirical literature. The data and the methodology is discussed in section 3. The findings are dissected in section 4 and, finally, section 5 imparts the concluding remarks.

2 Literature

2.1 Theoretical Literature

In the literature, early theoretical works by authors such as Bernard and Jensen (1999) and Melitz (2003), assume that productivity is exogenous. Melitz (2003) states that the more productive firms enter the export market, while less productive firms exit. Meantime, each firm faces initial uncertainty about its productivity level before making a decision to export. Thus, entry into the export market is costly, but the firm's decision to export occurs after it assesses its productivity. The Melitz (2003) framework is based on sunk costs and firm heterogeneity. As a consequence, the more productive firms produce for foreign markets while less productive firms continue to produce for the domestic market. On the other hand, in the theory of endogenous firm heterogeneity, productivity is considered endogenous, see Aw et. al (2011), Bustos (2011) and Harris and Moffat (2012). According to this view (in the theoretical studies), the most common assumption is that innovation generates new product and process outputs. Since product innovations and production processes increase the productivity level, firms enhance their productivity level via internal activities (such as R&D expenditure). Moreover, Kongmanila and Takahashi (2009) state that production process and product innovations have a different level impact on a firm's profitability by considering the size of the firm. On the other hand, as in the endogenous growth model (See Romer, 1990; Grossman and Helpman, 1991), firms need innovations to compete in foreign markets on the grounds that R&D intensity, scale effect and learning by exporting enhances the firm's intangible knowledge assets and leads to an increase in the ability to internalize external knowledge. It is the reason why exporting firms have the capacity to cover the large fixed and sunk costs of innovation. As a result, innovation leads to better export performance and profitability. As a consequence of endogenous firm heterogeneity, innovation and export decisions are independent, and both channels may endogenously affect the firm's future productivity (Aw et al., 2011). However, innovation and export performance have feedbacks to each other, as in stated in empirical literature in this study. Coşkun and Yıkılmaz (2018) claimed that causality relationship between profit and export intensity is bi-directional in the manufacturing sector. Thus, System-GMM is used for analyzing the relationship between innovation and export performance and profitability.

The relationship between productivity and export performance has been investigated by a substantial number of empirical studies. According to this literature, internationally competing firms illustrate higher productivity level than domestically competing firms; firms with a high level of productivity are expected to achieve high profits. However, there is no consensus in the literature about the relationship between export performance and profitability, by virtue of the fact that internationally competing firms deal with higher cost levels than domestically competing firms (Wagner 2012, van den Berg 2014). Even though it is inconclusive as to how exports should affect profitability due to the cost of exporting, there is a consensus in the literature that knowledge spillovers, learning by exporting and the firm's internal factors, such as R&D, enhance a firm's knowledge/skill sets. Thus, an increase in export intensity should effect the long-term profits of the firm. However, an increase profits may have happened by internal (export decision, learning by exporting, R&D etc.) or external (market structure, policy implications of government etc.) factors. On the other hand, Kuivalainen and Sundqvist (2006) state that the relationship between export performance and profitability is affected by the firm's size. In case of small firms, intra-firm factors (sales performance, profit performance etc.) affect the firm's export performance. On the other hand, in case of large firms, only profit performance affects the firm's export performance, as stated in Kongmanila and Tahahashi (2009) and Kuivalainen and Sundqvist (2006). Therefore, to evaluate the different impacts on profit to LEs, OEs and LEs, an analysis was made by considering the different scale of the firms.

2.2 Empirical Literature

Akyol and Akehurst (2003) investigated the relationship between export performance and export market orientation in the Turkish clothing industry. Özçelik and Taymaz (2004) examined the determinants of export performance of firms and innovations and R&D activities in the Turkish manufacturing industry. Zehir, Köle and Yıldız (2015) investigated the relationship between market orientation, innovation capability and export performance in the Turkish manufacturing sector. Esmeray and Esmeray (2016) evaluated the linkage between export and profit performance using the ordinary least square method. Although some of the studies in the literature have focused specifically on the causality relationship between export performance, innovation or productivity gap between exporting firms and non-exporting firms, there is a lack of empirical studies investigating the relationships between export performance, innovation and profitability taking into account endogeneity problem. Hence, the main contribution of this paper is to empirically examine the impact of export performance and R&D expenditure on profitability, and assist policy makers by taking the issue in terms of firm behaviour.

3 Data and Methodology

The data is extracted from the Central Bank of the Republic of Turkey between the years 2009 and 2019 from the sectoral balance sheet. The analyses were made for three different sizes of firms: small, medium and large enterprises (SE, ME, LE).

Tab. 1: *List of Variables*

Dependent Variable		
Return on Assets	ROA	Net Profit/Total Assets
Return on Equity	ROE	Net Profit/shareholders' equity
Return on Sales	ROS	Net Profit/Total Sales
Return on Assets for SE	SROA	Net Profit/Total Assets
Return on Equity for SE	SROE	Net Profit/shareholders' equity
Return on Sales for SE	SROS	Net Profit/Total Sales
Return on Assets for ME	MROA	Net Profit/Total Assets
Return on Equity for ME	MROE	Net Profit/shareholders' equity
Return on Sales for ME	MROS	Net Profit/Total Sales
Return on Assets for LE	LROA	Net Profit/Total Assets
Return on Equity for LE	LROE	Net Profit/shareholders' equity
Return on Sales for LE	LROS	Net Profit/Total Sales
Explanatory Variables		
Export Intensity	EXP	Foreign Sales/Total Sales
Export Intensity for SE	SEXP	Foreign Sales/Total Sales

Tab. 1: *Continued*

Dependent Variable		
Export Intensity for ME	MEXP	Foreign Sales/Total Sales
Export Intensity for LE	LEXP	Foreign Sales/Total Sales
Research and Development Expenditure	RandD	Research and Development Expenditure/ Total Sales
Research and Development Expenditure	SRandD	Research and Development Expenditure/ Total Sales
Research and Development Expenditure	MRandD	Research and Development Expenditure/ Total Sales
Research and Development Expenditure	LRandD	Research and Development Expenditure/ Total Sales
Control Variable		
Financial Leverage	FL	Total company debt/shareholder's equity
Financial Leverage for SE	SFL	Total company debt/shareholder's equity
Financial Leverage for ME	MFL	Total company debt/shareholder's equity
Financial Leverage for LE	LFL	Total company debt/shareholder's equity

Table 1 contains the details and calculations of the variables. To investigate the impact of R&D expenditure and export intensity on different profit indicators, an analysis was made of twenty-two manufacturing industries, with annual data between 2009–2019 for SEs and MEs, and thirteen LEs. Their return on assets (ROA), return on equities (ROE) and return on sales (ROS) were used for profitability indicators for their sector. Table 2 shows the manufacturing industry sectors used in the study and '*' denotes the thirteen sectors for LEs.

Tab. 2: *List of Manufacturing Sectors*

1*	Manufacture of food products
2	Manufacture of beverages
3*	Manufacture of textiles
4*	Manufacture of wearing apparel
5	Manufacture of leather and related products
6	Manufacture of wood, wood products and cork products (except furniture); manufacture of articles by knitting from reed, straw and similar materials
7*	Manufacture of paper and paper products

(continued on next page)

Tab. 2: *Continued*

8	Printing and reproduction of recorded media
9*	Manufacture of chemicals and chemical products
10	Manufacture of basic pharmaceutical products and pharmaceutical materials
11*	Manufacture of rubber and plastic products
12*	Manufacture of other non-metallic mineral products
13*	Main metal industry
14*	Fabrication of metal products (except machinery and equipment)
15	Manufacture of computers, electronic and optical products
16*	Electrical equipment manufacturing
17*	Manufacture of machinery and equipment not classified elsewhere
18*	Manufacture of motor vehicles, trailers (trailers) and semi-trailers (semi-trailers)
19*	Manufacture of other transport equipment
20	Furniture manufacturing
21	Other manufacturings
22	Installation and repair of machinery and equipment

4 Emprical Results

According to Kongmanila and Tahahashi (2009) and Kuivalainen and Sundqvist (2006) the causality link between export performance and profitability can be bi-directional for large firms, from profit performance to export performance. On the other hand, for small firms the causality link between export performance and profitability can be bi-directional between export performance and profitability, but only if there is an increase in profitability based on profit performance, otherwise the causality link between export performance and profitability should be unidirectional. As a consequence, Kuivalainen and Sundqvist (2006) state that the relationship between export performance and profitability is affected by the firm's size. Therefore, analyses were made of the three different size classification. The System-GMM estimator, which takes into account the endogeneity problem, was used in case of the possibility of bidirectional relationship between the explanatory and the dependent variable. This estimator requires deciding on optimal lag structure by considering AR tests and J statistics. According to AR tests and J test statistics, there is no autocorrelation and instrumental variable problem in Table 3, 4 and 5.

Tab. 3: *System-GMM Results for SE*

Dependent Variable	**SROA**	**SROE**	**SROS**
SROA(-1)	-0.12***		
SROA(-2)	0.43***		
SROE(-1)		0.07**	
SROS(-1)			0.13***
SEXP	0.43	1.04	-7.80***
SRandD	-1.30***	-2.72***	-2.31***
SFL	-1.39***	16.85***	-1.11***
J-statistic	21.73	20.90	21.36
J-probability	0.20	0.28	0.26
AR (1) test (prob.)	0.09	0.83	0.04
AR (2) test (prob)	0.18	0.67	0.10
Max lag (I.V)	2,1	1,1	1,1

*, **, *** present the 10%, 5% and 1% significance level.

Tab. 4: *System-GMM Results for ME*

Dependent Variable:	**MROA**	**MROE**	**MROS**
MROA(-1)	0.08***		
MROA(-2)	0.06***		
MROE(-1)		0.07***	
MROE(-2)		0.18***	
MROS(-1)			0.15***
MEXP	7.94***	22.67***	-1.79***
MRandD	1.34***	1.71***	2.96***
MFL	-13.65***	-2.21*	-11.00***
J-statistic	20.34	21.45	20.83
J-probability	0.26	0.21	0.29
AR (1) test (prob.)	0.00	0.00	0.04
AR (2) test (prob)	0.75	0.63	0.10
Max lag (I.V)	2,1	2,1	1,1

*, **, *** present the 10%, 5% and 1% significance level.

Table 3 indicates the System-GMM test results for SEs. Kongmanila and Tahahashi (2009) and Kuivalainen and Sundqvist (2006) claimed that the causality link between export performance and profitability should be unidirectional for SEs. The findings of the study may have evidence in favour of existence of this claim for ROA, ROS and ROE. On the other hand, ROA and ROE export intensity has a positive and significant coefficient. However, the ROS has negative coefficient, although for the ROS model export intensity is statistically significant at 1% significance level. R&D is significant and is statistically significant at 1% and its coeffeciant is also negative. LFs are statistically significant at 1%, 10% and 1%, significance level for ROA, ROE and ROS, respectively.

Table 4 illustrates the System-GMM test results for MEs. Findings revealed that export intensity and R&D expenditure are statistically significant at 1% significance level. Their coefficients are positive, except the export intensity coefficient for ROS and significant coefficients. Financial leverage (FL) was negative. Furthermore, these results support Kongmanila and Tahahashi (2009) and Kuivalainen and Sundqvist (2006) claims for ROA and ROE. However, although for the ROS, export intensity is statistically significant at 1% significance level, and has negative coefficient.

Tab. 5: *System-GMM Results for LE*

Dependent Variable:	**LROA**	**LROE**	**LROS**
LROA(-1)	0.28***		
LROE(-1)		0.21**	
LROS(-1)			-0.10***
LEXP	10.84*	30.03**	9.58
LR&D	-0.74	-2.28	12.34***
LFL	4.92	26.13***	0.16
J-statistic	12.11	11.28	3.17
J-probability	0.21	0.26	11.15
AR (1) test (prob.)	0.10	0.05	0.25
AR (2) test (prob)	0.25	0.47	0.39
Max lag (I.V)	1,1	1,1	1,1

*, **, *** present the 10%, 5% and 1% significance level.

Kuivalainen and Sundqvist (2006) state that the relationship between export performance and profitability is affected by the firm's size. Furthermore, Kongmanila and Tahahashi (2009) and Kuivalainen and Sundqvist (2006) state that the causality link between export performance and profitability should be bi-directional for large firms. Therefore, firm size clusteres are used and, due to the bi-directional relationship between the RandD, EXP and profitability, we used System-GMM. Table 5 demonstrates the System-GMM test results for LEs. Findings revealed that export intensity and R&D expenditure is statistically significant at 1% significance level just for ROS, and it has positive effect on ROS. R&D expenditure is not statistically significant for ROA and ROE. Although the export intensity is not statistically significant for ROS, it is statistically significant at 10% and 5% and it has positive coefficient for ROA and ROE respectively. FL is statistically significant just for ROE.

5 Conclusion

The motivation of this study is to examine the impact of export performance and R&D expenditure on profitability by considering the size of firms during the period between 2009–2019 for twenty-two manufacturing sub-sectors. For this purpose, three different clustered enterprises were used (SE, ME and LE) and three different profit measures (ROA, ROE and ROS) were used as a dependent variable As a result, nine models were estimated by using System-GMM estimator. As explanatory variables, R&D expenditure and export performance export intensity (EXP) were used. Besides, FL is included in the model as a control variable.

In the first group of data (SE), ROA and ROE export intensity has a positive and significant coefficient while export intensity has negative coefficient for ROS. However, R&D is statistically significant, but it has negative coefficient for all kind of profit indicators.

In the second group of data MEs, as in SEs group data for ROA and ROE export intensity, have a positive and significant coefficient, while export intensity has negative coefficient for ROS. On the other hand, R&D is statistically significant and positive except for ROS. According to the empirical analyses, it has significant and negative coefficient for ROS, but has positive and significant impact on ROA and ROE.

In the third group of data, LEs, findings revealed that export intensity is statistically significant for ROA and ROE, but it is not statistically significant for ROS. On the other hand, R&D is statistically significant and has positive coefficient for ROS, while it is not statistically significant for ROA and ROE.

In the light of these empirical results, the main conclusion is the firm size is a vital factor in understanding the relationship between profit, export performance and R&D.

References

Akyol, A., and Akehurst, G. (2003). An investigation of export performance variations related to corporate export market orientation. European Business Review, 15(1), 5–19.

Arellano, M., and Bover, O. (1995). Another look at the instrumental variable estimation of error-components models. Journal of Econometrics, 68(1), 29–51.

Aw, B. Y., Roberts, M. J., and Xu, D. Y. (2011). R&D investment, exporting, and productivity dynamics. American Economic Review, 101(4), 1312–44.

Bernard, A. B., and Jensen, J. B. (1999). Exceptional exporter performance: cause, effect, or both?. Journal of international economics, 47(1), 1–25.

Blundell, R., and Bond, S. (1998). Initial conditions and moment restrictions in dynamic panel data models. Journal of Econometrics, 87(1), 115–143

Bustos, P. (2011) Trade Liberalization, Exports, and Technology Upgrading: Evidence on the Impact of MERCOSUR on Argentinian Firms, American Economic Review, 101, 30440.

Coşkun, N., and Yıkılmaz Erkol, A., (2018) Causality Between Profitability and EXPort Performance: Evidence from Manufacturing Sectors in Turkey. Last Term Researches in Turkey. Lambert Academic Publishing.

Esmeray, A., and Esmeray, M. (2016). The relationship between profit and export performance revisited: Evidence from Turkish companies. International Journal of Economics and Financial Issues, 6(3).

Grossman, G., and E. Helpman. 1991. Innovation and growth in the global economy. cambridge, MA: MIT Press.

Harris, R. I., and Moffat, J. D. (2012). RandD, Innovation and Exporting in Britain: An Empirical Analysis (pp. 1–43). Centre for Public Policy for Regions, University of Glasgow.

Kongmanila, X., and Takahashi, Y. (2009). Innovation, export performance and profitability of Lao garment exporters. International Journal of Economics and Management, 3(2), 225–236.

Kuivalainen, O. and Sundqvist, S. (2006) Profitability of rapid internationalization: The relationship between international intensity and firms' export performance, Journal of Euromarketing, 16, 59–70.

Melitz, M. J. (2003). The impact of trade on intra-industry reallocations and aggregate industry productivity. Econometrica, 71(6), 1695–1725.

Özçelik, E., and Taymaz, E. (2004). Does innovativeness matter for international competitiveness in developing countries? The case of Turkish manufacturing industries. Research policy, 33(3), 409–424.

Romer, P. M. (1990). Endogenous technological change. Journal of political Economy, 98(5, Part 2), S71–S102.

The Central Bank of the Republic of Turkey, Sector Balance Sheets (2019), Available at: http://www3.tcmb.gov.tr/sektor/2020/#/tr, Date of Access: 02.03.2021.

van den Berg, M. (2014). Does internationalization foster firm performance? (Doctoral dissertation, Universiteit Utrecht).

Wagner, J. (2012). International trade and firm performance: a survey of empirical studies since 2006. Review of World Economics, 148(2), 235–267.

Zehir, C., Köle, M., and Yıldız, H. (2015). The mediating role of innovation capability on market orientation and export performance: An implementation on SMEs in Turkey. Procedia-Social and Behavioural Sciences, 207, 700–708.

Haydar Karadağ

The Relationship between the Happiness Index and Housing Prices in Selected EU Economies, Turkey and Russia

1 Introduction

Happiness is influenced by economic, social, cultural and political factors in society (Servet, 2017: 16). The happiness of individuals is also influenced by factors such as sex, age, education, income, marital status, health and social relationships networks (Beşel, 2015: 227, 228). In that sense, it can be said that there is excellent interaction between happiness and satisfaction in life (Şeker, 2009: 116). The happiness economy, which is influenced by individual and social lives, examines the macroeconomic signifiers such as economic growth, unemployment and inflation, and how institutional factors such as governance influence individuals' happiness (Deviren ve Yıldız, 2017: 236).

Economies aim to improve people's living standards by using economic politics to make people happier over time (Deviren ve Yıldız, 2017: 232). However, the happiness phenomenon may vary between individuals, countries and even periods (Servet, 2017: 16). According to purchasing power parity, GDP changes depending on the economy and period (Şeker, 2009: 117).

However, when people with high income are happier than the others, an increase of income does not increase the happiness level. This situation causes the 'Happiness Paradox' (Deviren ve Yıldız, 2017: 234). Similarly, Amartya Sen (1987) stresses that low-incomes decrease education, health and security services, leading to a decrease in welfare. People's confidence also decreases in places where political freedom is restricted (Akgiş, 2015: 70). The general aim of development plans is to increase individuals' average income to avoid the happiness paradox. However, now non-financial deprivations are considered much more in development plans (Akgiş, 2015: 69).

The study consists of five chapters, including the introductory part. In the second chapter, the relationship between the housing prices index and the happiness index is presented. In the third chapter, studies examining the relationship between housing prices and happiness are presented. In the fourth chapter, the relationship between the housing price index in selected economies and the happiness index is analysed. In the final part, which is the conclusion, the analysis findings are interpreted.

2 The Relationship between Housing Prices and the Happiness Index

Inflation and unemployment are two critical macroeconomic variables that indicate a countries' economic performance (Çondur, 2016: 1309). However, despite the world economy's growth and the increment of real GDP per capita, people's happiness does not increase because of unequal income distribution and the non-decreasing crime rates. When people maximize their financial earnings, they make sacrifices from their families, friends, friendships, sleeping and diets (Görmüş, 2015: 161–2). It is also important to note that since private property is sacred in the classical economy, and there is no need to distribute to needy people, resources and wealth gathers with certain people. Hence the injustice in income distribution increases. However, private property leads people to consume excessively; private property does not bring happiness to people (Görmüş, 2015: 164–5). However, that societies differ from each other in terms of happiness criteria is presented in the research. For example, family is of prime importance for 98.8% of people in Turkey (Şeker, 2009: 125, 128).

Individuals, countries, and competition conditions between the markets entered into a process of change with globalization. This change also changed individuals' needs and expectations, lifestyles and living standards (Karagöz et al., 2015: 248). The housing sector was also influenced by these changes (Coşkun, 2016: 202). Factors such as the differentiation of housing consumption habits lead to quantitative and qualitative changes in housing. People now want to live in safe houses with structural quality and interior design comfort in a globalized world. The location of the houses started to influence people's decisions to purchase a house (Memiş, 2018: 654). Since the housing is considered as a high-profit investment medium, the housing demand and prices strated to increase.Since there has been a consistent increase in housing prices, and individuals perceive housing as a protection against inflation, housing demand has increased. Thus, the change in housing prices started to infleunce the wealth of house owners positively which also contributed to the country's economy (Coşkun, 2016: 202–4). However, the mortgage crisis showed that credit risks stemming from housing price changes, especially in economies where housing and finance connections are strong, are essential. Thus, the rapid increase of housing prices showed that the housing price changes must be closely monitored (Coşkun, 2016: 202).

In this context, whether housing prices in developing countries such, Russia and Turkey or in selected EU countries, the influence individuals' happiness is researched in this study. Since the study is one of the detailed studies that measure how housing prices influence the happiness index, it contributes to the literature.

3 Literature

Aristotle asserted that life taking an individual to happiness could be provided with objective reasoning. Socrates stated that happiness could be obtained with knowledge. Farabi stressed that happiness is the highest goodness that can be reached as a supreme purpose. Bentham, adopting hedonist philosophy, emphasized the importance of feeling good when doing something (Deviren ve Yıldız, 2017: 235). The association of happiness to benefit started with Adam Smith. Smith asserted that social welfare could increase with the market mechanism. The benefit provided with wealth is the essential condition of happiness, so an individual can increase his/her benefits through work, resulting in happiness (Servet, 2017: 17–18).

In this context, a happiness economy stresses how economic growth, unemployment, inflation and institutional changes influence personal well-being (Veenhoven ve Dumludağ, 2015: 46). Duarte (2010) researched the relationship between different macro and individual variables influencing happiness to see how people perceive their living quality. According to Duarte (2010), for many people 'happiness is the ultimate aim of life', and happiness plays a vital role in people's perception of society.

In September 2002, one of the studies examining the happiness economy in terms of country economies, Smyth and Qian (2008), examined the relationship between inequality and happiness in thirty-one cities of China. Despite the difference between high-income and low-income individuals, people who think there is an income inequality report a lower level of happiness.

Gudmondsdottir (2011) examined how the decrease of income and an increase in unemployment influenced happiness following the 2008 economic crisis in Iceland. He used multiple linear regression analysis to find out how the relationship between economic factors and happiness, demographic factors, health and social relations explained the happiness changes between October 2007 and November 2008. He concluded that income and unemployment do not predict happiness, but financial difficulties negatively influence people's lives.

Coates et al. (2015) are trying to understand the relationship between sheltering and living satisfaction by revealing the connections between housing and housing satisfaction. They say that sheltering and inner circle may bring variable opportunities and liberty at the very centre of life. They also reveal that quality, and appropriate and affordable sheltering, provides individuals with healthy, secure and honourable lives.

Santipolvut (2015) examined the provincial development levels within the context of the eleventh National Economic and Social Development Plan (2012–2016) to observe, evaluate and report the performance of green and happy society in the Thailand economy. With the OLS analysis, he proved that wealthy people in the country were more likely to be happier than poor people.

Hu et al. (2020) examined the relationship between housing quality and people's well-being using the standard ordered probit model. Using 2016 data obtained from the Chinese Labour Force Dynamic Research, it was found that housing quality has a positive relationship with happiness. Furthermore, housing quality is more associated with local people's perceived happiness than immigrants who have lower happiness levels.

Öztürk and Suluk (2020) examined the relationship between happiness and economic growth between 2012 and 2018 with panel data analysis, using data from G8 countries, which are in the top rank with regard to terms of development. According to the results of GMM analysis, the greater the GDP the more happiness.

Studies also indicated a meaningful relationship between income and happiness in Turkey consistent with world literature. One of the studies examining the happiness economy in Turkey's economy was by Önemli and Avşar (2016), which examined regional inequality related to life satisfaction with a spatial perspective. In the study, alternative inequality criteria to solve the scale problem was examined, and they calculated the happiness inequality index on a regional basis. Then, with an analysis based on spatial approach, they associated the inequality of life satisfaction with the provinces' development level. As a result of the analysis they observed that as the development level increased in the provinces in the high development groups, in provinces with a low development level the inequality of happiness increases as the development level decreases. Ondes (2019) determined factors that affected the happiness level using the life satisfaction index, applied in Turkey in eighty-one provinces in 2015, using a spatial econometric approach. He first created the spatial weight matrix in the study and then applied diagnostic tests and spatial dependency tests. As a result of his analysis, it is seen that satisfaction rates regarding income-wealth, social life, health and working life increased the rate of happiness; he concluded that satisfaction rates regarding population ratio, housing, security and education decreased the happiness rate. Gür et al. (2020) state that housing and neighbourhood satisfaction affects neighbourhood residents' perceptions of happiness. They obtain their data using a stratified sample method in the Balat neighbourhood in Bursa, where Turkey's high-income residents live. They used the Chaid analysis to evaluate the data. According to the analysis results, the variable that most affects happiness is public housing satisfaction.

4 Empirical Analysis and Findings

The study aims to research the impact of the housing prices in eight selected EU countries and Turkey and Russia on the happiness index. Housing prices, the independent variable, was obtained from the OECD official website; the happiness economy, the dependent variable, was obtained from the Knoema website. In the study, the 2014–2019 period was analysed. The ten countries included in the analysis as samples were France, Spain, Italy, Portugal, Greece, Germany, Netherlands, Belgium, Turkey and Russia. In the analysis of the study, the Westerlund ECM (2007) cointegration test and the CCE mean group estimator were employed.

Tab. 1. *The Frequency Values belonging to Variables*

Variables	Observation	Mean	Std. Deviation	Min	Max
Happiness Index (HI)	60	6,2005	0,742176	4,86	7,49
Nominal House Prices (NHP)	60	108.19	12,132	86,2	141,5

In Table 1, the frequency values of the housing prices and happiness price index are presented.

Tab. 2. *Cross-section Dependence Results*

	Statistic	Prob
Breusch-Pagan LM	100,2416	0,0000
Pesaran scaled LM	5,22981	0,0000
Pesaran CD	-1,662870	0,0963

In Table 2, a cross-section dependence problem is observed. Although GMM is a method ignoring the cross-section dependence, the cross-section dependence test was employed in the study because the CCE group estimator was also used.

Tab. 3. *Autocorrelation and Heteroscedasticity Test*

	Test Statistics	**Probability Values**
Wooldridge test for autocorrelation in panel data	56,685	0,0000
HeteroscedasticityBreusch-Pagan/ Cook-Weisberg test	55,93614	0,0000

In Table 3, the autocorrelation and heteroscedasticity problem in variables is observed.

Tab. 4. *CADF and CIPS Unit Root Tests*

	CADF Test Statistical Values	**Critical Values**		
		%1	**%5**	**%10**
Happiness Index (HI)	-1.028	–6.40	–4.89	–4.00
Nominal House Prices (NHP)	-2.750	–6.40	–4.89	–4.00
	CIPS Value			
Panel	-1.028	-2.85	-2.47	-2.28

Note: *Fixed and trend effect model şs selected for the test model. Critical values are obtained from Table 1 (c) on page 276 in the article of Pesaran (2007), considering the country and period for each panel.*

In Table 4, since the CADF values belonging to both the dependent and independent variable are lower than the critical values in Pesaran's (2007) study, the hypothesis 'no unit roots in serials' is not accepted. The variables are not stable; that is, they carry unit root (Pesaran, 2007; 276; Şit, Çavuşoğlu ve Ekşi, 2020: 12). Similarly, when looked at the CIPS values for the panel's general, the serials carry unit roots.

Tab. 5. *Hsiao Homogeneity Test*

Hypothesis	F Statistics	Probability
H_1	102.4061	9.210228
H_2	5.100714	0.000132
H_3	113.9130	1.024829

H_2 hypothesis claiming the serials are homogenous is rejected. That is, according to the H_2 hypothesis, the variables are heterogeneous.

Tab. 6. *The Results of ECM Westerlund Cointegration Test*

	Statistics	P Values
Group_tau	-18.397	0.000
Group_alpha	-1.544	0.999
Panel_tau	-2.483	0.982
Panel_alfa	-0.603	0.995

Since the variables are heterogeneous, $Group_{ta}$ and $Group_{alpha}$ values are interpreted in the Hsiao homogeneity test in the table. Because the value of $Group_{ta}$ is lower than 1%, there seems a solid cointegrating relationship between the variables (Güney, 2017: 327).

Lastly, to determine the coefficient of the relationship between variables, the results of the CCE Coefficient Estimator are given below:

Tab. 7. *CCE Coefficient Estimator Results*

	Coefficient	Standard Error	Probability Value
Panel CCE	-0,2342058	0,2497251	0,348
Countries			
France	0,0274858	0,737267	0,97
Spain	-0,9854765	0,9836266	0,316
Italy	-0,5924015	0,8765431	0,499
Portugal	0,8268513	2,045601	0,686
Greece	0,1440152	0,3086167	0,641
Turkey	0,790649	0,2103886	0,000 ***
Germany	-1,823202	0,2240769	0,000 ***
Russia	-0,2976933	0,3839484	0,438
Netherlands	-0,1798891	0,624149	0,773
Belgium	-0,2523972	0,8312051	0,761

According to the CCE Group Estimator results, there is no relationship between housing prices for the general panel and the happiness index. However, when the CCE Estimator results are looked at based on countries, there appears to be a strong relationship between housing prices and the happiness index in Turkey and Germany in the 1% meaningfulness level. However, when looking at the coefficient values, the direction of both countries' relationship is the opposite. There is an isotropic relationship between the housing price index and the happiness index in Turkey; on the other hand, there is an opposite relationship in Germany. One unit change in the housing price index causes a 0.79 increase in Turkey's happiness index. In contrast, one unit change in the housing price index causes a 1.82 decrease in Germany's happiness index.

5 Conclusion

Researches about happiness economy and economic politics increasing individuals' happiness were conducted. People made self-sacrifices from their families, friends, sleep and regular diets while trying to maximize their finances in an intense and competitive working schedule. Since these sacrifices lead to work stress and social, psychological and health problems, they negatively influence happiness. That is, people's happiness does not increase immediately, even though their financial possibilities have increased. Despite being a welfare signifier, happiness is not valuable if it is not supported by liberty and justice.

No relationship between housing prices and the happiness index was observed at the end of the study. That is, an increase in housing prices neither increases nor decreases the happiness index. However, when the CCE estimator's results were looked at based on countries, there was a strong relationship between housing prices and the happiness index in Turkey and Germany at a 1% meaningfulness level. However, when the coefficient results were looked at, the relationships' direction is opposite in these two countries. There is an isotropic relationship between housing prices and the happiness index in Turkey. The increase in the housing prices in Turkey increases happiness. The savings of individuals in Turkey were dramatically evaluated in the housing market. The increase in housing prices increases an individuals' wealth. The happiness of individuals increases when their wealth increases. There is an opposite relationship in Germany. When housing prices increase in Germany, individuals cannot afford to purchase a new house. Thus, people's happiness level decreases when individuals cannot afford to purchase a house in Germany.

The results obtained from the study are consistent with the relationship between housing and happiness, which was established by Hu et al. (2020) for the Chinese economy and Gür et al. (2020) for the Turkish economy.

References

Akgiş, Ö. (2015). Bir Refah Göstergesi Olarak Türkiye'de Mutluluğun Mekânsal Dağılışı. Türk Coğrafya Dergisi, 65, 69–76.

Beşel, F. (2015). 2013 Yılı Yaşam Memnuniyeti Araştırması Sonuçlarının İl Bazlı Ekonomik, Sosyal ve Siyasi Analizi. Karabük Üniversitesi Sosyal Bilimler Enstitüsü Dergisi, 5 (2), 227–236.

Coates, D., Anand, P. and Norris, M. (2015). Housing, Happiness and Capabilities: A Summary of the International Evidence and Models. Open Discussion Papers in Economics, 81.

Coşkun, Y. (2016). Konut Fiyatları ve Yatırımı: Türkiye İçin Bir Analiz. Niğde Ömer Halisdemir Üniversitesi İktisadi ve İdari Bilimler Fakültesi Dergisi, 9 (2), 201–217.

Çondur, F. (2016). Türkiye'de Hoşnutsuzluk Endeksi Parametrelerinin Gelişimi. Atatürk Üniversitesi İktisadi ve İdari Bilimler Dergisi, 30 (5), 1309–1327.

Deviren, N. V. and Yıldız, O. (2017). Gayrisafi Milli Mutluluğun Ekonomik Kalkınmadaki Rolü: Bhutan Krallığı Örneği. Adnan Menderes Üniversitesi Sosyal Bilimler Enstitüsü Dergisi, 4 (4), 232–248.

Duarte, A. (2010). New Approaches in Transportation Planning: Happiness and Transport Economics. Netnomics, 11, 5–32. DOI: https://10.1007/s11066-009-9037-2.

Görmüş, Ş. (2015). İslam İktisadı İnsanlık İçin Bir İhtiyaç mı?. Uluslararası İslam Ekonomisi ve Finansı Araştırmaları Dergisi, 1 (2), 161–170.

Gudmundsdottir, D. G. (2013). The Impact of Economic Crisis on Happiness. Social Indicators Research, 110 (3), 1083–1101. DOI: https://10.1007/sl 1205-011-9973-8.

Güney, T. (2017). Governance and Sustainable Development: How Effective is Governance? The Journal of International Trade and Economic Development, 26 (3), 316–335. http://dx.doi.org/10.1080/09638199.2016.1249391.

Gür, M., Murat, D. and Sezer, F. Ş. (2020). The effect of housing and neighborhood satisfaction on perception of happiness in Bursa, Turkey. Journal of Housing and the Built Environment, 35, 679–697. https://doi.org/10.1007/s10901-019-09708-5.

Hu, M., Yang, Y., and Yu, X. (2020). Living better and feeling happier: An Investigation into the Association between Housing Quality and Happiness. Growth and Change, 51 (3), 1224–1238. https://doi.org/10.1111/grow.12392.

Karagöz, Y., Eş, A. and Yavuz, S. (2015). Nominal İlişki Ölçüleriyle Konut Satın Almaya Etki Eden Faktörlerin İncelenmesi: Bolu İli Örneği. Cumhuriyet Üniversitesi İktisadi ve İdari Bilimler Dergisi, 16 (1), 247–260.

Memiş, S. (2018). Tüketicilerin Konut Seçimini Etkileyen Faktörlerin Belirlenmesine Yönelik Bir Araştırma. International Journal of Academic Value Studies, 4 (20), 652–665. http://dx.doi.org/10.23929/javs.777.

Öndes, H. (2019). Türkiye'de Mutluluk Düzeyini Etkileyen Faktörler: Mekânsal Ekonometri Analizi. Dokuz Eylül Üniversitesi Sosyal Bilimler Enstitüsü Dergisi, 21 (4), 1039–1064. https://doi.org/10.16953/deusosbil.453325.

Önemli, M. B. and Avşar, N. A. (2016). Türkiye'de Yaşam Memnuniyetine İlişkin Mekânsal Bir Eşitsizlik Analizi. ODTÜ Gelişme Dergisi, 43, 607–634.

Öztürk, S. and Suluk, S. (2020). Mutluluk Ekonomisi: G8 Ülkeleri Açısından Ekonomik Büyüme ve Mutluluk Arasındaki İlişkinin İncelenmesi. Süleyman Demirel Üniversitesi Sosyal Bilimler Enstitüsü Dergisi, 37, 226–249.

Pesaran, M. H. (2007). A Simple Panel Unit Root Test in the Presence of Cross-Section Dependence. Journal of Applied Economics, 22, 265–312.

Santipolvut, S. (2015). The Development of a Provincial Green and Happy Society Index in Thailand: The Richer You Are, the Happier You Are. Asian Social Science, 11 (24), 48–61. http://dx.doi.org/10.5539/ass.v11n24p48.

Servet, O. (2017). Mutluluğun Türkiye'deki Belirleyenlerinin Zaman İçinde Değişimi. Akdeniz İktisadi ve İdari Bilimler Fakültesi Dergisi, 35, 16–42.

Smyth, R. and Qian, X. (2008). Inequality and Happiness in Urban China. Economics Bulletin, 4 (23), 1–10.

Şeker, M. (2009). Mutluluk Ekonomisi. Sosyoloji Konferansları Dergisi, 39, 115–134.

Şit, A., Çavuşoğlu, A., and Ekşi, İ. H. (2020). Finansal Risklerin Firma Değeri Üzerine Etkisi: Seçilmiş Bankalar Üzerine Uygulama. Uludağ Üniversitesi İktisadi ve İdari Bilimler Fakültesi Dergisi, 39 (1), 1–19.

Veenhoven, R. and Dumludağ, D.(2015). İktisat ve Mutluluk. İktisat ve Toplum, 58, 46–51.

Mehmet Şengür and Wilkista Lore Obiero

Validity of Okun's Law: Evidence from Kenya

1 Introduction

The presence of unemployment means there are people actively looking for a job at the current wage rate, but are not able to find one. There are several causes of unemployment, including the introduction of new technology since technology is cheaper and more efficient compared to human beings, increased competition between and within countries, and sometimes due to government regulations and policies. In every economy, both developed and underdeveloped, have some form of unemployment known as the natural rate of unemployment. This occurs from the changes in the economy causing the need for frequent structural adjustments (Parkin et al., 2005). Other existing forms of unemployment include seasonal unemployment and cyclical unemployment. Whereas seasonal unemployment is dependent on seasonal cycles and weather changes, cyclical unemployment on the other hand results from business cycles in the economy.

Kenya had an unemployment rate of 2.6% in 2018 and 2.98% in 2020 (Global economy, 2021) and this percentage is mostly comprised of natural and cyclical unemployment. Unemployment is one of the reasons why Kenya has not been able to achieve its development goals, while women also form a higher percentage of the unemployed (14%) as compared to men (Vuluku et al., 2013). There are various causes of unemployment in Kenya with a lack of matching job opportunities and corruption being the main causes of unemployment in this period (Abdirahman Farah and Abdi Ali, 2018). Unemployment is undesirable because it implies the presence of an underused labour force in the economy. This can lead to some economic evils like increased dependence, reduced output, slower economic growth and increased crime rates (Mose, 2019).

Based on these negative impacts of unemployment in the economy, Mavikela (2019) states that increasing the rate of economic growth in the economy is likely to translate to increased employment opportunities, thereby having a positive impact on unemployment. With economic growth more opportunities will be provided for increased labour force participation, thus reducing unemployment. The unemployment rate in Kenya is very high and this has led many people, especially youths, to become frustrated and lose faith in the system, preferring to look for work in other countries (Dikaniakina, 2014).

One of the ways of tackling the unemployment issue in the economy is through sustained economic growth, this relationship between economic growth and the unemployment rate is outlined using Okun's law. In this law, unemployment is outlined as being negatively related to economic growth and so it is examined by what percentage the economy must grow in order to reduce unemployment by 1%. However, this law does not hold for every economy, necessitating the current study on the Kenyan economy. Knowing this targeted growth level is important when setting the targeted economic growth rate for a specific year. This current study is aimed at analysing the applicability of Okun's law in Kenya; the elasticity of unemployment to real GDP growth rate was also calculated. In this study, analysis was made with the ARDL model with using annual data for the period 1991-2020: the ARDL model was used in this analysis. The contribution this study will make to the literature will provide updated data on the relationship between unemployment and economic growth in Kenya.

In the first chapter, a general introduction to the study subject was made. The second section is the literature and theoretical review section. The third is the data and methodology section. The fourth is the results discussion section, while the last section is the summary and policy recommendation section.

2 Theoretical Framework and Literature Review

The classical school of unemployment is based on a well-functioning labour market characterized by freely adjusted prices of labour. The supply of labour in this school of thought is a function of real wages. This implies that demand and supply for labour will adjust and an equilibrium level of wages shall prevail. Those who are unwilling to accept the prevailing wage rates end up being voluntarily unemployed. Involuntary unemployment only occurs when the market forces are not allowed to freely adjust. For instance, when the minimum wage rate is set above the prevailing equilibrium wage rate, firms may not be willing to employ many job seekers and some involuntary unemployment will be observed (Goodwin et al., 2006).

According to the Keynesian school of thought, wages are sticky downwards and people are reluctant to have their wages adjusted downwards. Labour supply is, therefore, a function of both real wages and money wages. The labour market is not as smooth functioning as classical economists postulate it to be and, therefore, unemployment is usually present in the economy (Edwards, 1959). Here, real wages determine the unemployment level, not the other way around. Firms have a fixed price for their goods and this price will determine aggregate output; how many people are employed will depend on this aggregate demand (Rodriguez, 2015).

This law was put forward by Arthur Okun in the early 1960s. It states that a negative relationship exists between unemployment and the rate of economic growth. This implies that when the country is experiencing very high unemployment rates, above the normal rates, then economic growth is affected. Therefore, a target growth rate can be set that will contribute to a reduction in the unemployment levels in the economy.

The gap version of Okun's law is shown below:

$$\frac{y-y^{*}}{y^{*}}=-\mu\left(c-c^{*}\right)$$

Where $y - y^{*}$ is the output gap, y^{*} is the potential GDP, y is the actual output, μ is the Okun coefficient, c is the current period's unemployment, while c^{*} is the previous year's unemployment.

The negative sign before the Okun coefficient represents the inverse relationship between unemployment and the growth rate. There are different versions of Okun's law namely: difference version, gap version, dynamic version and the production function version (Javeid, 2005).

In earlier studies, the Okun coefficient was estimated to exist at 3% change in unemployment for every 1% change in the GDP growth rate, but this has since changed with different studies obtaining different values for various economies (Prachowny, 2009).

Acaroğlu (2018) finds that Okun's law is applicable in some G20 countries, but not all of them. This is based on data for the period 1991–2014 and different techniques of data analysis. In this study however, it is noted that the G20 countries that are classified as developing countries did not fit Okun's law, while the developed countries all exhibited a negative relationship between economic growth and unemployment. The study attributes this difference in developing and developed countries to differences in population. Thesame conclusion was reached by Akeju and Olanipekun (2014) for Nigeria, which is a developing country; with an increased growth rate of the economy, unemployment levels did not reduce but, rather, continued to soar. This situation was ascertained due to the fact that Nigeria depends on oil for economic growth, leading to one-sided growth, which cannot reduce unemployment that exists in many sectors across the country. The inapplicability of Okun's law to low income and developing countries is further stated by An et al. (2016), and the issue put forward in this study to address this inapplicability is the existence of a different way of operation for the labour markets in low income and developing countries.

El Aynaoui and Ibourk (2016) in a study to prove the applicability of Okun's law in Africa, found that the law is only applicable to a few countries and this is attributed to differences in labour compositions across the continent. In majority of African countries, Okun's law was found to be invalid. Ball et al., (2019), in a study on how Okun's law is useful in decision making for both developing and developed countries, found that applicability in developing countries was for almost half when compared to developed countries.

For Indian economy, Bhat et al. (2019) found a negative relationship between unemployment and economic growth, implying that Okun's law could be applied in India. A further implication of this result is that the government can set growth targets aimed at reducing the unemployment rate. This is not, however, the case for Nigeria, as a study by Dankumo et al.,(2019) did not prove the existence of Okun's law in its economy. Despite Nigeria having experienced a high level of economic growth in the past, unemployment levels have also been rising, which is attributed to other factors like corruption and political instability. A similar study for Uganda by Kurayish and Joseph (2019) found that Okun's law is applicable in Uganda. Reducing the unemployment rate was proven to have a positive impact on the rate of economic growth. With these results, growth targets should be set to help reduce the unemployment rate in the country.

In a panel study of developing and developed countries, Furceri et al. (2020) concluded that Okun's law is more applicable in countries with a smaller portion of population employed in agriculture, but high for people employed in the public sector. Similar findings were arrived at by Hanusch (2014) for East Asian countries, whereby the countries that depend highly on agricultural sector experienced a jobless growth as compared to their counterparts with higher percentage of workers in the industrial sector. A similar study on Asian countries by Lal et al. (2010) failed to prove the existence of Okun's law. They based the inapplicability of Okun's law in these countries to the rate of inflation, which was fluctuating. Javeid (2005) was, however, able to confirm the existence of Okun's law in Pakistan, with a 1% increase in GDP growth leading to a 2.8% decrease in unemployment for the period under study.

In his thesis, Mavikela (2019) conducted an analysis of the South African economy to ascertain whether Okun's law was applicable for different economic time periods. Different values of Okun's coefficient were obtained, but just a few of them were significant for the period under study. To deal with the existing problem of high unemployment and slow growth, other growth targeting measures were recommended in the study. Michail (2015), in a study of the US economy, found than Okun's law was applicable, and still close to the initial value specified by Arthur Okun.

Mose (2019), in a study of the applicability of Okun's law in Kenya, found that a unit increase of GDP growth reduced the rate of unemployment by 0.12% . This implies that unless a higher rate of growth is achieved, it will take quite a long time to reduce unemployment rate to manageable levels. The results of this study were not similar to that of Acaroğlu (2018) and Akeju and Olanipekun (2014), who did not accept the applicability of Okun's law in developing countries such as Kenya.

Similarly, a study by Noor et al. (2007) accepted the applicability of Okun's law in Malaysia. This implies that measures taken to reduce unemployment in Malaysia will also contribute to an increase in the rate of economic growth. The study also found that a significant reduction in the unemployment position was only possible if the growth rate hit 8% per annum, which is quite high and not easily achieved. In an analysis of the applicability of Okun's law in BRICS and Turkey, Pehlivanoğlu and Tanga (2016) ascertained that the law is only applicable in India, Russia and China. These results only prove that unemployment and growth data relationship is different across economies and is dependent on the specific labour characteristics of the economy.

Taken together, the studies above indicate that there are different results obtained from studies testing the applicability of Okun's law in different countries. Even for studies on similar countries, but based on datasets for different periods and applying different methods of analysis, different results were arrived at. This prompted this study in order to provide an updated piece of literature on the relationship between GDP growth and unemployment in Pakistan.

3 Unemployment rates and GDP trends in Kenya

The unemployment values presented in Figure 1 show the unemployment trend as a percentage of labour force in Kenya for the period 1991 up to 2020. The labour force consists of people above the age of sixteen who can work and be paid at the existing wage rates. The unemployment rate was 2.8% in the year 1991, this rate increased to 2.9% in the year 1992, and further increased by up to 2.93% in the year 1995. The value then fluctuates up to 2008 when the unemployment rate fell to 2.66%. The unemployment rate then increased to 2.87% in 2013, before starting to fall again, hitting 2.60% in 2019 before rising again thereafter.

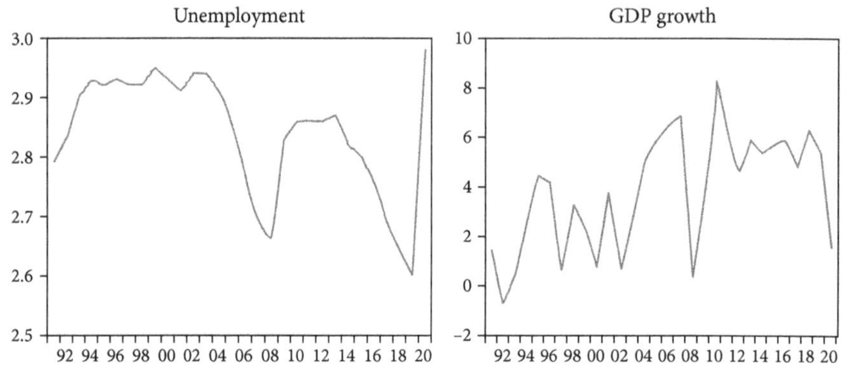

Fig. 1: *Unemployment and GDP in Kenya*
Source: Author's calculation based on the data

Figure 1 shows the trends in Kenya for the period 1991 to 2020. The GDP growth rate fluctuates through the period, the lowest GDP growth rate during this period was 0.2% in the year 2008; this was attributed to the effects of the post-election skirmishes experienced during the period. The GDP growth rate increased again in the following years, and reached 8.4% in 2010. The years that followed experienced fluctuating growth values, and the next period of low growth was observed in 2020 when the growth rate reduced to 1.5% because of the COVID 19 pandemic.

4 Data, Methodology and Findings

To understand whether Okun's law is applicable in Kenya, annual time series data for the period 1991 to 2020 was used. The data was sourced from the WDI data site. The two main variables used in the study were the unemployment data and the GDP growth rate data. Inflation was used as a control variable. The dependent variable was the GDP growth rate, while unemployment and inflation were independent variables. One desirable property of data is stationarity, therefore before the analysis was conducted, the ADF and KPSS methods were applied to test for stationarity.

Tab. 1: *Unit root tests*

		ADF		KPSS	
		Constant	**Constant and Trend**	**Constant**	**Constant and Trend**
Level	Unemployment	-2.2881	-3.2678*	0.4101*	0.1103
	GDP	-3.2267**	-3.8911**	0.5832**	0.1110
	Inflation	-2.9067*	-3.3142*	0.3636*	0.1058
First Difference	Unemployment	-2.3514	-1.9098	0.1164	0.1098
	GDP	-6.1930***	-6.2952***	0.2569	0.1568**
	Inflation	-7.6674***	-8.0160***	0.3690*	0.4269***

Source: Authors' calculation

From table 1, the unit root test results indicate that all the variables are stationary at level I(0). We then proceeded to conduct a ARDL test by to determine the cointegration property between these two variables. This is because ARDL can be applied whether the variables are I(0), I(1) or a mixture of both (Nkoro and Uko, 2016).

We proceeded to conduct the bounds test to determine whether a long run relationship existed between the variables. If the F value is greater than the I(0) and I(1) values, then it means a long run relationship exists between the variables. If the F value is smaller than the I(0) and I(1) values, then it implies the existence of a short run relationship. Otherwise, if the F value falls in between the I(0) and I(1) values, then a decision cannot be reached (Paul, 2014).

Tab. 2: *Bounds test*

Test static	**F value**	**Significance**	**I(0)**	**I(1)**
F stat	6.6145	10%	2.63	3.35
		5%	3.1	3.87
		2.5%	3.55	4.38
		1%	4.13	5

In table 2, the results from the bounds test indicates that the F value of 6.6145 is greater than all the I(0) and the I(1) values, alluding to the presence of a long run relationship between the variables.

Tab. 3: *Long-run ARDL*

Variable	Coefficient
Inflation	-0.1311** (-2.0833)
Unemployment	-16.4886*** (-3.2280)
Constant	52.4939*** (3.5890)

Source: Authors' calculation, the standard error values are in brackets.

From table 3, the long run results indicate the presence of a negative relationship between unemployment and GDP growth rate in Kenya. Inflation is also seen to present a negative impact on growth for the period under study.

Tab. 4: *Short-run ARDL.*

Variable	Coefficient
D(unemployment)	-16.6945*** (-4.0280)
D(unemployment(-1))	16.2111** (2.3736)
D(unemployment(-2))	14.9855* (1.9526)
ECM	-0.9530*** (-5.5161)

Source: Authors' calculation, the standard error values are in brackets.

The short run results also show in table 4 the existence of a negative relationship between debt and economic growth in Kenya for the period under study. The error correction term is negative and significant, showing that shocks to the system are cleared at an adjustment speed of 95% per annum. The tests conducted on the residual reveal that the data is reliable as it is normally distributed, free from autocorrelation and heteroscedasticity in table 5.

Tab. 5: *Residual tests*

Test	Null Hypothesis	Probability value
Normality test	The series is normal	0.6506
Correlation test	There is no Autocorrelation	0.4030
Heteroscedasticity	There is no Heteroscedasticity	0.6622

Source: Author's calculation

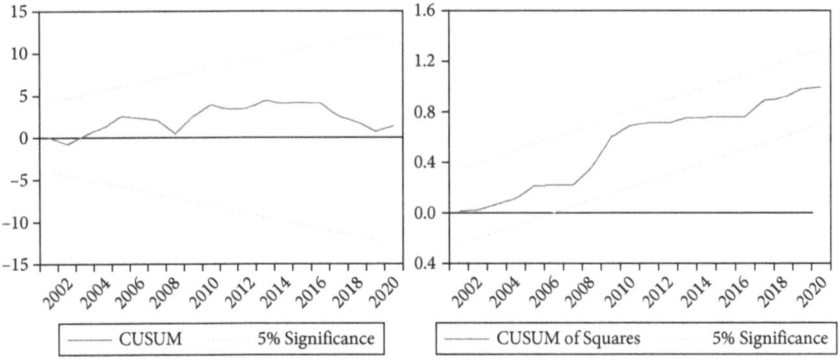

Fig. 2: *CUSUM and CUSUMSQ*

The residuals are stable, as can be observed in figure 2.

5 Conclusion

This study is aimed at proving the applicability of Okun's law in Kenya using data for the period 1991–2020. The ARDL model was used in the analysis. The GDP growth rate was the dependent variable, while unemployment (as a percentage of labour force) and inflation were the two independent variables used. The results revealed the presence of a negative and significant relationship between unemployment and economic growth for the period. This showed that unemployment in Kenya explained the changes in GDP, as postulated in Okun's law. These results are similar to those obtained by Mose (2019) and Javeid (2005) for Kenya and Pakistan respectively. Inflation also had a negative impact on growth for the period; however, Sattarov (2011) found a positive impact of inflation on growth for Finland.

Based on these results, the government should put measures to reduce unemployment as this will lead to a higher GDP growth rate in Kenya. This can be achieved through investment in developmental projects that create jobs, especially for the youths. The government can also set yearly targets of how much employment they want to create and work on achieving them. The partnering of the government and banks to make low interest rate loans available to investors will also go a long way in reducing unemployment and promoting GDP growth in the country.

References

Abdirahman F. S., and Abdi A. H. (2018). A Study on the Causes of Unemployment Among University Graduates in Kenya: A Case of Garissa County, Kenya. European Journal of Social Sciences Studies, 3(0), 183. https://doi.org/10.5281/zenodo.1312306

Acaroğlu, H. (2018). Çıktı Ve İşsizlik Arasında Bir Denge Var Mıdır? G-20 Ülkeleri İçin Okun Yasası'ndan Bir Kanıt. Eskişehir Osmangazi Üniversitesi İktisadi ve İdari Bilimler Dergisi, 13(2), 147–162. https://doi.org/10.17153/oguiibf.405529

Akeju, K. F., and Olanipekun, D. B. (2014). Unemployment and Economic Growth in Tanzania. Journal of Economics and Sustainable Development, 5(4), 138–144. https://doi.org/10.9734/jemt/2017/38500

An, Z., Ghazi, T., and Prieto, N. G. (2016). Okun's Law: Unfit for Low and Lower Income Countries? 2(4). https://doi.org/10.1111/j.0954-6820.1980.tb12883.x

Ball, L., Furceri, D., Leigh, D., and Loungani, P. (2019). Does One Law Fit All? Cross-Country Evidence on Okun's Law. Open Economies Review, 30(5), 841–874.

Bhat, T. A., Lone, T. A., and Din, T. M. U. (2019). The Validity of Okun's Law: Evidences from Indian economy. Theoretical and Applied Economics, XXVI(4), 273–278.

Dankumo, A. M., Ishak, S., Oluwaseyi, Z. A., and Onisanwa, I. D. (2019). Does Okun's Law Explain the Relationship between Economic Growth and Unemployment in Nigeria? Journal Economy Malaysia, 53(3), 153–162. https://doi.org/10.17576/JEM-2019-5303-12

Dikaniakina, E. S. (2014). The causes and Impacts of Youth Unemployment in Kenya: The Case Study of Nairobi, Doctoral dissertation, United States International University-Africa.

Edwards, E. (1959). Classical and Keynesian Employment Theories : A Reconciliation. The Quarterly Journal of Economics, 73(3), 407–428.

El Aynaoui, K., and Ibourk, A. (2016). Policy Lessons from Okun's Law for African Countries. In Paper Presented at the IMF-OCPPC Workshop on Global Labour Markets. Paris (Issue October).

Furceri, D., Tovar, J., and Loungani, P. (2020). On the Determinants of the Okun's Law : New Evidence from Time - Varying Estimates. Comparative Economic Studies, 62(4). Palgrave Macmillan UK. https://doi.org/10.1057/s41294-019-00111-1.

Global Economy, (2021).Retrieved from https://www.theglobaleconomy.com/Kazakhstan/unemployment_rate/

Goodwin, N. R., A.Julie, N., Frank, A., and Thomas, W. (2006). Theories of Unemployment the Classical Theory of Unemployment. In Global Development Environment Inst. https://www.saylor.org/site/wp-content/uploads/2010/11/Theories-of-Unemployment.pdf

Hanusch, M. (2014). Jobless Growth ? Okun's Law in East Asia, Policy Research Working Paper, The World Bank. (Issue March). https://doi.org/10.1142/S1793993313500142

Javeid, U. (2005). Validity of Okun's Law: Emperical Evidence from Pakistan. Unpublished Master's thesis, Sodertorn University, Sweden.

Kurayish, S., and Joseph, M. (2019). Estimating the Cost of Unemployment to Uganda' s Growth and Growth Trajectory 1980–2016 :'An auto-regressive distributed lag modelling approach.' International Journal of Econometrics and Financial Management, 7(1), 27–36. https://doi.org/10.12691/ijefm-7-1-4

Lal, I., Muhammad, S. D., Jalil, M. A., and Hussain, A. (2010). Test of Okun's Law in Some Asian Countries Co-Integration Approach. European Journal of Scientific Research, 40(1), 73–80.

Mavikela, N. (2019). Testing the Validity of Okun's Law in South Africa within the Democratic Era.

Michail, N. A. (2015). Examining the Stability of Okun's Coefficient. Working Paper 2015–2. Working Paper Series, December.

Mose, V. (2019). Does Okun's Law on Cyclical Unemployment Apply in Kenya ? International Journal of Current Research, 11(02), 1765–1770.

Nkoro, E., and Uko, A. K. (2016). Autoregressive Distributed Lag (ARDL) Cointegration Technique: Application and Interpretation. Journal of Statistical and Econometric Methods, 5(3), 63–91.

Noor, Z. M., Nor, N. M., and Ghani, J. A. (2007). The Relationship between Output and Unemployment in Malaysia : Does Okun's Law Exist ? International Journal of Economics and Management, 1(3), 337–344.

Paul, B. P. (2014). Testing Export-Led Growth in Bangladesh: An ARDL Bounds Test Approach. International Journal of Trade, Economics and Finance, 5(1), 1–5. https://doi.org/10.7763/ijtef.2014.v5.331

Parkin, M., Powell, M., and Matthews, K. (2005). Economics. Pearson Education, Inc.

Pehlivanoğlu, F., and Tanga, M. (2016). An Analysis on the Validity of Okun's Law : Case of Turkey and BRICS. International Congress on Political Economic and Social Studies, 24–26.

Prachowny, M. F. J. (2009). Okun's Law: Theoretical Foundations and Revised Estimates. The Review of Economics and Statistics, 75(2), 331–336.

Rodriguez, R. A. (2015). Classical versus Keynesian Theory of Unemployment: An approach to the Spanish Labour Market. Autonomous University of Barcelona.

Sattarov, K. (2011). Inflation and Economic Growth Analyzing the Threshold Level of Inflation-Case Study of Finland, 1980–2010, Umeå University. http://www.diva-portal.org/smash/get/diva2:484668/FULLTEXT01.pdf

Vuluku, G., Wambugu, A., and Moyi, E. (2013). Unemployment and Underemployment in Kenya: a Gender Gap Analysis. Economics, 2(2), 7. https://doi.org/10.11648/j.eco.20130202.11

Salih Türedi and Tunahan Hacıimamoğlu

Are Corruption and the Shadow Economy Complementary in Low Income Countries?

1 Introduction

Although they might vary in terms of the form and size between countries today, corruption and the shadow economy are two global phenomena that are observed in all countries throughout the world, and involve illegal activities. Even though there are different definitions of corruption in the literature, those made by Transparency International and the World Bank come to the forefront. According to Transparency International, corruption is defined as '*the abuse of entrusted power for private gain*' (T*ransparency* International, 2021), whereas the World Bank defines corruption, which includes various behaviours from bribery to stealing the public funds, as '*the abuse of public office for private gain*' (Worldbank, 2020). Corruption has important social, political and economic costs. It complicates access to education, health and justice services ,and especially negatively affects the poor, which is the most vulnerable segment of the society. It weakens democracy, degrades the rule of law and corrodes the trust in government. Moreover, it also results in wastage and misallocation of resources. It deteriorates the efficient functioning of market mechanisms, such as fair competition, and increases the cost of doing business. It also causes decreases in domestic and foreign investment and, consequently, results in reductions in economic growth and employment and increases inequality (OECD, 2014; Worldbank, 2021; Ferguson, 2018: 9). On the other hand, it is very difficult to make an exact definition of the shadow economy, which is also named the hidden, unofficial, informal and underground economy (Schneider and Enste, 2013: 6). According to a common definition, the shadow economy includes all the economic activities contributing to officially calculated GDP, but hidden from the official authorities due to certain monetary, regulatory and institutional reasons (hereby unregistered) (Schneider, 2012: 4–5; Medina and Schneider, 2018: 4). Not taxing the revenues generated by the shadow sector diminishes the tax revenues of governments and causes budget deficits and borrowing. Thus, the shadow economy negatively affects not only the main macroeconomic indicators but also the economic welfare of individuals (Batrancea et al., 2018: 1120). The link between the shadow economy and corruption, which have common characteristics such as being global, pervasive, illegal and unobservable, has been investigated in academic circles for a long time, at both theoretical and empirical levels.

In theoretical literature, there are two different approaches to the relationship between these variables. According to the first approach, claiming that there is a complementary (positive) relationship between corruption and shadow economy, the high level of the tax burden, besides the heavy bureaucracy and excessive regulations, forces the firms to go outside the economy. The firms comply with paying a reasonable tax, but they do not want to bear constant and arbitrary requests. Thus, the presence and increase of corruption (bribe requests) that functions as an extra tax leads firms to transfer their activities underground and, consequently, increases the size of shadow economy (Johnson et al., 1997: 169; Johnson et al., 1998: 387; Friedman et al., 2000: 460). Contrary to the first approach, the second approach claims that there is a substitution (negative) relationship between corruption and the shadow economy. For instance, according to Choi and Thum (2005), an entrepreneurs' option to go underground limits the corrupted government officer's corruption (requests for a bribe) for his/her private gains. For this reason, by decreasing corruption, one of the government-induced distortions, the shadow economy leads to an increase in activities in the formal economy. Examining how the institutional quality affected the relationship between the shadow economy and corruption, Dreher et al. (2009) also reported a similar result. Since it enables easier detection of illegal activities in formal economy, the increase in institutional quality and also the firms' option to go underground when facing a high bribe request decreases the level of public officers' corruption requests. In the presence of the shadow economy, the level of corruption is lower and the size of the formal economy is larger. Hence, the shadow economy and corruption are substitutes.

Finally, it was also emphasized in the theoretical literature that the relationship between corruption and the shadow economy varies depending on the income level of the countries. Dreher and Schneider (2006) stated that, if shadow economic activities in high-income countries are detected, giving a bribe to government officials is rarely an option. Moreover, since the firms/entrepreneurs can call corrupt government officials to account via the courts, they do not have to pay a bribe. Hence, corruption and the shadow economy might become independent of each other in high-income countries. Besides that, Schneider (2007) states that corruption, which is at low levels in high-income countries and is generally seen in the form of bribery, is an instrument of achieving certain advantages/making things easier, such as getting a huge contract from the public sector in the formal economy. In other words, in these countries bribery does not merely sustain the shadow economic activities, it produces more activity in the formal economy. Thus, the increase in the size of formal economy by corruption indicates that they are substitutes in high-income countries. Finally, Schneider (2007) and Vo et al. (2015), who had a similar approach, stated that detecting such activities in low-income countries, where all the firms are involved in underground (unregistered) activities, is easy. For this reason, in order to avoid being detected by the government, paying tax and being punished, they pay bribes to officials. Thus, the expansion of shadow economic activities brings more corruption. In conclusion, these two phenomena are complementary (positively correlated) in low-income countries.

The objective of this study is to test the relationship between corruption and shadow economy in seventeen countries, which are classified as low-income according to the classification of the World Bank for the period between 2002 and 2017. This study's contributions to the literature can be summarized as follows. First of all, this study tests the validity of the theoretical assumption that '*corruption and shadow economy are complementary in low-income countries*' because there are few studies that examine the relationship between these variables specifically in low-income countries. Second, corruption and the shadow economy are two important problems that make economic development more difficult in low-income countries, which needs to be effectively fought. Within this context, the results obtained from the present study might provide important clues for governments of countries struggling with these two phenomena. Third, the second-generation test methods considering the cross-sectional dependence and heterogeneity and providing more robust and consistent results when compared to the first-generation tests from this aspect are used in the empirical analyses. The rest of the paper is organized as follows. The previous studies on this subject are discussed in the second section, whereas the data and model used in this study are presented in the third section. The fourth section, where the econometric methodology is explained, is followed by the fifth section, where the empirical results are reported. Conclusions and suggestions are presented in the sixth and final section.

2 Literature Review

Besides the theoretical literature, the relationship between corruption and the shadow economy is also an important and current research field in the empirical literature. The studies carried out using different countries (or country groups), periods, and econometric approaches reported different results. In other words, some of the studies reported a substitution (negative) relationship between corruption and the shadow economy, whereas some studies reported a complementary (positive) relationship. Although there is no consensus about the relationship between these variables, it can be stated that the majority of empirical studies reported results indicating a complementary relationship between corruption and the shadow economy. For instance, in their study carried out on forty-nine countries in three different regions of the world (Latin America, the OECD and the former Soviet Bloc), Johnson et al. (1998) reported that there was a strong relationship between the shadow economy and corruption, and the level of the shadow economy was higher in countries with a higher level of corruption. Aiming to determine the global-scale determinants of the shadow economy, Chowdhury (2005), who conducted a study on ninety-six countries, discovered in cross-sectional regression analysis that corruption is one of the significant determinants of the shadow economy. Performing a cross-sectional analysis for 120 countries and panel data analysis for 70 countries, Dreher and Schnider (2006) and Schnider (2007), who conducted a panel data analysis for 145 countries (including developing, transition and highly developed OECD economies), determined that the shadow economy and corruption have a substitution relationship in high-income countries and a complementary relationship in low-income countries. In other words, the shadow economy decreases the level of corruption in high-income countries, but increases it in low-income countries. Virta (2010) aimed to show how the geographical location of a country affects the relationship between corruption and the shadow economy. For this purpose, the author used the Bootstrapping and IV regressions estimation and, according to the findings, it was determined that corruption doesn't affect the shadow economy outside the tropics. Instead, the increase in the shadow economy as a result of corruption is proportional to the size of country's tropic area. Manolas et al. (2013) investigated the determinants of the shadow economy in nineteen OECD countries by using a panel regression analysis for the period of 2002–2008, and they found that the improvements in control of corruption (a decrease in the level of corruption) had the effect of decreasing the size of the shadow economy. According to the results obtained by Vo et al. (2015), in a study performed for the period 1995–2014 on ASEAN countries (excluding the two high-income countries – Singapore and Brunei); (i) there was a complementary relationship between corruption and the shadow economy and (ii) the effect of corruption on the shadow economy was stronger than the effect of shadow economy on corruption. Emphasizing that the link between the shadow economy and corruption was investigated mainly at the country level, Gillanders and Parviainen (2015) examined the relationship between these variables at the regional level for Sub-Saharan Africa (thirty-six countries), Europe and Central Asia (twenty-six countries), Latin America and the Caribbean (twenty-three countries), and the rest of the world (fourteen countries). According to the results, there was a statistically significant and positive nexus between the shadow economy and corruption at a regional level.

Using cross-sectional regression analysis on twenty-eight European Countries (EU) in an empirical study, Borlea et al. (2017) revealed that there was a high and positive relationship between corruption and the shadow economy and, thus, a higher level of corruption includes a higher level of shadow economy. Using data from 193 countries and regions in their study carried out with moderation analysis, Batrancea et al. (2018) indicated that the shadow economy and corruption are complementary. Bayar et al. (2018) investigated the effect of corruption on the shadow economy in eleven transition economies, which are located in Central and Eastern Europe and are also members of the EU, by employing the cointegration test of Westerlund and Edgerton (2007) and causality test of Konya (2006). After determining that there was a long-term relationship between two variables, the cointegration coefficients were estimated using fully modified ordinary least squares (FMOLS) and dynamic seemingly unrelated regression (DSUR), which showed that this relationship was a complementary one. Moreover, according to the results of causality analyses, it was found that there was a bilateral causality between the shadow economy and corruption in all the countries. In another study, Navickas et al. (2019) performed a panel regression analysis for EU-member Eastern European countries (ten countries) and reported results similar to those specified by Bayar et al. (2018). In other words, for the period of 2003–2016, corruption was a significant determinant of the shadow economy and there was a positive (complementary) relationship between these variables. One unit increase in the level of corruption would increase the level of shadow economy by 0.2054%. The effect of the tax burden on the shadow economy was empirically examined by Unver and Koyuncu (2019) for the period of 1999–2013 and 154 countries by Kutbay (2020) for the period of 2000–2017, and sixteen emerging market economies. Incorporating corruption into their estimated regression models as a control variable, the authors reported that corruption has a positive effect on the shadow economy. In an empirical analysis using static (OLS, fixed effect) and dynamic (GMM) panel data estimators for thirty-four OECD-member countries, Baklouti and Boujelbene (2020) found that there was a complementary relationship between corruption and the shadow economy. Finally, in the panel regression analysis carried out by Gokcekus and Schnider (2020), considering fifty states in the USA for the period of 2001–2008, it was determined that the relationship between corruption and the shadow economy varied depending on the size of the shadow economy; there was a substitution relationship in states with a small shadow economy and a complementary relationship in the states with a large shadow economy. According to the estimation of the authors, it can be stated that the point where the relationship turns from negative to positive is where the shadow economy equals to 7.61% of state GDP.

3 Data and Model

In this study examining the relationship between corruption and shadow economy, the 2002–2017 annual data of seventeen low-income countries[1] were classified according to the income classification of World Bank.[2] In the estimation models, besides the *shadow economy* (shadow) and *control of corruption* (corrupt) used as the indicator of corruption, *trade openness* (trade), *foreign direct investment* (FDI), *unemployment* (unemp) and *GDP per capita growth* (growth) were included as control variables. The shadow economy data was obtained from Medina and Schneider (2019). The data of all other variables was procured from the World Bank's World Development Indicators database. The details of the variables used with natural values in the analysis are presented in Table 1.

Tab. 1: *The Variables and Definitions*

Variable	Definitions
Shadow	Size of the shadow economy (% of GDP)
Corrupt	Control of corruption index. (An increase in index value indicates a decrease in corruption)
Trade	Total foreign trade volume, import + export (% of GDP)
FDI	Foreign direct investment, net inflows (% of GDP)
Unemp	Unemployment rate (% of the total labour force)
Growth	GDP per capita growth (annual%)

1 Burkina Faso, Burundi, Chad, Gambia, Guinea, Haiti, Central African Republic, Liberia, Madagascar, Malawi, Mozambique, Niger, Rwanda, Sierra Leone, Tajikistan, Togo and Uganda.

2 World Bank classifies countries by their level of income per capita. According to this classification, the countries with an income per capita below $1,036 fall into the class of low-income countries.

In this study, the relationships between the variables were estimated using the models (1) and (2) below:

$$Shadow_{it} = \alpha_0 + \beta_1 Corrupt_{it} + \beta_2 Trade_{it} + \beta_3 FDI_{it} + \beta_4 Unemp_{it} + \beta_5 Growth_{it} + \mu_{it} \quad (1)$$

$$Corrupt_{it} = \alpha_0 + \beta_1 Shadow_{it} + \beta_2 Trade_{it} + \beta_3 FDI_{it} + \beta_4 Unemp_{it} + \beta_5 Growth_{it} + \mu_{it} \quad (2)$$

In Model (1), $Shadow_{it}$ is the dependent variable referring to the size of shadow economy of the ith country at the time t. In Model (2), $Corrupt_{it}$ is the dependent variable referring to the level of corruption in the ith country at the time t. Moreover, μ_t refers to error term, i to model's cross-sectional size, and t to the time dimension of model. In this study, where a balanced panel dataset was used, the empirical analyses were performed using the Gauss 20 program.

4 Econometric Methodology

4.1 Cross-Sectional Dependence and Homogeneity Tests

Breusch and Pagan (1980) developed the Lagrange multiplier (LM) test for testing the cross-sectional dependence (CD). LM test statistics is calculated as follows:

$$LM = T\sum_{i=1}^{N-1}\sum_{j=i+1}^{N}\hat{p}_{ij}^{2} \quad (3)$$

where $\hat{p}_{ij}$ is the estimated correlation coefficient of residuals obtained from OLS estimation in Equation (3). The LM test is more suitable for the panels with relatively small N and sufficiently large T. For the panels with $T \rightarrow \infty$ and $N \rightarrow \infty$, Pesaran (2004) introduced a scaled version of LM test. CD_{LM} test that has a normal distribution with $N(N\text{-}1)/2$ degree of freedom and asymptotic chi-square (χ^2) character:

$$CD_{LM} = \left(\frac{1}{N(N-1)}\right)^{1/2}\sum_{i=1}^{N-1}\sum_{j=i+1}^{N}\left(T\hat{p}_{ij}^{2} - 1\right) \quad (4)$$

The discussions on the homogeneity of slope coefficients date back to Swamy (1970). Since the Swamy test was developed for N<T panels, it is claimed that it cannot yield reliable results for the slope coefficient homogeneity in $N>T$ panels. In the Delta $\left(\tilde{\Delta}\right)$ test, a modified version of Swamy (1970) test is considered first:

$$\hat{S} = \sum_{i=1}^{N}\left(\hat{\beta}_i - \hat{\beta}_{WFE}\right)' \frac{X_i' M_\tau X_i}{\hat{\sigma}_i^2}\left(\hat{\beta}_i - \hat{\beta}_{WFE}\right) \tag{5}$$

$$\hat{\sigma}_i^2 = \frac{\left(y_i - X_i\hat{\beta}_i\right)' M_\tau \left(y_i - X_i\hat{\beta}_i\right)}{\left(T-k-1\right)} \tag{6}$$

Swamy statistics ($\hat{S}$) show asymptotic chi-square distribution with $k(N\text{-}1)$ degree of freedom. $\tilde{\Delta}$ and $\tilde{\Delta}_{adj}$ tests' standardized distribution statistics are defined as follows:

$$\tilde{\Delta} = \sqrt{N}\left(\frac{N^{-1}\tilde{S} - k}{\sqrt{2k}}\right) \tag{7}$$

Based on the condition that $(N,T) \to \infty$, $\tilde{\Delta}$ test has asymptotic standard normal distribution as long as $\sqrt{N/T} \to \infty$ and error terms have a normal distribution. The $\tilde{\Delta}$ test has small sample characteristics, whereas $\tilde{\Delta}_{adj}$ has been adjusted to include large sample characteristics.

$$\tilde{\Delta}_{adj} = \sqrt{N}\left(\frac{N^{-1}\tilde{S} - E\left(\tilde{z}_{iT}\right)}{\sqrt{Var\left(\tilde{z}_{iT}\right)}}\right);\ E\left(\tilde{z}_{iT}\right) = k, var\left(\tilde{z}_{iT}\right) = \frac{2k\left(T-k-1\right)}{T+1} \tag{8}$$

4.2 Panel Unit Root Test

The CADF test was developed by Pesaran (2007) by including the lagged cross-sectional averages into ADF regression. CADF regression, which can be used with *T*>*N* and *N*>*T* and considers the cross-sectional dependence and heterogeneity, can be expressed as follows:

$$\Delta y_{it} = \alpha_i + b_i y_{i,t-1} + c_i \overline{y}_{t-1} + d_i \Delta \overline{y}_t + e_{it} \tag{9}$$

CIPS (Cross-Sectionally IPS) panel unit root statistics obtained using the unit root statistics of each cross-section in CADF regression can be defined as follows:

$$CIPS(N,T) = t - bar = N^{-1} \sum_{i=1}^{N} t_i (N,T) \tag{10}$$

where t_i (N,T) is the CADF test statistic for each cross-section in the CADF regression (Pesaran, 2007: 276).

4.3 Panel Cointegration Test

Cross-sectional dependence is considered in Durbin-Hausman cointegration test developed by Westerlund (2008) and, on the condition that the dependent variable is I(1), independent variables are allowed to be I(0) or I(1). In this test, two different test statistics as (DH_p) and (DH_g) are proposed based on the homogeneity and heterogeneity of panel coefficients, respectively (Westerlund, 2008: 205).

Panel means (DH_p) and group means (DH_g) statistics are shown in the equations below, respectively:

$$DH_p = \hat{S}_n \left(\widetilde{\varnothing} - \widehat{\varnothing}\right)^2 \sum_{i=1}^{n} \sum_{t=2}^{T} e_{it-1}^2 \tag{11}$$

$$DH_g = \sum_{i=1}^{n} \hat{S}_i \left(\widetilde{\varnothing}_i - \widehat{\varnothing}_i\right)^2 \sum_{t=2}^{T} e_{it-1}^2 \tag{12}$$

(DH_p) statistic is calculated by summing (n) individual terms before multiplying them, whereas (DH_g) statistic is calculated by first multiplying and then summing various terms (Westerlund, 2008: 203).

4.4 Long-Term Coefficient Estimation Test

The long-term coefficient estimator, which was developed by Pesaran (2006) for estimating the panel data models with multifactorial error structure in general and named common correlated effects (CCE), allows potential cross-sectional dependence arising from multiple unobservable common factors. Moreover, the slope coefficient in the factors is sensitive to the heterogeneity and possible unit root (Pesaran, 2006: 969). CCE mean group (CCEMG) and CCE pooled (CCEP) estimators are derived as follows:

$$\hat{b}_{MG} = N^{-1}\sum_{i=1}^{N}\hat{b}_i \tag{13}$$

$$\hat{b}_i = (X_i'\bar{M}_w X_i)^{-1} X_i'\bar{M}_w y_i \tag{14}$$

CCEMG estimator is a simple mean of individual-specific CCE estimators $(\hat{b}_i)$. When the cross-section-specific slope coefficients (β_i) are the same, the efficiency gains are obtained by integrating the observations on the units from the same cross-section. Based on the assumption of $\beta_i = \beta$ and $\sigma_i^2 = \sigma^2$, the slope coefficient of common effects is allowed to vary alongside the *i*. Expressed with CCEP, the pooled β estimator is formulated as follows:

$$\hat{b}_P = \left(\sum_{i=1}^{N}\theta_i X_i'\bar{M}_w X_i\right)^{-1}\sum_{i=1}^{N}\theta_i X_i'\bar{M}_w y_i \tag{15}$$

$$\theta_i = \sigma_i^{-2} / \sum_{j=1}^{N}\sigma_j^{-2} \tag{16}$$

5 Empirical Results

5.1 CD and Homogeneity Test Results

The CD and homogeneity test results are presented in Table 2. According to the CD test results, the null hypothesis that there is no cross-sectional dependence was rejected at the significance level of 1%, and it was found that there was cross-sectional dependence in all the variables. Besides that, the presence of cross-sectional dependence was also detected in the results obtained from the models. Within this context, it was concluded that a shock in any country has an effect on the other countries. Based on the results of homogeneity test, the null hypothesis that the slope coefficients are homogeneous was rejected at the significance level of 1% for both models. Thus, it was determined that both panel data models are heterogeneous.

Tab. 2: *CD and Homogeneity Test Results*

CD Test	**Breusch and Pagan (1980) LM**	**Pesaran (2004) CD_{lm}**
Shadow	218.711***	5.015***
Corrupt	258.585***	7.433***
Trade	258.585***	7.433***
FDI	243.034***	6.49***
Unemp	568.514***	26.225***
Growth	268.711***	8.047***
Model (1)	159.033*	1.397*
Model (2)	163.32*	1.657**
Homogeneity test	**Delta Tilde**	**Delta Tilde_{adj}**
Model (1)	7.821***	10.197***
Model (2)	6.373***	8.309***

***, **, and * refer to statistical significance at 1%, 5%, and 10%, respectively.

5.2 Panel Unit Root Test Results

Since the cross-sectional dependence and heterogeneity were determined in variables and models using the relevant tests, the examination of the stationarity of variables was continued with the CIPS test, one of the second-generation panel unit root tests, which considers the heterogeneity and cross-sectional dependence. According to the test results, the null hypothesis assuming the presence of unit root was not rejected for *Shadow, Corrupt, Trade, and Unemp* variables, and it was found that these variables had unit root at the level. On the other hand, the null hypothesis was rejected for *FDI* and *Growth* at the significance level of 1%, and it was found that these variables were stationary at the level. In conclusion, determining that the stationarity levels of variables were different, it was decided to use a cointegration test considering this situation (Table 3).

Tab. 3: *CIPS unit root test results*

	Shadow	Corrupt	Trade	FDI	Unemp	Growth
Level	-2.171	-1.830	-1.048	-2.563***	-1.795	-3.160***
First difference	-3.484***	-2.873***	-2.512***	-2.228**	-2.497***	-3.286***

*** and ** refer to statistical significance at the level of 1% and 5%, respectively. The maximum lag is 3. Schwarz information criterion is used in calculating the optimal lag. The CIPS statistics critical values for the model with constant are -2.45, -2.22, and -2.11, for 1%, 5%, and 10%, respectively.

5.3. Panel cointegration test results

In order to determine the long-term relationship between the variables after the unit root test, the Durbin-Hausman panel cointegration test, considering the stationarity of variables at different levels, was applied and the results are presented in Table 4. Since Model (1) and Model (2) are heterogeneous, the DHg (group) test statistics were considered. Accordingly, since the DHg test statistics' value of probability was lower than 1% in both models, the null hypothesis assuming that there is no cointegration relationship was rejected and it was found that there was a cointegration relationship for some cross-sectional units. As a result, there is a long-term significant relationship between the variables in both models.

Tab. 4: *DH Cointegration Test Results*

Durbin-Hausman Test	Model (1)	Model (2)
DHg (Group)	6.392***	43.411***
DHp (Panel)	-0.324	7.005

*** refers to statistical significance at the level of 1%. kmax is 5. Schwarz information criterion is used.

5.4 Long-Term Coefficient Estimation Test Results

Finally, in the analysis, the long-term coefficients of the variables were estimated using an CCE estimator that can be used in heterogeneous panels. Given the results of Model (1), it can be seen that the coefficient of *corrupt* is significant and negative (-0.1037). Considering that a decrease (increase) in *control of corruption* index, that is used as an indicator of corruption, means an increase in the level of corruption (decrease), it can be stated that the increase in the level of corruption increases the size of the shadow economy in low-income countries. On the other hand, the negative and significant coefficients of *Trade* and *Growth* variables indicate that the increase in trade openness and economic growth causes an effect that decreases the shadow economy in low-income countries. Finally, unemployment and foreign direct investment inflows in these countries create no significant effect on the shadow economy. According to the results obtained from Model (2), the coefficient of the *Shadow* variable is significant and negative (-0.0202). This finding indicates that an increase in the size of the shadow economy in low-income countries causes a higher level of corruption. However, control variables create no significant effect on corruption. Considering all the findings within the scope of study, it can be stated that corruption and the shadow economy are complementary in low-income countries.

Tab. 5: *CCE Estimation Results*

Model (1) Dependent variable: Shadow	**coefficient**	**Model (2) Dependent variable: Corrupt**	**coefficient**
Corrupt	-0.1037**	Shadow	-0.0202**
Trade	-0.0667**	Trade	-0.0004
FDI	0.0344	FDI	0.0088
Unemp	3.2778	Unemp	0.1604
Growth	-4.9798**	Growth	0.1690

** refers to statistical significance at the level of 5%.

6 Conclusions and Suggestions

In this study, the relationship between corruption and the shadow economy, seen in all countries throughout the world but at different levels and forms, was investigated for low-income countries. Detecting the relationship between these two important global problems complicated sustainable development due to their significant social, political and economic costs, which is important since it guides governments in their efficiency struggle with these problems. On the other hand, in the relevant literature (theoretical and empirical), it was emphasized that the relationship between corruption and the shadow economy varies depending on factors such as countries' institutional development and income levels – complementary (positive) or substitution (negative) – and, hence, this relationship is uncertain. According to Dreher and Schneider (2010), these variables have a substitution relationship in high-income countries and a complementary one in low-income countries. In this study, which was carried out on seventeen low-income countries for the period 2002–2017 using panel data methods such as Westerlund (2008) cointegration test and CCE estimator, the aim was to contribute to the literature by answering the question '*if corruption and shadow economy are complementary*'. According to the empirical results obtained; (i) corruption and the shadow economy have a long-term relationship, (ii) corruption and the shadow economy positively affect each other, but the effect of corruption on the shadow economy is stronger than the effect of the shadow economy on corruption, and (iii) in parallel with the theoretical expectations, corruption and the shadow economy are complementary. Based on these findings, which are consistent with the results reported by Schneider (2007), Dreher and Schneider (2010), and Vo et al. (2015), it can be specified that the governments in low-income countries should incorporate policies that aim to decrease the shadow economy (*corruption*), in their strategy to fight against corruption (*shadow economy*).

References

Baklouti, N. and Boujelbene, Y. (2020). Shadow economy, corruption, and economic growth: An empirical analysis. The Review of Black Political Economy, 47(3), 276–294.

Batrancea, L., Nichita, A., Batrancea, I. and Gaban, L. (2018). The strenght of the relationship between shadow economy and corruption: evidence from a worldwide country-sample. Social Indicators Research, 138, 1119–1143.

Bayar, Y., Odabas, H., Sasmaz, M. U. and Ozturk, O. F. (2018). Corruption and shadow economy in transition economies of European Union countries: a panel cointegration and causality analysis. Economic Research, 31(1), 1940–1952.

Borlea, S. N., Achim, M. V. and Miron, M. G. (2017). Corruption, shadow economy and economic growth: An empirical survey across the European

Union countries. Studia Universitatis "Vasile Goldis" Arad. Economic Series, 27(2), 19–32.

Breusch, T. S. and Pagan, A. R. (1980). The Lagrange multiplier test and its applications to model specification in econometrics. The Review of Economic Studies, 47(1), 239–253.

Choi, J. P. and Thum, M. (2005). Corruption and the Shadow Economy. International Economic Review, 46(3), 817–836.

Chowdhury, H. U. (2005). Informal economy, governance, and corruption. Philippine Journal of Development, 32(2), 103–134.

Dreher, A. and Schneider, F. (2006). Corruption and the shadow economy: an empirical analysis. CESifo Working Paper No: 1653.

Dreher, A. and Schneider, F. (2010). Corruption and the shadow economy: an empirical analysis. Public Choice, 144(1), 215–238.

Dreher, A., Kotsogiannis, C. and McCorriston, S. (2009). How do institutions affect corruption and the shadow economy?. International Tax and Public Finance, 16, 773–796.

Ferguson, Gerry. (2018). Global corruption: Law, theory and practice. 3rd edition, Victoria, BC: University of Victoria. Available at: https://dspace.library.uvic.ca//handle/1828/9253.

Friedman, E., Johnson, S., Kaufmann, D. and Zoido-Lobatón, P. (2000). Dodging the grabbing hand: the determinants of unofficial activity in 69 countries. Journal of Public Economics, 76, 459–493.

Gillanders, R. and Parviainen, S. (2015). Corruption and the shadow economy at the regional level. MPRA Paper No: 64510, 1–18.

Gokcekus, O. and Schneider, F. (2020). Are shadow economy and corruption in US states substitutive or complementary? An empirical investigation. Sosyoekonomi, 28(46), 11–23.

Johnson, S., Kaufmann, D. and Shleifer, A. (1997). The unofficial economy in transition. Brookings Papers on Economic Activity, 2, 159–239.

Johnson, S., Kaufmann, D. and Zoido-Lobatón, P. (1998). Regulatory discretion and the unofficial economy. The American Economic Review, 88(2), 387–392.

Kutbay, H. (2020). The effect of tax burden on the shadow economy: panel data analysis for emerging market economies (in Turkish). Journal of Selcuk University Vocational School of Social Sciences, 23(1), 226–239.

Manolas, G., Rontos, K., Sfakianakis, G. and Vavouras, I. (2013). The determinants of the shadow economy: the case of Greece. International Journal of Criminology and Sociological Theory, 6(1), 1036–1047.

Medina, L. and Schneider, F. (2018). Shadow Economies Around the World: What Did We Learn Over the Last 20 Years?. IMF Working Papers No: 18/17.

Medina, L. and Schneider, F. (2019). Shedding light on the shadow economy: A global database and the interaction with the official one. CESifo working Paper No: 7981.

Navickas, M., Juščius, V. and Navickas, V. (2019). Determinants of shadow economy in Eastern European countries. Scientific Annals of Economics and Business, 66(1), 1–14.

OECD (2014). The rationale for fighting corruption. CleanGovBiz Integrity in Practice Available at: https://www.oecd.org/cleangovbiz/49693613.pdf (15.11.2020)

Pesaran, M. H. (2004). General diagnostic tests for cross-sectional dependence in panels. CESifo Discussion Paper No:1229.

Pesaran, M. H. (2006). Estimation and inference in large heterogeneous panels with a multifactor error structure. Econometrica, 74(4), 967–1012.

Pesaran, M. H. (2007). A simple panel unit root test in the presence of cross-section dependence. Journal of Applied Econometrics, 22(2), 265–312.

Pesaran, M. H., and Yamagata, T. (2008). Testing slope homogeneity in large panels. Journal of econometrics, 142(1), 50–93.

Schneider, F. and Enste, D. H. (2013). The shadow economy: An international survey. 2nd edition, New York: Cambridge University Press.

Schneider, F. (2007). Shadow Economies and Corruption all over the World: New Estimates for 145 Countries. Economics Discussion Paper No: 9.

Schneider, F. (2012). The Shadow Economy and Work in the Shadow: What Do We (Not) Know?. IZA Discussion Paper No: 6423.

Swamy, P. A. (1970). Efficient inference in a random coefficient regression model. Econometrica: Journal of the Econometric Society, 38(2), 311–323.

Transparency International (2021). What is Corruption?. Available at: https://www.transpa rency.org/en/what-is-corruption (15.03.2021).

Unver, M. and Koyuncu, J. Y. (2019). Does Tax Burden Foster Shadow Economy? An Empirical Analysis. XII. International Balkan and Near Eastern Congress Series on Economics, Business and Management-Plovdiv/ Bulgaria.

Virta, H. (2010). The linkage between corruption and shadow economy size: does geography matter? International Journal of Development Issues, 9(1), 4–24.

Vo, D. H., Ha, D. T. T., and Ly, T. H. (2015). Shadow Economy and Corruption in the ASEAN: Complement or Substitute? In A New Paradigm for International Business, 151–169. Springer, Singapore.

Westerlund, J. (2008). Panel cointegration tests of the Fisher effect. Journal of Applied Econometrics, 23(2), 193–233.

World Bank (2020). Anticorruption Fact Sheet. Available at: https://www.worldbank.org/en/news/factsheet/2020/02/19/anticorruption-fact-sheet (21.02.2021).

World Bank (2021). Combating Corruption. Available at: https://www.worldbank.org/en/topic/ governance/brief/anti-corruption (15.03.2021).

Esra Balli and Muammer Tekeoglu

Catching Up: Advanced and Falling Behind Countries

1 Introduction

Over the last two centuries the world economy has experienced unprecedented growth. Between 1820 and 1997, the world's Gross Domestic Product (GDP) increased by 2.2% annually, six to seven times more than in the period 1500–1820. However, this growth was not evenly distributed around the world. The GDP of America, Japan and Northwest Europe increased much faster than the rest of the world (Van Ark, Kuipers and Kuper, 2000: 1).

In the second half of the eighteenth century, large-scale technological breakthroughs in textile production in Great Britain and the application of steam power to production had a profound effect on that period and other periods. In the nineteenth century, the term industrial revolution was used to describe these developments. In addition to being the first industrialized country and the technological leader of the world economy, Great Britain has been a model for other countries. The manufacturing industry became the main engine for accelerating economic growth in the nineteenth century. Manufacturing technologies spread to other countries, thus starting a global industrialization race. European countries such as Belgium, Switzerland and France were the first countries to follow the industrialization process. In the nineteenth century, the United States pursued a different path of industrialization based on raw material exports, abundance of land and resources, and labour shortages (Szirmai, 2012: 406).

According to Diamond (1997), fourteen factors played an important role in the development of technology. The first was prolonged life expectancy. Prolonged life expectancy provided the necessary years for technical knowledge. Therefore, greatly increased life expectancy, as a result of modern medicine, may have contributed to the increase in the number of inventions. The five factors that follow include the economy or the organization of society: (1) while the existence of cheap slave labour in the classical period did not encourage innovative activities, technological solutions have come to the fore today because of rising wages and a decrease in labour supply; (2) patents and other property laws; (3) modern industrial societies offer wide opportunities for technical education; (4) modern capitalism, unlike the ancient Roman economy, was organized in a way that rewarded capital investment for technological development; and (5) the strong individualism of US society allows successful inventors to make gains for themselves. The following four explanations have ideological characteristics: (i) the first-taking behaviours required for innovation are more common in some societies; (ii) the modern technological superiority of post-Renaissance European society arises from their scientific perspective; (iii) tolerance to different perspectives promotes innovation, while a traditional perspective suppresses innovation; and (iv) religions' views on technological innovations differ greatly. The remaining four hypotheses consist of war, central rulers, climate and abundance of resources. (1) Throughout history, wars have often been the precursor to technological innovation. (2) Powerful central governments increased technology in Germany and Japan in the late nineteenth century and led to the decline of technology in China in the sixteenth century. (3) Many northern Europeans assume that technology was formed in a dense climate where it was impossible to survive without technology. (4) There is also a debate that technology is the result of an abundance or scarcity of environmental resources. While water mill technology in rainy northern Europe has funded the development of inventions that use these resources, why hasn't watermill innovation been realized in rainy New Guinea more quickly? Why hasn't deforestation had the same effect in China, with deforestation cited as the reason behind the onset of coal technology? (Diamond, 1997, 249–51).

According to Schwab (2016), the world is now entering its fourth industrial revolution. During the third industrial revolution, digital technologies changed computer hardware, software and networks, while transforming society and the global economy. With the fourth industrial revolution, the transition to intelligent and interconnected systems, nanotechnology and quantum computers began. The technologies and innovations created in this revolution are spreading faster than in previous periods. However, the consequences of the second industrial revolution have still not had an impact on 17% of the world's population; 1.3 billion people do not have access to electricity. The same is true of the third industrial revolution. Half the world's population lacks internet access. While it took 120 years for the first industrial revolution to spread out of Europe, the spread of internet technology spanned less than a decade (Schwab, 2016, 8–9).

Rodrik (2014) proposed six stylized facts about economic growth. First, economic growth has occurred over time. According to economic historians, since 1780 the total factor efficiency has been 0.5% annually. This rate is considered good compared to previous periods when technological development was about 0%. The second stylized fact is the fact that convergence is more of an exception than a rule (Rodrik, 2014, 19–22). It constitutes the third stylized fact that economic development will work together with productivity differentiation. Accordingly, as economies get bigger, they become less specialized and more differentiated. The fourth stylized fact is that, historically, the export of industrialization and manufacturing products are the most trusted components for rapid and continuous growth. The fact that the manufacturing industries have a 'special' status in terms of unconditional convergence shows the fifth stylized fact. The last stylized fact constitutes that economies with minimal state intervention are not the most successful economies (Rodrik, 2014: 23–7).

Abramovitz (1986) showed that differences between countries in terms of productivity levels created a strong convergence between these levels in the future, provided that countries had adequate 'social capacity' to absorb more advanced technologies. He defined a country's social capacity, at least for western countries, as a technical competence characterized by its political, commercial, industrial and financial institutions, which it assumes will be a rough proxy variable. The institutional and human capital-related components of social capacity are developing quite slowly as the layers of education and organization respond to the requirements of technological possibilities and the experience of using technology. The degree of their development is seen as a limiting function of technological potential. In addition, the speed at which the capture potential is implemented depends on a number of other conditions that govern the dissemination of information, the fluidity of resources and the rate of investment (Abramovitz,1986: 405–6).

However, despite this long-term deviation in productivity and income, there are a number of examples of countries that have initially lagged behind, closing the productivity and income gap between them and their counterparts; They resist this trend and try to catch it at different times trend (Fagerberg and Godinho, 2005). Therefore, the catching hypothesis suggests that being backward in terms of efficiency level has the potential for rapid progress. (Abramovitz, 1986: 386). According to Fagerberg and Godinho (2005), 'catching' alone is associated with a country's ability to catch the productivity and income gap compared to a leading country, while 'convergence' refers to the tendency to reduce the total difference in productivity and income in the world as a whole.

2 Literature

Several researchers investigated economic convergence and the catching up process from a country level. Gao (2015) reviewed the state's technology and innovation intervention mechanism in the context of China's catching experience, and its findings confirm the argument that there are different innovation points and different challenges in the stages of technology development and the dissemination of technology, which pushes the state to intervene with a mixed policy of legal, financial and administrative tools. The state must take advantage of the corporate environment, R&D and industrialization capacity, and the technological characteristics of innovation when identifying tasks and challenges in the field of innovation and determining the intervention strategy. It should explore the potential for intervention by taking advantage of the national economy and industry under its control and using various legal tools; for example, the leading role of government institutions should be taken into account in the field of innovation. Fagerberg, Srholec and Knell (2007) analysed the key factors behind the growth rate and trade performance differences between countries using the Schumpeterist framework. Four dimensions of competitiveness, namely technology, capacity, demand and price have been determined. As a result of this analysis, for ninety countries based on different levels of development for the period 1980–2002, they found that competitiveness in the fields of technology, capacity and demand was important for growth and development. According to the results, deteriorating competitiveness in the fields of technology and capacity, and an unfavourable export structure, are the main hindrance factors to the potential of many developing countries to capture in terms of technology and revenue. When unfavourable geography, nature and climatic conditions are added to these effects, serious problems with competitiveness may arise.

Castellacci and Archibugi (2008) investigated the distribution of information through a sample of several developed and developing countries for the 1990s. The results reveal that there are three different groups in the field of technology, determined by significantly different levels of development. These include the advanced technology group (advanced infrastructure and skill level, high innovation), the follower group (medium-advanced infrastructure and skills, low innovation) and the marginal group (inadequate infrastructure and skill level, fairly low innovation). The high-tech group consists of a small number of industrialized economies that account for about 40% of the world's GDP (15–21 countries, less than 15% of the sample population). This group includes traditional leaders such as the United States and Japan, as well as the economies of northern Europe, as well as their western extensions (Australia, Canada, Israel, and New Zealand). The membership structure in this cluster has presented a stable picture over time, and the main differentiation has been with the introduction of the newly industrialized Asian economy (Hong Kong, South Korea, Singapore) into this restricted club. This cluster also exhibits a dynamic structure over time, especially during the period 1900–2000, with rapid growth rates in technological competencies, patents (40% growth), internet usage (986% growth), telephone

(104% growth) and higher education enrollment rates in science and engineering (approximately 60% growth).

The following group consisted of approximately seventy countries, which represented about 27% of the sample population in 1990, and held 36% of the world's GDP at the beginning of the period. The membership structure in this group was very stable during the period 1990–2000, and its focus was on countries in the catch dynamics from Southeast Asia and southern Europe, as well as Turkey, former Soviet countries and the Middle East. In the early 1990s, the gap between the high-tech group and the follower group was remarkably high (16:1 in the patent field, 9:1 in the article area and 11:1 in the number of internet users). During a ten-year period, the distance in the field of information was gradually closed in terms of patents and articles, and much faster for internet users. However, when the innovation gap was compared, those countries in the advanced technology group remained significantly ahead at the end of the decade.

In 1990, the marginal group was the largest group of countries, representing 60% of the sample population, but at the beginning of the decade it produced only 23% of the world's GDP. The groups of countries that stand out in this cluster are the major Asian economies as well as all African countries. While the membership structure in this group was relatively stable in the 1990s, it was able to achieve a limited number of dynamic economies and join the more developed follower group in 2000 (e.g. China, Indonesia, Vietnam, Iran, Oman and a small number of countries from Central America and Africa). In terms of its ability to generate advanced information and mimic new technologies, this group is not just a high-tech group, it also a follower group.

Furman and Hayes (2004) conducted research covering twenty-three countries for the period 1978–1999, allowing emerging innovative economies to demonstrate successful catch-up practice, while exploring factors that led some of the more innovative countries to experience relative declines in innovative productivity. The focus of their analysis has been the estimation of a manufacturing function for innovations on the technical edge of the world. According to the results, they divided countries into four categories: leading innovative countries, middle-class innovative countries, third-tier innovative countries and emerging innovative countries in terms of the historical route followed by their innovative capacities. The results suggest that innovation-changing policies and developing infrastructures are essential for leadership in innovation, but they will be inadequate unless they are increasingly combined with financial and human capital investments in innovation.

In their study of the unequal distribution of knowledge, Castellacci and Archibugi (2008) argued that a country in the process of catching should not only follow or imitate the league's leaders, but rather draw their own paths and follow their own, considering the possibility of successfully increasing their existing knowledge competencies and position. Specifically, they have argued that a nation's ability to build its capacity by developing basic levels of education and technological infrastructure is a prerequisite for further innovation competencies and, therefore, a successful and sustainable economic performance.

Fagerberg and Srholec (2005) compared countries' growth rates between 1820 and 2003 and found that Austria, Belgium, Denmark, Finland, France, Germany, Greece, Italy, The Netherlands, Norway, Portugal, Spain, Sweden and the United Kingdom grew by an average of 1% annually between 1820 and 1950, with the lowest average growth rates of these countries in the period from 1950 to 2003 – the lowest rate of 2.2% was in the United Kingdom. Between 1820 and 1950, the average growth rate in Australia, New Zealand, Canada and the United States was 2.1%, 2.4%, 1.6% and 1.6%, respectively. These countries did not lose their growth rate in 1950–2003, they grew at an average annual rate of 2.2%, 1.4%, 2.3 and 2.2%, respectively. Between 1820 and 1950, China, which was in the class of countries coming from behind, grew by -0.2%, India by 0.1%, Indonesia by 0.2% and Japan by 0.8%. It is seen that the growth performance of these countries increased between 1950 and 2003, which averaged 4.6% for China, 2.4% for India, 2.8% for Indonesia and 4.8% for Japan. Between 1950 and 2003, they grew at an average annual rate of 4.5% in Singapore, 6% in South Korea and 5.8% in Taiwan.

Soete and Verspagen (1993) examined the validity of the convergence and capture hypothesis between countries with cluster analysis to include 114 countries, dividing into five clusters between 1960–1973 and 1973–1988. The analysis included the average annual growth rate of countries, population, the average R&D density, the average investment rate in GDP and countries' initial catching potential variables. In the period 1960–1973, the countries were divided into three main groups: those left behind, the catchers and the leading countries. According to the results, they showed that the investment rate is one of the most important factors in the catching hypothesis. R&D density was seen to be high in technologically leading countries. In the period 1960–1973, Turkey was ranked in the class of the left behind countries, between 1973–1988 Turkey was included in the group of newly catching countries.

3 Analysis and Conclusion

Following Fagerberg and Srholec (2005), this paper investigated the convergence status of countries for the period 1980–2015. Data extracted from the World Bank database. Table 1 represents the

Tab. 1: *Four quadrants*

(II) Losing Momentum	(I) Moving Ahead
(III) Falling Further Behind	(IV) Catching Up

Source: Fagerberg and Srholec (2005)

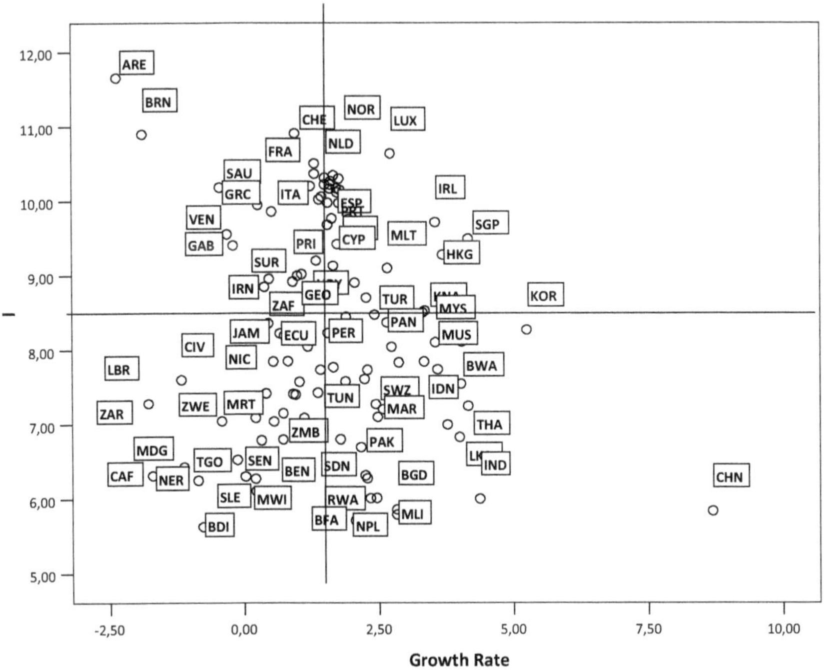

Fig. 1: *Convergence-Divergence In GDP Per Capita Over 1980–2015*

Figure 1 shows annual average growth of GDP per capita over the period 1980–2015 (horizontal axis) against the level of GDP per capita in 1980 (vertical axis). All variables extracted from World Bank, World Development Indicators,

Table 1 also represents the four quadrants that emerged. The findings are in line with the results of Fagerberg and Srholec (2005) which produced four fields Accordingly, although the countries on the left side of the axis (I) had high initial GDP per capita, the average growth rate was relatively low. For this reason, these countries are called 'countries that have lost their momentum' in the terminology of Fagerberg and Srholec (2005). These countries included Gabon and Venezuela. In contrast, the countries in the right corner (II) continued to grow rapidly. These countries constitute the class of 'moving ahead'. Countries in this group include European Union countries, Singapore and Uruguay. The countries in the right corner (IV) below constitute the class of 'catching-up countries'. Although these countries initially had a low GDP, they grew above average. These countries included China, South Korea and Turkey, upper middle income countries. The countries in the left corner (III) below are in the class of countries that were initially poor, as well as slow-growing countries. These countries constitute the 'Falling Further Behind' class. These include under-developed African countries such as Burindi, Central African Republic, Senegal, Cameroon and poor countries under heavy debt burdens.

As a result, it is seen that historically developed countries continue to be in the class of advancing countries. One of the results obtained in the study of Soete and Verspagen (1993) was that Turkey, which was in the 'countries left behind' class in the period 1960–1973 and 'newly captured countries' in 1973–1988, is still in the 'catching-up countries' class.

Acknowledgment

This paper is derived from the author's doctoral dissertation titled 'The Relationship between Technology, Innovation and Economic Growth: An Investigation of High and Upper Middle Income Countries'.

References

Abramovitz, M. (1986). Catching up, forging ahead, and falling behind. The journal of economic history, 46(2), 385-406

Castellacci, F., and Archibugi, D. (2008). The technology clubs: The distribution of knowledge across nations. Research Policy, 37(10), 1659–1673.

Diamond, J. (1997). Guns. Germs and Steel: The Fates of Human Societies, Vintage.

Fagerberg, J., & Godinho, M. M. (2005). Innovation and catching-up. In the Oxford handbook of innovation, Fagerberg, Jan, Mowery, D.C., Nelson, R.(eds) Oxford university press.

Fagerberg, J., & Srholec, M. (2005). Catching up: What are the Critical Factors for success. Vienna, UNIDO, Background paper for the UNIDO Industrial Development Report.

Furman, J. L., and Hayes, R. (2004). Catching up or standing still?: National innovative productivity among 'follower'countries, 1978–1999. Research Policy, 33(9), 1329–1354.

Gao, P. (2015). Government in the catching-up of technology innovation: Case of administrative intervention in China. Technological Forecasting and Social Change, 96, 4–14.

Godinho, M., and Fagerberg, J. (2005). Innovation and catching-up. chap, 19, 514–543.

Rodrik, D. (2014). The past, present, and future of economic growth. Challenge, 57(3), 5–39.

Schwab, K. (2016). The fourth industrial revolution. Geneva: World Economic Forum.

Soete, L., and Verspagen, B. (1993, January). Convergence and divergence in growth and technical change: an empirical investigation. In AEA Annual Meeting in Anaheim, CA.

Szirmai, A. (2012). Industrialisation as an engine of growth in developing countries, 1950–2005. Structural Change and Economic Dynamics, 23(4), 406–420.

Van Ark, B., Kuipers, S. K., and Kuper, G. H. (Eds.). (2000). Productivity, technology and economic growth. Springer Science and Business Media.

World Bank. World Development Indicators.

Hüseyin Çağatay Karabıyık and Mahmut Nevfel Elgün

The Sales Improvement Paradox: Theoretical Foundations of Sales Development and the Theory-Practice Incompatibility in Today's Practice

1 Introduction

One of the most important factors in the transition from the modern science period to the postmodern science period is the theory-practice harmony. Postmodern approaches and their assumptions started with the recognition of a nonlinear and mutually interactive ontology after the Second World War (Bauman, 1988; Hayles, 1991), and criticism of modernist approaches and positivist determinism has gradually increased (Devers et al., 2014). In other words, despite the theoretical internal consistency and strong structure of modern science, what is expected from a theory in the postmodern period is the ability to explain the practice as closely as possible. This change, Kurt Lewin (1952) said, was "A good theory is practice". he expressed it successfully. In other words, if the subject is to produce postmodern science, a theory should explain what is happening in practice and what should be done rather than structural integrity. In fact, the emergence and importance of marketing as a science took place in the period when this postmodern understanding of science was accepted. Adding to this, that marketing is an applied science, marketing has become one of the sciences that have the strongest connections with practice. For this reason, the existence of a marketing theory that conflicts with practice will experience a scientific crisis, as stated in Kuhn's (1977) paradigm, stemming from the theory-practice incompatibility. One of the most important theory-practice incompatibilities in today's marketing practice is seen in the sales development theory, which needs to be revised depending on developments in practice. This paradox, the context of which is the short-term nature of sales development, constitutes the basic problem of this study. In this context, the literature on sales development was first reviewed. Then, the literature on postmodern consumer behaviour was reviewed in order to understand the facts in practice correctly. Finally, the emerging paradox has been identified, defined and proposed solutions within the framework of these two literature.

2 Promotion and Sales Development

2.1 Promotion

Sales development is positioned as a sub-component of promotion, one of the components of the Marketing Mix (4P). For this reason, it is necessary to talk briefly about the promotion. Promotion is defined as the coordination of personal sales, advertising, public relations, sales development, direct and digital marketing tools in the general framework of integrated marketing communication in order to increase sales, support and ensure the permanence of the products in market conditions in a sustainable way with all kinds of abstract and concrete positioning (Karabıyık, 2021). Theories developed on the main dynamics of promotion share a common view, that it is a communication set (Dacko, 2008; Perreault Jr. et al., 2012; Kotler and Armstrong, 2018).In other words, promotion components are essentially seen as tools for developing a sustainable relationship with consumers. In some specific studies it was also stated that promotion should be defined and evaluated through perception as the main purpose rather than communication (Lawrence et al., 2003). However, since such positioning also indicates that promotion is a tool for developing relationships with consumers, it should be accepted that promotion is a relationship development set. In this context, it is possible to say that each of the promotion components is one of the tools for the relation development. Although there is no direct context to this study, the subcomponents of promotion consist of personal selling, advertising, public relations, sales development and direct and digital marketing. In other words, all these subcomponents are essentially tools used to develop relationships with consumers, and sales development is one of these tools. After the theoretical positioning of sales development, the definition of sales development and the systematics of sales development should be specifically examined.

2.2 Sales Development

Sales development methods, which can provide brands with significant competitive advantages in dynamic and competitive market conditions draw attention, especially in terms of being determinant in consumer attitudes (Ogden-Barnes and Minahan, 2015). Sales development, which is important because it shows the aforementioned effects, is defined by the Institute of Sales Promotion as 'broad marketing tactics applied to add value to a product or service within the framework of strategic marketing and to achieve specific sales and marketing goals'. There are also studies in which the definition of sales development is summarized as temporary applications that create added value to the brand in order to achieve specific marketing goals (Horchover, 2002). When the definitions of the concept of sales development are examined, it is seen that sales development theory and practices are formed within the framework of three main features. These features are as follows:

1. Sales development creates added value.
2. Sales development tactics are used to achieve specific marketing goals.
3. According to classical definitions, sales development consists of temporary applications.

The sales development paradox, which is the main argument of this study, stems from the third feature of sales development, which consists of temporary applications – discussions on this have been made in the conclusions section. The aim of this section is to review the classic literature of sales development. While sales development continues its application in the markets within the framework of these three features, it uses three basic tools to achieve these goals. In other words, a sales development communication must contain three basic features. These features are as follows (Brassington and Pettitt, 2007):

1. Communication
2. Incentive
3. Invitation

The theoretical background of promotion and sales development shows that these components include practices focused on developing relationships with consumers. In order to realize these practices, there should be an invitation to establish a relationship with consumers and an incentive element for the invitation to be received by the consumer. However, when it comes to sales development, it is seen that this communication is temporary.

After understanding sales development as a structure and a process, the question of what temporary relationship development tools are arises. The framework of these tools of sales development is drawn with the phrase 'all tools other than the other components of promotion'. For example, practices such as temporary discounts, 'buy one get one free', coupons and sweepstakes are seen as practical equivalents of sales development.However, as can be understood from the definition, it is not possible to draw a limit on sales development practices. Because different sales development practices may arise according to the situational conditions that can be seen in each market. Regardless, these applications are seen as temporary applications.

On the one hand, while theoretical and applied research on sales development continues, on the other hand, sales development continues to gain importance in practice. Because, in the globalized economic world, competition in the markets is increasing rapidly. While the brands that cannot adapt to these competition conditions disappear, the brands that survive also use all marketing tools intensively to ensure sustainability. The economic factors that set the groundwork for sales development to gain importance in this period have been systematized by marketing science as follows (Fahy and Jobber, 2015):

- **Increase in Unplanned Purchases:** One of the most important facts showing the integration of consumption into social life is the emergence of shopping mall lives. Now, consumers are so intertwined with the brand and virtual and physical sales environments that they cannot avoid being exposed to the marketing strategies implemented by the brands. Because marketing has become an ordinary part of the postmodern consumer life, this has enabled a sales development that is effectively implemented at the time of sale and at the sales points to gain importance.
- **Increase in the Cost of Advertising and a Decrease in the Marginal Efficiency of Advertisements:** The prices of advertisements that make it possible to reach the most consumers are increasing. On the other hand, consumers who are exposed to too many advertisements are less likely to remember them. However, considering that a consumer who is close enough to the store is closer to the purchasing action, it becomes inevitable for brands to give importance to sales development activities.
- **Shortening the Time Horizons of Products:** The shortening of the total product life cycle of the products necessitates a rapid sales increase graphic in marketing planning. In this context, sales development programs should also be considered in order to achieve the necessary increases in sales.
- **Activities of Competitors:** Due to the competitive market conditions mentioned above, in a market where there are competitors performing sales development activities other brands are also obliged to implement sales development activities.
- **Measurability:** Since sales development activities are expected to reflect directly on sales, a measurement indexed to sales is possible. This measurable nature is one of the factors that leads to more implementation of sales development.

Some studies have examined the following factors as a cause in addition to the factors mentioned above (Peattie and Peattie, 1993):

- **Micro-marketing Approach: A** sales development which focuses on micro-targets as part of its marketing strategy is more suitable to adapt to targets than promotion tools based on mass communication.
- **The 'Snowball' Effect:** Some studies have reached findings and comments that sales enhancement can have a multiplier effect (Lattin and Bucklin, 1989). In the literature, it is stated that this situation occurs as a result of the effect of sales development on consumer attitudes (Ortmeyer et al., 1991) and a sales development application that includes at least two tools is proposed to create this effect (Blythe, 2006).
- **Manageability:** Sales development has a less risky structure in terms of manageability due to both cost and time flexibility (Pauwels et al., 2004). Manageability plays an important role in the efficient use of sales development due to the flexibility factor in today's markets, which are in a rapid change where businesses with flexible organizational structures gain importance.

All these developments show that sales improvement penetrate to marketing and adds great importance in practice. However, in order for marketing strategies to find a response in the markets, consumer behaviour must also be compatible with the theory. Consumer behaviours that respond to changes in sales development are examined within the framework of postmodern consumer behaviours in marketing literature. For this reason, in order to understand the paradox in sales development correctly, it is necessary to understand postmodern consumer behaviours.

3 Postmodern Consumer Behaviours

Especially since the 1980s, there has been a marked transformation in consumer behaviour. While this transformation created a consumption-oriented society, it also caused products to be socialized. These changes, seen in practice, were analysed within the framework of consumer behaviour. This contradiction makes it difficult for consumers who try to develop relationships with brands and see brands as individuals.The characteristics of postmodern consumers are examined in the consumer behaviour literature as follows (Ackerman, 1997; Gabbott, 2008; Featherstone, 2007):

- **Asocial Individualism:** Although socialization and social integration process has accelerated, postmodern consumers do not like to be affected by social or economic structures. This feature does not express the indirect effect of social culture, but that consumption behaviour is not changed upon a direct suggestion. Although this situation of individualism coincides with the concept of

'Generation Me' (Twenge, 2006) in psychology, it is a phenomenon observed not just in consumption, but also in many human behaviours.
- **Greed:** The postmodern consumer has made consumption a part of his/her life and is constantly seeking to consume more and better. Some studies based on these behaviours of consumers call this period the 'mass consumption age' (Glickman, 2012).
- **Meta Compliance:** Postmodern consumers want to have more information about the products they want to have. In this context, the widespread use of approaches and practices, such as experiential marketing that ensure commodity harmony, has occurred as a result of the need to ensure commodity harmony in postmodern consumers (Skandalis et al., 2019). This situation can be seen as one of the consumer characteristics that laid the groundwork for the emergence of the concept of 'customer focus', with the effect of advancing marketing competition, as well as the positioning of products in consumers' lives.

These features of the postmodern consumer show that today consumption plays a determining role in social structures. As a result of this situation, consumption is included in models as a central structure in sociological and anthropological studies that examine the postmodern period (Elliot, 1999).

In the era of postmodern consumer behaviour, products and brands are no longer seen only as a means of meeting the wants and needs. In addition, products and brands are used as a tool in the formation of individuals' social identities and in showing this identity socially. This also shows that brands have become individuals in society. Undoubtedly, the relationships individuals develop with brands they see as individuals will have a much more complex structure. For example, the same products and brands begin to gain symbolic values in a structure where products and brands are seen as individuals, while symbolic values are not attributed to the product, which is seen as an object of need. As a matter of fact, the fact that phenomena such as symbolic consumption are included in the marketing literature parallels these developments.

The emergence of the sales development paradox is also seen at the intersection of the characteristics of postmodern consumer behaviour and the short-term viability of sales development in classical approach.

4 Conclusion

Postmodern consumer literature shows that consumers are now adapting products and brands to their lives and essentially making consumption social. This means that not only brands, but also consumers, are in the process of developing a relationship. In other words, the consumer who chooses a brand does not only meet his needs but creates his own identity using that brand. At this point, the behaviours of consumers also constitute the structure of the brand-consumer relationship. In other words, brands tend towards a long-term relationship development process. At the same time, sales development practices continue to be accepted as short-term in the literature due to market competition. This contradiction makes it difficult for consumers who try to develop relationships with brands, and see brands as individuals, to position them. Especially in the sales development practices of brands in the luxury segment, which damages brand values and may even cause some brands to go bankrupt.

Although it seems that sales development is experiencing a crisis in practice, there are also studies in marketing science which state that sales development is a short-term program. However, whether they are aware of it or not, studies of this approach in marketing cause this paradox to deepen and begin a scientific crisis. On the other hand, marketing experts who have close relations with practice point out the devastating effects this paradox causes. For example, Trout and Ries (2020) state that the same mistake that occurs in practice is due to short-term financial reservations of businesses although, in theory, sales development focuses on the short-term with a theoretical myopia.

Some studies that are aware of this scientific crisis in theoretical studies divide sales development into 'temporary purchaser programs' and 'loyalty marketing programs' (Kaser, 2013). While temporary purchaser programs focus on short-term solutions of sales development in the classical sense, loyalty marketing programs focus on the long-term effects of sales development programs (Karabıyık, 2020). However, brands that cannot avoid sales development practices due to intense competition in the market should focus their sales development practices on loyalty marketing programs in order not to be exposed to the sales development paradox. Similarly, marketing theory should be in this orientation. In today's world where target markets are becoming more specific, the number of businesses that maintain their market share, especially with discounts, is increasing, and these practices lead to a sales development paradox. Because in today's markets, there are brands such as WalMart that make low prices a brand image and design the entire organizational structure accordingly. In fact, these brands create a brand image by turning price discounts, one of the most frequently used tools of sales development, into a loyalty marketing program. This enables a stable low-price application. This approach reveals a differentiation that is difficult to imitate. However, brands trying to implement the same low prices within the framework of temporary purchaser programs lose their sustainability against others while, at the same time, damaging their brand position in the consumers' mind. This example is one of the most typical examples of the practical response of the sales development paradox.

As a result, the sales development paradox is defined as the use of purchaser programs developed with the view that sales development is short-term; even though sales increase in the short term, it harms the image, positioning and sustainability of the brand in the long term. In order to prevent this, brands should pay attention to the fact that the sales development applications they plan in practice have the characteristics of differentiation and compatibility with the brand image. In theory, the distinction between buyer programs and loyalty marketing programs should be taken into account in sales development studies. In addition to this, more studies should be done on loyalty marketing programs, which have not yet gained scientific depth, and thus scientific depth in this field should be provided.

References

Ackerman, F. (1997). Consumed in Theory: Alternative Perspectives on the Economics of Consumption. Journal of Economic Issues, 31(3): 651–664.

Brassington, F. and Pettitt, S. (2007). Essentials of Marketing. Harlow: Prentice Hall.

Bauman, Z. (1988). Sociology and Postmodernity. The Sociological Review, 36(4), 790–813.

Blythe, J. (2006). Essentials of Marketing Communications. Harlow: Prentice Hall.

Dacko, S.G. (2008). The Advanced Dictionary of Marketing: Putting Theory to Use. New York: Oxford University Press.

Devers, C.E., Misangyi, V.F. and Gamache, D.L. (2014). Editors' Comments: On the Future of Publishing Management Theory. Academy of Management Review, 39(3), 245–249.

Elliot, R. (1999). Symbolic Meaning and Postmodern Consumer Culture. In the Rethinking Marketing Towards Critical Marketing Accountings, Brownlie, D., Saren, M., Wensley, R., Whittington, R. (eds.), London: Sage Publications.

Fahy, J. and Jobber, D. (2015). Foundations of Marketing. London: McGraw-Hill Education.

Featherstone, M. (2007). Consumer Culture and Postmodernism. London: Sage Publications.

Gabbott, M. (2008). Consumer Behaviour. In the The Marketing Book, Baker M.J., Hart, S.J. (eds.), Oxford: Butterworth-Heinemann.

Glickman, L.B. (2012). Consumer Activism, Consumer Regimes, and the Consumer Movement: Rethinking the history of Consumer Politics in The United States. In the The Oxford Handbook of the History of Consumption, New York: Oxford University Press.

Hayles, N.K. (1991). Chaos and Order: Complex Dynamics in Literature and Science. Chicago: University of Chicago Press.

Horchover, D. (2002). Sales Promotion. Oxford: Capstone Publishing.

Karabıyık, H.Ç. (2020). Pazarlamaya Psikolojik Bir Yaklaşım: Merchandising Uygulamalarını Çıpalama Teorisi Bağlamında İnceleyen Deneysel Bir Araştırma. Doctoral Thesis, Konya: Necmettin Erbakan University Institute of Social Sciences.

Karabıyık, H.Ç. (2021). Pazarlama İlkeleri and Bir Meta-Pazarlama Tartışması: Tüketici Perspektifli Karşı Pazarlama Modeli. Konya: NEÜ Yayınları.

Kaser, K. (2013). Advertising and Sales Promotion. Mason: South-Western Cengage Learning.

Kotler, P. and Armstrong, G. (2018). Pazarlama İlkeleri. İstanbul: Beta.

Kuhn, T. (1977). The Essential Tension. Chicago: The University of Chicago Press.

Lattin, J.M. and Bucklin, R.E. (1989). Reference Effects of Price and Promotion on Brand Choice Behaviour. Journal of Marketing Research, 26(3), 299–310.

Lawrence, E., Newton, S., Corbitt, B. and Lawrence, J. (2003). Internet Commerce: Digital Models for Business. Australia: John Wiley and Sons.

Lewin, K. (1952). Field Theory in Social Science: Selected Theoretical Papers by Kurt Lewin. London: Tavistock.

Ogden-Barnes, S. and Minahan, S. (2015). Sales Promotion Decision Making: Concepts, Principles, and Practice. New York: Business Expert Press.

Ortmeyer, G., Lattin, J.M. and Montgomery, D.B. (1991). Individual Differences in Response to Consumer Promotions. International Journal of Research in Marketing, 8(3), 169–186.

Pauwels, K., Silva-Rosso, J., Srinivasan, S. and Hanssens, D.M. (2004). New Products, Sales Promotions, and Firm Value: The Case of the Authomobile Industry. Journal of Marketing, 68(4), 142–156.

Peattie, K. and Peattie, S. (1993). Sales Promotion – Playing to Win?. Journal of Marketing Management, 9(3), 255–269.

Perreault Jr., W.D. Cannon, J.P. and McCarthy, E.J. (2012). Essentials of Marketing. New York: McGraw Hill-Irwin.

Skandalis, A., Byrom, J. and Banister, E.(2019). Experiential Marketing and the Changing Nature of Extraordinary Experiences in Post-Modern Consumer Culture. Journal of Business Research, 97: 43–50.

Trout, J. and Ries, A. (2020). Pazarlamanın 22 Kuralı, İstanbul: MediaCat.

Twenge, J.M. (2006). Generation Me. New York: Free Press.

Ceren Ece Göcen and Meral Balcı

Populism: An Evaluation by the Cultural Political Economy Approach

1 Introduction

'Populism' was chosen as the word of the year by the Cambridge Dictionary in 2017 (University of Cambridge, 2017) and is one of the most important phenomena shaping the international order of the twenty-first century. This rise of populism affects social relations and the political economy, as well as the process of cultural transformation. In this context, the relationship between the concept of Cultural Political Economy (CPE) and populism becomes important.

CPE examines the relationship between meaning and practices, including approaches such as cultural transformation, discourse, rhetoric, interpretation and identity. It allows identifying how politics is determined in a dialectical interaction between discourse and material selectivity (Jessop, 2010: 337–41). Choosing the CPE approach constitutes an important and different perspective to understand how and why a policy trend like populism is legitimized with discourses. It has a close relationship with populism in the context of its features, such as handling cultural transformation in the political economy, examining the elements that shape the social structure, benefiting from semiotics and linguistics, and technology consolidating hegemony (Jessop, 2010; Jessop and Sum, 2010).

It is an important lack that the relationship between CPE and populism has not been examined in the international relations literature. We recognize that the concept of CPE is closely related to semiotics and linguistics; it is an appropriate approach to explain the reflection of the discourses affected by the cultural transformation on the political economy through populist discourses. Accordingly, this study will provide an original perspective by evaluating the causes and consequences of success in the rise of populism via the CPE approach, which had not been previously covered in the literature. In addition, the study aims to identify the impact of cultural transformation on populism in countries, and the determinants of the relationship between CPE and populism.

2 A Literature Review on CPE and Populism

The rise of populism and populist tendencies makes populism concept more important today than in the past. The features of populism and populist tendencies differ according to the political, economic, social and cultural structures of the countries. In this direction, firstly, it is very important to understand these two concepts to discuss populism in terms of CPE and to compare the results.

The concept of CPE entered the international relations literature in the 1990s, and has been introduced to understand the interaction of economic and cultural dynamics in social development. Some of the academics from Lancaster University contributed to the development of the concept of CPE. Jessop (2004) defines CPE as an approach that aims to draw a path between 'soft cultural economy' and the 'hard orthodox economy'. According to him, CPE explores the role of the process of showing signs for the exploration of political and economic activities, institutions and social order. This is a post-disciplinary approach that embraces cultural transformation without neglecting the interconnectedness of politics and economics with wider social formations. According to Dannestam (2008), Sum (2013), Hauf (2015) and Sum and Jessop (2017), CPE separates the semiotics, linguistics and structural (material) dimensions of social relations, and aims to make a cultural turn within the political economy. Sum (2015) defines CPE as a broad theoretical trend that combines cultural transformation with critical political economy. Ayhan (2017) draws attention to the impact of the mentioned cultural transformation on the economy and social structure, and states that this transformation affects the political economy in line with the rationality of neoliberal dominant governments.

Jessop (2010) and Sum (2013) see CPE as a tool that points to the discursive role of individual and institutional actors in reconstructing social relations. On the other hand, Jessop (2004, 2010), Jessop and Oosterlynck (2008), Makarovič et al. (2014), Hauf (2015) and Staricco (2016) see it as a tool that generates analytical and practical solutions for the change, selection and storage of strategic discourses. Jessop and Oosterlynck (2008) state that the CPE sees the political society and social society as a whole and examines the state within a social network of relations. Jessop (2010), Sum (2015), Staricco (2016) and Sum and Jessop (2017) state that these relationships can be investigated with some selectivity methods and explain them by listing them structurally, discursively, technologically, and agenda. According to Jessop and Oosterlynck (2008), this approach offers a macro-theoretical framework based on Foucault, Marks, Gramsci and Poulantzas. According to Belfrage and Hauf (2015), it adopts the studies of Gramsci and post-structuralist theories to explain the importance of discursive orders.

Jessop (2004), Dannestam (2008), Jessop and Oosterlynck (2008), Makarovič et al. (2014) and Staricco (2016) explain the three characteristics of CPE: Firstly, it emphasizes the importance of both history and institutions in political and economic dynamics, and is against transhistorical analysis. Secondly, unlike many trends in evolutionary and institutional political economy, it takes cultural transformation seriously by emphasizing the complex relationships between meanings and practices. Finally, it focuses on the evolution of semiotics and their impact on the structure and dynamics of capitalist formations.

In summary, CPE is in a very close relationship with semiotics and linguistics within the framework of these explanations in the literature. Therefore, it is a suitable approach to explain the reflection of the discourses affected by the cultural transformation on the political economy through populist discourses.

Populism is explained by four approaches in the literature. The first is 'populism as ideology'. This approach is based on the division of society into two homogeneous and opposing groups, 'the pure people' and 'the corrupt elites'. The moral dimension of the populist discourse that makes this distinction reflects the tendency to define the will of the people as good and the elite as bad (Mudde, 2004: 543; 2016: 26). The second is 'populism as discourse'. It focuses on how the distinction between 'the people' and 'the elites' is constructed by political actors within populism. In this context, populism is a phenomenon that structures politics as a moral and ethical struggle between the people and the oligarchy. The third is 'populism as a strategy'. According to this approach, populism refers to a strategy in which personal and charismatic leaders seek or implement government power through the people-elite opposition, using a direct salutation and developing customer relationships (Gidron and Bonikowski, 2013: 5–11). It is defined by Weyland (2001) and Mudde and Kaltwasser (2017) as a political strategy in which a leader, and a large number of unorganized followers, seeks or implements state power directly, without intermediaries and without institutions. Finally, the 'populism as performance' approach focuses on the interaction of personal and charismatic leaders and the established political communication processes while examining populism. Leaders' emotions, the way they speak, dress, behave and their tastes gain importance in this respect (Moffitt and Tormey, 2013).

According to Kenny (2017), the boundaries and definitions of the concept of populism are not clear, and it creates a need for classification to be analysed according to the system where it emerged: inclusive populists and exclusive populists. Inclusive populism describes a form of economic populism that tries to unite ordinary people against a wealthy ruling class. Exclusive populism refers to an international populism that protects the rights and interests of the indigenous, where 'pure people' oppose cultural elites defined by ethnic pluralism. According to Stanley (2008), populism is not an inevitable product of abstract formal logic, but emerges empirically and conditionally through the explanation and articulation of concepts. It is an ideology aimed at defining people as a privileged subject of politics. It is based on the adoption of the people and the denial of the elite. It has become more 'mainstream' in recent years as a result of the increasing independence and commercialization of popular media and the increased cognitive mobilization of a better-educated public.

Populist discourses developed based on 'people' and 'elites' have three common characteristics. Mudde (2004: 543) listed these as follows: (1) the essence of the definition of populism is that the society consists of two homogeneous and opposing groups as 'the pure people' and 'the corrupt elites'; (2) populist leaders are representatives of the general or national will of the people; and (3) since populism is a weak-centred ideology, it necessarily needs a stronger host ideology to become operational. According to Jagers and Walgrave (2007: 322), these characteristics are listed as follows: (1) populists always appeal to the public and legitimize their actions and policies through this discourse; (2) populism is fueled by anti-elite sentiments; and (3) populism regards the people as a single, homogeneous piece without differences, except a certain excluded group. Ertan (2019) states that this homogeneity and unity creates a will for populists and gives them representation power. Bulut and Hacıoğlu (2018: 190) state that within the framework of these features, populism is a political organization style, a political communication style, or a 'weak-centred' ideology. The fact that populism is a political communication style makes the language and discourses used by political actors and leaders important. In this context, populist political actors place the established institutions and current elites in the other part of their populist discourse, arguing that the public interests are ignored by the corrupt elite and this disrupts the welfare order of the society.

3 Populism Evaluation by the CPE Approach

CPE examines the relationship between meaning and practices, including approaches such as cultural transformation, discourse, rhetoric, interpretation and identity. It allows identifying how politics is determined in a dialectical interaction between discourse and material selectivity (Jessop, 2010: 337–41). Choosing a cultural political economy approach constitutes an important and different perspective to understand how and why a policy trend like populism is legitimized with discourses. It has a close relationship with populism in the context of its features, such as handling cultural transformation in the political economy, examining the elements that shape the social structure, benefiting from semiotics and linguistics, and technology consolidating hegemony (Jessop, 2010; Jessop and Sum, 2010, 2017).

Today, populist leaders attach importance to technological elements such as social media, and being in direct contact with the public in their election processes is an indicator of cultural transformation. The cultural transformation that takes place in the form of populist leaders seeking state power directly, without intermediaries and institutions, affects the economy and social structure. This affect's evaluation in the field of the CPE. In addition, the discourse of these populist leaders is a huge factor in their preference in election processes. Again, an approach that can be used in this regard, CPE draws attention to the discursive role of individual actors. Therefore, 'populism as discourse' and 'populism as performance' approaches can be explained with CPE.

In this study – by preventing to ignoring non- western countries – the populist prime minister of India, Narendra Modi's political attitude is chosen as a case study. Because the case study of India and Modi give us clues about how populist approaches trigger cultural transformation and how this in turn affects the political economy. Modi's populist approaches, namely discourse and performance, will be examined by using the CPE approach.

3.1 A Case Study: Narendra Modi in Context of India

Populist trends in mainstream politics started with Indira Gandhi in India in the 1960s. Today, it has been on the rise with the discourses of Narendra Modi, who was elected as prime minister from the Bharatiya Janata Party (Indian People's Party) as a result of the 2014 elections (Jaffrelot and Tillin, 2017: 112). During the election campaign, Hindu nationalist Modi pledged to rid India of the corrupt elite and to follow the policy of 'India first'. He shaped his discourses with populist and nationalist logic. In addition, he declared that foreign policy should be decided not by the 'elite' politicians, but by the people in Delhi during this process (Wojczewski, 2019). This shows that Modi preferred an 'as discourse' populist approach.

The rise of populism with Modi occurred through a process of cultural transformation. Modi has used different social media platforms to reach different social groups to run his campaign. This situation personalized his campaign and enabled him to rise from a local leader to the prime minister in 2014 (Chakravartty and Roy, 2015; Sinha, 2017). In this direction, Plagemann and Destradi (2009) also state that Modi's leadership is highly centralized and personalized. Therefore, Modi has established a hegemony by integrating his populist approach with cultural transformation. He has created a personal, centralized, technocratic leadership that bypasses representative institutions and uses the media and symbolism in populist ways (Chacko, 2018) which shows his populism 'as performance'.

The political attitude of Modi, who embraces populism as a discourse and as a performance, is highly related to cultural transformation. With CPE, which examines the relationship between meaning and practices through concepts such as cultural transformation, discourse, rhetoric and interpretation, it is correct to explain that this situation affects both social relations and political economy as a whole. In terms of political economy, Modi's populist rhetoric and charismatic leadership came to the fore, especially during the election process. The economic reforms carried out in India, which was struggling with an economic crisis, did not produce the desired result and the country remained in trouble economically. However, because of the Kashmir Crisis with Pakistan in February 2019, which brought the two countries to the brink of war, Modi increase his vote (Bag, 2019). As a matter of fact, despite the deteriorating economic situation in the country, Modi prioritized national security in all of his actions and discourses, and increased his votes even in rural areas where economic problems such as unemployment and poverty existed. Thus, he was elected prime minister again in 2019 (Bayram, 2019). In summary, Modi adopted populism as a discourse and as a performance and, in this context, despite the problems in India's political economy, he was able to win the election.

One of the problems in the political economy of India is related to the agricultural sector, which is very important for the country's economy and is a part of the culture. The Modi government's reform of the agricultural sector at the end of 2020 has not been supported by farmers. The laws were protested by one of the world's most massive strikes, with the participation of 250 million people. The government tried to suppress these protests using the security forces. Also, as a result of the cultural transformation, the government has applied technological pressure and threatened social media platforms for the removal of anti-government social media posts supporting the protests (Sofuoğlu, 2021). Therefore, Modi's adoption of a populist political behaviour with both his rhetoric and performance brings along an autocratic transformation along with the cultural transformation.

4 Conclusion

CPE has a close relationship with populism in the context of its features, such as handling cultural transformation in the political economy, examining the elements that shape the social structure, benefiting from semiotics and linguistics and technology consolidating hegemony. This study, as a pioneer in literature, focused on the relationship between CPE and 'populism as discourse' and 'populism as performance'. Thus, it aimed to create a new perspective by bringing the relationship between populism and CPE in the international relations discipline. The case study of India and Modi has given us clues about how populist approaches trigger cultural transformation and how this in turn affects the political economy. As a matter of fact, Modi's populist rhetoric and charismatic leadership enabled him to win the elections despite all the difficulties in India's political economy. In addition to winning the elections, Modi, who adopted populist policy behaviour during his tenure, strengthened his hegemony by combining this populism and autocracy with cultural and technological transformation. In this direction, it is correct to say that populism, which enables leaders – like Modi – to strengthen their hegemony and autocratic power, gains support with CPE, which prioritizes cultural transformation. Although it is not known what Modi's populism will lead to in the future, it is clear that the link between cultural transformation and political economy will have important implications for the future of populism.

Acknowledgement

This chapter is derived from Ceren Ece Göcen's doctoral dissertation titled 'Kültürel Politik Ekonomi Perspektifinden (Neo)Popülizm: Hindistan ve Türkiye'.

References

Ayhan, B. (2017). Cultural Political Economy of Financial Literacy in Turkey (PhD Thesis). Onraio: McMaster University.

Bag, M. (2019). "Hindistan'da aşırı sağcı, Hindu milliyetçisi Narendra Modi yeniden başbakan seçildi". Euronews, 23.05.2019. https://tr.euronews.com/2019/05/23/hindistan-da-asiri-sagci-hindu-milliyetcisi-narendra-modi-yeniden-basbakan-secildi (06.04.2021).

Bayram, D. (2019). "Hindistan'da ikinci Modi dönemi". Anadolu Ajansı, 11.06.2019. https://www.aa.com.tr/tr/analiz/hindistanda-ikinci-modi-donemi/1501128 (06.04.2021).

Belfrage, C. and Hauf, F. (2015). Operationalizing cultural political economy: towards critical grounded theory. Journal of Organizational Ethnography, 4(3), 324–340.

Bulut, A. and Hacıoğlu, N. (2018). Bir Siyasi İletişim Stili Olarak Popülizm: Akp'nin Popülist Siyasal Söyleminin Karşılaştırmalı Analizi. Siyasal: Journal of Political Sciences, 27(2), 187–219.

Chacko, P. (2018). The Right Turn in India: Authoritarianism, Populism and Neoliberalisation. Journal of Contemporary Asia, 48(4), 541–565.

Chakravartty, P. and Roy, A. (2015). Mr. Modi Goes to Delhi: Mediated Populism and the 2014 Indian Elections. Television and New Media, 16(4), 311–322.

Dannestam, T. (2008). Rethinking Local Politics: Towards a Cultural Political Economy of Entrepreneurial Cities. Space and Polity, 12(3), 353–372.

Ertan, M. (2019). Bir Kavramın İzini Sürme Çabası: "Popülizm Nedir?". Hacettepe Üniversitesi İletişim Fakültesi Kültürel Çalışmalar Dergisi, 6(1), 255–259.

Gidron, N. and Bonikowski, B. (2013). Varieties of Populism: Literature Review and Research Agenda. Weatherhead Working Paper Series, No. 13-0004.

Hauf, F. (2015). The Paradoxes of Decent Work in Context: A Cultural Political Economy Perspective. Global Labour Journal, 6(2), 138–155.

Jaffrelot, C. and Tillin, L. (2017). Populism in India. Kaltwasser, C., Taggart, P, Espejo, P and Ostiguy, P. (Eds.). In The Oxford Handbook of Populism (pp. 231–250). New York: Oxford University Press.

Jagers, J. and Walgrave, S. (2007). Populism as political communication style An empirical study of political parties' discourse in Belgium. European Journal of Political Research, 46(3), 319–345.

Jessop, B. (2004). Critical Semiotic Analysis and Cultural Political Economy. Critical Discourse Studies, 1(2), 159–174.

Jessop, B. and Oosterlynck, S. (2008). Cultural Political Economy: On Making the Cultural Turn without Falling into Soft Economic Sociology. Geoforum, 39, 1155–1169.

Jessop, B. (2010). Cultural Political Economy and Critical Policy Studies. Critical Policy Studies, 3(3–4), 336–356.

Jessop, B. and Sum, N. (2010). Cultural Political Economy: Logics of Discovery, Epistemic Fallacies, the Complexity of Emergence, and the Potential of the Cultural Turn. New Political Economy, 15(3), 445–451.

Kenny, P. (2017). Populism and Patronage: Why Populists Win Elections in India, Asia, and Beyond. New York: Oxford University Press.

Makarovič, M., Šušteršič, J. and Rončević, B. (2014). Is Europe 2020 Set to Fail? The Cultural Political Economy of the EU Grand Strategies. European Planning Studies, 22(3), 610–626.

Moffitt, B. ve Tormey, S. (2013). Rethinking Populism: Politics, Mediatisation and Political Style. Political Studies, 62(2), 381–397.

Mudde, C. (2004). The Populist Zeitgeist. Government and Oppositio, 39(4), 541–563.

Mudde, C. (2016). Europe's Populist Surge: A Long Time in the Making. Foreign Affairs, 95(6), 25–30.

Mudde, C. ve Kaltwasser, C. (2017). Populism: A Very Short Introduction. Oxford: Oxford University Press.

Plagemann, J. and Destradi, S. (2019). Populism and Foreign Policy: The Case of India. Foreign Policy Analysis, 15, 283–301.

Sinha, S. (2017). Fragile Hegemony: Modi, Social Media, and Competitive Electoral Populism in India. International Journal of Communication, 11, 4158–4180.

Sofuoğlu, Y. (2021). "Tüm yönleriyle Hindistan'ı ayağa kaldıran çiftçi eylemleri: Milyonlarca kişiyi sokağa döken protestolarda neler oluyor?". Independent Türkçe, 27.02.2021. https://www.indyturk.com/node/321341/d%C3%BCnya/t%C3%BCm-y%C3%B6nleriyle-hindistan%C4%B1-aya%C4%9Fa-kald%C4%B1ran-%C3%A7ift%C3%A7i-eylemleri-milyonlarca-ki%C5%9Fiyi (07.04.2021).

Stanley, B. (2008). The Thin Ideology of Populism. Journal of Political Ideologies, 13(1), 95–110.

Staricco, J. (2016). Putting Culture in its Place? A Critical Engagement with Cultural Political Economy. New Political Economy, 22(3), 1–14.

Sum, N. (2013). A Cultural Political Economy of Crisis Recovery: (Trans-) national Imaginaries of 'BRIC' and Subaltern Groups in China. Economy and Society, 42(4), 543–570.

Sum, N. (2015) Cultural Political Economy of Competitiveness, Competition, and Competition Policy in Asia. Distinktion: Scandinavian Journal of Social Theory, 16(2), 211–228.

Sum, N. and Jessop, B. (2017). Cultural Political Economy and Critical Policy Studies: Developing a Critique of Domination. F. Fischer, D. Torgerson, A. Durnová ve M. Orsini (Ed.). Handbook of Critical Policy Studies (ss. 128–150) içinde. UK: Edward Elgar Publishing.

University of Cambridge (2017). " 'Populism' revealed as 2017 Word of the Year by Cambridge University Press", 30.11.2017. https://www.cam.ac.uk/news/populism-revealed-as-2017-word-of-the-year-by-cambridge-university-press#:~:text=The%20word%20'populism'%20has%20been,2017%20Word%20of%20the%20Year (07.12.2020).

Weyland, K. (2001). Clarifying a Contested Concept: Populism in the Study of Latin American Politics. Comparative Politics, 34(1), 1–22.

Wojczewski, T. (2019). Populism, Hindu Nationalism, and Foreign Policy in India: The Politics of Representing "the People". International Studies Review, 0, 1–27.

Selami Erdoğan

Historical Development of Turkish Democracy in the Ottoman Period (1876–1923)

1 Introduction

The phenomenon of democratization in Turkish political history has emerged as a result of modernization efforts starting from the nineteenth century. At that time, the Ottoman Empire was an underdeveloped state compared to European states in many respects. Especially, the defeats in the military field led the leading administrators of the state to seek new solutions. Reforms have been continuously made since the early 1800s to reduce the growing development gap with Europe. In this context, important documents such as Sened-i İttifak, Tanzimat Edict, Islahat Edict and Kanun-i Esasi (First Constitutional Era) were created. With these reforms, the Ottoman State struggled to adapt its political, military, administrative and legal system to Europe.

As a result of the Enlightenment age in Europe, the Industrial Revolution and the French revolutions, the countries in this region have made significant progress in terms of both economic and liberal freedoms. Again, in this context, it is seen that national democratic institutions actually emerged with the American and French revolutions (Huntington, 2011: 28). A period in which parliaments became more functional, written constitutions were made and political parties started to be established. Western states, which have built successful institutions in the political sense, entered a rapid development process with the help of the rational policies they implement.

Reformist Ottoman Sultans and statesmen tried to understand the developments in Europe. Therefore, Sultan III. Selim and Sultan II.Mahmud made reforms in the military and administrative fields. In addition, they opened modern schools and brought consultants from countries such as France. In 1839, with the initiatives of Mustafa Reşit Pasha, a reformer statesman, the Tanzimat Edict was declared. This edict is accepted as one of the important steps inTurkish modernization. Thanks to these reforms, relations between the Ottoman and European states developed. Intellectual movements in Europe influenced Turkish intellectuals and students. At this point, liberal ideas came to the fore. Turkish intellectuals admired the political institutions and systems of Europe. They thought that if we adopted western institutions, we will get rid of the plight we are in. In this context, it is seen that opposition movements demanding the restructuring of the state administration emerged. The first of these movements was the intellectual movement known as the New Ottomans (Yeni Osmanlılar), of which Namık Kemal was the leader. It became widespread among the elite strata over time. This formation brought the declaration of the First Constitutional Era and the first Constitution in 1876. Another opposing movement, İttihad Terakki (The Committee of Union and Progress), which is a continuation of them, was founded in 1889. This movement was the most influential factor in the declaration of the II. Constitutional Monarchy.

The Unionists (The Committee of Union and Progress) had a long struggle against the Sultan Abdulhamid regime. At the end of this struggle, they achieved the democratic and libertarian regime they aimed for. The II. Constitutional Monarchy period is described as a democratization movement in the real sense. In fact, according to the Tarık Zafer Tunaya, an accepted and respected historian, this period was like a laboratory of the Republic of Turkey (Tunaya, 2009: 18). On the other hand, a single-party regime was established in 1923, and attempts were made to transition to multi-party life twice – in 1924 and 1930. The scope of this study was limited by the democratization studies carried out between 1876–1923. In other words, political developments and intellectual movements in the period between the First Constitutional Monarchy and the proclamation of the Republic will be analysed.

2 New Ottomans (Yeni Osmanlılar) and I. Constitutional Era

Reforms such as the Tanzimat and Islahat Edict made by the Ottoman state caused social dissatisfaction. The so-called New Ottomans was born and developed in such an atmosphere (Ahmad, 2007: 45). In 1865, Namık Kemal and his friends established a secret movement called İttifak-ı-Hamiyet. This movement took the Carbonari community in Italy as an example (Zürcher, 2011: 109). Namık Kemal and his friends accused the Tanzimat bureaucrats for giving too many privileges to the Europeans. They claimed that the Reform Edict was a document that reinforced economic imperialism. At the same time, for them the Tanzimat reforms brought cultural imitation. In addition, they claimed that the Muslim population was reduced to second class during this period (Mardin, 2012a: 87).

A large majority of opposition movement members were journalists. People like Agah Efendi, Şinasi and Namık Kemal were journalists (Akşin, 2007: 34). Namık Kemal, who was the leader of this movement, opposed the imitation of Europe. He wanted the state to be transformed into a legitimate administration.

Ottoman reformers were educated in the western style and spoke French. Namık Kemal was brought up in the Translation Room where foreign languages were taught very well. Therefore, they were well aware of the currents of liberalism and nationalism within European thought (Zürcher, 2011: 107). The Ottoman Empire, which was disturbed by their activities, made regulations prohibiting freedom of thought. At this point, the leaders of this movement had to flee abroad for a certain period of time because of their opposing views. When they went to Europe, Mustafa Fazıl Pasha provided the greatest support to them. When Namık Kemal returned to the country, he started work as editor for a newspaper called İbret (in 1872). However, this newspaper was closed shortly afterwards (Karpat, 2012: 65).

When Kemal was in exile in Europe, he understood the importance of the technological development of the West in that era. However, he underlined that the two essentials for the material development of the Ottomans were the concepts of freedom and development. During the years he was in Europe, he published a newspaper called 'Hürriyet' with his friends (Ahmad, 2007: 47; Zürcher, 2011: 111). In the first issue of the newspaper, published in 1868, Namık Kemal wrote an article titled 'Love for homeland comes from faith'. Yet another article in the same issue emphasized the importance of consultation. Similar topics would be emphasized predominantly in the articles to be published in subsequent issues (Lewis, 2017: 212).

On the other hand, Ottomanism wanted to maintain a supreme identity and keep all elements of the empire together. According to Namık Kemal, everyone living in the Ottoman homeland was a citizen, regardless of religion and language. He explained this with the concept of 'ittihad-ı anasır' (Akşin, 2007: 37). Thanks to this concept, they believed that all ethnic groups could live together under the umbrella of the Ottoman state. The ideology they defended was the ideology of Ottomanism. However, they used Islamic motifs to a great extent in their writings. The new Ottomans based their democratic understanding on the principles of the Islamic religion. They argued that the liberal values of Europe could match the Islamist tradition. They claimed that a structure with a parliament resembled the consultation method in Islam. On the other hand, the idea of freedom and constitutionalism, which had developed since the Tanzimat influenced the intellectual circles, became an organized opposition movement for the first time (Tanör, 2017: 129). This organized opposition was sometimes called the New Ottomans and sometimes the Young Ottomans at that time.

With the Tanzimat, the influence of bureaucrats in the administration of the Ottoman state started to increase day by day. In time, the idea of constitutionalism spread among top bureaucrats. For them, the only source of crises was the repressive regime. An assembly formed by an election would completely solve the problem (Tunaya, 2009: 5). In other words, the ideas advocated by the New Ottomans movement started to be adopted by senior managers. Now, high-ranking bureaucrats were in a stronger position than the Sultan. However, Abdülaziz, the sultan of the period, did not adopt the idea of constitutionalism. For this reason, Sultan Abdulaziz was dismissed from his post and the Fifth Murad was made sultan in his place.

However, he was forced to leave his post after a short time due to health problems. In this context, Crown Prince Abdulhamid met with Mithat Pasha, one of the leaders of the New Ottomans movement. Abdulhamid promised reformers a constitutional government. Therefore, Abdülhamid was appointed as the sultan with the support of the New Ottomans (Karatepe, 1993: 82–86). As soon as he was enthroned, he drew the profile of a libertarian sultan. A special commission was established to prepare the first Constitution of the Ottoman state, Kanun-i Esasî. This commission examined most of the written constitutions in the world during the preparation phase. In particular, the French Constitution and the Belgian Constitution were reviewed in detail (Tunaya, 2009: 7–8). The first Ottoman constitution prepared by the commission was announced by the Sultan in the last days of 1876. This constitution had not been submitted to a referendum. For this reason, it was made with the Ferman method, which is one of the monocratic constitution making methods (Gözler, 2018: 166). In fact, the 1876 Constitution was born largely as the work of Mithat Pasha and the New Ottomans who helped him (Karpat, 2012: 79–80). However, this document, called Kanun-i Esasi, was a very weak when compared with western constitutions.

Elections were held in 1877 and the first Ottoman parliament started its activities in March. Most of the deputies were elected by the provincial councils. The first Ottoman parliament was formed with two wings – Meclis-i Mebusan and Heyet-i Ayan. It was not possible to talk about political parties at that time. The candidates for parliament announced their candidacy individually. This first experience of democracy in the Ottoman State did not last long. Because, on 14 February 1878, Abdulhamid suspended the Constitution, citing the Ottoman-Russian war in that period as a reason. He also suspended the parliament (Tanör, 2017: 160).

It is not possible to say that Kanun-i Esasi brought a real limited monarchy, because the legislative and executive powers were mostly in the hands of the Sultan. Perhaps the strongest aspect was that the judicial task was given to independent courts (Gözler, 2018: 169). In fact, this Constitution did not come into being at the request of the bourgeoisie or the demands of the people. Anyway, the economic structure of the Ottoman State did not have a structure that allowed capital accumulation. In fact, this Constitution was prepared in a top-down method as a result of the efforts of statesmen and intellectuals. In this context, there could not be a democratic method in terms of its preparation. Regardless, the short life of parliament has been an ideal example for future generations. Ottoman intellectuals and young students would long for the reopening of the parliament and the implementation of the Constitution.

In the Ottoman state, there was a period without a parliament and a constitution for about thirty years. But in the process, a very strong opposition movement would emerge, aiming to bring the Constitution and parliament back. The first core of the new opposition was formed at the military medical school, with a few students coming together (Findley, 2016: 161). This organization increased its power day by day. At the end, they ensured the re-declaration of the II. Constitutional Monarchy.

3 İttihad Terakki Cemiyeti (The Committee of Union and Progress) and the II. Constitutional Era

Leaving deep marks in the history of the Ottoman state, the Committee of Union and Progress was first established in 1889 in a military medical school under the name İttihad-i-Osmani. In the past, it continued its activities secretly. In particular, it spread among students and bureaucrats studying at elite schools. This movement would operate abroad in the future. Due to the pressure of the Sultan Abdülhamid administration, the leaders of the movement fled abroad. Dissidents who went abroad published newspapers named Meşveret and Mizan. In fact, they sent these newspapers back to Istanbul and other cities in various ways (Karabekir, 2009: 22).

Upon the suggestion of Ahmet Rıza, one of the leaders of the movement, the name of the committe became İttihad ve Terakki. They were called the Young Turks when they were active in Europe. In fact, this formation was a political movement that was a continuation of the earlier dissident movement, the Young Ottomans. They were already secretly reading the patriotism works written by Namık Kemal and his friends. The new generation of Ottoman youth, who were educated in schools such as Mülkiye (administration) and Harbiye (military), adopted liberal ideas (Zürcher, 2011: 135). Students studying in these elite schools even planned a coup to overthrow Sultan Abdulhamid. However, the plan failed because one of them confessed to this plan. In fact, many students were exiled to Fezzan for this reason (Karabekir, 2009: 27). These students believed that the Constitution and parliament were necessary institutions for the country. They opposed the absolutism and oppression regime and demanded the reinstatement of the 1876 Ottoman Constitution (Tanör, 2017: 169). It is not possible to say that this movement had a consistent and monist political thought (Mardin, 2012b: 24). Despite the differences of opinion between the Young Turks, there were two issues on which they agreed. First, they were western fans and, secondly, they were against the oppressive rule of Sultan Abdulhamid (Tunaya, 2010: 25).

Shortly after the establisment of the committee, the movement was divided in two. One side of this division was the liberal wing, the other was the nationalist wing. Broadly speaking, the liberal wing advocated decentralization while the other wing advocated a centralized administration (Lewis, 2017: 289). This difference of opinion emerged most clearly at the First Young Turk Congress. This congress was held in 1902 with the initiatives of Prince Sabahattin. Sabahattin, the leader of the liberal wing, defended the idea that the Abdulhamid regime should be destroyed with the help of foreign states. However, nationalists such as Ahmet Rıza and Yusuf Akçura, the leader of the nationalist wing, rejected this idea. Thus, the congress ended in conflict. This movement united with the Ottoman Freedom Association in 1907, and became a much stronger organization. In the same year, II. The Young Turk Congress convened. In this meeting, a consensus was reached on the destruction of the Abdulhamid regime by taking arms (Akşin, 2007: 50–1). By 1908 the movement had become a very strong body composed of soldiers, civilian bureaucrats, intellectuals and minorities living in the Balkans. In this context, reformers intensified the pressure they exerted on Abdulhamid. These pressures paid off. The Young Turks sent many telegrams to the Yıldız Palace, where the sultan resided. Sultan Abdulhamid had to reactivate the Constitution and parliament (Karatepe, 1993: 103). It was a turning point in Turkish political history. The declaration of the II. Constitutional Monarchy was welcomed with enthusiasm in the Ottoman Empire.

Ottoman citizens of different ethnic backgrounds celebrated this event like a holiday. People in the country adopted this important change as the 'Declaration of Freedom'. The Committee of Union and Progress, which played an active role in the declaration of the Constitutional Monarchy, became the most important political power of the empire. However, he was not fully in power (Afyoncu, 2016: 332). After the proclamation of the II. Constitutional Monarchy, a libertarian environment emerged, especially in terms of political organization. We can say that many political parties have been established. The first ones that came to mind were the following: the Party of Union and Progress, the Freedom Party, the National Constitutional Party, the Freedom and Reconciliation Party, the People's Party, the İttihad-ı Muhammedi Party and the Ottoman Democrat Party (Tekin and Okutan, 2019: 54). Even the Ottoman Socialist Party was established.

Minority groups also had the opportunity to establish their own associations. It became free to defend even the most extreme ideas. In this libertarian period, for the first time in Ottoman history, intellectual movements had the opportunity to express themselves. The strongest of these were Islamism, Turkism, westernism and socialism. During the II. Constitutional Monarchy, every writer or intellectual adopted one of these movements. Members of the intellectual movements were generally those who fought against the Abdulhamid regime. Again, these people said, 'How can this state be saved?' They were looking for an answer to the question. Because in those years, the Ottoman state was very weak. The state, which had a hard time in the face of western countries, was at risk of disintegration. Representatives of these movements were trying to produce formulas to save their own country (Tunaya, 2010: 66).

The press were able to write whatever they wanted without the threat of censorship. Representatives of thought movements were able to defend their thoughts and theses from 1908 to 1922. Some of these thinkers had important political positions, even after the transition to the Republican regime., Ziya Gökalp, Şemsettin Günaltay, Fuad Köprülü and Mehmet Akif are the first names that come to mind (Tunaya, 2010: 67).

On the other hand, those in exile began to return to Istanbul from Europe, Egypt and various parts of the empire (Ahmad, 2007: 61). Thanks to this revolution, general elections were held for the first time in 1908 and a parliament was established. The candidates of the İttihad Terakki Party and the Ahrar Party competed in the elections. The Ahrar Party was a very weak party in terms of organization. They did not nominate a deputy candidate in the elections in many regions. However, İttihad Terakki had established a very good network of organizations in every region of the empire. The candidates of Union and Progress won the elections by a clear margin. At that time, two newspapers, named Serbesti and Volkan, were very strong in opposition. Hasan Fehmi, the editor-in-chief of the Serbesti newspaper, was assassinated. This journalist was probably killed by a Unionist. This incident mobilized the opposition to İttihad Terakki (Zürcher, 2011: 149). A large crowd gathered on the day of the funeral ceremony. This ceremony turned into a show of power of the groups opposing the Committee of Union and Progress. As a result of all these events, the rebellion movement, known as the 31 March Incident, began (Afyoncu, 2016: 334). In fact, the starting date of the event was 13 April 1909, according to the Gregorian calendar.

There were madrasah students, uneducated soldiers and members of the opposition party among the rebels. They wanted a regime based on religion.

They also demanded the dissolution of the Council of Ministers. Another wish was for women to withdraw from social life. Sultan Abdulhamid accepted all the requests of the rebels. During the rebellion, some members of İttihad Terakki were killed. Again, the deputies close to the İttihad Terakki fled from Istanbul. Apparently, the İttihad Terakki seemed to have been defeated (Ahmad, 2007: 65). The army in Istanbul was reluctant to intervene in the events. Thereupon, the 'army of movement' moved from Thessaloniki to Istanbul in order to suppress the rebellion. Mustafa Kemal was in this army (TekinandOkutan, 2019: 54), which was successful in suppressing the rebellion.

The İttihad Terakki suffered a great shock due to the rebellion movement. They made radical changes to restore their authority. At the end of this event, Abdulhamid was dismissed by the İttihad Terakki. Instead of him, Sultan Mehmet Reşat, known as a passive person, was made the sultan (Lewis, 2017: 294–5). However, discussions about the March 31 incident are still going on today. After the rebellion movement was suppressed, very important changes were made to the Constitution in August 1909.

With these changes, the powers of the sultan were reduced while the powers of the Assembly were increased. From now on, the Council of Ministers would be accountable to the Assembly. The absolute veto power of the sultan was taken away. The right of termination, which was an important trump card in the hands of the Sultan in the past, was rendered otiose (Tanör, 2017: 193–4). In fact, the transition to a true parliamentary democracy was made with these changes.

İttihad Terakki also formed a party in 1909. Even if he had suppressed the rebellion, it was not possible to say that the İttihad Terakki had full sovereignty over the Assembly. The power of İttihad Terakki was mainly based on the army (Afyoncu, 2016: 340). There were opposition groups inside and outside the Assembly that were uncomfortable with the behaviour of the Unionists. All of these groups founded the Hürriyet ve İtilaf Party in 1911, against the İttihad Terakki Party. General elections were held in 1912. These elections became known as 'elections with sticks' in Turkish political history (Zürcher, 2011: 158) – because the Party of Union and Progress won these elections by applying policies of threats and violence. However, this time the officers opposing the Union and Progress took action. These officers called themselves 'Saviour Officers'. With their declarations, they forced the current government to resign in July 1912. Before long, İttihad Terakki took the rematch by carrying out the January 1913 Bab-ı Ali Raid. What they did was actually a military coup because the Council of Ministers was forced to resign by force of arms. Now, the Unionists themselves took over the state administration. The Union and Progress established a despotic administration after this date (TekinandOkutan, 2019: 58–60), and established a single-party regime between 1913 and 1918.

When the Ottoman state entered the First World War in 1914, the İttihad Terakki party was in power. When the war ended with defeat in 1918, its principal leaders fled the country. Nevertheless, at the end of the war the party held its final congress. Since the unionists did not want to see their parties buried in history, they turned their parties into a party called Teceddüd. However, this party was not allowed to operate (Tunaya, 2011: 29).

In the post-war period, some regions of the Ottoman state were occupied. As a reaction to this, Turkish resistance movements started. The Turkish Grand National Assembly (TBMM) was opened to manage this resistance, while at the same time protecting the country's administration. The Turkish War of Independence was successful won, with the TBMM under the leadership of Mustafa Kemal. Mustafa Kemal realized one of his biggest dreams on 29 October 1923 and a republic was declared. After the proclamation of the republic, efforts to transition to a multi-party democratic life ended in failure, both in 1924 and in 1930. Multi-party life began in the real sense after the Second World War in Turkey.

4 Conclusion

It is not possible to claim that there was a stable democracy during the Ottoman period, there are no conditions for the consolidation of democracyThere was no strong social support for a civil society. The groups that were influential in the democratization process were generally intellectuals and students studying in elite schools. These groups were aware political and democratic developments in Europe. In particular, they were influenced by liberal ideas because they spoke foreign languages and even lived there. The state administrators were generally disturbed by democratization attempts and liberal demands. It was very risky to express demands for democracy within the Ottoman Empire. Therefore, Ottoman reformers often had to continue their activities abroad. The Young Ottomans provided the first Ottoman Constitution (Kanun-i-Esasi) and the proclamation of the first Constitutional Era. The Committee of Union and Progress, which followed them in a sense, enabled the Constitution to be re-enacted and for parliament to reopen.

On the other hand, the Unionists, who took their power from the army, defended libertarian and democratic principles for a certain period of time. Indeed, a climate of freedom and democracy emerged after the II. Constitutional Monarchy was declared. Multi-party elections were held for the first time. But this beautiful climate was short-lived. First, the 31 March Incident (1909), then the Saviour Officers Incident (1912) frightened the İttihad Terakki. Unionists forced the government to resign at gunpoint. After they took over, they turned to despotic practices. Unionists started to act like the administrations they criticized. This time they continued the tradition of a strong state and crushed opposition movements. They established a single party power. The press was silenced and freedom of association was forgotten. As before, the opposition had to flee abroad. So, not much changed compared to the past. Even after the transition to the republican regime, it was necessary to wait a long time for multi-party life.

References

Afyoncu, E. (2016). Askeri İsyanlar ve Darbeler. İstanbul: Yeditepe.

Ahmad, F. (2007). Bir Kimlik Peşinde Türkiye. İstanbul: Bilgi Üniversitesi.

Ahmad, F. (2015). Modern Türkiye'nin Oluşumu (Yavuz Alagon Trans.). İstanbul: Kaynak.

Akşin, S. (2007), Kısa Türkiye Tarihi. İstanbul: Türkiye İş Bankası.

Findley, C. (2016). Modern Türkiye Tarihi. İstanbul: Timaş.

Gözler, K. (2018). Anayasa Hukukuna Giriş. Bursa: Ekin.

Huntington, S. (2011). Üçüncü Dalga (Ergun Özbudun Trans.). Ankara: Kilit.

Karabekir, K. (2009). İttihad ve Terakki Cemiyeti. İstanbul: YKY.

Karatepe, Ş. (1993). Darbeler, Anayasalar ve Modernleşme. İstanbul: İz.

Karpat, K. (2012). Kısa Türkiye Tarihi. İstanbul: Timaş.

Lewis, B. (2017). Modern Türkiye'nin Doğuşu. Ankara: Arkadaş.

Mardin, Ş. (2012a). Türk Modernleşmesi. İstanbul: İletişim.

Mardin, Ş. (2012b). Jöntürklerin Siyasi Fikirleri 1985–1908). İstanbul: İletişim.

Tanör, B. (2017). Osmanlı-Türk Anayasal Gelişmeleri. İstanbul: YKY.

Tekin, Y. and Okutan, Ç. (2019). Türk Siyasal Hayatı Ankara: Orion.

Tunaya, T. Z. (2009). Türkiye'de Siyasal Gelişmeler (1876–1938) İstanbul: İstanbul Bilgi.

Tunaya, T. Z. (2010). Türkiye'nin Siyasi Hayatında Batılılaşma Hareketleri. İstanbul: Bilgi

Tunaya, T. Z. (2011). Türkiye'de Siyasal Partiler-Cilt 3- . İstanbul: İletişim.

Zürcher, E. J. (2011). Modernleşen Türkiye'nin Tarihi (Yasemin Saner Trans.) İstanbul: İletişim.

Hasan Hakses and Arzu Al

Effects of the Belt and Road Initiative on the Global Political Economy[1]

1 Introduction

The history of the Silk Road forming the centre of global trade dates to seventh century. The Silk Road, enabling the wealth of east to transfer to west, also made the circulation of cultures and ideas possible. The Silk road, starting from China and extending to Europe, cxame under the general name of Caravan Lines. Thanks to inventions in the area of Astronomy, caravans had information about distances and routes between cities. In addition, caravansaries were built for caravans to rest (Ersöz, Tüğen, 2019: 637). Thus, trade continued non-stop for many years. Controlling this trade route was of great importance to many, in every era.

During the battles in Asia, Chinese efforts to protect the well-known Great Wall of China led, in some ways, to them limiting their own geography. As a result, throughout the geography of the Silk Road, which stretches from China to Europe, it is fair to conclude that regional authority has been in the hands of Turks for many years (Okur, 2017: 50).In parallel with the discovery of new continents and the emergence of alternative trade roads, the Silk Road lost its importance (Sak, 2015). The seaways and railways became attractive for world trade, once again, which serviced large markets like Asia. The modernization of the Silk Road, enabling the transfer of wealth from the east to the west, required the development of many projects. Among the most comprehensive projects, the Belt Road Project, developed by China, attracts the greatest attention. Outlining the Belt Road project and its effect on international trade, and the views of global actors to the project, will be analysed in terms of interactions political economy.

1 This study is based on the first author's PhD thesis, which he completed at Marmara University's Department of International Relations under the supervision of the second author

2 Belt and Road Project

The Belt and Road project, focused on reanimating the historical Silk Road, was initially named as the Silk Road Economic Belt and the 21st Century Maritime Silk Road. Later, an abbreviation in the form of 'One Belt One Road' began to be used (Chin et al., 2015: 2). The route overland was expressed as 'One Belt', and the route over the sea 'One Road'. In the second section, the scope of the Single Way and Single Belt projects will be examined under the separate headings.

2.1 One Belt

As President Xi Jinping said in September 2013 during his Kazakhstan visit, for the revitalization of the historical Silk Road, the general name for the project routes, developed by China, over land was named as One Belt (Minghao, 2015: 2). As stated in the introduction, in historical scale, the trade existing between Asia and Africa directly improved through short lines. It would be a truism to describe the Silk Road lines as networks of roads rather than being a single road through which local trade centres are interconnected.

The Belt, which starts in Asia and extends to Europe, has six different six routes. These are New Eurasia Intercontinental Bridge, China-Mongolia-Russia, China-Pakistan, China-Indonesia, Bangladesh-China-India-Myanmar, and China-Central Asia-West Asia economic corridors (Winter, 2016).

Today, the goal is to eliminate infrastructural flaws in this route, which is still supported by railway lines, in order to enable speedier and more effective coordination. In the routes where bidirectional trade flow is planned, shortening long waiting periods at the points of customs clearance and fiscal control are among the priorities for the project in Belt dimension. In this scope, the first freight train going nonstop from China to Europe was the China Railway Express in 2019 (Kenderdine and Bucsky, 2020). The road, extending to approximately 12,000 kilometers was completed in just twelve days. For bidirectional trade flow, the first export train departing from Turkey in the late 2000s, logged about 9 thousand kilometers before reaching China (MFA, 2020). Thus, it is possible to say that this was a win-win policy for all parties.

2.2 One Road

President Xi Jinping said that a sea route was also planned during Indonesia visit in October 2013 in conjunction with the modernization of the Silk Road. The project, expressed as the Maritime Silk Road, was a maritime route extending from Asia to Europe was described as the new Silk Road Line. This line, extending over sea was also called 'Road' (Chin et al., 2015: 2).

As regards the scope of Road, lines were drawn from the China Sea to important ports in Europe. A route proceeding from the south reached continental Africa. Hence, the Belt Road Project is considered to extend over a greater area than the historical Silk Road. The project is considered to extend over a greater area than the historical Silk Road. The fact that disruptions caused by port countries result in commercial losses is one of the reasons behind the creation of the Road. In this context, China purchased 'port businesses' with dual contracts (UTIKAD, 2010). In addition, it is also planning to build facilities where large ships can dock, and increasing the capacity of the ports. Piraeus in Greece and Gwadar Port in Pakistan fall within this scope (Zhen, 2015). Due to the potential of a trade increase in the Mediterranean, the Aliağa (İzmir) Port in Turkey – a facility in which large ships can dock –was built (Atlı, 2020: 49).

In the last period, the Arctic Ocean was evaluated as an alternative route to and from China. this is shorter and less costly than the Suez Canal route has a quality, which provides an advantage for all parties.

2.3 Fund Resource of Belt and Road Initiative

For the infrastructural investments planned by China, it is necessary to mention domestic resources. These are Silk Road Fund, the New Development Bank and the Asian Infrastructural Investment Bank (CLSA, 2015).

The Silk Road Fund, when compared to other resources, is mostly a fund that China formed itself. In 2014, in partnership with the China Exim Bank, the Development Bank, and the Public Foreign Exchange Administration and Investment Company, a public limited company was formed. The foundation budget was $40 billion (Silk Road Fund, 2016).

The New Development Bank was founded with the participation of the BRICS countries (Brazil, Russia, India, China and South Africa) in 2015, although the bank has no direct connection with the Belt and Road project. The New Development Bank, having a budget of $100 billion, will provide finance for the projects that fall within this geographic area (NDB, 2021). Lastly, the Asian Infrastructural Investment Bank is a fund resource that has a larger participation. The bank founded in 2016 is thought to be an alternative to the Asia Development Bank. Among the reasons for the foundation of bank was the fact that the World Development Bank and the Asian Development Bank could not supply the necessary fund resources for the infrastructural projects planned in the Asian. On the other hand, it can be said that the bank, being a founder member in the Asian region, contributes to a diverse financial system. It has a total of eighty-five members, forty-six of which are regional countries, and thirty-nine are from outside of the region. They financially supported the 106 infrastructural projects planned as of 2021(NDB, 2021).

3 The Effect of Belt and Road Initiative on International Trade

The year 2013, when the project was announced, coincided with the period when the world economy recovered from the adverse effects of the global financial crisis. Thus, the project attracted the attention of the world public opinion.

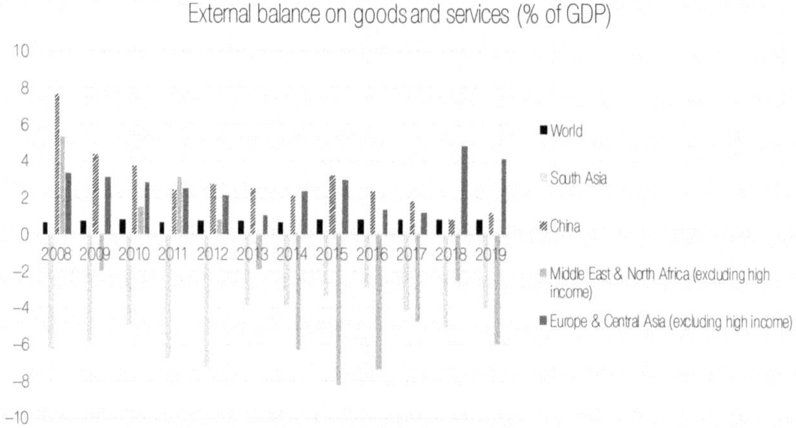

Fig. 1: *External Balance on Goods and Servicesi (% of GDP)*
Source: World Development Indicators, 2021.

According to the data from the World Bank, between the years 2008–2019 the percentage of foreign balances in goods and services in GNP fluctuated all over the world. It is conceivable to claim that foreign balance s are below the world average in the Asian, European, Middle Eastern, and North African regions, analyzed as part of the Belt and Road Project. China has a particularly good potential in terms of foreign balances compared to the other regional groups. In the recent years, it is shown in the graph above that European and Central Asian countries positively decompose about foreign balance.

4 Security Structure of Belt and Road Initiative

In terms of the security perspective of the Belt and Road Initiative, since there are not any countries that are in direct conflict in this geographic area, it is possible to examine this project in dimension of routes. Upon that Soviet Union decomposes in land basin, Turkic Republics established in Central Asia and new border definitions of these countries with China take place. Together with the Turkish republics that has gained their independenc, the thoughts of the desire of the Uyghur Turks in Xinjiang Region of China to become independent have strengthened even more. However, the establishment of Uyghur Turkish in this region will cut the connection between China and Central Asia, and has resulted in China making an oppressive intervention. It is plausible to argue that the Turkish Republics' efforts to deal with their own domestic concerns, as well as their limited ability to act together, preclude them from establishing a policy against China.

In 1992, after President Turgut Özal visited Turkish Republics that gained their independence, Turkey took steps to develope policies and strategies for this region. In this scope, the foundation of Turkish Cooperation and Coordination can be shown as an example (Hatipoğlu, 2018: 106. However, at the point of political will, that agency is deprived of the power to sufficiently maneuver has led to the efforts taken in this direction to be able to provide feedback in a short period of time. Thus, by means of penetration and political interests in the region, the effects of Russia and China were felt. When looking at the Belt's scope in terms of route scale, it can be noted that it is far off from ongoing hostilities such as those seen along the Iran-Iraq-Syria line to the south, as well as the fact that terrorist groups operating in the region have a commerce agenda. In the scope of the Road, the presence of discussible issues experienced in the China Sea shows that the project, which promises a global peace environment, exhibits an approach that is far away from solving the problems in starting region (Kim, 2015: 132). On the other hand, because it is constrained in South Asia and the Indian Ocean basin, it is in a position to stifle competition with China. Finally, the discourses of China about a set of pearl strategy and discussions about that the facilities, to which nuclear submarines can land in infrastructural projects in the countries it carries out port businesses, form a threat in terms of port countries (Manhas, 2020: 18).

5 Approaches of Global Actors Belt and Road Initiative

For the Belt and Road Initiative to operate as planned, coordination and cooperation is necessary. The approach of global actors in the project are important. In this section, the approaches of Russia, India, Turkey, the Europe Union and United States of America will be evaluated.

5.1 Russia

Russia has land in both Europe and Asia. Hence, due to its having trade lines extending from Asia to Europe, it has an advantageous position. It is fair to say that Russia, from the outset, as one of the region's founding parts, has viewed the Belt and Road Initiative in a distant manner. On the other hand, it is a natural state for Russia, which wants to leverage regional cooperation from an economic and political standpoint in a platform like the Eurasia Economic Union, which it can transfer from its own perspective, to approach Belt and Road from a distance.

One of the goals of regionalization might be the Eurasia Economic Union. Russia and China see the Asian region as a competition zone in this context. However, the close relationship between presidents Xi and Putin, and the fact that project will be profitable for all concerned, has changed Russia's approach, and Russia has begun to support the project (Özdaşlı, 2015: 592). In the possible routes extending from Asia to Europe, the China-Mongolia-Russia line passes through the least number of countries before it reaches Europe, to the advantage of Russia. In the energy-economy equation, the long-term agreements China made with Russia have been evaluated as a gain to Russia.

5.2 India

India participates in the Belt and Road Initiative. The border problems experienced with Pakistan, and infrastructural investments made by China in Pakistan, negatively affect . In the scope of China-Pakistan economic corridor, it is planned to provide transit pass for both energy transmission lines and a railway line that will extend from Gwadar Port to the city of Kashgar. Due to the fact that 40% of international energy transmission are made through this region, the region has a strategic position (Gökten, 2019: 165).

In meeting the increasing energy needs of China, the China-Pakistan economic corridor has an advantage in terms of cost due to its short distance. However, the fact that the energy transmission traffic in the Indian Sea Basin decreases is disadvantageous to India (Pant, 2017).

5.3 Turkey

Turkey, which has one of important junctions in the Belt and Road Initiative, has an advantageous position from a strategic point of view. Turkey, which has a central position between the Asian and European continents, has been one of the closely followed countries from the advent of the announcement of the Belt and Road Initiative. Turkey, which is among the founder members of Asian Infrastructural Investment Bank, also has an optimum position at the point of possible routes for the project. Railway lines, planned to reach Europe using the Caspian transit corridor through Central Asia, were evaluated as the most suitable point for two-way flow in terms of cost and utility level. Within the scope of Belt and Road Initiative, a total of eleven projects financed by Asian Infrastructural Investment Bank were carried out in Turkey, that is: the Salt Lake Turkey Gas Depot Enlargement Project; the Sustainable Energy and Infrastructure Loaning Facility' the Renewable Energy and Energy Effectiveness Loaning Facility; the Istanbul Seismic Risk Reduction and Emergency Case Preparation Project; the Efeler 97.6 MWE Geothermal Power Plant Enlargement Project; the Halkalı-Çerkezköy Railway Project; the COVID-19 Credit Line Project; the İzmir Underground Enlargement Stage 4; the Fahrettin Altay – Narlıdere Line Project; the COVID -19 Medical Emergency Response (MER) Project; the Akbank COVID-19 Crisis Relief Facility; and the Eximbank COVID-19 Credit Line Project. Within the scope of these projects, under the headings of liquidity, energy, and transportation, approximately $2.5 billion of investment was made (AIIB, 2021).

5.4 The European Union

The approach of the European Union to Belt and Road Initiative is generally positive. However, it is not possible to say that the EU has a common view. Venice, Italy, accepted as a finish point of the Silk Road, causes Italy to be seen in the position of an important partner in Europe in terms of China. With Italy, one the founder members of Europe Union, signing an agreement to develop the project, this can be seen as a diplomatic achievement for China (Zeneli, 2019).

The Cooperation Platform Agreement China made with European countries was signed by sixteen countries, eleven of which were EU members (Pepermans, 2018: 2). This shows that China tried to form an economic influence area within the borders of the EU. Thus, China forms a platform that can compete with Germany, the most important economic power in the EU.

While China uses the sea for commercial transportation at a rate of 59%, Europe uses the highway at a rate of 70%. It is considered that China will have positive effect on European trade with infrastructural improvement and the building of railway and highway connections. Furthermore, because China has a weighed share in financing, the European Union has the opportunity to enjoy trade benefits without incurring long-term costs (Herrero and Xu, 2016: 4).

5.5 The United States of America

Following the Second World War, it is possible to say that the US, one of the major actors of world order, has dominated the world economy for many years. With the breakup of the Soviet Union, while global responsibilities undertaken negatively effect the American economy, this has led to more competitive economies emerging in the system (Gilpin, 2015: 103). The fact that the global financial crisis arose, which seriously effected continental Europe, enabled China to effect public opinion, developing an alternative discourse. Although the West cannot promise a positive future in a commercial sense, the fact that China emerged with the Belt and Road Initiative attracted attention to Continental Asia. That China is catching USA economically forms a serious threat. In the light of all of these developments, that the USA cannot develop a policy as a global actor has increased the ability of China to act.

When the China-US relationship is evaluated, it will be seen that trade wars and sanction policies have affected the hegemonic position of the US (Schuman, 2019). On the other hand, the American military presence in continental Asia reveals that discussions regarding this case is costly (in terms of providing regional security). The fact that China does not accept any responsibility to provide security on the regional scale, and that it uses its commercial advantages, are among US criticisms of China.

It is not possible to say that the US introduces a clear alternative policy against the Belt and Road Initiative. In the framework of the decisions made by Barrack Obama, the transfer of American soldiers in Asia to the Pacific Ocean was interpretated as US policy to surround China from the sea, not from the land. While the US, which attempts to develop close relationships with Pacific countries, meets at the common point of competition with China, it does not seem to be an easy relationship (Athari and Ejazi, 2020: 52).

6 Conclusion and Discussion

The Belt and Road Initiative has a comprehensive vision, addressing to three continents, seventy-five countries, and more than half of the world's population. For the project to be successful, it is necessary to install multilateral cooperation rather than unilateral coordination. To achieve this, China suggests that countries revise their development policies to include common targets. Moving forward, it is apparent that countries' development initiatives can be realized once they are in sync with project goals. In terms of developing mutual trade, the project has an advantageous aspect for all parties. The infrastructural projects completed have increased the participation of countries in international trade and encouraged a more competitive environment.

When the effects of Belt and Road Initiative on the political economy are examined, besides the fact that the project is advantageous in an economic sense, it is possible to say that it carries a risk in terms of security. It can be seen that the discourse of China is to develop cooperation. Examining which areas of foreign direct investments concentrate on allows for more detailed studies in terms of testing China's discourses from this perspective. Examining Chinese companies in those countries taking place in the Belt and Road Initiative on a micro scale comes to our attention as issues that need to be researched.

References

Athari, Assadollah. and Ejazi, Ehsan. (2020). Çin-ABD Rekabeti Gölgesinde Kuşak ve Yol Girişimi, Çev: Ebru Şahin, BRIq Journal 1/4, 44–54.

Atlı, Altay. (2020). Kuşak, Yol ve Saat Kulesi Çin ile Ekonomik İlişkilere İzmir ve Ege Bölgesi'nden Bakış, EGİAD Çin Raporu, 6–67.

AIIBa. (2021). Our Projects, Available at: https://www.aiib.org/en/projects/list/year/All/member/Turkey/sector/All/financing_type/All/status/All (06.02.2021)

AIIBb. (2021). Our Projects List, Available at: https://www.aiib.org/en/projects/list/index.html (08.02.2021)

Chin, Helen, Lau, Fang, He, Winnie, and Cheung, Timothy. (2015). The Silk Road Economic Belt and the 21st Century Maritime Silk Road, Hong Kong: Fung Business Intelligence Centre, 7–30.

CLSA, (2015). A Brilliant Plan: One Belt, One Road, Available at: https://www.clsa.com/special/onebeltoneroad/ (09.02.2021)

Ersöz Tüğen, A. (2019). Tarihi İpekyolu'nda Bir Durak: Akhan Kervansarayı, Kent Akademisi, 12(3), 634–643.

Gilpin, Robert. (2015). The Political Economy of International Relations, Kripto Yayınları, 95–105.

Gökten, K. (2019). Çin-Pakistan Ekonomik Koridoru ve Yeni Güney Asya Jeopolitiği, Fiscaoeconomia, 3 (1), 160–177.

Hatipoğlu, O. (2018). Farklı Bir Kamu Kurumu Olarak Tika: Örgüt Yapısının Dönüşümü Hakkında Bir Analiz, Türkiye Siyaset Bilimi Dergisi, 1 (1), 99–116.

Herrero, Alicia Garcia and Xu, Jianwei. (2016). China's Belt and Road initiative: can Europe expect trade gains?, Bruegel Working Paper Issue 5, 2–19.

Kenderdine, Tristan and Bucsky, Péter. (2020). Rail Freight Use on China's Iron Silk Road Underdelivers, Available at: https://thediplomat.com/2020/11/rail-freight-use-on-chinas-iron-silk-road-underdelivers/ (11.01.2021)

Kim, Jihyun. (2015). Territorial Disputes in the South China Sea: Implications for Security in Asia and Beyond, Strategic Studies Quarterly, s. 107–141.

Manhas, Neeraj. (2020). China's Policy of 'String of Pearls', International Journal of Social Impact, 5(3), 18–25.

MFA. (2020). Press Release Regarding the Departure of the First Export Train from Turkey to China, No: 314, Available at: https://www.mfa.gov.tr/no_-314_-turkiye-den-cin-e-gidecek-ilk-ihracat-treninin-yola-cikmasi-hk.en.mfa (03.02.2021)

Minghao, Zhao. (2015). China's New Silk Road Initiative. Istituto Affari Internazionali, IAI Working Papers 15/37, 2–12.

NDB. (2021). New Development Bank About Us, Available at: https://www.ndb.int/about-us/essence/history/ (03.03.2021)

Okur, M . (2017). "Bir Kuşak, Bir Yol" Projesi'nin Jeopolitiği, Türk Kuşağı ve Uygurlar, Akademik Hassasiyetler, 4 (8), 45–55.

Özdaşlı, Esme. (2015). Çin'in Yeni İpek Yolu Projesi Ve Küresel Etkileri, International Periodical for the Languages, Literature and History of Turkish or Turkic, Turkish Studies, 10/14 (Fall 2015), 579–596.

Pant, H.V. (2017). India challenges China's intentions on One Belt, One Road Initiative, Observer Research Foundation, Available at: https://www.orfonline.org/research/india-challenges-china-intentions-one-belt-one-roadinitiative/ (19.10.2020)

Pepermans, A. (2018). China's 16+1 and Belt and Road Initiative in Central and Eastern Europe: economic and political influence at a cheap price, Journal of Contemporary Central and Eastern Europe, 1–23.

Sak, G. (2015). Türkiye'nin Bir İpek Yolu Stratejisine İhtiyacı Var, TEPAV Günlük, Available at: http://www.tepav.org.tr/tr/blog/s/5177/Turkiye___nin+bir+Ipek+Yolu+stratejisine+ihtiyaci+var. (11.02.2021)

Schuman, M. (2019). The U.S. can't make allies take sides over China, The Atlantic, Available at: https://www.theatlantic.com/international/archive/2019/04/us-allies-washington-china-belt-road/587902/ (19.02.2021)

Silk Road Fund. (2016). About, Available at: http://www.silkroadfund.com.cn/enweb/23773/index.html (20.05.2020)

UTIKAD. (2010). Çin'in Pire Limanı Atağı lojistik sektörünü Nasıl Etkileyecek?, Available at: https://www.utikad.org.tr/Detay/Sektor-Haberleri/6317/cinin-pire-limani-atagi-lojistik-sektorununasil-etkileyecek (07.02.2021)

Zeneli, Valbona. (2019). Italy Signs on to Belt and Road Initiative: EU-China Relations at Crossroads?, Available at: https://thediplomat.com/2019/04/italy-signs-on-to-belt-and-road-initiative-eu-china-relations-at-crossroads/ (09.01.2021)

Zhen, S. (2015). Chinese firm takes control of Gwadar Port free-trade zone in Pakistan, South China Morning Post, Available at: http://www.scmp.com/business/companies/article/1877882/chinese-firm-takes-control-gwadar-port-free-trade-zone-pakistan (10.02.2021)

Winter, Tim. (2016). One Belt, One Road, One Heritage: Cultural Diplomacy and the Silk Road, Available at: https://thediplomat.com/2016/03/one-belt-one-road-one-heritage-cultural-diplomacy-and-the-silk-road/ (05.01.2021)

World Bank. (2021). Data Bank World Development Indicators, Available at:https://databank.worldbank.org/indicator/NY.GDP.MKTP.KD.ZG/1ff4a498/PopularIndicators (09.03.2021)

Oğuzhan Özçelik

Sustainability of Foreign Trade Balance in African Countries: A New Generation Panel Data Analysis

1 Introduction

Adam Smith's 'The Wealth of Nations', published in 1776, underlines how important it is for economies to engage in the division of labour, specialization and free foreign trade based on absolute advantage. International trade later evolved with the theory of comparative advantage by David Ricardo (1817) and has still been keep going in line with this theory. According to this, economies should specialize in whichever goods they produce at relatively lower costs. Going for comparative advantage in international trade in terms of the efficient use of scarce resources generally improves economic effectiveness. But this phenomenon does not mean that all economies will benefit from trade. Although international trade allows resources to be distributed more efficiently, and provides potential gains to societies, there will still be losers and winners in this mechanism (Acemoglu et al. 2015). From this point of view, ensuring and sustaining a foreign trade balance is of great importance (WTO, 2012: 3). Foreign trade balance, which can be measured by the difference between exports and imports or the ratio of exports to imports (Kharroubi, 2011: 34), is one of the most important reasons for the profitability or indebtedness of countries against the external world. The ongoing foreign trade war between the US and China, the departure of the UK from the European Union and the replacement of NAFTA, which has been in practice with the US, Mexico and Canada since 1994 by USMCA[1] on 1 July 2020, are all due to the efforts by sovereign countries to improve their foreign trade balance (Condon, 2018: 30).

Although African countries gained their independence after the colonial period, their foreign trade balances and volumes have never been able to reach the desired levels. Today, a great majority of the African countries[2] experience foreign trade deficit problems. Foreign trade deficit is the most important reason behind current account deficit, with high current account deficits

1 USMCA: United States-Mexico-Canada Trade Agreement

2 Thirty-one of the thirty-nine countries had a foreign trade deficit problem in 2019.

having the potential to drag those countries into economic crisis. At this point, Dornbusch and Fischer (1990) consider it a sign of crisis when the ratio of current account deficit to national income exceeds 4 %, whereas this threshold is 5% and 6% according to Freund (2000) and Labonte (2010), respectively. It is therefore quite important to frequently analyse the current account deficits of countries, and the foreign trade deficits that cause them, and to take necessary measures without delay. It is noteworthy that developed and developing economies, including China in particular, have been engaging in an increasing amount of foreign trade with underdeveloped African countries since the early 2000s. Jeanneney and Hua (2015) showed that the trade between the African countries and China negatively affects the commercial relations of African countries with each other. In other words, over time underdeveloped continental Africa has become more inclined to trade with developed and developing economies. The differences in GDP between developed and underdeveloped countries have led African countries to export goods with low added value and to import goods with relatively high added values, as expected. This phenomenon has raised foreign trade deficits in continental Africa, and the sustainability of such deficits has become more problematic.

In this study, the sustainability of the foreign trade balance in thirty-nine African countries, whose data could be accessed, was analysed using the new generation panel data analysis method for the period of 1980–2019. The analyses were not only made for the entire period, they were also repeated for the periods of 1980–1999 and 2000–2019. The countries included in the sample accounted for 86.74% of the total national income of all countries in the African continent as of 2019 (UCTAD, 2021), which shows the high representative power of the sample. This study presents a literature review on the subject in its second section, the third section includes the methodology, the fourth section offers a review of the sample, the fifth section involves analyses, and finally the sixth section arrives at the conclusions.

2 Literature Review

In the literature review on the subject, it was observed that the sustainability of foreign trade deficits was not discussed much, and researchers generally focused on the sustainability of the current account deficit. Researching the sustainability of the foreign trade deficits in Turkey for the period of January 1981 to February 2000 using the two regime self-exciting threshold autoregressive unit root test by Kapetanios and Shin (2006), the study by Guris and Kiran (2011), which was one of the limited number of studies that were available, concluded that Turkey's foreign trade deficit was unsustainable, since the foreign trade series was non-stationary at that level. Examining the sustainability of Turkey's foreign trade deficits for the period of 1989–2015, Celik and Ilkay (2016) found that there was a positive relationship between exports and imports, and that there was also a causality relationship from an increase in imports towards exports, but the sustainability of the foreign trade deficit in Turkey was weak in the long run, in spite of all of these. Yavuz Tiftikcigil et al. (2017) searched the sustainability of Turkey's foreign trade deficit in the field of energy for the period of 1969–2013 by linear and non-linear unit root tests and found that Turkey's energy trade was unsustainable.

Perera and Varma (2008) examined the sustainability of the foreign trade deficits in Sri Lanka for the period of 1950–2006 by a unit root test with a single break, and decided that the foreign trade deficits in this country were unsustainable, since the foreign trade balance series was nonstationary at that level. Tiwari (2010) examined the sustainability of the foreign trade deficits in India using the HEGY unit root test of Hylleberg et al. (1990), by using the data from the period April 1984 to March 2009 and decided that the foreign trade deficit in India was sustainable in that period, since the foreign trade deficit series was stationary. Nag and Mukherjee (2012) analysed the sustainability of the foreign trade deficits in India via a unit root test with structural breaks for the period of January 1950 to September 2008 and found that the macroeconomic policies implemented in India were not effective to achieve a foreign trade balance in the long run. Al-Khulaifi (2013) examined the sustainability of the foreign trade balance in Qatar using the ADF and PP unit root tests; the series became stationary in the first difference, therefore Qatar's foreign trade deficits were unsustainable in the period 1980–2011. In the study by Salman Abdou and Monastiriotis (2018), the sustainability of net export in MENA countries was analysed by using the ADF and Ng-Perron unit root tests and it was found that the net export was sustainable in Egypt, Morocco and Tunisia, but unsustainable in Algeria, Jordan and Lebanon.

3 Methodology

Foreign trade balance can be calculated in two different ways: The first of these is the coverage ratio of export to import, while the second is the ratio of the difference between exports and imports to national income. These can also be represented by the following equations, respectively (Rath et al. 2020: 401–402):

$FTB_1 = \frac{X}{M} * 100$ and $FTB_2 = \frac{X - M}{GDP} * 100$ Where FTB is the foreign trade balance, X is Export, M is Import, and GDP is Gross Domestic Product. The sustainability of the foreign trade balance can be decided by looking at the stationarity of the series produced by using these equations (Perera and Varma, 2008; Nag and Mukherjee, 2012). When these series are found to be stationary in their level values or at higher degrees as a result of the unit root tests, the foreign trade balance in the respective economy is sustainable or unsustainable, respectively (Bozoklu and Yilanci, 2014: 255). Jha and Sharma (2004) also expressed this situation in their study, in which they examined the financial sustainability of India by a unit root test with two structural breaks. This method is frequently used in academic studies today. For example, Ceylan, Uz and Cevis (2018) analysed the sustainability of the current account deficit in the fragile five countries by the KSS and AESTAR non-linear unit root tests, and decided that the current account deficits in Brazil were unsustainable because the series was nonstationary, while the current account deficits in other countries were sustainable because the series was stationary. Gurdal et al. (2018) tested the sustainability of the current account deficits in Turkey by the Fourier ADF unit root test and decided that the current account deficit in Turkey for the period of 1972–2017 was sustainable, since the series was stationary at the level. Demir (2019) examined the sustainability of current account deficits by unit root tests with structural breaks, and decided that the current account deficits in Turkey were unsustainable, since the series was nonstationary.

In this study, the sustainability of the foreign trade balance in African countries was analysed by using new generation panel unit root tests. As the countries included in the analysis were located in the same geographical region (continent), it was possible to find a cross section dependence among them. For this reason, the LM, LM_S, CD and LM_{BC} cross section dependence tests were performed first, before proceeding with the Pesaran (2007) CADF unit root test, which works by taking into account the cross section dependence among countries, and is able to generate results for each country as well as the overall panel.

3.1 Cross Section Dependence Tests

Cross section dependence means that an economic or political shock on one country also affects the other members of the group (Baltagi and Pesaran, 2007). It is very important to test the existence of cross section dependence between the countries that make up the panel and, in case of its presence, to use the Second-Generation panel data analysis methods that take this situation into account. The first study to test cross section dependence belonged to Breusch and Pagan (1980), who were followed by Pesaran (2004) and Baltagi, Feng and Kao (2012). The null hypothesis of these tests are '*There is no cross section dependence among the countries*'.

3.2 CADF Panel Unit Root Test

The Cross-Sectional Augmented Dickey Fuller (CADF) panel unit root test developed by Pesaran (2007) is the panel data analysis version of the ADF test in time series analyses, which works under cross section dependence. In the CADF test, the unit root test statistics of panel (CIPS), can be calculated by using individual unit root statistics. The hypotheses of the CADF and CIPS tests are '*The series is nonstationary*'. The critical values required to test these hypotheses are given in Pesaran (2007: 279–281).

4 Sample

The analyses in this study was based on annual data from the period of 1980–2019 of thirty-nine countries. The total national income of the thirty-nine countries was USD 2.2 trillion for 2019; this data was found to account for 86.74% of the 2019 national income of fifty-seven countries in the African continent, which was USD 2.54 trillion. This is important as it shows that the analysis performed strongly represents the sample. The main macroeconomic data of the countries included in the analysis is provided in Table 1.

Tab. 1: *Main Macroeconomic Data of the Countries (2019)*

Country	Export (Billion $)	Import (Billion $)	GDP (Billion $)	GDPPC ($)	X/M (%)	(X-M)/ GDP (%)
Algeria	36	42	171	3974	85	-4
Angola	35	14	89	2791	246	23
Benin	3	4	14	1219	82	-5
Botswana	5	7	18	7961	80	-7
Burkina Faso	3	5	16	787	65	-12
Burundi	0	1	3	261	20	-23
Cabo Verde	0	1	2	3604	8	-37
Central African Rp.	0	1	2	468	25	-21
Chad	3	2	11	710	127	5
Comoros	0	0	1	1370	22	-15
Congo, Dem. Rep.	7	6	50	581	110	1
Congo, Rep.	7	3	12	2280	231	33
Egypt	29	71	303	3019	41	-14
Equatorial Guinea	5	3	12	8132	193	20
Ethiopia	3	15	96	856	19	-12
Gabon	7	3	17	7767	238	26
Gambia	0	1	2	778	21	-27
Ghana	16	13	67	2202	117	3
Guinea-Bissau	0	0	1	697	71	-7
Kenya	6	18	96	1817	33	-12
Lesotho	1	2	2	1118	49	-44
Madagascar	3	4	14	523	67	-9
Malawi	1	3	8	412	30	-27
Mali	4	5	17	879	75	-7
Mauritania	2	3	8	1679	86	-5
Mauritius	2	6	14	11099	40	-24
Morocco	29	51	120	3204	57	-18
Namibia	5	8	12	4957	64	-22
Niger	1	2	13	554	51	-9
Nigeria	63	55	448	2230	113	2
Senegal	4	8	24	1447	51	-17
Sierra Leone	1	2	4	528	44	-20

Tab. 1: *Continued*

Country	Export (Billion $)	Import (Billion $)	GDP (Billion $)	GDPPC ($)	X/M (%)	(X-M)/ GDP (%)
South Africa	90	108	351	6001	84	-5
Sudan	4	9	31	442	43	-17
Togo	1	2	5	679	53	-18
Tunisia	15	22	39	3317	69	-17
Uganda	3	8	35	794	46	-12
Zambia	7	7	23	1305	98	-1
Zimbabwe	4	4	21	1464	122	4

Source: World Bank (2021). Note: X; Export, M: Import, GDP: Gross Domestic Product.

Table 1 shows that the country with the highest level of exports among the African countries for 2019 was South Africa, with annual exports amounting to USD 90 billion, followed by Nigeria and Algeria with USD 63 billion and USD 36 billion, respectively. Looking at imports, South Africa ranks first with USD 108 billion, which is followed by Egypt and Nigeria with USD 71 billion and USD 55 billion, respectively. Looking at national incomes, it is noteworthy that Nigeria is the biggest economy in Africa with USD 448 billion, followed by South Africa and Egypt with USD 351 billion and USD 303 billion, respectively. For GDPPC, it is seen that Mauritius ranks first with USD 11,099, followed by Equatorial Guinea and Botswana with USD 8,132 and USD 7,961, respectively. It is seen that the country with the worst foreign trade balance (X / M) is Cabo Verde with 8%, followed by Ethiopia and Burundi with 19% and 20%, respectively. It is also seen that nine countries, including Nigeria and Ghana, had a foreign trade surplus in 2019. The top three countries with the worst ratio of foreign trade deficit to national income were Lesotho (-44%), Cabo Verde (-37%) and the Gambia (-27%). Given the situation, Dornbusch and Fischer (1990), Freund (2000) and Labonte (2010) are of the opinion that these African countries face a serious risk of economic crisis. The top three countries with the highest positive ratio of foreign trade surplus to national income were determined to be the Congo Republic (33%), Gabon (26%) and Angola (23%).

5 Results

In the study, the LM , LM_S, CD and LM_{BC} tests were performed to test the presence of a cross section dependence in terms of the foreign trade balance among the African countries included in the analysis, the results of which are presented in Table 2. The series used in these procedures are those that are defined in Equation (1) and Equation (2).

Tab. 2: *Results of the Cross Section Dependence Tests*

Test	FTB_1	FTB_2
Breusch-Pagan LM	4909.03*** (0.00)	4805.32*** (0.00)
Pesaran scaled LM	104.54*** (0.00)	101.91*** (0.00)
Bias-corrected scaled LM	104.02*** (0.00)	101.40*** (0.00)
Pesaran CD	4.25*** (0.00)	8.95*** (0.00)

Note: *** shows a significance level of 1%. The values in parentheses are prob. values.

According to the results in Table 2, the null hypothesis was strongly rejected in the cross section dependence test conducted for African countries; it was decided that a cross section dependence did exist between these countries. This result is in line with our prior expectations, and it would be usual for an economic or political shock on one of the countries in the same geographical region to affect the other ones. Accordingly, while developing their foreign trade policies, African countries should consider the policies implemented by other African countries and the political and economic changes they experienced.

As a cross section dependence was found among the countries, the CADF panel unit root test was preferred, which is a new generation panel data analysis, taking this situation into account in unit root testing. The results of the CADF panel unit root test for each country and the results of the CIPS statistics for the overall panel are shown in Table 3.

Tab. 3: *Results of the CADF Panel Unit Root Test (Period of 1980–2019)*

Countries	FTB_1		FTB_2		Countries	FTB_1		FTB_2	
	Intercept	Intercept and Trend	Intercept	Intercept and Trend		Intercept	Intercept and Trend	Intercept	Intercept and Trend
Algeria	-3.71**	-3.69*	-3.95***	-3.90**	Lesotho	-0.35	-2.77	-0.30	-4.74***
Angola	-2.11	-2.79	-2.93	-3.03	Madagascar	-2.65	-2.84	-2.62	-2.93
Benin	-3.23*	-3.24	-3.53**	-3.85**	Malawi	-1.13	-3.33	-1.11	-3.48*
Botswana	-2.97*	-3.06	-3.10*	-3.26	Mali	-1.99	-3.20	-1.48	-2.36
Burkina Faso	-1.81	-5.35***	-3.48**	-5.94***	Mauritania	-1.55	-2.32	-2.13	-2.98
Burundi	-1.70	-3.09	-1.06	-1.88	Mauritius	-0.10	-1.99	-1.20	-2.38
Cabo Verde	-0.81	-1.98	-3.01*	-3.47*	Morocco	-1.63	-1.78	-0.56	-1.21
C. African R.	-1.17	-1.66	0.07	-1.49	Namibia	-1.86	-4.17**	-2.07	-3.76*
Chad	-3.02*	-3.82**	-3.24*	-3.48*	Niger	-2.56	-4.92***	-3.59**	-4.23**
Comoros	-2.19	-3.06	-1.31	-1.53	Nigeria	-3.68**	-3.62*	-4.09***	-4.04**
Congo, D. R.	-2.89	-2.94	-3.26*	-3.30	Senegal	-1.65	-2.73	-1.13	-2.25
Congo, R.	-2.58	-2.90	-2.59	-3.15	Sierra L.	-2.02	-2.21	-3.26*	-4.61***
Egypt	-2.33	-3.18	-3.13*	-3.59*	S. Africa	-1.53	-3.47*	-1.79	-3.65*
Eq. Guinea	-2.37	-3.70*	-2.17	-2.44	Sudan	-3.22*	-3.44*	-2.93	-3.43
Ethiopia	-2.30	-3.17	-2.44	-1.86	Togo	-2.98*	-3.12	-2.36	-2.68
Gabon	-1.17	-1.35	-4.18***	-3.96**	Tunisia	-3.00*	-4.19**	-2.84	-3.47*
Gambia	-2.18	-2.26	-3.87**	-4.43**	Uganda	-2.31	-2.81	-2.68	-3.43
Ghana	-2.67	-2.53	-3.25*	-3.26	Zambia	-2.78	-2.83	-2.34	-2.50
Guinea-B.	-0.84	-2.39	-1.24	-2.47	Zimbabwe	-2.21	-2.00	-2.95*	-2.76
Kenya	-0.60	-2.04	-1.23	-1.48	CIPS	-2.13**	-2.98***	-2.43***	-3.15***

Note: The CADF critical values at the significance levels of 1%, 5% and 10% were taken from Pesaran (2007: 275) (intercept only) and were -3.95, -3.27 and -2.94, respectively, while the critical values at the significance levels of 1%, 5% and 10% from Pesaran (2007: 276) (intercept and trend) were -4.47, -3.78 and -3.44, respectively. The critical values for the CIPS test were taken from Pesaran (2007: 280) (intercept only) and were -2.23, -2.11 and -2.05, respectively, while the critical values at the significance levels of 1%, 5% and 10% from Pesaran (2007: 281) (intercept and trend) were -2.72, -2.60 and -2.50, respectively. ***, ** and * show that the series is stationary at significance levels of 1%, 5% and 10%.

According to the results in Table 3, both the export/import coverage ratio and the share of the foreign trade deficit in national income were sustainable in Algeria, Benin, Botswana, Burkina Faso, Chad, Namibia, Niger, Nigeria, South Africa and Tunisia. Only the export/import coverage ratio was sustainable in Equatorial Guinea and Sudan. Similarly, only the share of the foreign trade deficit in the national income was sustainable in Cabo Verde, the Democratic Republic of Congo, Egypt, Gabon, the Gambia, Ghana, Lesotho, Malawi, Sierra Leone and Zimbabwe. The fact that the share of the foreign trade deficit in national income was found to be more sustainable indicates that not only the export and import data, but also the share of the difference between them in national income, should be considered for the foreign trade balance and, in fact, the latter is probably a more accurate indicator than the former. It was determined that both the export/import coverage ratio and the share of the foreign trade deficit in the national income was sustainable in the overall panel.

These analyses were repeated for the periods of 1980–1999 and 2000–2019. The main reason for such distinction is the effort to distinguish the effects of the dramatic changes that appeared in the world trade in the early 2000s. The findings obtained for the period of 1980–1999 are presented in Table 4.

Tab. 4: *Results of the CADF Panel Unit Root Test (Period of 1980–1999)*

Countries	FTB_1		FTB_2		Countries	FTB_1		FTB_2	
	Intercept	**Intercept and Trend**	**Intercept**	**Intercept and Trend**		**Intercept**	**Intercept and Trend**	**Intercept**	**Intercept and Trend**
Algeria	-2.89	-3.01	-4.09***	-4.91***	Lesotho	-1.02	-4.36**	-1.65	-3.63*
Angola	-1.55	-0.84	-1.47	-1.64	Madagascar	-2.13	-2.18	-1.99	-2.65
Benin	-3.21*	-2.91	-2.04	-1.96	Malawi	-1.91	-1.84	-1.70	-1.71
Botswana	-2.87	-2.65	-2.20	-3.00	Mali	-0.20	-4.96***	-1.68	-2.65
Burkina Faso	-1.61	-2.43	-3.80**	-3.64*	Mauritania	-0.90	-1.64	-0.94	-2.17
Burundi	-1.89	-1.87	-1.44	-1.33	Mauritius	-3.04*	-2.35	-2.94*	-2.34
Cabo Verde	-1.18	-1.40	-2.26	-2.91	Morocco	-1.10	-1.77	-2.39	-2.14
C. African R.	-1.48	-2.17	-2.35	-3.27	Namibia	-1.94	-3.47*	-2.38	-2.80
Chad	-1.31	-1.99	-2.21	-2.15	Niger	-3.37**	-5.76***	-5.61***	-6.80***
Comoros	-0.76	-2.72	-2.77	-2.96	Nigeria	-2.88	-2.63	-3.19*	-3.25
Congo, D. R.	-1.71	-2.12	-2.52	-2.56	Senegal	-1.89	-2.30	-2.49	-2.46
Congo, R.	-1.65	-1.55	-3.03*	-2.83	Sierra L.	-0.24	-1.45	-1.37	-1.64
Egypt	-1.14	-1.43	-2.24	-2.59	S. Africa	-1.29	-2.78	-0.96	-2.81
Eq. Guinea	-0.12	-3.73*	1.46	0.48	Sudan	-2.97*	-2.78	-1.21	-2.97
Ethiopia	-2.01	-2.00	-0.31	-1.06	Togo	-2.03	-2.25	-2.61	-2.47
Gabon	-1.43	-1.87	-2.38	-2.13	Tunisia	-2.04	-2.23	-1.87	-1.72
Gambia	-1.47	-2.95	-3.14*	-3.20	Uganda	-1.44	-3.09	-1.72	-3.07
Ghana	-1.89	-2.34	-2.42	-3.05	Zambia	-3.08*	-2.45	-3.03*	-2.04
Guinea-B.	1.07	-0.43	-1.07	-1.48	Zimbabwe	-1.62	-1.44	-1.06	-1.74
Kenya	-1.97	-1.91	-2.37	-2.01	CIPS	-1.73	-2.42	-2.12*	-2.55

Tab. 5: *Results of the CADF Panel Unit Root Test (Period of 2000–2019)*

Countries	FTB_1		FTB_2		Countries	FTB_1		FTB_2	
	Intercept	Intercept and Trend	Intercept	Intercept and Trend		Intercept	Intercept and Trend	Intercept	Intercept and Trend
Algeria	-3.25*	-3.03	-3.60**	-1.42	Lesotho	-2.09	-1.87	-1.84	-1.28
Angola	-0.69	-2.58	-1.84	-1.63	Madagascar	-3.40**	-3.21	-3.13*	-3.24
Benin	-0.97	-1.11	-2.06	-2.39	Malawi	-1.33	-3.40	-1.15	-4.96***
Botswana	-2.32	-2.25	-2.18	-2.02	Mali	-3.08*	-3.27	-2.31	-2.99
Burkina Faso	-3.32**	-3.53*	-3.83**	-3.97**	Mauritania	-1.97	-2.25	-2.59	-2.52
Burundi	-2.32	-2.54	-0.85	-1.49	Mauritius	-2.00	-2.47	-0.20	-2.19
Cabo Verde	-1.40	-1.61	-3.54**	-3.26	Morocco	-1.58	-1.36	-0.22	-1.41
C. African R.	-1.70	-2.95	-0.98	-2.24	Namibia	-2.79	-2.92	-1.79	-1.73
Chad	-2.76	-2.12	-2.18	-3.56*	Niger	-3.29**	-3.31	-3.63**	-3.51*
Comoros	-0.59	-0.77	0.06	0.32	Nigeria	-1.75	-2.32	-1.99	-2.24
Congo, D. R.	-4.79***	-5.15***	-4.04***	-4.44**	Senegal	-0.53	-1.39	-1.06	-3.13
Congo, R.	-0.43	-0.69	-0.83	-1.28	Sierra L.	-2.46	-2.82	-3.92**	-3.77*
Egypt	-3.25*	-2.01	-1.22	-4.03**	S. Africa	-2.72	-2.36	-1.64	-2.37
Eq. Guinea	-3.24*	-3.10	-2.04	-0.94	Sudan	-2.73	-2.43	-2.75	-2.59
Ethiopia	-1.64	-1.24	-2.30	-1.29	Togo	-1.53	-3.27	-0.70	-1.19
Gabon	0.23	0.20	-1.44	-1.70	Tunisia	-2.76	-2.37	-1.29	-1.25
Gambia	-0.92	-0.92	-1.98	-1.85	Uganda	-3.29**	-2.85	-7.25***	-5.38***
Ghana	-2.17	-2.07	-4.06***	-6.52***	Zambia	-1.67	-2.03	-1.36	-1.76
Guinea-B.	-3.53**	-4.06**	-3.01*	-3.79**	Zimbabwe	-1.24	-1.11	-1.96	-2.33
Kenya	0.98	-0.68	0.71	0.38	CIPS	-2.08	-2.29	-2.29**	-2.49

According to the results in Table 4, both the export/import coverage ratio and the share of the foreign trade deficit in the national income were sustainable in Lesotho, Mauritius, Niger and Zambia. While only the export/import coverage ratio was sustainable in Benin, Equatorial Guinea, Mali, Namibia and Sudan, only the share of the foreign trade deficit in the national income was sustainable in Algeria, Burkina Faso, the Congo Republic and the Gambia in the overall panel for the 1980–1999 period. It can be seen that the export/import coverage ratio was unsustainable in the overall panel. These analyses were also carried out for the period 2000–2019; the findings are presented in Table 5.

According to the results in Table 5, both the export/import coverage ratio and the share of the foreign trade deficit in national income were sustainable in Algeria, Burkina Faso, the Democratic Republic of Congo, Guinea-Bissau, Madagascar, Niger and Uganda. While only the export/import coverage ratio was sustainable in Mali and Uganda, the share of the foreign trade deficit in the national income was only sustainable in Cabo Verde, Ghana, Malawi and Sierra Leone in the overall panel for the period 2000–2019. It is seen that the export/import coverage ratio was unsustainable in the overall panel.

6 Conclusions

In this study, the sustainability of the foreign trade deficits in African countries was analysed using the new generation panel data analysis method for 1980–2019 period based on thirty-nine countries whose data could be obtained. The presence of a cross section dependence among countries was examined by using the LM, LM_s, CD and LM_{BC} methods, and it was observed that there was a cross section dependence among African countries in terms of foreign trade. For African countries, this structural relationship points out the importance of considering the policies implemented by other African countries and the political and economic changes they experience while determining their own foreign trade policies.

Whether or not the countries' export/import coverage ratio and their foreign trade deficit share in the national income was sustainable was examined by the CADF panel unit root test, which also produces individual results for the countries. The results for the overall panel were obtained using the CIPS method. The analyses were not only made for the period of 1980–2019, but were also repeated for the periods of 1980–1999 and 2000–2019. Looking at the findings in general, it can be said that the sustainability of foreign trade balance was lower in the period of 1980–1999 and increased, even if relatively, in the period after 2000. In Guinea-Bissau, Madagascar and Uganda the foreign trade balance was unsustainable in the period before 2000; however, certain improvements were seen in this area in the period after 2000. According to the analyses for the overall panel, the ratio of foreign trade deficits to national income was sustainable in both sub-periods, while the export/import coverage ratio was unsustainable.

Based on the findings of this study, it can be stated that the foreign trade balances in African countries is unsustainable in general, and that international organizations such as the IMF, IBRD and the World Bank need to take urgent measures to ensure the foreign trade balance of such countries, and to prevent them from being forced to exit the global foreign trade network in the long run. It is also important that the administrators of the developed countries that trade with African countries prioritize not only short-term high profits, but also long-term and sustainable trade, and consider the commercial interests of the other country accordingly. As for the local administrators of these countries, it is important that they are aware of the disturbances in their foreign trade balances, and that they rearrange their national production and consumption in a way to improve this balance.

References

Acemoglu, D., Laibson, D. and List, J. (2015). Microeconomics. Pearson Education Inc., Prentice Hall.

Al-Khulaifi, A.S. (2013). Exports and Imports in Qatar: Evidence from Cointegration and Error Correction Model, Asian Economic and Financial Review, 3(9), 1122–1133.

Baltagi, B.H. and Pesaran, M.H. (2007). Heterogeneity and Cross Section Dependence in Panel Data Models: Theory and Applications, Journal of Applied Econometrics, 22, 229–232.

Baltagi, B.H., Feng, Q. and Kao C. (2012). A Lagrange Multiplier test for Cross-sectional Dependence in a Fixed Effects Panel Data Model, Journal of the Econometrics, 170, 164–177.

Bozoklu, S. and Yilanci, V. (2014). Current Account Sustainability in Emerging Markets: An Analysis with Linear and Nonlinear Panel Unit Root Tests, Ataturk University Journal of Economics and Administrative Sciences, 28(4), 251-264.Breusch, T. S. and Pagan, A.R. (1980). The Lagrange Multiplier Test and Its Applications to Model Specification Tests in Econometrics, Review of Economic Studies, 47, 239–253.

Celik, T. and Ilkay, S.C. (2016). Testing the Relationship between Export and Import in Turkey for the Period of 1989–2015, Suleyman Demirel University,

The Journal of Faculty of Economics and Administrative Sciences, 21(3), 961–969.

Ceylan, R., Uz, I. and Cevis, I. Sustainability of Current Account Deficits in Fragile Five: Evidence from Non-Linear Unit Root Tests, Ege Academic Review, 18(1), 121–134.

Condon, B.J. (2018). From NAFTA to USMCA: Two's Company, Three's a Crowd, Latin American Journal of Trade Policy, 2, 30–48.

Demir, M.A. (2019). Current Account Deficit Sustainability in Turkey Under the Concept of Structural Break Unit Root Tests, Third Sector Social Economic Review, 54(1), 261–273.

Dornbusch, R. and Fischer, F. (1990). Macroeconomics, McGraw-Hill, International Editions.

Freund, C.L. (2000), Current Account Adjustment in Industrialized Countries, Board of Governers of the FED International Finance, Discussion Papers, No. 692.

Gurdal, T., Kirca, M., Inal, V. and Degirmenci, T. (2018). Sustainability of Current Account Deficit: Fourier Unit Root Test, Business and Organization Research International Conference, 12–14 September, Safranbolu/Karabuk.

Guris, B. and Kiran, B. (2011). Foreign Trade Deficit Sustainability of Turkey, Economic Studies journal, Bulgarian Academy of Sciences - Economic Research Institute, 11(1), 167-174. Jeanneney, S.G.and Hua, P. (2015). The impact of Chinese competition on Africa's manufacturing. Fondation Pour Les Etudes et Recherches Sur le Dévelopement International (FERDI) Working Paper, No: 131.

Jha, R. and Sharma, A. (2004). Structural Breaks, Unit Roots, and Cointegration: A Further Test of the Sustainability of the Indian Fiscal Deficit, Public Finance Review, 32(2), 196–219.

Kharroubi, E. (2011). The Trade Balance and The Real Exchange Rate, BIS Quarterly Review, September, 33–42.

Labonte, M. (2010), Is the U.S. Current Account Deficit Sustainable?, Congressional Research Service, 7–5700.

Pesaran, M.H. (2004). General Diagnostic Tests for Cross Section Dependence in Panels, Cambridge Working Papers in Economics, No. 1240.

Nag, B. and Mukherjee, J. (2012). The Sustainability of Trade Deficits in the Presence of Endogenous Structural Breaks: Evidence from the Indian Economy, Journal of Asian Economics, 23(5), 519–526.

Perera, N. and Varma, R. (2008). An Empirical Analysis of Sustainability of Trade Deficit: Evidence from Sri Lanka, International Journal of Applied Econometrics and Quantitative Studies, 5(1), 79–92.

Pesaran, M.H. (2007). A Simple Panel Unit Root Test in The Presence of Cross-Section Dependence, Journal of Applied Econometrics, 22, 265–312.

Rath, S.S., Dash, S. and Sharma, M.K. (2020). Dynamic Relationship between Trade Balance and Macroeconomics Variables in India, Test Engineering and Management, 83, 399–418.

Ricardo, D. (1817). The Principles of Political Economy and Taxation. https://web.archive.org/web/20020806175422/http://socserv2.socsci.mcmaster.ca/~econ/ugcm/3ll3/ricardo/prin/index.html. (18.07.2021).

Salman Abdou, D.M. and Monastiriotis, V. (2018). External and Internal Imbalances in South Mediterranean Countries, FEMISE Research Papers, No. FEM42–13.

Tiwari, A.K. (2010). Is Trade Deficit Sustainable in India? An Inquiry, MPRA Paper, No. 24454, University Library of Munich, Germany.

UCTAD (2021). Gross Domestic Product: Total Annual, Available at: https://unctadstat.unctad.org/wds/TableViewer/tableView.aspx?ReportId=96, (29.03.2021). World Bank (2021). Indicators, Available: https://data.worldbank.org/indicator, (25.03.2021).

WTO (2012). Mainstreaming trade to attain the Sustainable Development Goals. Available at: https://www.wto.org/english/res_e/booksp_e/sdg_e.pdf, (27.03.2021).

Yavuz Tiftikcigil, B., Yasgul, Y.S. and Guris, B. (2017). Sustainability of Foreign Trade Deficit in Energy: The Case of Turkey. Chapter in "Business Infrastructure for Sustainability in Developing Economies". IGI Global Publisher of Timely Knowledge.

Semra Altingöz Zarpli

The Evolution of the Power of the Purse Concept in Turkey

1 Introduction

The power of the purse, defined as the right to determine and approve the type and amount of public expenditure (Yılmazcan, 2000: 163) together with the revenues obtained from taxes and other sources, plays a significant role in the functioning and implementation of the public economy (Bağlı, 2012: 48). The efficiently functioning of the public economy is made possible through the effective implementation of fiscal policies. A proper determination of public revenues and expenditure, which are the primary fiscal policy elements, and a controlled borrowing, will ensure the financial policy objectives. It is not possible to deny the share of the power of the purse in achieving the targets of fiscal policy.

This study investigated the development of the power of the purse in Turkey by considering its conceptual framework and evaluated its stages in the 1921, 1924, 1961 and 1982 Constitutions chronologically.

2 The Power Of The Purse Concept

Aristotle argues that what is legal is right. In other words, the right is that the rules comply with the laws. About the concept of right, some theories are dominated by various ideas, including the will theory, the interest theory and the hybrid theory. The hybrid theory, which has a compromising spirit, can be seen as a combination of the will and interest theories. The right qualitatively needs some will, some benefit and some explanation. These concepts have no meaning alone (Çetin, 2010: 5).

According to James Madison, the power of the purse is an efficient, evergrowing, flawless tool providing the force that no legal entity can provide to the nation's representatives to solve all kinds of problems and implement all neutral and beneficial measures (Avcı, 2015: 70). It is not possible to talk about the power of the purse in totalitarian administrations because all authorities regarding the power of the purse are under the control of the ruler (Edizdoğan and Çetinkaya, 2010: 21)

The power of the purse is the authority to decide on the type and amount of public services and the collection of public revenues to meet these services

(Karaarslan, 2006: 139). The power of the purse has emerged as a part of the democratic management approach. The mechanism giving the budget an 'earned right' character, and developing it as an institution arises from society's rational and questioning behaviour style (Bağlı, 2012: 46). In non-democratic management structures, administrative people demand material benefits for the services they offer to the public. The public does not always respond voluntarily for the taxes that the administrators request. People question the activities they finance because they are concerned about the necessity of the taxes and their usage areas. When these concerns begin to dominate society in general, the budget concept now begins to be accepted as a right (Selen and Tarhan, 2014: 2).

The development process of the power of the purse is completed in three main stages. In the first stage, to legalize the budget's revenue part, parliament approves that taxes and other income sources are available. In the second stage, parliament approves the expenditure. At the last phase, the approval process of the state's revenues and expenses, which completed the preparatory processes in the previous stages, is usually carried out by parliament every year, in principle.

While executive power has the power of decision on public policies affecting communities, parliament plays a significant role in budget law enactment. While the executive power is empowered to draft budget laws, the authorities of review, approval and change belong to parliament which oversees the executive's activities. This control is an imposition mechanism of positive law (Özer, 1999: 30). One of the main reasons for the existence of the 'Court of Accounts' is the legislative's inspection duty on the authority given to the executive power by parliament through the budget, and this task is also defined in the power of the purse. Therefore, the court of accounts reports can be described as significant outputs of the power of the purse (Parlak, 2016: 2).

Answers to questions such as why the power of the purse should be presented by public units, what types and amounts of the service to be provided, who will participate in its financing, who will be authorized to find financing and produce works, and which preferences will be considered while providing the service, suggests that the budget has a political aspect (Altuğ, 2004: 3).

The power of the purse and control are inseparable concepts. The Public Financial Management and Control Act No 5018 says, 'The public financial management is executed according to the Power of the Purse of Turkey Grand National Assembly'. In the same law, public financial management is defined as legal and administrative systems and processes that will ensure the effective, budgetary and efficient use of public resources per the defined standards. Similar to our country, the public financial management approach in the world focuses on three points. The first is the effort to increase fiscal discipline to use public resources efficiently, the second is the official regulations for ensuring the accountability of public institutions and organizations, and the last, increasing the efficiency of the legislative bodies in the budgeting process and the use of resources (Yılmaz and Biçer, 2010: 205). The power of the purse is a system formed by the nations assigning their sovereignty and authority over public revenues and expenditure to the parliament in the processes that democracies have undergone until today; and as a financial institution it is a 'right', whose borders have been drawn by the constitutions. With this expression, budgets turn into contracts. While one of the parties in the agreement is the parliament representing the people, the other party is the executive itself (Narter, 2012: 37).

The most pronounced process of the power of the purse, which parliaments constitutionally hold, is the supervision of the budget approval and implementation processes. Domination and representation are revealed in these processes. The inspection of budgets by parliament ranks first among the basic requirements of the national will principle. The legality of the budget and the parliament's control give it a concrete character. The executive body needs to receive permission from the legislature to collect revenues and realize expenditure; therefore, it should act according to the budget. It should be determined whether or not the executive power is used under the law. In this respect, the power of the purse can be described as a whole, continuing from the budget preparation process to the implementation and ends with the supervision of the implementation results (Bağlı, 2010: 140).

3 Development of the Power of the Purse in England

The power of the purse first appeared in England. Britain was a state governed by a monarchy at that time, as in other European states. However, the road to democracy and parliamentarism emerged earlier here, and Britain has been an example to other countries in this regard. When British political history is examined, the power of the purse concept is seen to emerge because of the authority conflict between the king and the parliament, first, in the twelfth century. Indeed, the political, economic and social revolutions that reached their peak in the seventeenth century allowed the issues regarding tax collection and disposition to be under parliament control. In this context, there is a linear connection between the birth of the power of the purse and the development of parliamentarism in England. After this process was born in England, it spread to Europe and America, and then to the world (Doğan and Şentürk, 2017: 354). The UK first adopted the right to impose taxes on 19 June 1215 with the great freedom edict (the Magna Carta Libertatum). The Magna Carta Libertatum resulted, inter alia, from the people's revolt against the king's excessive taxation (Gürsoy, 1980: 74–80). After that, the taxing power was left to the people's representatives for approval. However, the English kings did not want to respect these conditions, and troubles were experienced over a number of centuries. These troubles ended when the new king finally accepted the parliament's superiority in the taxation issue after the events that led to the king being deposed in 1688 (Eş, 2002: 72).

The Bill of Rights, published after the British Revolution in 1688, is the second text on the power of the purse. Human rights laws have brought significant restrictions in the financial field on rulers. The ruler's authority on taxes and expenditure was narrowed, and the permission to determine military and administrative expenses, which are critical expenditure items, was assigned to the parliament consisting of people's representatives (Edizdoğan, Çetinkaya, and Gümüş, 2012: 368). With the Consolidated Fund Act, which was established for the first time in 1787, the state could handle income and expenditure items together. Thus, more emphasis was placed on public expenditure. Until 1822, only actual expenses were included in the budget. Later, estimated budgets covering future revenues and expenses were prepared. With these developments in democracy, the budget found its meaning (Orhaner, 2007: 34–35).

In the West, a radical change was made in public financial management understanding in the 1980s. As a result of developments called 'government failures' before 1980 (an increase in budget deficits, unfunctional economic planning in many countries etc.), efforts to establish an efficient public sector were made. Efforts in three areas were seen as a guarantee to create such a public sector. First, the establishment of an adequately informed public decision-making process. Second, apparent determination and separation of political and administrative (bureaucratic, technical) responsibilities in the public service production. The third, forming a system that responds quickly and works effectively (Konukman, 2015: 26).

4 The Power of the Purse Development in Turkey

England pioneered the concept of the power of the purse. The notion spread rapidly to European countries after England. Unlike European countries, Turkey has met the budget concept late in the modern sense. Our country faced the approval and audit concepts in budgeting only in the nineteenth century (Çiçek and Dikmen, 2015: 96).

During the Ottoman Empire, scholars and bureaucrats were responsible for preparing reports to follow the state's revenues and expenditure, organizing sultans' expenses and regulating treasury transactions. The Ottoman Empire had a sharia budget that was suitable for the Islamic financial system at that time. This budget system was also far from being a systematic budget. In 1839, although the Imperial Edict of Reorganization (Tanzimat Fermanı), which was the first democratization step in Turkish history, enforced provisions regarding the fiscal field, such as tax collection per ability to pay, salary system's regulation, the formation of the state's treasury combining the sultan's treasury and the state's expenses, the budget concept was not in this regulation. However, with the Edict of Reform (Islahat Fermanı), which was prepared during the Ottoman Empire's collapse in 1856, budget regulations were formed. With the budget regulations, all income and expenses were prepared and presented to the sultan. Arrangements were made for budgetary techniques. With these regulations, the budget preparation and approval authority was given to a council established with an appointment (Edizdoğan and Çetinkaya, 2019: 33).

The Finance Reform Commission made the first Ottoman budget in the modern sense in 1863–1864. The purpose of preparing this budget is to show the state's financial situation to foreign countries and to facilitate borrowing when necessary. A new regulation was made in 1872, and a different budget commission was established. Before the budget project was forwarded to the Board of Deputies, the newly formed budget commission reviewed the project. There were bank and financial institutions' representatives among the commission members in İstanbul; therefore, that period's budgets had no political, legal or technical nature (Edizdoğan and Çetinkaya, 2019: 34).

Turkey met the power of the purse for the first time in 1876 with the Fundamental Law (Kanuni Esasi). In this Constitution, concerning the power of the purse, there was the principle that approved taxes could be collected from all citizens based on their ability to pay according to the law. This Constitution included annual taxation, the approval of the revenue and expenses in separate sections, an annual budget, the final account law principles, and the Court of Accounts' inspection. However, this law could not be implemented and was shelved due to other events (Edizdoğan and Çetinkaya, 2019: 34).

With the Second Constitutional Era in 1908, the Constitution was put into effect again. In 1909, the first contemporary budget was prepared. This first budget was prepared, discussed, approved and put into practice by the Assembly under the unity and generality principles. In the 1921 Constitution budget-related provisions were not available, but information on the budget's revenues and expenditure existed. In the 1924 Constitution, the power of the purse was fully implemented. The legality principle was thus brought into taxation. In 1927, the General Accounting Law No.1050 was put into effect. With this law, basics such as revenue collections, expenditure and state property administration were regulated. In the 1961 Constitution, the Draft Budget Law legal structure and its approval process in the legislature were specified in detail. The most significant part of the 1961 Constitution was the Ministers Boards' National Budget Estimate supplements to the budget draft, to be submitted to the Parliament three months before the beginning of each fiscal year (Edizdoğan and Çetinkaya, 2019: 35).

The 1982 Constitution stipulated that the state would fulfill its duties determined in the social and economic fields, considering the protection of economic stability to the extent of financial resources. It stated that laws were the sole authority to impose taxes. The executive body had no force to impose taxation. The most important innovation brought by the 1982 Constitution compared to the 1961 Constitution was regarding the Final Account Draft Laws. If the law does not decree a shorter period, the Cabinet submits Final Account Draft Laws to the Grand National Assembly of Turkey, beginning at the end of the fiscal year to which they relate, and not later than seven months. The Court of Auditors submits to the Grand National Assembly of Turkey the general compliance statement at the latest within seventy-five days, beginning with the draft final account law submission. The Final Account Draft Law is then put on the Budget Commission agenda together with the new year budget draft law. The Budget Commission submits the draft budget law and the final account draft law together to the General Assembly, and the General Assembly discusses the final account law draft together with the new year budget draft and decides on it (Constitution of the Republic of Turkey, article: 164) (Repealed: 21 January 2017 – 6771, art. 16).

In the PFMC No. 5018, published in the Official Gazette in 2003, public administrations outside the budget's scope were included in the budget's sphere to ensure the effectiveness of the power of the purse. Thus, the budget's purview was further expanded. Within the same law, the creation of an information system aimed to increase the TBMM's effectiveness in the power of the purse realization. In Article 1 of the law, the purpose was expressed as, '*in line with the policies and targets included in the development plans and programs, to regulate the public financial management's structure and function, public budgets' preparation and implementation, all financial transactions' recognition and reporting, financial controlling, to ensure the efficient acquisition and use of public resources, accountability and financial transparency*'.

The Constitution Article 16 and its caption were amended with Law No. 6771, amending the Constitution of the Republic of Turkey. '*The president of the Republic offers the budget law proposal to the Turkey Grand National Assembly at least 75 days before the fiscal year. The Budget Commission discusses the budget proposal. The commission confirms the text within 55 days, then discusses it in the General Assembly and concludes until the fiscal year. The President of the Republic submits the Central Government Final Accounts Law proposal to Turkey's Grand National Assembly within six months, starting from the end of the current fiscal year. The Court of account submits the general conformity statement to the General Assembly within 75 days at the latest, starting from the final account law proposal submission. The submission of the Final Account Law proposal and General Compliance Statement to Turkey's Grand National Assembly does not prevent the audit and accounting trial that could not be finalized by the Court of Accounts for the relevant year and mean they are settled.'* (T.C. Constitution, Article 161). One of the significant changes coming to the fore in the article is the statement: 'The President submits the budget law proposal to the Parliament at least 75 days before the fiscal year.' With this regulation, the Ministerial Cabinet's authority was transferred to the President of the Republic in submitting the budget to the parliament. Article 162 covering the budget negotiations, article 163 covering the principles of changing budgets, and article 164 covering statements about final accounts were repealed.

With these regulations in place in the legal structure, significant transformations have been experienced with the power of the purse process. The legal, political and institutional infrastructure are three substantial pillars that determine the power of the purse. The legal structure generally frames the functioning process of the institutions and determines the jurisdiction and the procedures to be followed (Küçükaycan and Çelikay, 2019: 352).

5 Conclusion

The power of the purse, defined as the right to determine and approve the types and amounts of public expenditure and public revenues predominantly formed by taxes, has great significance in public economics. At the same time, the power of the purse ensures the effective implementation of fiscal policies. The power of the purse, which completes the development process in three stages, must get the parliament's approval with its tax and other income sources in the first stage. In the second stage, the parliament must approve the expenses. In the third stage, the parliament must perform the approval of income and expenditure every year.

In this study, the reflections of the changes experienced due to the 5,018 public financial management and control laws in Turkey on the central government's budget preparation process were examined. By examining the legal regulations made in the central government budget process, a gradual change has been revealed. With Act No. 6771, dated 21 January 2017, the statement, '*In the budgeting process if a shorter period is not adopted in the law, the Ministerial Cabinet submits final account draft laws to Turkey Grand National Assembly within no later than seven months from the end of the relevant fiscal year'* has been replaced with the statement *'the central government's final accounts law proposal is submitted by the President of the Republic to Turkey Grand National Assembly at the latest six months after the relevant fiscal year-end.'* Again, one of the significant changes brought by the same law is the Republic's President's submission of the budget bill to the TBMM at least seventy-five days before the fiscal year.

References

Altuğ, F. (2004). Kamu Bütçesi, 2. Baskı, Ezgi Kitabevi, Bursa.

Avcı, M. A. (2015). Yasamanın Birincil Güçlü Silahı Bütçe Hakkı: Teorik Bir Yaklaşım. Atatürk Üniversitesi Sosyal Bilimler Enstitüsü Dergisi, S.1, s. 69–80.

Bağlı, M. S. (2010). TBMM'nin Bütçe Sonuçlarını Denetleme Süreci, Yasama Dergisi, No: 16. ss.103–143. (Online) http://www.yasader.org/web/yasama_dergisi/2010/sayi16/103-143.pdf, 15 Mayıs 2016

Bağlı, M. S. (2012). Teorik ve Tarihsel Açıdan Bütçe Hakkı, Yasama Dergisi, No: 20. ss.39–77. (Çevrimiçi) (http://www.yasader.org/web/yasama_dergisi/2012/sayi20/39-77.pdf, 20 Mayıs 2016

Çetin, G. (2010). "Mükellef Hakları ve Vergiye Gönüllü Uyum", Celal Bayar Üniversitesi Sosyal Bilimler Enstitüsü, Basılmamış Doktora Tezi.

Çiçek, H. G., and Dikmen, S. (2015). Osmanlı Devleti'nde bütçenin ve bütçe hakkının tarihsel gelişimi. Ekonomik ve Sosyal Araştırmalar Dergisi, 11(2), 83–98.

Doğan, K. C., and Şentürk, S. H. (2017). İngiltere'de On Yedinci Yüzyıl Devrimler Çağı Ve Parlamentarizmin Gelişimi Doğrultusunda Bütçe Hakkı. Karadeniz Teknik Üniversitesi Sosyal Bilimler Enstitüsü Sosyal Bilimler Dergisi, 7(14), 353–373

Edizdoğan, N. ve Çetinkaya, Ö. (2010). Kamu Bütçesi, Ekin Yayınları, Bursa.

Edizdoğan, N. ve Çetinkaya, Ö. ve Gümüş, E. (2012). Kamu Maliyesi, 4.Baskı, Ekin Yayınları, Bursa.

Edizdoğan, N. ve Çetinkaya, Ö. (2019). Kamu Bütçesi, Ekin Yayınları, Bursa.

Eş, M. (2002). Kamu Maliyesi, Ekspres Matbaa, Kütahya.

Gürsoy, B. (1980). Kamusal Maliye, İkinci Cilt, A.Ü.S.B.F. Yayınları, Ankara.

Karaarslan, E. (2006). Kamu Harcama Hukuku, Yaklaşım Yayınları, Ankara.

Konukman, A. (2015). Türkiye'de bütçe hakkının kullanımı: sorunlar ve çözüm önerileri. Artvin Çoruh Üniversitesi Uluslararası Sosyal Bilimler Dergisi, 1(1), 23-65

Küçükaycan, D. ve Çelikay, F. (2019). Bütçe Teorisi Perspektifinden Cumhurbaşkanlığı Hükümet Sisteminin Bütçeleme Süreci Ve Bütçe Hakkı Üzerindeki Etkileri. Güncel Maliye Tartışmaları - 2, 109–124.

Narter, R. (2012). Anayasal Açıdan Bütçe Hakkı, Erzincan Üniversitesi Hukuk Fakültesi Dergisi, C:XVI, S: 1–2, ss.35–52.

Parlak, N. (2016). Bidayeten Zimmettarlıktan Kusurlu Sorumluluğa Hesap Yargısı. Journal of Turkish Court of Accounts/Sayistay Dergisi, 103.

Orhaner, E. (2007). Kamu Maliyesi, Siyasal Kitabevi, Ankara.

Özer, M.A. (1999). "Parlamentolar ve Denetim Fonksiyonları", Sayıştay Dergisi, No: 33, ss.24–61.

Selen, U. ve Tarhan. A.B (2014). Türkiye'de Bütçe Hakkı Algısı, Star Ajans Basım, Bursa.

Yılmaz, H.H ve Biçer M. (Ocak- Haziran 2010). Parlamentonun Bütçe Hakkını Etkin Kullanımının Yeni Bütçe Sistemi Çerçevesinde Değerlendirilmesi, Maliye Dergisi, C.158, ss. 201–225. (Online) https://dergiler.sgb.gov.tr/calismalar/maliye_dergisi/yayinlar/md/158/10.H.Hakan.YILMAZ_Mustafa.BICER.pdf (10 Şubat 2016).

Reyhan Leba

Global Taxation Issues and Developing Countries

1 Introduction

Privatization, deregulation and liberalization of foreign trade and capital movements are among the fundamental economic policies in the globalization process that have led to radical changes in expenditure, taxation and borrowing policies of governments. It can be seen that these developments on a global scale since the 1980s have greatly affected the tax systems of many countries. As Tanzi stated, with these developments the potential tax base of a country is no longer limited to the territory of that country alone. In other words, it has expanded as to cover the rest of the world. These developments as of the 1980s have deeply affected the economies of developing countries.

International tax competition, and in this context tax havens, harmful preferential tax regimes and transfer pricing, are scrutinized in this study, which aims to analyse and evaluate the globalization-induced tax issues that influences the tax policies of developing countries, which is generally evaluated in the conclusion to this chapter.

2 Globalization-induced Tax Issues

The globalization phenomenon with cultural, social, technological and economic dimensions led to some important changes in the field of economics, finance and taxation, along with the changing concept of government, especially in the period after 1980.

After stating that the developments on a global scale since the 1980's greatly influenced taxation systems of countries, Tanzi (4–6) listed the most important of these developments as:

a) Foreign expansion of economies and extraordinary growth of international trade,
b) Trade growth accompanied by a significant increase in cross-border capital flows,

c) A great increase in the importance of multinational corporations both in financing direct investments and in promoting trade between divisions of the same businesses in different countries,
d) These international activities, accompanied by rising per capita incomes, falling transportation costs and policy changes have led to a high mobility of indviduals in their roles as either economic agents or consumers.

Because of these developments, the potential tax base of a country is no longer limited to the territory of that country. In other words, it has expanded as to cover the rest of the world (Tanzi: 6).

International tax competition, which is one of the most important tax issues caused by globalization; in this context tax havens and harmful preferential tax regimes are included below, and then transfer pricing is discussed.

2.1 International Tax Competition

2.1.1 The Concept and Theory of Tax Competetion

In general, tax competition is an effort by administrative units to make their administrative units attractive compared to competing administrative units, where administrative units (states or sub-units) desire to increase their competitiveness at a company and national level and have the authority to tax. For this purpose, the tax burden of productive factors with potentially high mobility (especially skilled labour and capital) are reduced or kept low (Aktan and Vural, 2004: 2).

Despite the numerous studies in the literature on tax competition, there are two models that are the references for these studies, which are considered as the building blocks of tax competition. They are the models suggested by Tiebout in 1956 and by Zodrow and Mieszkowski in 1986. (Yurdadoğ and Albayrak, 2017: 123).

The Tiebout model is based on the view that local governments in countries with a federal state structure will compete with each other in the delivery of public services. Local governments will not want to lose the support of their voters, who are also taxpayers. In the relevant model it is assumed that voters are fully mobile and will move to the territory that best meets their preference patterns, having full knowledge of the differences between income and outlay patterns and react to these differences. There are many territories that voters can move to; people's work does not prevent living in different territories – for instance, people living on dividend income and public outlays do not create any externality between territories. Accordingly, the variables that affect the choice of the local government territory that voters want to live in is emphasized. For instance, while a territory that delivers a quality education service can be a motive for a family with kids, another person may prefer a territory with golf courses. The applicability and quality of facilities and services, such as beaches, parks, police protection, roads and parking lots will influence the decision-making process. Therefore, a voter who wants a high quality public service may prefer a territory that imposes higher taxation, otherwise a voter who wants to pay less tax will prefer to live in a territory that delivers lower quality and limited public services. Thus, voters will try to maximize their benefits by preferring the most appropriate territories for them. They will continue to move until each territory reaches the optimal size. Tax competion in the Tiebout model operates similarly to market competition Local governments offer different public outlay-tax combinations according to the expectations and preferences of voters. Territories have to keep their production costs to a minimum due to competition with other territories and the efficiency of urban governors. According to Tiebout, an urban governor or an elected official who cannot keep their costs (taxes) low when compared to similar territories will his/her job in this model, and in real life. Urban governors may be under more pressure than company managers in the market to minimize costs. This is due to 1) public reluctance to pay taxes and, more importantly, 2) the costs of competitors – other territories – are a matter of public register and can be easily compared. As can be seen, according to Tiebout model, competition between local governments works for the benefit of voters, i.e. citizens (Tiebout, 1956: 418–422).

The Tiebout model was especially criticized for the fact that its hypotheses do not fully reflect the truth. That being said, a model developed to analyse federal countries in which different local tax rates are applied will not be sufficient to express the tax competion of countries in an international system with different qualifications.

Zodrow and Mieszkowski systematized the tax competition through their study in 1986. The model includes two countries that desire to attract an international mobile tax base (capital). Under the assumption that the tax revenue of one country depends on the tax rate of the other country, the tax policies of both countries are interdependent. The model predicts that this interdependence will trigger a 'race to the bottom' in taxation because each country tries to attract the mobile tax base of the other. In equilibrium, tax rates are lower in both countries than they would otherwise, resulting in a sub-optimal supply of tax-financed public goods (Genschel and Schwarz, 2011: 341).In the following years the Zodrow and Mieszkowski model was expanded a little more within the framework of two elements. It was indicated in conducted studies (Bucovetsky,

1991; Wilson, 1991; Kanburi and Keen, 1993) that the differences in country size changed the estimations of the main model. Accordingly, if competing countries are of equal size, they apply similar incentives to lower taxes and suffer equal welfare losses (symmetric tax competition). However, if country sizes are different, the smaller country will have to apply stronger incentives to lower tax rates than the larger one, and suffer less in competitive equilibrium (asymmetric tax competition). This is because, for a small country, the revenue loss from tax reduction, i.e. revenues initially lost from the domestic tax base, is relatively smaller compared to the large income revenues from the introduction of part of a large country's foreign tax base. As a result, the small country will get more revenues from the incoming foreign capital than it lost from its domestic tax base as a result of a reduction in tax rates. Wilson stated this situation as 'advantage of smallness' in tax competiton (Genschel and Schwarz, 2011: 341–2).

The second element in the expansion of Zodrow and Mieszkowski model is related to domestic constraints. In main model it is assumed that countries are completely free to identify their national tax rates as a part of tax competition. However, some political scientists stated in their studies (Hallerberg and Basinger, 1998; Hays, 2009) that governments today are subject to corporate constraints. In this framework, it is emphasized that some compensatory measures (Ganghof, 2000: 624) curb or delay (Swank and Steinmo, 2002; Genschel, 2002; Ganghof, 2006) policy adjustment against competitive pressures. Corporate constraints are mostly related to the number and ideologies of those who disagree with players involved in making tax policy. What underlies these constraints is the thought that tax reductions on mobile factors will damage the principle of equality and justice due to the limited budget revenues and the high tax burden on non-mobile factors. Including these constraints in the main model alleviates competitive downward pressure on tax rates and reveals new asymmetries. Namely, countries with lower domestic constraints will be able to set lower tax rates to attract the international mobile tax base than countries with strong domestic constraints, thus making a competitive advantage (Basinger and Hallerberg, 2004; Plümper et al., 2009).

2.1.2 *Types of Tax Competition*

Despite various classifications in different studies on tax competition, there are two generally accepted distinctions. Tax competition is classified as horizontal and vertical in terms of administrations, and is beneficial or harmful (bad) according to its impact.

2.1.2.1 Classifications In Terms of Administrations

2.1.2.1.1 Horizontal Tax Competition

There is a horizontal tax competition when two (or more than two) governments of the same level tax a mobile tax source. For instance, it is horizontal tax competition when two local (or two national) governments tax the same mobile tax source; the tax rate set by any one of the jurisdictions then affects the tax revenues of the other jurisdiction (Goodspeed, 1998: 581). Here, the important point is that all competing governments are at the same level (Wilson, 1999: 289). The tax competition among countries in the international system is also horizontal tax competition, as in local governments within a political union or federal state (Kılıçaslan, 2005: 19). Therefore, tax competiton among countries today is discussed in this classification, which is also called international tax competition (Yurdadoğ and Albayrak, 2017: 126).

2.1.2.1.2 Vertical Tax Competition

Vertical tax competition happens between two (or more than two) governments of different levels. For instance, it occurs when central and state governments tax the same source in countries with federal state structures. Here, again, as in horizontal tax competition, the tax rate set by one of the parties affects tax revenues of the other (Goodspeed, 1998: 581).

2.1.2.2 Classification According to İmpacts

2.1.2.2.1 Good Tax Competition

A certain level of tax competition is considered to be beneficial in reducing high tax rates to the optimal level. According to public choice theory, governments have to reduce their outlays on inactive fields as a result of decreasing tax revenues with the tax competition. This limits the powers of politicians and ensures that citizens' choices are considered in what direction public outlays will be made. Therefore, this type of tax competition, which enables the most efficient use of resources, is effective in increasing social welfare (Günaydın and Benk, 2003: 147–8).

That being said, the decrease in tax rates due to tax competition creates a more favourable atmosphere in terms of economic growth and development (Mitchell, 2001; Aktan and Vural, 2004: 16). Low tax rates also positively affect the voluntary tax compliance of taxpayers (Aktan and Vural, 2004: 16).

2.1.2.2.2 Harmful (Bad) Tax Competition

Harmful tax competition: it is the fact that the advantages they provide due to the competitive tax policies followed by the countries create diversion effects on the mobile production factors and, in this way, the tax bases of other countries are eroded (Saraç, 2006: 140; Taş and Karaca, 2004: 424).Harmful tax competition is a competition type that leads to diversions in international investment decisions and an erosion in national tax base of other countries, and works to the detriment of everyone due to the race to the bottom as a result of the reactions of countries subsequently damaged (Taş and Karaca, 2004: 424). In this case countries may find themselves in a 'prisoner's dilemma' or 'prisoner's deadlock'[1] (OECD, 1998: 34).

The fact that tax competition can become harmful was brought forward mostly in the studies carried out within the OECD. The harmful impacts of tax competition were identified in the report published by the OECD in 1998, in which harmful tax competition is addressed as a rising global issue. Aiming to prevent these harmful impacts, the OECD developed the study launched in 1998 with progress reports in 2000, 2001, 2004 and 2006, and continues this struggle today (Yurdadoğ and Albayrak, 2017: 141).

2.1.3 Practice Forms of International Tax Competition

'Tax havens' and 'harmful preferential tax regimes' are stated in the relevant OECD report published in 1998 as harmful tax competition practices.

2.1.3.1 Tax Havens

The concept of tax haven has no definite internationally accepted definition. However, tax havens are highly attractive for corporate and individual investors because they offer an opportunity to minimize taxes and obtain fiscal secrecy (OECD, 1998: 20,22).

Although the concept of tax haven has been used frequently in recent years, the appearance of tax havens coincides with the appearance period of tax. In Ancient Greece, merchants stored their goods on islands off Athens to avoid the 2% of tax on imported products. Switzerland is considered to be the oldest of

1 According to game theory, it is an example that two or more rational parties may not be able to cooperate even though it is in their best interests to do so. Here, it is emphasized that lack of knowledge curbs cooperation. It can be expressed as the departure of two or more parties from cooperation with similar intentions in the absence of mechanisms that provide communication and create trust (Duffy, 2015: 31: Aktaş, 2016: 37).

the modern tax havens as it is a safe and less costly shelter for the capital fleeing other territories. Switzerland, which attracted capital during the Second World War with its safe harbour identity further consolidated its status after the war as the former combatants increased their tax rates (Aktan and Vural, 2004: 11). The number of tax havens began to increase rapidly as of 1980's. Globalization, improvement in telecommunication services and liberalization in foreign exchange movements effected this increase (Bilici, 2004: 602).

In the 1998 report by the OECD (OECD, 1998: 23) it was pointed out that although there is no precise definition of the concept of tax haven, there are four important factors indicating that a country or territory is a tax haven. These factors are as follows:

a) No taxes or only nominal taxes,
b) Lack of effective exchange of information,
c) Lack of transparency in administritive practices about taxation,
d) No substantial economic activity.

The damages caused by tax haven or harmful preferential tax regime practices in other countries are listed in the relevant report by the OECD (OECD, 1998: 16) as follows:

a) Changing the direction of real investment flows both financially and indirectly,
b) Destroying the integrity of tax structures and causing injustice,
c) Affecting voluntary compliance of taxpayers with tax adversely,
d) Causing changes in the amount and combination of taxes and public outlays,
e) Causing an unfair shift in the tax burden from mobile resources to less mobile resources, especially labour, and from income to consumption,
f) Causing an increase in administrative and compliance costs for tax administrations and taxpayers.

In a study by Damgaard, Elkjaer and Johannesen (2018: 51), it was estimated that the funds held in countries considered as tax havens amount to $19 trillion ($12 trillion of which belongs to multinational companies and $7 trillion to individuals). This amount corresponds to approximately 27% of world GDP.

Tax havens become a more important issue day by day due to reasons such as they lead to capital flight and a decrease in tax rates through harmful tax competition; they faciliate illegal activities such as tax evasion and money laundering; and they cause financial instabilities to spread rapidly. As a result of all this, tax havens lead to serious disparities in global income distribution and adversely affect fighting strategies against global poverty (Arslan, 2011: 47). In addition, it is estimated that the losses of developing countries due to tax haven countries amount to three times the aid they receive from developed countries, which is an important resource that can be used to finance development (Öztürk and Ülger, 2016: 244).

2.1.3.2 Harmful Preferential Tax Regimes

Another practice form of harmful tax competition besides tax havens is harmful preferential tax regimes. In the 1998 report by the OECD (27) there is no definition for harmful preferential tax regimes such as tax havens. However, as in tax havens, the characteristics of harmful preferential tax regimes were identified by the specified factors (four main and eight auxiliary factors). According to this, main factors used in identifying harmful preferential tax regimes are:

a) Low or no effective tax rate,
b) The creation of free tax zones within the regime,
c) A lack of transparency in the operation of the system,
d) A lack of effective exchange of information.

As can be seen, three of the main factors used in determining harmful preferential tax regimes are also used in determining tax havens. Here, unlike tax havens, the advantages are limited to a specific territory or subject. Therefore, the created regime is isolated from the domestic market. This can be achieved in a number of ways (OECD, 1998: 27), including:

→ The regime may explicitly or implicitly exclude full taxpayers from taking advantage of the offered benefits,
→ Businesses benefiting from the mentioned tax regime may be prohibited from operating in the domestic market, either explicitly or implicitly.

In addition, transactions with the national currency in an isolated area may not be allowed in order to ensure that the national monetary system is not affected by the regime. Thus national economies are protected from the adverse impacts of the regime on the domestic market (OECD, 1998: 28).Auxiliary factors used in determining harmful preferential tax regimes are (OECD, 1998: 30–4):

a) Artificial or fraudulent definition of the tax base,
b) Failure to adhere to international transfer pricing principles,
c) Exemption of foreign source income from the residence country tax,
d) Negotiable tax rate and/or tax base,
e) Existence of secrecy provisions,
f) Access to a wide network of tax treaties,

g) Regimes promoted as tax minimization vehicles,
h) Regimes encouraging purely tax-driven operations and arrangements.

That being said, some free zone practices have been evaluated in the context of harmful preferential tax regimes. According to the OECD, one of the important points to pay attention to where a tax regime shifts existing activities from one country to another, one that offers preferential tax regime instead of creating new activities. However, it is difficult to determine whether the investment represents a new investment or a shift from another location in order to exploit tax differentials. Answering this question requires an analysis of both the host preferential tax regime and the tax and business environment of the home country or countries. The OECD accepts that a company may wish to move out of an unfavourable economic or political environment to a more favourable business environment, regardless of the tax incentive offered It is also accepted that the domestic tax provisions in some countries may indirectly serve to discourage or drive out investment that is independent of the tax policies pursued in other countries.Another important point for the OECD is that if the preferential tax regime is an initial priority for where an activity will be, this may indicate that the related regime is potentially harmful. In practice, it is recognized that it is not always easy for tax authorities to evaluate the priority of investors because non-tax factors, such as the quality of the infrastructure, the legal and regulatory framework, labour costs etc. may also influence location decisions (OECD, 1998: 34–5). In addition, the cases in which special tax incentives or tax regimes may be required are accepted in order to offset non-tax disadvantages for countries with certain structural disadvantages, such as poor geographical location, lack of natural resources etc. Likewise, less developed territories in countries usually have trouble in promoting their development, and they may benefit from more attractive tax regimes or tax incentives for certain activities at certain stages in their development. All indicate that many factors affect the overall competitive position of a country in itself. Although the international community has concerns about potential spillover effects, these practices are acceptable to the countries in question (OECD, 1998: 15). The point that the OECD emphasizes here is that a country directs capital and financial flows and revenue from other jurisdictions with an aggressive tax regime from the tax base of other countries. This effect is described as 'poaching' as the tax base belongs to the other country. From this point of view, if the spillover effects of certain tax practices are so important that it can be concluded that other countries poach tax bases, these practices will be described as 'harmful tax competition' (OECD, 1998: 16). Therefore, as stated in 1998 report by the OECD, all relevant factors should be considered when investigating whether a particular tax regime is harmful or not (OECD, 1998: 26).

Harmful preferential tax regimes facilitate tax evasion and money laundering, just like tax havens, as a natural consequence of the lack of effective exchange of information. Harmful preferential tax regimes that cause the meltdown of tax bases in other countries, and tax losses, lead to harmful impacts in those countries similar to tax havens.

Transfer pricing is another global tax issue that harms tax systems of countries.

2.2 Transfer Pricing

In general terms, transfer pricing can be defined as the pricing applied by businesses in the purchase and sales of goods or services, and similar operations between the units such as affiliates, departments, partnerships, sub-units or headquarters which are in the same interest group and are directly or indirectly affiliated in terms of profit sharing. When the affiliated companies are located in different countries, the pricing used is called international transfer pricing (Öncel and Öncel, 2004: 17).

The phenomenon of globalization that began to gain momentum in the 1980's contributed to the reduction of risks when entering markets in different countries, and increased the volume of international trade along with the development of e-trade. In addition, the increase in the number of multinational companies, and the mergers in parallel, led the transfer pricing practices of multinational companies to increase (Çak, 2008: 36). As a matter of fact, transfer pricing has become synonymous with the pricing of multinational companies in countries with different taxation powers as among themselves. For that reason, transfer pricing today, unless otherwise stated in literature, is considered as the pricing applied by multinational companies in the transfer of goods and services across the (Öncel, 2003: 5).

Changes (manipulations) in transfer prices have economic, political, international micro-scale business economy dimensions and relevant objectives as well as tax.However, tax dimensions and the objectives of manipulations in transfer prices are emphasized today (Öncel, 2003: 5).

As a result of the manipulations in transfer pricing, the affiliated companies can minimize the final tax burden of the relevant company community by shifting their profits, i.e. their tax bases, from countries with higher tax rates to countries with lower or no tax rates (Miesel et al., 2003). Multinational companies can determine the transfer price as higher or lower than the market price by abusing it for transactions within the group. The most important reason is the effort by multinational companies to minimize the amount of tax they pay. Considering that companies with high intracompany sales at the international level pay less tax in total than other companies, it is understood that these companies use transfer prices to reduce their total tax burden (Günaydın and Benk, 2003: 159– 60).The purposes of manipulations in transfer pricing in terms of taxation are as follows (Öncel, 2003: 6–8):

a) Maximizing the total profit after taxation,
b) Minimizing the taxes from foreign trade,
c) Receiving an excessive tax refund by changing export prices,
d) Narrowing or concealing the tax base in cases where withholding tax is applied to the price one has to pay,
e) Reducing the tax base in countries with high tax rates by shifting the costs of headquarters to the affiliated companies in countries with higher tax rates than others,
f) Overcoming the constraints of countries on foreign trade or profit transfer by changing transfer prices and therefore reducing the tax burden indirectly.

As a result of the use of transfer pricing in accordance with the purposes mentioned above, multinational companies maximize their profits or minimize their losses and, therefore, erode the tax bases of countries (Işık, 2005: v). The relevant practices cause adverse impacts on the taxation authority, national income, resource allocation, income distribution, the unemployement rate, customer prices, production inputs and balance of payments of, especially, developing countries (Günaydın and Benk, 2003: 160; Öncel, 2003: 18). Many countries adopted transfer pricing acts in order to curb tax loss and other problems caused by changes in transfer prices, and the number of regulations have been gradually increasing due to the importance of the issue in recent years (Günaydın and Benk, 2003: 160). However, national measures alone are not sufficient to find solutions to the issues caused by the globalization. In terms of international tax competition and transfer pricing, both the participating countries and communities such as the OECD and the EU have different measures and regulations, and the struggle continues in this context (Öncel and Öncel, 2004: 18).

To sum up, with the acceleration of the globalization process as of the 1980s, capital can escape from tax authorities by ways such as: international tax competition, tax havens, harmful preferential tax regimes and transfer pricing, which cause remarkable tax losses. This led public taxation authorities to experience challenges in the taxation of the capital. These events also caused significant changes in the combination of taxes. Taxation authorities preferred to include new indirect taxes into their system to compensate for the decreasing tax revenue.

Direct tax-weighted tax systems have now been replaced by a structure where indirect taxes are predominant, and indirect tax revenue has exceeded 60% of the total tax revenues on average, especially in many developing countries. The main payer of these taxes is the labour sector, which has to allocate a significant part of its income to consumption. That being said, while the share of corporate taxes within direct taxes decreased, especially the taxes on labour, incomes (payroll taxes) began to be a significant part of income tax revenue. Therefore, the challenge to tax the capital in globalization process caused the tax burden to increase and this created an unfair structure (Balseven, 2019: 15).

In addition, the challenges facing governments to create funds in this process made borrowing an ordinary public financing method. The growing financial markets created various opportunities for governments in domestic and foreign borrowing, but increased interest rates due to macroeconomic instability, while crises increased the cost of borrowing and thereto the burden of borrowers. Governments as well as households and companies began to bear high debt burdens that increased year by year. When taxation and borrowing policies in the globalization process were evaluated together, it was seen that these policies led to adverse impacts on income distribution and were ineffective in creating funds, and in this respect they limited governmental opportunities to deliver redistributive goods and services (Balseven, 2019: 16).

3 Evaluation and Conclusion

As of the 1980s, when globalization process gained momentum, significant changes have been experienced in governments' economic, fiscal and social functions. In this process the factor of capital that managed to escape from tax authorities through ways such as international tax competition, tax havens, harmful preferential tax regimes and transfer pricing began to cause remarkable tax losses. Harmful tax competition was discussed as a rising global issue in the 1998 report by the OECD. Tax havens and harmful preferential tax regimes facilitate tax evasion and money laundering as a natural consequence of the lack of effective exchange of information. In addition, with the tax policies they implement, they cause tax losses and the erosion of the tax base of other countries. The manipulations in transfer prices also cause adverse impacts on taxation authority, national income, resource allocation, income distribution, unemployment rates, customer prices, production inputs and balance of payments, especially for developing countries. These practices, which increased with the acceleration of globalization after 1980, greatly affected the tax systems of countries and caused significant changes in the composition of taxes. In general, the change caused by globalization in taxation policies was especially in the form of a reduction in tax rates on capital and an increase in the weight of indirect data and tax incentives. As a result of the increase in the weight of indirect taxes in the tax systems, indirect taxes began to be almost two-thirds of the total tax revenues, especially in many developing countries. The challenge in taxation of capital during the globalization process played a significant role in making the tax structure unfair. Borrowing became a common public financing method due to governments' challenges in generating funds by this process. Increasing interest rates increased the cost of borrowing and the burdens of borrowers. All these policies affected income distribution adversely, and the ineffectiveness in creating funds caused erosion in governments' social policy practices.

Developing countries had to be involved in the globalization process before they could develop their economic, social, cultural, physical infrastructures sufficiently; i.e. they could not complete their own development moves. For that reason, the relevant countries were much more affected by the adverse impacts of this process when compared to developed countries.

However, national measures alone will not be sufficient to solve the problems caused by globalization. In addition to these measures, countries should act together to find common solutions to the taxation problems caused by globalization. As national measures, a registration system should be extended, especially in developing countries, and efficiency in tax administration and audit should be ensured in order to reduce tax losses and evasion. Therefore, the tax base should be broadened by recording the informal economy. In this way, it will be possible to reduce tax rates that cause a decrease in tax revenues to a reasonable level. In addition, informality in the country of capital outflow plays an important role in capital movements towards tax havens and harmful preferential tax regimes. For that reason, curbing informality is of great importance in terms of keeping the capital in the country. In addition, it is necessary to concentrate on the international struggle to create a fair tax competition atmosphere and to increase international cooperation Only in this way will it be possible to force countries that are tax havens, and countries implementing harmful preferential tax regimes, to exchange information and to be more transparent.

References

Aktan, C. C. and Vural, İ. Y. (2004). Vergi Rekabeti, Erciyes Üniversitesi İktisadi ve İdari Bilimler Fakültesi Dergisi, (22), 1–18.

Aktaş, M. C. (2016). Küresel Kamu Mallarının Uluslararası İşbirliklerinde Kullanımı ve Türkiye İçin Öneriler, (Uzmanlık Tezi), Ankara: T.C. Kalkınma Bakanlığı, No. 2959.

Arslan, M. O. (2011). Vergi Cennetleri ve Küresel Yoksulluk, Vergi Raporu, (142), 42–48.

Balseven, H. (2019). Küreselleşme ve Kamu Maliyesi, Uluslararası Kamu Maliyesi (Ed.: Tekin, F. and Arslan, M. O.), Eskişehir: T.C. Anadolu Üniversitesi Açık Öğretim Fakültesi Yayını, No. 3961/2745, 2–25.

Basinger, S. and Hallerberg, M. (2004). Remodeling the Competition for Capital: How Domestic Politics Erases the Race to the Bottom, American Political Science Review, 98, 261–276'dan Genschel, P. and Schwarz, P. (2011). Tax Competition: A Literature Review, Socio-Economic Review, 9, 339–370.

Bilici, N. (2004). Vergi Cennetleri ile Mücadele (Tebliğ, 19. Türkiye Maliye Sempozyumu, Antalya, Türkiye, 10–14 Mayıs), 601–620.

Çak, M. (2008). Uluslararası Vergi Rekabeti Transfer Fiyatlaması ve Vergilendirme, Ankara: T.C. Maliye Bakanlığı Strateji Geliştirme Başkanlığı Yayını, No. 2008/385.

Damgaard, J., Elkjaer, T. and Johannesen, N. (2018). Some $12 Trillion Worldwide is Just Phantom Corporate Investment, Finance and Development, 51–53, https://www.imf.org/external/pubs/ft/fandd/2018/06/inside-the-world-of-global-tax-havens-and-offshore-banking/damgaard.pdf (21.01.2021).

Duffy, J. (2015). Game Theory and Nash Equilibrium, Thunder Bay: Lakehead University.

Genschel, P. and Schwarz, P. (2011). Tax Competition: A Literature Review, Socio-Economic Review, 9, 339–370.

Goodspeed, T. J. (1998). Tax Competition, Benefit Taxes And Fiscal Federalism, National Tax Journal, 51(3), 579–586.

Günaydın, İ. and Benk, S. (2003). Globalleşmenin Vergi Sistemlerinde Ortaya Çıkardığı Sorunlar ve Çözüm Önerileri – I, Vergi Sorunları, (179), 138–161.

Işık, H. (2005). Çok Uluslu Şirketlerde Örtülü Kazanç ve Örtülü Sermaye, Uluslararası Düzenlemeler ve Uygulamalar ile Türk Vergi Sisteminin Karşılaştırılması ve Öneriler, Ankara: T.C. Maliye Bakanlığı Araştırma, Planlama ve Koordinasyon Kurulu Başkanlığı, No. 2005/370.

Kılıçaslan, H. (2005). Avrupa Birliği'nde Vergi Rekabeti ve Türkiye, İstanbul: İktisadi Araştırmalar Vakfı.

Miesel, V. H., Higinbotham, H. H. and Yi, C. W. (2003). International Transfer Pricing, The International Tax Journal, Winter'dan Öncel, T. and Öncel, Y. (2004). Uluslararası Vergi Rekabeti, Maliye Araştırma Merkezi Konferansları, Kırküçüncü-Kırkdördüncü Seri, İstanbul Üniversitesi İktisat Fakültesi Maliye Araştırma Merkezi Yayını, 1–25.

Mitchell, D. (2001). A Tax Competition Primer: Why Tax Harmonization and Information Exchange Undermine America's Competitive Advantage in the

Global Economy, The Heritage Foundation, https://www.heritage.org/taxes/report/tax-competition-primer-why-tax-harmonization-and-information-exchange-undermine (17.01.2021).

OECD (1998). Harmful Tax Competition, An Emerging Global Issue, https://www.oecd.org/tax/harmful/1904176.pdf (06.12.2018).

Öncel, T. and Öncel, Y. (2004). Uluslararası Vergi Rekabeti, Maliye Araştırma Merkezi Konferansları, Kırküçüncü-Kırkdördüncü Seri, İstanbul Üniversitesi İktisat Fakültesi Maliye Araştırma Merkezi Yayını, 1–25.

Öncel, Y. (2003). Transfer Fiyatlaması, Örtülü Kazanç Dağıtımı ve Vergilendirme, Maliye Araştırma Merkezi Konferansları, Kırkbirinci Seri, İstanbul Üniversitesi İktisat Fakültesi Maliye Araştırma Merkezi Yayını, 1–19.

Öztürk, S. and Ülger, Ö. (2016). Vergi Cennetlerinin Küresel Finansal Kriz Üzerine Ekonomik Etkileri: Vergi Kaçırma, Vergiden Kaçınma ve Kara Para Aklamadaki Rolü, Niğde Üniversitesi İktisadi ve İdari Bilimler Fakültesi Dergisi, 9(1), 237–254.

Plümper, T., Troeger, V. E. and Winner, H. (2009). Why Is There No Race to the Bottom in Capital Taxation?, International Studies Quarterly, 53, 761–786'dan Genschel, P. and Schwarz, P. (2011). Tax Competition: A Literature Review, Socio-Economic Review, 9, 339–370.

Saraç, Ö. (2006). Küresel Vergi Rekabeti ve Ulusal Vergi Politikaları, Türkiye Değerlendirmesi, Ankara: Maliye ve Hukuk Yayınları.

Tanzi, V. Globalization, Tax System and the Architecture of the Global Economic System, 1–23, https://publications.iadb.org/publications/english/document/Globalization-Tax-System-and-the-Architecture-of-the-Global-Economic-System.pdf (10.01.2021).

Taş, B. and Karaca, Y. (2004). Küreselleşmenin Vergi Sistemleri Üzerindeki Etkileri Açısından İki Önemli Konu: Vergi Rekabeti ve Elektronik Ticaret (Tebliğ, 19. Türkiye Maliye Sempozyumu, Antalya, Türkiye, 10–14 Mayıs), 421–463.

Tiebout, C. M. (1956). A Pure Theory of Local Expenditure, The Journal of Political Economy, 64(5), 416–424.

Wilson, J. D. (1999). Theories of Tax Competition, National Tax Journal, 52(2), 269–304.

Yurdadoğ, V. and Albayrak, M. (2017). OECD Ülkelerinde Vergi Rekabeti, Sosyoekonomi, 25(32), 121–148.

Şebnem Ekeryilmaz

Force Majeure in Turkish Tax Law

1 Introduction

In Turkish Tax Law, *force majeure* is defined by Article 13 of the Tax Procedure Law (TPL). *Force majeure* is an event or circumstance beyond the control of the taxpayer that prevents the taxpayer from fulfilling his/her tax obligations.

The law states that *force majeure* occurs in circumstances such as a serious accident, a severe disease, imprisonment, natural disasters, involuntary absence and involuntary loss of tax books and documents. However, the use of the phrase *'circumstances such as'* at the end of the article describing *force majeure* stipulates that uncited events beyond the taxpayer's control that prevent the fulfillment of tax obligations are to be regarded as *force majeure* events.

Force majeure also suspends tax processes, and tax payments are postponed until the *force majeure* event ceases. Moreover, if the occurrence of the *force majeure* event is common knowledge or can be proven by the taxpayer with documents, a tax penalty is not imposed.

It is critical to examine the institution of *force majeure* which suspends tax processes and prevents the imposition of tax penalties. Within the scope of the measures implemented because of the ongoing COVID-19 pandemic, the institution of *force majeure* gained prominence. This study provides a detailed examination of the institution of *force majeure* in judicial decisions to concrete cases, discusses issues with the institution of *force majeure* and proposes solutions.

The institution of *force majeure*, a matter of prime importance to tax cases, is examined conceptually in Section 2. Section 3 discusses the *force majeure* provisions in the TPL and *force majeure*-related judicial decisions in detail. Lastly, Section 4 discusses issues with the institution of *force majeure*, as well as solution proposals.

2 Conceptual Analysis of *Force Majeure*

The Turkish Language Association's dictionary characterizes the concept of force majeure as an unforeseeable and, notwithstanding measures taken by any party, unavoidable event that prevents the fulfillment of a debt beyond the control of the liable party.

Based on this definition, *force majeure* in tax law signifies serious unavoidable circumstances outside the control of the taxpayer that hinders the fulfillment of financial and formal tax obligations.

In another definition, *force majeure* was described as compelling reasons that occur unexpectedly (Pehlivan, 2020: 120).

In Decision No. 2007–6248 by the Eleventh Chamber of the Council of State, *force majeure* was defined as '*an unpredictable and irresistible event*'. This decision also delineates the characteristics of *force majeure* as unforeseeability, unavoidability and inculpability.

Within each branch of law, there are natural or artificial circumstances that related parties cannot foresee or prevent, but which constitute *force majeure* (Erol, 2012: 201). On the other hand, in the domain of private law, *force majeure* involves the occurrence of an unforeseeable and unavoidable event unrelated to the debtor's business activity that prevents the fulfillment of a debt or a general liability. An incident must involve the elements of externality, unpredictability and irresistibility to be characterized as a *force majeure* event (Yıldırım, 2019: 1521).

Although laws do not provide a definition of *force majeure*, they set forth events that might constitute *force majeure*. Law articles on *force majeure* comprise a list of events that constitute *force majeure*, as well as the characteristics of a *force majeure* event to cover circumstances not indicated on the list (Theroux and Grosse, 2011: 402).

In Decision No. 2020–5962 by the Eleventh Chamber of the Council of State, unforeseeable circumstances and *force majeure* events were used interchangeably. *Force majeure* encompasses unforeseeable circumstances, as well as events that are unavoidable, even if foreseeable. Therefore, a *force majeure* event is more comprehensive than unforeseeable circumstances.

The common characteristics of a *force majeure* event are as follows (Şenyüz, 2020: 302–303):

- They occur outside the taxpayer's control. The taxpayer does not contribute to their occurrence.
- They are extraneous and irresistible events that are impossible to foresee and, even if foreseen, to avoid.
- They are beyond the taxpayer's control and prevent the fulfillment of tax duties, rendering completion of tax duties impossible outside the taxpayer's will.
- In the presence of *force majeure* conditions, the taxpayer cannot be considered to be at fault.

In tax law, *force majeure* has legal consequences if taxpayers fail to perform their tax obligations on time or exercise their tax-related rights, protecting taxpayers (Ekmekci et al., 2020: 1077).

3 *Force Majeure* Provisions in the Tax Procedure Law

In the TPL, *force majeure* events that hinder taxpayers from fulfilling their tax obligations are classified in four categories:

- Serious accident, severe disease or imprisonment preventing fulfillment of tax obligations.
- Natural disasters such as fire, earthquake and flood preventing fulfillment of tax obligations.
- Involuntary absence beyond the taxpayer's control.
- Loss of books and documents due to reasons beyond the taxpayer's control.

Circumstances that fulfil the first *force majeure* condition are serious accident, severe disease or imprisonment which prevents the taxpayer from fulfilling his/her tax obligations. According to this provision, the accident, disease or imprisonment must be severe enough to prevent fulfillment of tax obligations. For instance, suffering minor injuries in a traffic accident would not be regarded *force majeure* as per this provision.

The unexpected prolongation of the ongoing COVID-19 pandemic is an example of a *force majeure* event. The inability of taxpayers, who contracted the disease and suffered severe symptoms and long-term problems, to perform their tax duties can be regarded as *force majeure*.

In the TPL General Communique No. 524 dated 25 January 2021, taxpayers whose activities were suspended within the scope of the COVID-19 measures imposed by the Ministry of the Interio, were acknowledged to be under *force majeure* from 1 February 2020 until the date they resumed their normal activities.

The General Communique extended the time limit for withholding tax, value added tax and Form BA/BS declarations whose legal submission dates coincided with the *force majeure* period – and thereby were required to be submitted within this period – until the end of the 26th day of the month following the date of termination of the *force majeure* conditions, for those taxpayers considered to be subject to *force majeure*. Furthermore, payment periods for taxes accrued on the basis of these declarations were extended until the end of the following month, for each successive period, beginning with the month following the declaration period specified in the legislation.

For instance, C.M. has income and value added tax obligations. C.M.'s business activity was temporarily suspended within the scope of the Ministry of the Interior's measures for COVID-19, which was regarded as a *force majeure* event in accordance with the Communique. If C.M. recommences business on 1 May 2021, s/he is required to submit VAT and Form BA/BS declarations by the end of 26 May 2021.

The Turkish Constitutional Court Individual Application Judgment No. 2013–4690 ruled that if the applicant cannot submit an individual application on time due to an acceptable excuse, such as *force majeure* or severe illness, the applicant can apply within fifteen days after the end of the excuse, with evidence documenting the excuse, establishing that an acceptable excuse such as *force majeure* or severe illness would extend the application period.

Circumstances that constitute the second *force majeure* condition are natural disasters such as fire, earthquake and flood that prevent taxpayers from fulfilling tax obligations. Although the said provision does not cite all natural disasters with examples, other uncited natural disasters that can hinder the fulfillment of tax obligations are included via the phrase '*natural disasters such as*'. However, if the occurrence of a natural disaster does not hinder the fulfillment of tax obligations, the presence of *force majeure* conditions will not be accepted (Biyan, 2020: 99).

Circumstances that create the third *force majeure* condition are compulsory absences beyond the taxpayer's control that prevent taxpayers from fulfilling tax obligations. For instance, being in quarantine due to the ongoing COVID-19 pandemic constitutes a *force majeure* situation for taxpayers.

Within the scope of *force majeure*, serious illness or involuntary absence due to COVID-19 will result in tax-related extensions of time (Karadağ, 2020: 402).

Circumstances that constitute the third *force majeure* condition include the loss of books and documents due to reasons beyond the taxpayer's control. The loss of books and documents must be involuntary and out of the taxpayer's control. Therefore, a taxpayer who has destroyed tax books and documents cannot claim *force majeure* (Karakoç, 2019: 214).

The General Assembly on the Unification of Judgments of the Council of State (Decision No. 2019–1) ruled that failure to present tax books and documents due to *force majeure* was cause for ex-officio assessment.

Article 15 of the TPL, entitled postponement in case of *force majeure*, prescribes the suspension of tax processes during a *force majeure* event as follows: 'In the event of any of the force majeure incidents prescribed in Article 13, processes are suspended until the end of the force majeure incident, and the statutes of limitations for tax collection are extended for the duration of the suspension. For this provision to be implemented, the force majeure incident must be evident or be proved or documented by related parties.'

In addition, the Turkish Constitutional Court Decision No. 2019–72 states that the five-day statutory period set out in the TPL regarding electronic tax declaration would be suspended in case of a *force majeure* event.

With the occurrence of a *force majeure* event, the statutes of limitations for tax collection are suspended in favour of the administration. Although the suspension of tax processes benefits taxpayers, the suspension of the statutes of limitations for tax collection is a disadvantageous outcome for taxpayers (Karadağ, 2012: 1031).

In the event of a *force majeure* incident, this article also authorizes the Ministry of Treasury and Finance to declare a state of *force majeure* in places affected by the *force majeure* incident and to identify the taxpayers who would not be able to fulfill their tax obligations. The Ministry of Treasury and Finance is further entitled to redesignate tax declaration deadlines or revoke the obligation of tax declaration, pursuant to the authorization granted by the law.

Article 111 of the TPL, regulating tax payment periods, authorizes the Ministry of Treasury and Finance to postpone payment of taxes, fines and default interests with a payment period that corresponds to a later date than the occurrence of a natural disaster, for a maximum period of one year after the respective deadlines, in places where the *force majeure* was declared.

A tax penalty is not imposed if the occurrence of the *force majeure* event is common knowledge or can be proven by the taxpayer with documentation. In Turkish criminal law, the manifestation of a *force majeure* incident is one of the causes of removal of culpability (Karakoç, 2019: 355).

Turkish criminal Llaw does not resort to punishment for lack of control or intent, based on the impossibility of the offender to abide by the law due to *force majeure*. As it impossible for the offender to comply with the law, there is no criminal liability (Şenyüz, 2020: 302). Moreover, the existence of *force majeure* circumstances is considered to be a legitimate defence in tax evasion offences (Çakar and Saraçoğlu, 2014: 417).

The TPL does not stipulate an absolute requirement of form for proving the existence of *force majeure* conditions; a certificate of loss from commercial courts, as well as legally valid documents obtained from the concerned authority can be used as evidence. The quality of the evidence is assessed by competent courts according to the characteristics of the incident (The General Assembly on the Unification of Judgments of the Council of State Decision No. 2019–1 dated July 25, 2019).

In Decision No. 2020–3699, the Fourth Chamber of the Council of State decided imposed a triple tax penalty for failure to submit a certificate of loss, despite the claimant's statement that the books and documents for the year 2009 were destroyed when the workplace was flooded.

The decision of the Fourth Chamber of the Council of State is legitimate with respect to Article 373 of the TPL, which stipulates two conditions for waiving a tax penalty on account of *force majeure*:

- The occurrence of the *force majeure* event must be public knowledge,
- The occurrence of the *force majeure* event must be documented and proven by the taxpayer.

Only one of these two conditions needs to be met for the rejection of a *force majeure* claim. In the abovementioned case, the taxpayer was not able to prove the existence of a *force majeure* situation by submitting a certificate of loss, despite claiming the books and documents were destroyed due to flooding. Therefore, the decision of the Fourth Chamber of the Council of State was appropriate, given the claimant's failure to fulfill the stipulation of evidence.

4 Conclusion

In tax law, *force majeure* indicates serious unforeseeable, and even foreseeable, unavoidable events beyond the control of the taxpayer that prevents the fulfillment of financial and formal tax obligations.

The occurrence of a *force majeure* event suspends tax processes and statute of limitations for tax collection, precludes the imposition of tax penalties and, as per the Turkish Constitutional Court Individual Application Judgment No. 2013–4690, extends the prescribed period to litigate a claim.

Circumstances that constitute a *force majeure* event are classified in only four categories in the TPL: serious accident, severe illness and imprisonment; natural disasters; involuntary absence; and involuntary loss of books and documents.

Utilization of the phrase *'circumstances such as'* in the relevant article of law is appropriate as it is possible for events that cannot be foreseen by lawmakers to befall taxpayers, preventing the fulfillment of tax duties.

Due to the impossibility of listing all *force majeure* circumstances in the law, the tax administration is authorized with determining whether any *force majeure* circumstances other than those listed in the law has occurred. In addition to the tax administration, the judiciary also provides a judicial interpretation on whether the said circumstances constitute a *force majeure* event when a taxpayer goes to court in case of a tax dispute.

Notwithstanding the impossibility of citing all *force majeure* events in the law, it would be expedient for both taxpayers and the state to conduct a more comprehensive regulation on *force majeure* in the TPL in order to promote the comprehensibility of the institution of *force majeure* on important issues such as taxation law.

Furthermore, Paragraph 2 of Article 13 on *force majeure* contains the phrase '*natural disasters, such as fire, earthquake and flood, that prevent the fulfillment of tax obligations*'. It would be appropriate to transcribe this phrase as '*natural disasters that prevent the fulfillment of tax obligations*' for the sake of brevity.

The institution of *force majeure* has gained prominence with the ongoing COVID-19 pandemic. The declaration of *force majeure* for taxpayers and the suspension of tax duties due to the ongoing pandemic in accordance with the TPL General Communique No. 524 has been an expedient measure imposed for the benefit of taxpayers.

References

Biyan, Ö. (2020). Mali Hukuk Açısından Mücbir Sebep. 1. Baskı, İstanbul, Legal Yayıncılık.

Çakar, E. P., and Saraçoğlu, F. (2014). VERGİDE ÖZGÜRLÜK İLKESİ. Ankara Hacı Bayram Veli Üniversitesi Hukuk Fakültesi Dergisi, 18(3), 409–434.

Ekmekci, E., Güneş, G., Kaşıkcı, M., and Gümüşkaya, G. (2020). Vergi Hukukunda Mücbir Sebep ve Hukuksal Sonuçları Üzerine Eleştirisel Bir Yaklaşım ve Öneriler. İstanbul Hukuk Mecmuası, 78(2), 1069–1138.

Erol, A. (2012). Mükellef Hakkı Olarak Mücbir Sebepler ve Sonuçları. TBB Dergisi, 103, 200–222.

Karadağ, N. C. (2012). Zamanaşımı sürelerine etkisi açısından "mücbir sebepler" ve "ödeme" ye eleştirel bakış. Ankara Üniversitesi Hukuk Fakültesi Dergisi, 61(3), 1017–1056.

Karadağ, N. C. (2020). Covid-19 Pandemisi Ve Alinan Önlemlerin Vergi Hukuku Açisindan Değerlendirilmesi. Çukurova Üniversitesi Sosyal Bilimler Enstitüsü Dergisi, 29(3), 400–413.

Karakoç, Y. (2019). Vergi Ceza Hukuku (2. Baskı). Ankara: Yetkin Yayınları.

Pehlivan, O. (2020). Vergi Hukuku Genel Hükümler ve Türk Vergi Sistemi. Celepler Matbaacılık, Trabzon.

Theroux, M., and Grosse, A. D. (2011). Force majeure in Canadian law. Alberta Law Review, 49, 397–425.

Yıldırım, T. (2019). Danıştay Kararlarında Mücbir Sebep Kavramı. Marmara Üniversitesi Hukuk Fakültesi Hukuk Araştırmaları Dergisi, 25(2), 1520–1538.

Şenyüz, D. (2020). Vergi Ceza Hukuku, 11. Baskı, Bursa, Ekin Kitabevi.

Türk Dil Kurumu, https://sozluk.gov.tr/, Date of access: 05.02.2020.

Tax Procedure Law dated, January 4, 1961.

Tax Procedure Law General Communique No. 524 dated, January 25, 2020.

In Decision No. 2020–5962, File No. 2020-4852 by the Eleventh Chamber of the Council of State dated December 18, 2020.

Turkish Constitutional Court Decision No. 2019–72, File No. 2018-144 dated September 19, 2019.

The Turkish Constitutional Court Individual Application Judgment No. 2013–4690 dated February 25, 2016.

The General Assembly on the Unification of Judgments of the Council of State Decision No. 2019–1, File No. 2013-3 dated July 25, 2019.

In Decision No. 2020–3699, File No. 2016-20354 the Fourth Chamber of the Council of State dated October 12, 2020.

In Decision No. 2007–6248, File No. 2005-1353 by the Eleventh Chamber of the Council of State dated June 29, 2007.

Melike Torun and Ezgi Demir

Performance Ranking of the Istanbul Stock Exchange Traded Turkish Banks with Fuzzy Sets

1 Introduction

In todays worldwide competitive financial markets it is vital for banks and other financial institutions to evaluate their performance compared to others – to stand and stay alive. As uncertainty increases in the financial markets, investor and policy makers' need for dependable instructions rises too. Therefore, a proper evaluation of the performance of the banks and financial institutions is crucial in the banking sector, as well as the financial system. While performance measurements clearly reveal the status of banks, bank managers may also have consequences such as evaluating the sustainability of the bank in question within the financial system, identifying the strengths and weaknesses of their banks, and determining new targets and practices if necessary.

Meanwhile, the commercial banks carrying out deposit collection and lending activities as their main intermadiary role take a significant place both in the banking sector and the real sector (Torun and Altay, 2019). Therefore, the measurement of commercial banks' performance is necessary to evaluate the country's economy. In this regard, the aim of this study is to analyse the performance ranking of the Turkish commercial banks and the Istanbul Stock Exchange with multi criteria decision-making methods. After the establishment of the Banking Regulation and Supervision Agency, which manages the risks of the Turkish banking sector, heavily affected by the 1994 and 2001 banking crises, it can be stated that the performance of the Turkish banking sector has improved.

In the literature, scientific studies conducted the CAMELS method and applied credit ratings in an attempt to evaluate the performance of the banking sector in many countries. The CAMELS analysis includes six components, which are: capital adequacy (C); asset quality (A); management quality (M); earnings (E); liquidity (L); and senstivity to market risk (S). As a part of CAMELS the financial ratio analysis is broadly utilized for the evaluation of the banks performance. Moreover, some of the studies applied variables, such as financial ratios, from CAMELS components. Broadly used financial ratios from CAMELS components are; **Capital Adequacy Ratio** (HYPERLINK \l "Koetter et al.,2007; Helhel and Varshalomidze, 2014; HYPERLINK \l "Mandic et al.,2014; HYPERLINK \l "Sun et al. 2017);

Total Loans and Receivables / Total Assets (Helhel and Varshalomidze, 2014); **ROA** (HYPERLINK \l "Bian and Deng, 2017; HYPERLINK \l "Saeed et al. 2020; Simoens and Vennet 2020); **ROE** (Helhel and Varshalomidze, 2014; HYPERLINK \l "Bian and Deng, 2017; HYPERLINK \l "Saeed et al. 2020); **Loans to Deposits**; (HYPERLINK \l "Saeed et al. 2020); **Assets/ Total Sector Assets**; (HYPERLINK \l "Saeed et al. 2020); **Net Interest Margin** (Gerhardt and Vennet, 2017; HYPERLINK \l "Sun et al. 2017; Simoens and Vennet 2020); **Non-performing Loans to Total Loans** (NPL Ratio) (Epure and Lafuente 2014; HYPERLINK \l "Bian and Deng, 2017; Gerhardt and Vennet,2017; HYPERLINK \l "Saeed et al. 2020).

All these studies indicate convincing signs about the bank performance and credit rating (Yuksel et al.,2015). To the best of our knowledge, the studies generally used used financial ratios from the banks' balance sheet; few of them used bank-specific macro variables, but few global variables affect the country's economy. Therefore, to fill the gap in the scientific literature, we included financial ratios, macro variables and global indicators: the global financial markets carry a lot of risks that should be included in the analysis. For the Turkish real sector, most foreign trade transactions are done with European countries; therefore, European Gross Domestic Product (EU GDP) was also analysed.

In our analysis, the macro variables **Exhange Rate and Gross Domestic Product (GDP)** for Turkey and global variables **GDP for European, GDP of World** have been applied as well as bank-specific financial ratios (**Capital Adequacy Ratio, Sensitivity to Capital Adequacy Ratio, Liquid assets / Total Assets (Asset Quality), Current Ratio, ROA, ROE, NPL ratio, Net Interest Margin, Deposit Interest Rate, Rediscount rate** and **Overnight Interest Rate**, to evaluate the performance ranking of the Istanbul Stock Exhange and traded Turkish banks. For this purpose, financial data of the Istanbul Stock Exchange traded banks, which are ten commercial banks and two investment banks. The banks, included in the analysis were Akbank, Denizbank, Garanti BBVA, Halkbank, ICBC Bank, İş Bank, Türkiye Kalkınma Yatırım Bankası, Türkiye Sınai Kalkınma Bankası, Şekerbank, Vakıflar Bankası, Yapı Kredi and QNB Finansbank. In order to achieve the aim, the points structure of the CAMELS method was utilized to maintain weights for the diverse criteria in the Netrosophic AHP method.

This chapter has been organized into an introduction part, a literature review part, a methodology and analysis part and a conclusion, respectively.

2 Literature Review

In the literature, many studies analysed the determinants affected the peformance of the banks by performing different empricial techniques. In our study, as we preferred the Fuzzy Analytic Hierarchy Process (AHP) to evaluate the bank performance, the relevant literature covering multi-criteria decision method conducted studies are investigated in this review part. So we used Neutrosophic AHP method to weight the criteria. And the included banks have been sorted by the Neutrosophic Technique for Order Preference by Similarity to Ideal Solution (TOPSIS) method. Commonly-applied research methodologies with variable and country details can be summarized as seen in Table 1.

In our study, one of the most utilized multiple criteria decision-making techniques, the Analytic Hierarchy Process (AHP) method, developed by Saaty (2000) was choosen to evaluate the ranking of the commercial banks and the investment bank's peformances traded in the Stock Exchange. AHP is a tool that utilizes pairwise comparisions in conjunction with professional decisions for the evaluation of both qualitative and intangible criteria. Also it helps to sustain a link among measurable value functions and ratio judgements, utilizing numerical values taken from the principal scale of 1–9 (Greco et al., 2016).

Several studies were conducted to evaluate the performance of the banks by utilizing the AHP method. Che et al. (2010) tried to determine a precise and effective decision-making module together with the loan weightings to determine the substantial indicator of the assesment of loans for small and medium sized enterprises in Taiwan. First, they utilized a fuzzy AHP for the evaluation of bank loan decisions and then used the DEA method in order to avoid the overdue loans.

The study of Stankevičienė and Mencaitė (2012) employed an AHP method as a multicriteria decision-making model to evaluate the performance of Lithuanian commercial banks. The result of the study confirmed that this method was appropriate for the comparision of banks and brings to light their ranking and specifies the banks leading positions in the banking system.

Ferreira et al. (2014) utilized an AHP-based approach in the credit scoring system for the evaluation of credit risks for mortgage loans. With the aim of regulating trade-offs between assessment criteria and maintaining a more transparent mortagage risk evaluation framework for the decision-makers, some studies conducted hybrid models, such as by combining the fuzzy AHP and TOPSIS methodologies (Mandic et al., 2014) and the AHP approach and VIKOR method (Chang and Tsai, 2016). The purpose of Mandic et al. (2014), by utilizing both Fuzzy AHP and TOPSIS methods as a hybrid model, was to assess the financial performance of the Serbian banking sector from 2005 to 2010.

Chang and Tsai (2016) performed both AHP and VIKOR approaches to measure the performance of Taiwan's seven wealth management (WM) banks. The result of their study highlighted that risk control, consumer confidence and service are higher key factors than the other factors such as performance and professionalism.

Tab. 1: *The Studies of Bank Performance Measurement with Multi Criteria Decision Methods*

Author/Authors	Country	Method*	Variables	Measurement
Ayadi et al. (1998)	Nigeria	Data Envelopment Analysis (DEA)	Interest income, total expenses, total loans, total deposits and non-interest income of ten banks, on the Nigerian Stock Exhange (1991–1994)	Bank performance
Lin and Chiu (2013)	Taiwanese Domestic Banks, Research period is 2009.	Network DEA together with Independent Component Analysis (ICA)	Fixed assets, equity, operating expenses, deposits, loans, interest revenue and profit.	Bank performance of the Taiwanese domestic banking
Fukuyama and Matousek (2017)	Japanese Banks, from September 2000 to March 2013.	Network DEA Approach	Deposits, interest income, premises and real estate, number of workers, securities investment, NPL and performing loans.	Bank performance of the Japanese banks from 2000 to 2013.
Doumpos and Zopounidis (2010)	18 Banks in Greece (From 2001 to 2005)	PROMETHEE* II Method	In accordance with the CAMELS framework (14 qualitative and 17 quantitative criteria)	Bank performance of the Banks in Greece
Ic et al. (2020)	Turkish Commercial Banks (From 2011 to 2016)	VIKOR** Method	Total Equity/Total Assets, Total Loans/ Total Assets, Liquid Assets/ Total Assets, Net Interest Income after Special Provisions/ Total Assets, Net Interest Income after Special Provisions/ Total Operating Income (expenses), Consumer Loans/ Total Loans and Receivables, Total Deposits/ Total Assets	Bank performance
Ic (2021)	13 industries, each sector with seven financial ratios.	Multi-objective on the basis of ratio analysis (MOORA) Method and Goal Programming (GP)	(Both qualitative and quantitative criteria.) As for financial ratios: Ratio of Net Earning to Equity, Ratio of Operating Profits to Net Sales, Ratio of Net Earnings to Net Sales, Ratio of Bank Debt to Equity, Ratio of Total Liabilities to Total Assets, Current Ratio and Liquidity Ratio	Credit evaluation process

* Preference Ranking Organization Method for Enrichment of Evaluation (PROMETHEE).
** VIseKriterijumska Optimizacija I Kompromisno Resenje (VIKOR)

The recent study of Fernando and Siagian (2021) used the AHP Method within credit analysis evaluation, known as the 5C analysis (Capital, Capacity, Character, Conditions of economy and collateral) to estimate the bank credit offer. The result of the study indicated that the method helped to evaluate the decision to give a loan, or not, to the applicant.

3 Methodology

Fuzzy logic is a mathematical theory put forward by Zadeh in 1965 in her work 'Fuzzy Sets' published in the journal 'Information and Control'. Zadeh defined fuzzy clusters as sets of graded and continuous membership objects. Fuzzy set elements, unlike classical sets, are elements assigned by a membership function with degrees of membership ranging from 0 to 1 (Zadeh, 1965). The judgements made in case of uncertainty are not final. It gives results close to the actual result. In general, incomplete information sources such as complexity and uncertainty that occur in different forms are called fuzzy resources. Fuzzy means that complete and imprecise information expresses. Fuzzy means that complete and imprecise information expresses. Fuzziness is to express linguistically for the information received. People use verbal and linguistic expressions while expressing their judgements about various problems in their daily and business lives, and in solving these problems. Understanding and expressing fuzziness in these situations, involving verbal expressions and using them to solve problems, is related to the concept of 'fuzzy logic'. Fuzzy logic has been used when there is a need for personal evaluations, opinions and thoughts due to the lack of sufficient information and data about a situation or event. Thus, it is possible to use intuition and other abilities to solve problems.

In this study, 2019, the variables of the Istanbul Stock Exchange Traded Turkish banks were taken. The data from ten commercial banks and two investments banks were taken into consideration. Later, this data was transformed into a fuzzy model. Then, the fuzzy model Neutrosophic Fuzzy Ahp and the criteria of the banks were classified. Later, the banks were listed using the Neutrosophic TOPSIS method.

3.1 Fuzzy Numbers and Operations in Fuzzy Numbers

Fuzzy sets have been expressed in membership functions. Membership of an element in the fuzzy set is determined between 0 and 1 with the membership function. Each of the fuzzy basic sets can be thought of as a fuzzy number. Fuzzy numbers represent a range value with a lower and an upper bound. Fuzzy sets are the same concepts as their membership functions since they have been defined by membership functions. Fuzzy numbers approximate roughly, as if they could be characterized by verbal expressions.

3.2 Neutrosophic AHP

The following steps have been applied while performing Neutrosophic AHP.

1. A decision matrix has been created.
2. Paired comparisons have been made to create a neutrosophic assessment matrix that represents the opinions of decision makers. The neutrosophic binary evaluation matrix ($\breve{X}$) is as in Equ. 1.

$$\tilde{X} = \left[\tilde{1} \tilde{x}_{12} \cdots \tilde{x}_{1n} :::: \tilde{x}_{n1}\, \tilde{x}_{n2} \cdots \tilde{1} \right] \quad (1)$$

According to Eq(1) $\tilde{x}_{ji} = \tilde{x}_{ij}^{-1}$ is valid.

3. Neutrosophic rating matrix has been made using the Neutrosophic scale as in Table 2.

Tab. 2: *Scale Conversed for Neutrosophic Triangular Numbers*

Value	Explanation	Neutrosophic triangular scale
1	Equally influential	$\tilde{1} = \langle (1,1,1); 0.5, 0.5, 0.5 \rangle$
3	Slightly influential	$\tilde{3} = \langle (2,3,4); 0.3, 0.75, 0.7 \rangle$
5	Strongly influential	$\tilde{5} = \langle (4,5,6); 0.8, 0.15, 0.2 \rangle$
7	Very strongly influential	$\tilde{7} = \langle (6,7,8); 0.9, 0.1, 0.1 \rangle$
9	Absolutely influential	$\tilde{9} = \langle (9,9,9); 1, 0, 0 \rangle$
2 4 6 8	Intermediate values between two close scales	$\tilde{2} = \langle (1,2,3); 0.4, 0.65, 0.6 \rangle$ $\tilde{4} = \langle (3,4,5); 0.6, 0.35, 0.4 \rangle$ $\tilde{6} = \langle (5,6,7); 0.7, 0.25, 0.3 \rangle$ $\tilde{8} = \langle (7,8,9); 0.85, 0.1, 0.15 \rangle$

4. Thanks to the Neutrosophic pairwise evaluation matrix, a deterministic pairwise evaluation matrix has been gathered to determine the weights of the criterion in Eq. (2), (3), (4), (5) and (6):

Assume that $\tilde{x}_{ij} = \langle (g_1, h_1, k_1), \alpha_{\tilde{x}}, \theta_{\tilde{x}}, \beta_{\tilde{x}} \rangle$ be a single valued neutrosophic number, score and accuracy degrees of $\tilde{x}_{ij}$ have been computed in Eq. (2), (3), (4), (5), (6):

$$S(\tilde{x}_{ij}) = \frac{1}{16}[d_1 + e_1 + f_1] x (2 + \alpha_{\tilde{x}} - \theta_{\tilde{x}} - \beta_{\tilde{x}}) \quad (2)$$

$$A(\tilde{x}_{ij}) = \frac{1}{16}[g_1 + h_1 + k_1] x (2 + \alpha_{\tilde{x}} - \theta_{\tilde{x}} + \beta_{\tilde{x}}) \quad (3)$$

To get the score and accuracy degree of $\tilde{x}_{ij}$ Eq. (4) and (5) have been used.

$$S(\tilde{x}_{ji}) = 1 / S(\tilde{x}_{ij}) \quad (4)$$

$$A(\tilde{x}_{ji}) = 1 / A(\tilde{x}_{ij}) \quad (5)$$

Deterministic pairwise evaluation matrix has been formed by score value of each triangular neutrosophic number in neutrosophic pairwise evaluation matrix. Gathered deterministic matrix can be seen in Eq. (6):

$$X = \left[1 x_{12} \cdots x_{1n} \vdots\vdots\vdots\vdots x_{n1} \; x_{n2} \cdots 1 \right] \quad (6)$$

Ranking of priorities as eigen vector X has been gathered according to following:

a) Firstly column values have been normalized by dividing each value to the sum of column
b) Averages of rows have been summed.

5. Consistency index (CI) and consistency ratio (CR) values have been calculated to evaluate the inconsistency of decisions in all pairwise evaluation matrixes. If the CR is greater than 0.1, the process must be repeated due to untrustworthy decision-makers' decisions.

CI has been calculated according to following steps:

a) Each value in first column of the pairwise evaluation matrix has been multiplied by the priority of first criterion and this process has been applied for entire columns. Values have been summed across the rows to construct the weighted sum vector.
b) The elements of the weighted sum vector have been split by corresponding the priority of each criterion. Then the average of values have been handled and represented by λ_{max} .
c) The value of CI has been computed as Eq.(7):

$$CI = \frac{\lambda_{max} - n}{n-1} \tag{7}$$

where number of elements being contrasted have been defined by n.

After the value of CI has found, CR has been calculated in Eq. (8):

$$CR = \frac{CI}{RI} \tag{8}$$

where RI defines the consistency index for randomly generated pairwise evaluation matrix and can be shown as Table 3.

Tab. 3: *RI used for computing CR value*

Order of random matrix (n)	0	2	3	4	5	6	7	8	9	10
Related RI value	0	0	0.58	0.9	1.12	1.24	1.32	1.4	1.45	1.49

4 Analysis

In this study, pre-covid 2019 data of ten commercial banks and two investment banks were taken into account. The data are as shown in Table 4. Criteria weights of existing criteria have been blurred. Then, criterion weights have been determined by Neutrosophic AHP.

Tab. 4: *The data of the Istanbul Stock Exchange Traded Turkish Banks*

Banks	CAR	LIQUID ACTIVES / TOP ACTIVITIES (ACTIVE QUALITY)	Current Ratio	ROA	ROE	Sensitivity to CAR	NPL RATIO	NET INTEREST MARJIN	Deposit interest Rate	Exchange Rate	Rediscount Rate	Overnight Interest Rate	TR GDP	EU GDP	WORLD GDP
Akbank	21,0	12,9	24,1	1,6	11,0	56,0	7,3	183,6	25,64	5,674	12,75	10.50	7,54412E+11	1,55928E+13	8,77515E+13
Denizbank	17,69	13,6	22,5	0,9	8,1	42,5	10,4	162,0	25,64	5,674	12,75	10.50	7,54412E+11	1,55928E+13	8,77515E+13
Garanti BBVA	19,57	16,3	27,3	1,6	12,3	56,7	6,9	192,1	25,64	5,674	12,75	10.50	7,54412E+11	1,55928E+13	8,77515E+13
Halkbank	14,33	8,4	13,5	0,4	5,6	53,5	5,1	129,4	25,64	5,674	12,75	10.50	7,54412E+11	1,55928E+13	8,77515E+13
ICBC Bank	18,64	24,0	50,2	0,2	3,4	-26,9	1,8	143,0	25,64	5,674	12,75	10.50	7,54412E+11	1,55928E+13	8,77515E+13
İş Bank	17,87	14,1	24,3	1,4	11,2	70,6	6,5	185,7	25,64	5,674	12,75	10.50	7,54412E+11	1,55928E+13	8,77515E+13
Kalkınma Bank	22,29	12,8	905,4	2,5	23,7	-0,6	0,8	266,4	25,64	5,674	12,75	10.50	7,54412E+11	1,55928E+13	8,77515E+13
Sınai Kalkınma Bank	17,80	3,4	65,1	1,7	13,5	73,6	3,5	246,0	25,64	5,674	12,75	10.50	7,54412E+11	1,55928E+13	8,77515E+13
Şeker Bank	13,40	13,1	19,5	-2,2	-31,4	119,1	13,1	140,8	25,64	5,674	12,75	10.50	7,54412E+11	1,55928E+13	8,77515E+13
Vakıflar Bank	16,61	10,1	18,6	0,7	9,1	92,0	5,9	144,8	25,64	5,674	12,75	10.50	7,54412E+11	1,55928E+13	8,77515E+13
Yapı Kredi	17,81	19,2	35,2	1,0	9,0	84,4	7,6	170,6	25,64	5,674	12,75	10.50	7,54412E+11	1,55928E+13	8,77515E+13
QNBFinans Bank	15,73	12,5	22,2	1,5	16,8	176,5	7,0	170,4	25,64	5,674	12,75	10.50	7,54412E+11	1,55928E+13	8,77515E+13

Tab. 5: *The weight of the criteria*

Criteria	CAR	LIQUID ACTIVES / TOP ACTIVITIES (ACTIVE QUALITY)	Current Ratio	ROA	ROE	Sensitivity to CAR	Npl Ratıo	Net Interest Marjin	Deposit Interest Rate	Exchange Rate	Rediscount Rate	Overnight Interest Rate	TR GDP	EU GDP	WORLD GDP
Weight of Criteria	0,062	0,059	0,063	0,071	0,066	0,069	0,066	0,068	0,071	0,057	0,073	0,070	0,076	0,071	0,061

Tab. 6: *Ranking of the banks*

Banks	Akbank	Denizbank	Garanti BBVA	Halkbank	ICBC Bank	İs Bank	Kalkınma Bank	Sınai Kalkınma Bank	Şeker Bank	Vakıflar Bank	Yapı Kredi	QNBFinans Bank
Results	0,169	0,121	0,203	0,158	0,70	0,147	0,98	0,92	0,102	0,128	0,135	0,120
Ranking	2	7	1	3	12	4	10	11	9	6	5	8

This data has been blurred with Neutrosophic AHP. The significance level of 15 criteria was determined. In this context, the weights of the criteria are as in Table 5.

Afterwards, the performance analysis of the Istanbul Stock Exchange Traded Turkish banks has been performed with Neutrosophic TOPSIS and the banks have been ranked in Table 6.

5 Conclusion

In this study the performance of the commercial and investment banks quoted on the Istanbul Stock Exchange have been sorted by using neutrosophic the AHP-based neutrosophic TOPSIS approach. For this purpose, related criteria for evaluating performance factors have been denoted according to depth literature review resources and weighted neutrosophic sets based the AHP approach. And the twelve alternatives have been sorted by using neutrosophic sets based TOPSIS method.

Neutrosophic sets have been chosen as for the advantage of in contrast to crisp, fuzzy, interval-valued and intuitionistic sets due to efficiency, flexibility and easiness for explaining decision-makers' indeterminate judgements.

For further research, the criteria related to performance analysis in the Istanbul Stock Exchange Traded Turkish banks can be expanded, applications can be diversified, and results can be contrasted with different multi-criteria decision-making methods. Also other hybrid techniques can be used for decision-making to provide solutions for real world investment problems.

References

Ayadi, O. F., Adebayo, A. O., and Omolehinwa, E. (1998). Bank performance measurement in a developing economy: An application of data envelopment analysis. Managerial Finance, Vol. 24 No.7, pp.5–16.

Bian, W., and Deng, C. (2017). Ownership dispersion and bank performance: Evidence from China. Finance Research Letters, 22, 49–52.

Chang, S. C., and Tsai, P. H. (2016). A hybrid financial performance evaluation model for wealth management banks following the global financial crisis. Technological and Economic Development of Economy, 22(1), 21–46.

Che, Z., Wang, H. S., and Chuang, C. L. (2010). A fuzzy AHP and DEA approach for making bank loan decisions for small and medium enterprises in Taiwan. Expert Systems with Applications, 37(10), 7189–7199.

Epure, M., and Lafuente, E. (2015). Monitoring bank performance in the presence of risk. Journal of Productivity Analysis, 44(3), 265–281.

Fernando, E., and Siagian, P. (2021). Proposal to use the analytic hierarchy process method evaluate bank credit submissions. Procedia Computer Science, 179, 232–241.

Ferreira, F. A., Santos, S. P., and Dias, V. M. (2014). An AHP-based approach to credit risk evaluation of mortgage loans. International Journal of Strategic Property Management, 18(1), 38–55.

Fukuyama, H., and Matousek, R. (2017). Modelling bank performance: A network DEA approach. European Journal of Operational Research, 259(2), 721–732.

Greco, S., Figueira, J., and Ehrgott, M. (2016). Multiple criteria decision analysis (Vol. 37). New York: Springer.

Gerhardt, M., and Vander Vennet, R. (2017). Bank bailouts in Europe and bank performance. Finance Research Letters, 22, 74–80.

Ic, Y. T., Celik, B., Kavak, S., and Baki, B. (2021). Development of a multi-criteria decision-making model for comparing the performance of Turkish commercial banks. Journal of Advances in Management Research, Vol. 18 No.2, pp.250–272.

Ic, Y. T., Celik, B., Kavak, S., and Baki, B. (2020). Development of a multi-criteria decision-making model for comparing the performance of Turkish commercial banks. Journal of Advances in Management Research.

Javalgi, R. G., Armacost, R. L., and Hosseini, J. C. (1989). Using the analytic hierarchy process for bank management: Analysis of consumer bank selection decisions. Journal of Business Research, 19(1), 33–49.

Koetter, M., Bos, J. W., Heid, F., Kolari, J. W., Kool, C. J., and Porath, D. (2007). Accounting for distress in bank mergers. Journal of Banking and Finance, 31(10), 3200–3217.

Lin, T. Y., and Chiu, S. H. (2013). Using independent component analysis and network DEA to improve bank performance evaluation. Economic Modelling, 32, 608–616.

Mandic, K., Delibasic, B., Knezevic, S., and Benkovic, S. (2014). Analysis of the financial parameters of Serbian banks through the application of the fuzzy AHP and TOPSIS methods. Economic Modelling, 43, 30–37.

Otchere, I., and Chan, J. (2003). Intra-industry effects of bank privatization: A clinical analysis of the privatization of the Commonwealth Bank of Australia. Journal of Banking and Finance, 27(5), 949–975.

Saeed, H., Shahid, A., and Tirmizi, S. M. A. (2020). An empirical investigation of banking sector performance of Pakistan and Sri Lanka by using CAMELS ratio of framework. Journal of Sustainable Finance and Investment, 10(3), 247–268.

Saaty, T. L. (2000). Fundamentals of decision making and priority theory with the analytic hierarchy process (Vol. 6). Pittsburgh: RWS Publications.

Simoens, M., and Vander Vennet, R. (2020). Bank performance in Europe and the US: A divergence in market-to-book ratios. Finance Research Letters, 101672.

Sun, P. H., Mohamad, S., and Ariff, M. (2017). Determinants driving bank performance: A comparison of two types of banks in the OIC. Pacific-Basin Finance Journal, 42, 193–203.

Stankevičienė, J., and Mencaitė, E. (2012). The evaluation of bank performance using a multicriteria decision making model: a case study on Lithuanian commercial banks. Technological and economic development of economy, 18(1), 189–205.

Torun, M., and Altay, E. (2019) Ticari Bankacılık Sektöründe Sorunlu Kredileri Etkileyen Faktörlerin Analizi. Yönetim ve Ekonomi Araştırmaları Dergisi, 17(1), 179–200.

Yuksel, S., Dincer, H., and Hacioglu, U. (2015). CAMELS-based determinants for the credit rating of Turkish deposit banks. International Journal of Finance and Banking Studies (2147–4486), 4(4), 1–17.

Hüseyin Sevgi

Labour Exploitation on Social Media: The Relationship Between Free Labour and Digital Labour

1 Introduction

As social media spreads rapidly and becomes a part of people's daily life, people start spending more and more time every day on social media. The time spent on social media may seem like a harmless fun activity at first. However, the time spent on social media and what people do on these platforms is used as raw material by social media companies. In time this raw material is turned into a commodity, something purchased and discarded in the market (Niemeyer, and Keightley, 2020: 1640; Birtchnell et al., 2020)

While the concepts of free labour and digital labour are older than social media, they have taken on different dimensions with the popularity of social media. The wide accessibility of social media via mobile applications and networks has caused free labour to expand into a larger part of society, and has become more invisible.

Free labour, by the nature of social media, is visible in the digital environment and requires active participation from users. Web 2.0 and the active intervention of users in the digital content has created a different dimension of digital labour visible on social media. The concept of digital labour, which was first raised in post-Fordist economies, has expanded its scope to include the labour spent on social media through information communication technologies. Thus, rapidly advancing social media has allowed users to create their content and brought importance to digital labour as seen on social media.

The most significant relationship between free labour and digital labour is that digital labour in the form of texts, photographs, videos, audios, live streams, etc. has been turned into free labour by social media companies, and made concrete. Social media companies make profits by commercializing the content created by users on social media. Free labour often emerges as unpaid digital labour in this commodification process.

And free labour and digital labour have a symbiotic relationship in this regard. These two concepts are parts of an inseparable whole that feed each other. The symbiotic relationship between free labour and digital labour has led to the emergence of an order that exploits users' labour. The content created by users on social media with digital labour is commodified by social media companies. The most significant aspect of this commodification process is turning the digital labour of users into free labour. Therefore, each social media user produces free labour for social media companies in some way. In this regard, the concept of 'social factory' is highly associated with social media. In the concept of social factories, production has gone beyond traditional places such as factories and manufacturing plants. The value for the capital is produced by the general public (Hardt and Negri, 2000: 243).

In this respect, the research question of the study is: 'Are there any relations between free labour and digital labour in the context of labour exploitation on social media?' To find the answers to the research question, systematic literature review was carried out with the terms free labour, digital labour, prosumer, produser, produsage, playbor, user-generated content and participatory culture.

In this study, the concepts of free labour and digital labour are examined separately and their relationship addressed. The place of these concepts in the context of intangible labour will also be evaluated. Different concepts that have a different take on labour exploitation on social media and how they are turned into free labour will be discussed. In the last chapter, there will be a theoretical discussion on labour exploitation and commodification on social media, and how labour exploitation becomes widespread and profound via social media.

2 Free Labour

Free labour is a comprehensive concept approached from different angles in the literature. Thus, it is not easy to have a single definition for the concept. For example, in the classical labour theory developed by Karl Marx about the labour market and productive labour in the nineteenth century, free labour is oxymoronic. According to Marx, labour refers to a paid action that becomes concrete with work. Therefore, it cannot be regarded as labour if it is not paid for (Marx, 1973: 300).

When we look into the concept of free labour within the framework of information and communication technologies, it takes on a much different meaning. According to Terranova, one of the theoreticians of free labour in media and culture, free labour is a labour that is voluntary, simultaneous, related to content production on the Internet and brings some kind of joy to the producer of the content, but is exploited and unpaid at the same time (Terranova, 2000: 33). In this regard, the scope of free labour has been expanded with technological developments.

This study addresses three main theoretical dimensions of free labour: *Forced labour (slavery), unpaid work* and *free labour*. The first dimension of free labour is forced labour (slavery). The concept of forced labour, frequently emerging in eighteenth-century colonialism, takes part in the literature as free labour and slave labour. Forced free labour refers to a labour market that was regulated by law in eighteenth century Anglo-American geography and the United Kingdom, which functioned using slave labour. This dimension of free labour has a political and economic background and needs to be addressed within the purview of basic human rights (Drescher, 1999: 399); (Earle, 1978: 51–2); (Taylor, 2015: 486–7).

The second dimension of free labour is the much-debated concept of unpaid work. Free labour on social media and unpaid work are two very different concepts. By their nature, both concepts are used to refer to unpaid labour; however, 'labour' means two different things in these two concepts. Unpaid work is often mentioned in women's labour. The most fundamental reason for this is the direct relation of unpaid work with domestic affairs and care work. In this regard, unpaid work is directly related to gender inequality and one of the outcomes of the patriarchal social order. Unpaid work, addressed as the daily house chores and child/elderly care labour of women, refers to the daily routine and unpaid works of women. Therefore, it becomes very difficult to measure and determine the limits of unpaid work (Luxton, 1997: 431–2); (Shelton, 2006: 376). Unpaid work also found itself a place in feminist theory studies as a women's labour issue. In feminist theory, unpaid work is addressed more as a class inequality where the capitalist male exploits women's labour in domestic affairs by taking on the role of the husband. In this respect, unpaid work is regarded as one of the means of exercising men's dominance over women (Primeau, 1992: 984).

The third and important aspect of free labour for this study is the free labour occurring with media consumption. Free labour in media studies is based on the theory that mass media is not only a means of communication, but also social means of production. This aspect of means of communication was described by Marks as, '*The class which has the means of material production at its disposal, consequently also controls the means of mental production,*' (Marx, 1998: 67). Describing the media as a means of production with the 'audience commodity' theory, Smythe emphasizes that the material side of communication is the work, exploitation and the sale of audiences as commodities to advertisers and that television viewers are not just audiences but also employees of the advertisers (Smythe, 1977: 3–5). Similarly, Williams states that the media's mission is not only communication. According to Williams, media reproduces social relations, culture, art, ideology and many social structures as a means of production tool (Williams, 1983: 203–4).

The idea that media is not only a means of communication has become more widespread and concrete with advancing information and communication technologies. Passive users of traditional mass media such as television, newspapers, the radio etc. now have the chance to become as active as never before. The popularization of social media platforms with Web 2.0 has allowed users to be more active on the Internet. Web 2.0 has turned the Internet into a collective field. Instead of having their gardens, individuals have come together to work in cooperation in a shared area (Gauntlett, 2011: 4). In this regard, Web 2.0 provides a basis for free labour on social media. With users being a part of the production, social media is differentiated from the traditional media and has its unique structure. Users play a dominant role in producing, distributing and reproducing content on social media.

Terranova defines the hours spent every day and the millions of content produced on social media by the users as free labour. According to Terranova, users produce the raw materials needed by companies as they spend time on social media. These raw materials (content produced by users, behaviour compasses and directly-provided personal information) are processed and used by social media companies to create large profits. This kind of labour is called free labour as users are not charged for the time they spent in this process (Terranova, 2013: 46–8).

The commodification of information on social media is now intertwined with free labour. The fact that users spend time on social media (the online consuming process) works as a process that justifies the commodification of information. Social media platforms provide access to internet tools, access and content without selling it as a commodity. Instead of this they commodify users' data; they provide communication mediums to social media users in return for the commodification of data. For example, a person who drinks a bottle of water does not produce value for the company that is producing the water while drinking/consuming this, s/he only pays money for the water. The consuming process requires online communication and utilization time on social media. The whole time is not only a reproduction time but also labour time that produces data commodities for the companies advertising on social media. The consumption time on social media is also the time for commodity production. The simultaneity of the times of production and consumption of the commodity makes it difficult to determine the limits of free labour. Users are both the producers and the consumers of the content on social media. In Toffler's terms, users have turned into 'prosumers' (Toffler, 1984: 214); (Fuchs, 2014: 136–8).

As to the concept of the prosumer, suggested by Toffler in 1984, by combining the words 'producer' and 'consumer' (in terms of traditional mass media) is referred to together with the social transformation called The Third Wave. According to Toffler, a prosumer is someone who both produces and consumes the media content (Ritzer and Jurgenson, 2010: 17). With the development of technology, the Internet and social media have caused users to be both consumers and producers. Thus, the concept of prosumer has been reshaped in the form of free labour.

3 Digital Labour

We see two different meanings for digital labour in the literature, as conventional and modern. With the development of information and communication technologies, digital labour in the conventional sense is used to define labour spent by employees in this sector. For example, the labour that a software developer invests when working every day is identified as digital labour. Conventionally, digital labour is shaped by the processing of information and culture. Therefore, conventional digital labour partly intersects with intangible labour (Lazzarato, 1996: 133).

Digital labour in a modern sense is a concept becoming more widespread with Web 2.0 and social media platforms, and is related to user labour spent in the digital environment. In this context, digital labour in a modern sense and the prosumer concept complement each other. There is a relationship of support between these two concepts. Digital labour in a modern sense is embodied mostly with the concept of prosumer (Fuchs, 2014: 354–5). The driving force of digital labour in the modern sense is that users emerge with Web 2.0 and turn into prosumers. Therefore, in this study, digital labour will be not discussed conventionally, but in a modern sense.

The relationship of labour exploitation on social media with digital labour emerges in the axis of the prosumer. There is a multidimensional and highly complex relationship between digital labour and prosumers. This process consists of the voluntary production of digital content by users, consuming the content produced by other users at the same time, and the commodification of all their resulting labour by social media companies. The commodification of a part or all of the user's labour brings about free labour. Labour exploitation on social media is the digital labour that has been turned into free labour by the social media companies after digital labour emerged when the users evolved into prosumers. The concept of labour exploitation here takes on a different meaning than in traditional labour markets.

However, this approach has been criticized because labour on social media is voluntarily spent by users and cannot constitute exploitation. Digital labour and free labour on social media are by their nature very different from labour in the traditional labour market. Thus, the exploitation here will inevitably be different. The fact that users voluntarily spend time on social media and spend digital labour does not mean that there is no labour exploitation. Users produce value with or without being aware of it. This value is commodified by social media companies without paying anything and converted into profit (Andrejevic, 2013: 154).

How do social media companies commodify digital labour? How does this commodification process work? Most importantly, how is the digital labour of users converted into plus value? The answer to all these questions is directly related to the time that users spend on social media. This value, converted into surplus-value, is everything users do while spending time on various social media platforms. In this regard, the total time spent on social media platforms such as Facebook, Twitter, Instagram and YouTube is processed by social media companies, sold especially to advertising companies, and thus generating surplus value (Ekman, 2012: 166–7).

The exploitation of digital labour by converting it into a surplus-value is similar to the socially necessary labour time in the classical labour theory. In the classical labour theory, Marx distinguishes between workforce and the labour force. The workforce is the ability of the individual to work. The labour force is a process of creating value. Marx approaches this process from a social perspective. To Marx, social production is made by a complex and compound workforce and this labour unit consists of very different working people who need each other to survive and to generate wealth (Marx, 2007: 26–7). In this context, to turn digital labour into surplus-value on social media it needs to be socialized. Content produced by a user on social media has no value for social media companies. Therefore, the way to exploit digital labour by commodification is the production and consumption of it by a large number of users. Only in this way will digital labour be turned into free labour, which is exploited by social media companies.

The commodification of digital labour by socialization is similar to the difference between the use-value and exchange-value of labour in the classical labour theory. The use-value of labour is the value demonstrating usefulness in use and occurring only during the consumption process. The exchange value of labour is the average social labour time necessary to produce a commodity (Marx, 2007: 70). In this context, whereas content produced by a social media user carries an intangible use-value, such as personal satisfaction, the whole of the content produced by billions of social media users are commodified by social media companies and obtain exchange value.

4 Digital Transformation and Digital Labour

The reshaping of labour exploitation with new technologies and social media forms a part of digital transformation. Digital labour is recognized as a labour exploitation strategy in the digital economy. In this context, strategies applied for digital transformation reshape both the economy and digital labour. The digital economy (also referred to as the Internet Economy, New Economy, Web Economy), is defined as doing business via web-based markets based on internet and computer technology. The digital economy has become an important factor that globally creates value with the spread of the Internet, which has increased use of smart mobile devices and the popularization of social media. The digital economy is increasingly intertwined with the traditional economy. That is why it is hard to identify the notion. The digital economy is based on the online connection between billions of people using the internet daily, enterprises, devices, data and processes. It is also based on the strong connection between the Internet, mobile device technologies and the Internet of Things (IoT) (Ertz and Boily, 2019: 87).

The digital transformation strategy is seen as a formal plan structured throughout the digital transformation process of the entire economy. In this way, digital transformation strategies comprehensively address all positive and negative scenarios associated with digital technologies. Inclusive of the unique nature of all business units and organizational characteristics includes multiple coordination mechanisms: first, consistent with business strategy and, second, consistent with other actions (Albukhitan, 2020: 665).

According to traditional definitions, a strategy is a series of plans to achieve long-term goals. The package of measures consists of a large number of individual measures that maintain a consistent relationship with each other. Expanding the classical definition, digital strategy describes an economy's overall vision in the context of digitalization, including strategic measures to achieve digitalization. It defines specific, short-term, medium-term and long-term digital goals and plans in every aspect of the economy (Lipsmeier et al., 2020: 175).

The digital transformation of the economy and digital strategies has made digital labour emerging in social media more visible. Digital labour, created by millions of users and offered completely free to the digital environment, has become a new exploitation field in the digital transformation of the economy. In this context, the relationship between digital transformation, digital strategies and new communication technologies enables digital labour and the exploitation of it.

5 Conclusion

When Smythe first mentioned audience labour, he emphasized that capitalism was creating a new area of exploitation through media technologies. Audience labour does not only refer to the time that people sitting in front of the TV spend to make use of their spare time. Audience labour refers to turning the leisure time of most of the population into a working time through television. In this context, the tangible aspect of communication is the working of the audience, exploiting and selling them as commodities to the advertisers.

The concept of audience labour put forward by Smythe has led to all concepts such as digital labour, free labour, prosumer, produser and playbor with the development of information and communication technology. While the audience labour individuals used to be defined as passive consumers in the media production-consumption period, the passive audience has transformed with the development of the Internet, Web 2.0 and social media. The popularity of social media has changed the status of social media users from consumers to active producers and consumers. Now, while the individuals produce their content, they have also started to consume the content of other users rather than consuming the content produced from a single centre. Thus, individuals have turned into users that can intervene in the production process in the digital environment.

The producer and consumer status of the individual has not changed the facts about the working of the audience, exploiting and selling them as commodities to advertisers, as emphasized by Smythe. The efforts of capitalism for expanding and spreading have deepened the exploitation of intangible labour created by users. Appearing as prosumer, produser, playbor, etc. free labour has become much more accessible for companies with information and communication technologies. The portable smart devices and mobile internet networks becoming more widespread have made social media a part of our daily lives. In this way, companies can easily access the free labour spent by billions of social media users and the free content created by them, and exploit these by using social media as a free source of raw materials.

And the most dangerous aspect of exploitation on social media is that it can be easily masked due to the voluntary participation of users. Users voluntarily participate in the production-consumption process on social media as prosumers or produsers. They enjoy being a part of this production-consumption process on social media (playbor). For this reason, materializing the exploitation of labour on social media and correlating it with the traditional 'exploitation of labour' becomes hard to do. The voluntary participation of users on social media or the fact that they enjoy being there does not eliminate the exploitation of free labour.

On the contrary, this makes the exploitation larger and deeper. From this aspect, the exploitation of labour on social media has similarities with the traditional exploitation of labour.

In the traditional sense, exploitation of labour occurs with surplus-value. The capital has two ways to expand the surplus-value and increase the exploitation of labour: *expansion of exploitation* and *deepening of exploitation*. Expansion of exploitation is made possible by increasing the working times. The deepening of exploitation refers to increasing production by making the production process more efficient. When we look at the production-consumption dynamics on social media in this regard, the number of users and the time spent on social media have always increased over the years (expansion of exploitation). However, the type of content on social media has differed in parallel to technological advancements. In the beginning posts contained texts but, due to technological advancements, these have turned into posts with photos, videos and live broadcasts (deepening of exploitation).

Despite its short history, social media has been able to become a part of the capitalist economy with the economic dynamics it contains. And the fact that it has become a part of capitalism has made social media a suitable place for the exploitation of labour. Even though the form and method of labour exploitation may differ, it happens through companies that want to increase their profit by extracting the surplus value on social media. However, the exploitation process is not clear and visible as in traditional exploitation of labour, and it is relatively more abstract.

References

Albukhitan, S. (2020). Developing Digital Transformation Strategy for Manufacturing. Procedia Computer Science, 170, 664–671. https://doi.org/10.1016/j.procs.2020.03.173

Andrejevic, M. (2013). Estranged Free Labour. In: Digital Labour the Internet as Playground and Factory. New York: Routledge.

Bernal, P. A. (2010). Web 2.5: The Symbiotic Web. International Review of Law, Computers and Technology, 24(1), 25–37. https://doi.org/10.1080/13600860903570145

Bhatti, S. S., Gao, X. and Chen, G. (2020). General Framework, Opportunities, and Challenges for Crowdsourcing Techniques: A Comprehensive Survey. Journal of Systems and Software, 167, 2–27. https://doi.org/10.1016/j.jss.2020.110611

Birtchnell, T., McGuirk, P., Moore, C. and Vettoretto, L. (2020). Pay to play? Subverting the digital economy of Pokémon go in the Smart City. Digital Geography and Society. https://doi.org/10.1016/j.diggeo.2020.100004

Brabham, D. C. (2008). Crowdsourcing as a Model for Problem Solving: An Introduction and Cases. Convergence, 14(1), 75–90. https://doi.org/10.1177/1354856507084420

Bruns, A. (2006). Blogs, Wikipedia, Second Life, and Beyond: From Production to Produsage, New York: Peter Lang Publishing.

Campbell, C. (2015). The Craft Consumer: Culture, Craft, and Consumption in a Postmodern Society. Journal of Consumer Culture, 5(1), 23–42. https://doi.org/10.1177/1469540505049843

Chaffey, D. (2020). Global Social Media Research Summary 2020. Retrieved from https://www.smartinsights.com/social-media-marketing/social-media-strategy/new-global-social-media-research/

Çömlekçi, M. F. and Başol, O. (2019). Research on Social Media News Trust And News Verification Awareness. Galatasaray University Journal of Communication, 30, 55–77. https://doi.org/10.16878/gsuilet.518697

Dibbell, J. (2007). The Life of the Chinese Gold Farmer. Newyork Times. Retrieved from https://www.nytimes.com/2007/06/17/magazine/17lootfarmers-t.html

Dijck, V. J. (2009). Users Like You? Theorizing Agency in User-Generated Content. Media, Culture and Society, 31(1), 41–58. https://doi.org/10.1177/0163443708098245

Drescher S. (1999) Free Labour vs Slave Labour: The British and Caribbean Cases (1999). In: From Slavery to Freedom. London: Palgrave Macmillan.

Earle, C. (1978). A Staple Interpretation of Slavery and Free Labour. Geographical Review, 68(1), 51–65. https://doi.org/10.2307/213510

Ekman, M. (2012). Understanding Accumulation: The Relevance of Marx's Theory of Primitive Accumulation in Media and Communication Studies, Journal of Global Sustainable Information Society, 10(2), 156–170. https://doi.org/10.31269/triplec.v10i2.407

Ertz, M. and Boily, E. (2019). The Rise of The Digital Economy: Thoughts on Blockchain Technology and Cryptocurrencies for the Collaborative Economy. International Journal of Innovation Studies, 3(4), 84–93. https://doi.org/10.1016/j.ijis.2019.12.002

Fink, A. (2020). Conducting research literature reviews: From the internet to paper. Fifth Edition. Los Angales: Sage.

Fisher, E. (2015). Audience Labour on Social Media: Learning from Sponsored Stories. In: Reconsidering Value and Labour in the Digital Age. New York: Palgrave Macmillan.

Fuchs, C. (2014). Digital Labour and Karl Marx. New York: Routledge.

Gauntlett, D. (2011). Making Is Connecting: The Social Meaning of Creativity, From DIY and Knitting to Youtube and Web 2.0, Cambridge: Polity Press.

Goggin, J. (2011), Playbour, Farming and Leisure. Ephemera Journal, 11(4), 357–368. http://www.ephemerajournal.org/contribution/playbour-farming-and-labour

Grinnell, C. K. (2009). From Consumer to Prosumer to Produser: Who Keeps Shifting My Paradigm? (We Do!). Public Culture, 21(3), 577–598. https://doi.org/10.1215/08992363-2009-009

Hardt, M. and Negri, A. (2000). Empire. Cambridge: Harvard University Press.

Harvey, D. (2003). The New Imperialism, Oxford: Oxford University Press.

Jevkins, H., Ford, S., and Green, J. (2013). Spreadable Media: Creating Value and Meaning in a Networked Culture. New York: New York University Press.

Jevkins, H. (2008). Convergence Culture, New York: New York University Press.

Kiatsuranon, K. and Suwunnamek, O. (2017). Determinants of Thai Information and Communication Technology Organization Performance: A Structural Equation Model Analysis. Kasetsart Journal of Social Sciences, 40(1), 113–120. https://doi.org/10.1016/j.kjss.2017.08.004

Kücklich, J. (2005). Precarious Playbour: Modders and the Digital Games Industry, The Fibreculture Journal, (5). http://five.fibreculturejournal.org/fcj-025-precarious-playbour-modders-and-the-digital-games-industry/

Lazzarato, M. (1996). Immaterial Labour. In: Radical Thought in Italy: A Potential Politics. Minnesota: University of Minnesota Press.

Lipsmeier, A., Kühn, A., Joppen, R., and Dumitrescu, R. (2020). Process for the development of a digital strategy. Procedia CIRP, 88, 173–178. https://doi.org/10.1016/j.procir.2020.05.031

Lund, A: (2015). A Contribution to a Critique of the Concept Playbour. In: Reconsidering Value and Labour in the Digital Age. London: Palgrave Macmillan

Luxton, M. (1997). The UN, Women, and Household Labour: Measuring and Valuing Unpaid Work. Women's Studies International Forum, 20(3), 431–439. https://doi.org/10.1016/S0277-5395(97)00026-5

Manovich, L. (2001). The Language of New Media. Cambridge: MIT.

Marx, K. (1818–1883 [1998]). The German Ideology. New York: Prometheus Books

Marx, K. (1857–1861 [1973]). Grundrisse: Foundations of the Critique of Political Economy. London: Penguin

Marx, K. (1867 [2007]). Capital (Volume 1: A Critique of Political Economy). Kansas: Digireads.com Publishing

Marx, K. (1885 [1992]). Capital Volume 2. London: Penguin Books.

Massaro, M., Dumay, J., and Guthrie, J. (2016). On the Shoulder of Giants: Undertaking a Structured Literatüre Review in Accounting. Accounting, Auditing and Accountability Journal. 29 (5), 767–801. https://doi.org/10.1108/AAAJ-01-2015-1939

Nakamura, L. (2013). Don't Hate the Player, Hate the Game The Racialization of Labour in World of Warcraft, In: Digital Labour The Internet as Playground and Factory. London: Routledge.

Niemeyer, K., and Keightley, E. (2020). The Commodification of Time and Memory: Online Communities and the Dynamics of Commercially Produced Nostalgia. New Media and Society, 22(9), 1639–1662. https://doi.org/10.1177/1461444820914869

Primeau, L.A. (1992). A Woman's Place: Unpaid Work in the Home. American Journal of Occupational Therapy, 46, 981–988. https://doi.org/10.5014/ajot.46.11.981

Ritzer, G. and Jurgenson, N. (2010). Production, Consumption, Prosumption: The Nature of Capitalism in the Age of the Digital 'Prosumer.' Journal of Consumer Culture, 10(1), 13–36. https://doi.org/10.1177/1469540509354673

Ritzer, G. (2015), Prosumer Capitalism. The Sociological Quarterly, 56, 413–445. https://doi.org/10.1111/tsq.12105

Shelton, B. A. (2006) Gender and Unpaid Work. In: Handbook of the Sociology of Gender. Handbooks of Sociology and Social Research. Boston: Springer

Smythe, D. W. (1977). Communications: Blindspot of Western Marxism. Canadian Journal of Political and Social Theory, 1(3), 1–29. https://journals.uvic.ca/index.php/ctheory/article/view/13715/4463

Somerfield, K. and Mortimer, K and Evans, G. (2008). The Relevance of Images in User-Generated Content: A Mixed Method Study of When, and Why, Major Brands Retweet. International Journal of Internet Marketing and Advertising, 12(4), 340–357. https://doi.org/10.1504/IJIMA.2018.095360

Taylor, R. (2015). Volunteering and Unpaid Work. In: The SAGE Handbook of the Sociology of Work and Employment. London: Sage.

Terranova, T. (2000). Free Labour: Producing Culture For The Digital Economy. Social Text, 18 (2), 33–58. https://doi.org/10.1215/01642472-18-2_63-33

Terranova, T. (2013). Free Labour. In: Digital Labour: The Internet as Playground and Factory, London: Routledge.

Toffler, A. (1984). The Third Wave. New York: Bantam Books.

Torres, L., Royo, S., and Garcia-Rayado, J. (2019). Social media adoption by Audit Institutions. A comparative analysis of Europe and the United States. Government Information Quarterly, https://doi.org/10.1016/j.giq.2019.101433

Vincent, S. and Vickery G. (2007). Participative Web and User-Created Content: Web 2.0, Wikis and Social Networking. Paris: OECD Publications.

Wang, T. (2016). From News Receiver to News Produser—The New Relationship between Journalists and Audience in Web 2.0. Advances in Journalism and Communication, 4, 55–66. https://dx.doi.org/10.4236/ajc.2016.42006

Selim Tüzüntürk

Robust Counterparts of Two Independent Samples t and One-Way ANOVA Tests: Welch and Brown-Forsythe Tests

1 Introduction

Hypothesis tests are one of the focal points of inferential statistical analysis. Parametric hypothesis tests such as two independent samples t and one-way ANOVA tests are the two well-known statistical tests[1] that require a normal distribution assumption. This normality assumption is one of the main distinction points in deciding whether to conduct a parametric tests or non-parametric tests.[2] In testing the normality assumption, 'H_0: The population is normally distributed. H_1: The population is not normally distributed.' hypotheses are tested by using one of the following popular univariate normality tests: the Anderson-Darling test, the Kolmogorov-Smirnov test, the Shapiro-Wilk Test, the Ryan-Joiner test and the Jarque-Bera test.

Besides the requirement of normality assumption for the two independent samples t and one-way ANOVA tests, another important assumption, which is called the homogeneity of variances assumption, also needs to be satisfied. In testing the homogeneity assumption, Levene's (1960) test, Hartleys's (1950) test (or Hartley's F_{max}) and Bartlett's (1937) test can be used. 'H_0: The variances of the populations are equal (Homogeneity). H_1: The variances of the populations are not equal (heterogeneity)' hypotheses are tested for the two independent samples t test and 'H_0: The variances of the populations are equal (Homogeneity). H_1: At least one population variance is different (heterogeneity)' hypotheses are tested for the one-way anova test.

In practical applications, it is observed that contrary to the normality assumption, the homogeneity of the variances tests seem to be ignored by the researchers. Hence, without testing the stated homogeneity of variances assumption and reporting its results, it was seen that two independent samples t and one-way ANOVA testing continues, which is not the true acceptable procedure. The aim of this text is to draw researchers' attention to conducting the homogeneity of

1 See Tüzüntürk (2020) for the multivariate versions of these tests.

2 See Aytaç, (1991, 2004); Aytaç and Arlı (2018); andTüzüntürk (2015) for details.

variances test and in reporting its results, besides the normality check and report in their research reports. Depending on this purpose the aim of this text is also draw researchers' attention in conducting the existing robust tests, which are the counter parts of the two independent samples t and one-way ANOVA tests in case of the violation of the homogeneity of variances assumption. To do so, in Section 2 a brief review of the two independent samples t and one-way ANOVA tests are made. Besides, in Section 2 the violation of the two most important assumptions and their solutions are also explained. Section 3 composes of the robust tests in case of the violation of the homogeneity of variances assumption. And, finally, Section 4 comprises the conclusions.

2 Two Independent Samples t Test and One-Way ANOVA Test

Two independent samples t test is a parametric test that enables researchers to compare two independent population means. This test is a small sample (n<30) test of means. Before testing the hypotheses below, some assumptions must be met. If you fail to satisfy the assumptions, you might not be able to trust the results.

$$H_0: \mu_1 = \mu_2$$
$$H_1: \mu_1 \neq \mu_2 \quad (1)$$

The assumptions of the two independent samples t test are as follows:

- Normality: Each population from which a sample is taken is assumed to be normal.
- Random sample/Independency: All samples are randomly selected and independent.
- Homogeneity: The populations are assumed to have equal variances.
- Outlier: No outliers involved inside of the groups.

Under these assumptions, the t test statistics

$$t = \left| \frac{\bar{x}_1 - \bar{x}_2}{s_{\bar{x}_1 - \bar{x}_2}} \right| \quad (2)$$

is computed with the standard error in the equation shown below:

$$s_{\bar{x}_1 - \bar{x}_2} = s_p \sqrt{\frac{1}{n_1} + \frac{1}{n_2}} \tag{3}$$

Here, 's_p' stands for the standard deviation which is called the pooled standard deviation:

$$s_p = \sqrt{\frac{(n_1 - 1)s_1^2 + (n_2 - 1)s_2^2}{n_1 + n_2 - 2}} \tag{4}$$

The degrees of freedom (df.) is '$v = n_1 + n_2 - 2$'. And, by comparing the calculated t test statistic with the t table value decision is given which is to reject or not to reject the null hypothesis.

Fisher's one-way ANOVA test (or F test) is also a parametric test that enables researchers to compare more than two (k>2) independent population means. Before testing the hypotheses below, some assumptions must be met. If you fail to satisfy the assumptions, you might not be able to trust the results.

H_0: $\mu_1 = \mu_2 = \ldots\ldots\ldots\ldots = \mu_k$
H_1: At least one population mean (μ) is not equal to the others (5)

The assumptions of the one-way ANOVA test are as follows:

- Normality: Each population from which a sample is taken is assumed to be normal.
- Random sample/Independency: All samples are randomly selected and independent.
- Homogeneity: The populations are assumed to have equal variances.
- Outlier: No outliers involved inside of the groups.
- Variables: The factor is a categorical variable and the response is a numerical variable.

Outlier research is very important before starting the analysis. Especially before checking the assumptions such as normality and homogeneity with the hypothesis tests, it must be determined whether there is an outlier (or outliers) among the data. It should be noted that the inclusion of an outlier among the data may cause the wrong decision to be made in the hypothesis testing. Under the stated assumptions above, the valid F test statistics is computed as is shown in the following table below:

Tab. 1: *One-Way ANOVA Table*

Source of variation	**Sum of Squares (SS)**	**df.**	**Mean Square**	**F Ratio**
Between Groups (Factor)	SSR	k-1	MSR=SSR/k-1	$\left(F=\dfrac{\text{MSR}}{\text{MSE}}\right)$
Within Groups (Error)	SSE	n-k	MSE=SSE/n-k	
Total	SST	n-1		

Here, SSR is the regression sum squares, SSE is the error sum squares and SST is the total sum squares. And, by comparing the calculated F test statistic with the F table value a decision is given, which is to reject or not to reject the null hypothesis.

2.1 Violation of the Normality Assumption and its Solutions

Violation of normality assumption is a big issue. When the normality assumption is not met in both of the two independent samples t and one-way ANOVA tests, some practical solutions can be helpful to cope with this problem. Outliers can be the sources of this type of assumption violation. So, one of the solutions is to examine carefully the sample data to find out whether there is an outlier (or outliers), or not, within it. To do so, some graphical methods such as a box-whiskers plot, a histogram, a dot plot or a probability plot may be applied. Once they are detected, they should be removed from the data set.

A second solution is to increase the sample size (n); the researcher will have to collect more data. The third solution is to use normality transformations. These transformations depend on the distribution shape of the current sample data. For the right skewed distribution, square root and logarithmic transformations can be useful. On the other hand, for the left skewed distribution, the data should should first be reflected to the right skewed distribution, then square root and logarithmic transformations can be used. If none of these solutions work, nonparametric counterparts of these two independent samples t and one-way ANOVA tests can be applied.

2.2 Violation of the Homogeneity Assumption and its Solutions

Although the assumption of normality is met, the violation of homogeneity is another major problem. The two independent samples t test and the one-way ANOVA test are both sensitive to unequal variances. If your groups have unequal variances, the classic t test and the one-way ANOVA test (F test) yield biased results and lead to invalid statistical inferences (Delacre et al., 2017: 92; Delacre et al., 2019: 1). The solution for this problem is to be found in Welch's (1947, 1951) and Brown-Forsythe's 1974 (a) and 1974 (b) studies.

When the normality assumption is met in the two independent samples t test, Welch's t test, which is a robust test in case of the violation of the homogeneity of variances assumption, can be applied. On the other hand, when the normality assumption is met in one-way an ANOVA test, Welch's F test or Brown-Forsythe's F test, which are robust tests in case of the violation of the homogeneity of variances assumption, can be applied. These robust tests are unaffected by unequal variances.

3 Robust Tests for the Violation of Homogeneity of Variances Assumption

Welch's t test and F test, and Brown-Forsythe's F test, are the robust counterparts of the two independent samples t and one-way ANOVA tests for the violation of homogeneity of variances assumption in parametric hypothesis tests. Welch's F test and Brown-Forsythe's F test are only available with one-way ANOVA tests.

3.1 Welch's t Test

Welch's t test is the robust counterpart of the two independent samples t test. This test is more reliable than the classic two independent samples t test when two samples have unequal variances. The hypotheses that are tested in the two independent samples t test again stay the same in the Welch's t test. The assumptions are also the same, but with one exception. The homogeneity assumption does not exist here. If the equal variance assumption has been violated, then an adjusted t statistic can be used. Under the mentioned assumptions, Welch's t test statistics is computed

$$t = \left| \frac{\bar{x}_1 - \bar{x}_2}{SE_{W(\bar{x}_1 - \bar{x}_2)}} \right| \tag{6}$$

with the standard error in the equation shown below:

$$SE_{W(\bar{x}_1-\bar{x}_2)} = \sqrt{\frac{s_1^2}{n_1}+\frac{s_2^2}{n_2}} \tag{7}$$

Welch's t test statistic has a distribution very close to the t distribution. And, the standard deviation is computed as follows:

$$s = unpooled = \sqrt{\frac{\Sigma\left(x-\bar{x}\right)^2}{n-1}} \tag{8}$$

The degrees of freedom (df.) is as follows:

$$df = \frac{\left(\frac{s_1^2}{n_1}+\frac{s_2^2}{n_2}\right)^2}{\frac{\left(\frac{s_1^2}{n_1}\right)^2}{n_1-1}+\frac{\left(\frac{s_2^2}{n_2}\right)^2}{n_2-1}} \tag{9}$$

The same comparison that is the comparison of the calculated Welch's t test statistic with the t table value is conducted in order to make decision to reject or not to reject the null hypothesis.

Two independent samples t test and Welch's t test differs in two ways. The first difference is the difference between standard errors. While the standard deviation is calculated in the two independent samples t test, the pooled standard deviation is calculated by taking the weighted mean.

In the Welch's t test the standard deviations of each sample are calculated separately by taking simple averages. The standard error calculated in the Welch's t test is called the Satterhwaite (1946) convergence. With this equation, both unequal variances and unequal sample sizes are taken into account at the same time. The second difference is the difference in the degrees of freedom. In the two independent sample t tests, the degrees of freedom is the sum of the numbers of observations minus two $\mathrm{v} = \mathrm{n}_1 + \mathrm{n}_2 - 2$, while in Welch's t test the degrees of freedom is calculated with a mixed formula.

3.2 Welch's F Test and Brown-Forsythe's F Test

Welch's F test and Brown-Forsythe's F test are robust counterparts of the one-way ANOVA test. This test is more reliable than the classic one-way ANOVA test when more samples have unequal variances. The Welch's F test is more powerful than the Brown-Forsythe F test. The hypotheses that are also tested for the Welch's F test and Brown-Forsythe's F test, which are tested for the one-way ANOVA test, again stay the same. The assumptions are also the same with one exception. The homogeneity assumption does not exist here. If the equal variance assumption has been violated, then an adjusted F statistic can be used. Under the mentioned assumptions, respectively, Welch's F test statistics and Brown-Forsythe's F test statistics are as follows:

$$F_{Welch} = \frac{\sum_{l=1}^{k}\left[\left(\overline{T}_l - \tilde{X}\right)^2 \Big/ (k-1)\right]}{1 + \frac{2(k-2)}{(k^2-1)}\sum_{l=1}^{k}\left[\left(1 - \frac{\omega_l}{u}\right)^2 \Big/ W_l - 1\right]} \tag{10}$$

$$F_{BF} = \frac{\sum_{l=1}^{k} W_l\left(\overline{T}_l - \overline{G}\right)^2}{\sum_{l=1}^{k}\left(1 - W_l \big/ W\right) s_l^2} \tag{11}$$

If the variances are unequal, these two techniques (Welch one-way ANOVA and Brown-Forsythe one-way ANOVA) allow for this assumption violation, and make it available to continue to conduct the parametric test under these conditions. If the null hypothesis is rejected with either the Welch's F test statistic or the Brown-Forsythe's F test statistic, then the Games-Howell post hoc test is an appropriate post hoc test under the conditions of the unequal variances assumption violation. So, the group that makes the difference can be found.

3.3 How to Run the Robust Tests in Statistical Packages

Minitab and SPSS are popular statistical packages that are generally used by the practitioners in all type of statistical analyses. These packages enable researchers to conduct the robust tests.[3]

In Minitab 17, you can run the robust test of Welch's t test by clicking Stat / Basic Statistics / 2 Sample t, then clicking 'Two Sample t: Options' and unchecking 'Assume equal variances'. By doing so, Welch's t test results are obtained.

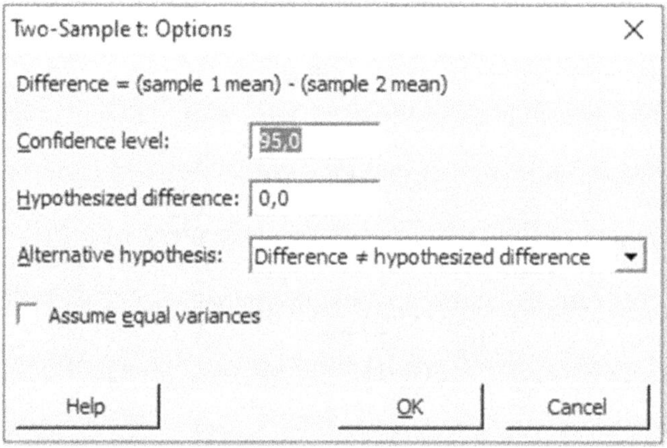

Fig. 1: *Minitab Welch's t Test Selection Screen*

In Minitab 17, you can also run the robust test of Welch's F test by clicking Stat / ANOVA / One-Way, then clicking 'One-Way Analysis of Variance: Options' and unchecking 'Assume equal variances'. By doing so, Welch's F test results are obtained.

3 See Tüzüntürk (2018) for application details with these packages.

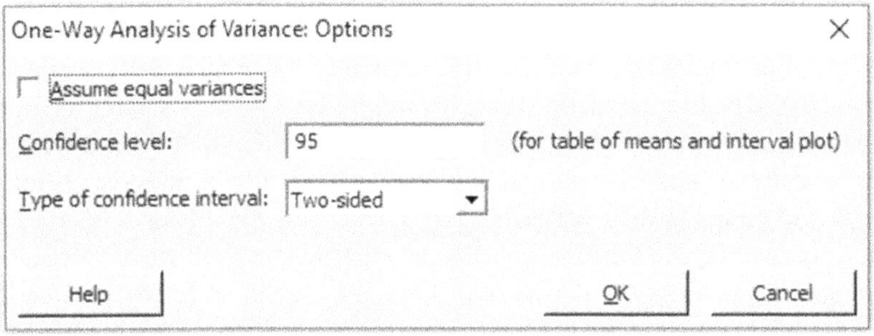

Fig. 2: *Minitab Welch's F Test Selection Screen*

In SPSS 23, you can run the robust test of Welch's t test by clicking Analyse / Compare Means / Independent Samples t test. And, automatically, the SPSS statistical package gives both results for the two independent samples t test and for Welch's t test at the same output table. The line with the 'Equal variances assumed' are the results for the two independent samples t test, and the line with the 'Equal variances not assumed' are the results for Welch's t test.

In SPSS 23, you can run the robust test of Welch's F test and Brown-Forsythe's F test by clicking Analyse / Compare Means / One-Way ANOVA, then clicking 'One-Way ANOVA: Options' and checking the Brown-Forsythe and Welch boxes, as seen below.

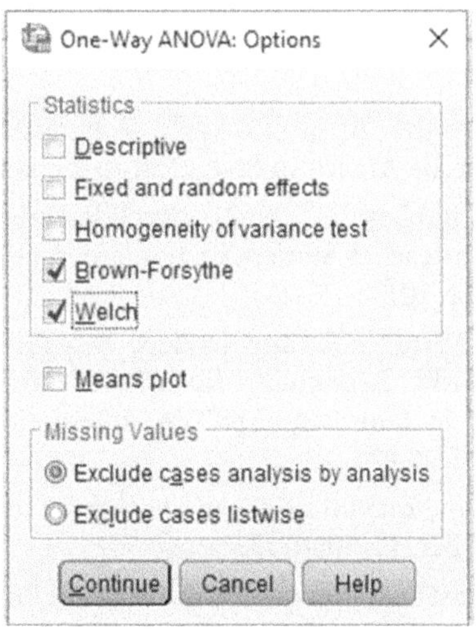

Fig. 3: *SPSS Welch's and Brown-Forsythe F Tests Selection Screen*

4 Conclusions

Assumptions of parametric tests, such as normality and homogeneity, are needed to be satisfied before conducting these hypothesis tests. As stated in the introduction, the aim of this text is to draw the researchers' attention in conducting the homogeneity of variances test, and in reporting its results, besides the normality check, and report in their research reports, and draw the researchers' attention when conducting the existing robust tests, especially in the case of violation of homogeneity assumption. Biased results are obtained in both two independent samples t and one-way ANOVA tests in case of violation of the homogeneity assumption. Results are no longer reliable and statistical inferences are invalid. In such situations, researchers should use Welch's and Brown-Forsythe's tests as stated.

References

Aytaç, M. (1991). Uygulamalı Parametrik Olmayan İstatistik Testleri, Bursa: Uludağ Üniversitesi Basımevi.

Aytaç, M. (2004). Matematiksel İstatistik, Bursa: Ezgi Kitabevi.

Aytaç, M. and Arlı, N. B. (2018). Sosyal Bilimlerde Parametrik Olmayan İstatistiksel Yöntemler, Bursa: Ezgi Kitabevi.

Bartlett, M. S. (1937). Properties of sufficiency and statistical tests. Proceedings of the Royal Statistical Society. Series A, 160, 268–282.

Brown, M. B. and Forsythe, A. B. (1974(a)). The small sample behaviour of some statistics which test the equality of several means. Technometrics. 16, 129–132.

Brown, M. B. and Forsythe, A. B. (1974(b)). Robust tests for the equality of variances. Journal of the American Statistical Association. 69, 364–367.

Delacre, M, Lakens, D. and Leys, C. (2017). Why Psychologists Should by Default Use Welch's t-test Instead of Student's t test, International Review of Social Psychology, 30(1), 92–101.

Delacre, M, Leys, C. Mora, Y. L. and Lakens, D. (2019). Taking Parametric Assumptions Seriously: Arguments for Use of Welch's F-test instead of the Classical F-test in One-Way ANOVA, International Review of Social Psychology, 32(1): 13, 1–12.

Hartley, H. O. (1950). The maximum F-ratio as a short cut test for homogeneity of variance. Biometrika. 37, 308–312.

Levene, H. (1960). Robust tests for equality of variances. In Ingram Olkin, Harold Hotelling, et al. (Eds.), Contributions to Probability and Statistics: Essays in Honor of Harold Hotelling. Stanford, CA: Stanford University Press, pp. 278–292.

Satterthwaite, F. E. (1946). An Approximate Distribution of Estimates of Variance Components, Biometrics Bulletin, 2(6): 110–114.

Tüzüntürk, S. (2015). Performing Parametric and Nonparametric Statistical Methods Using Higher Education Service Quality Data. Paradoks Economics, Sociology and Policy Journal, 11(1): 265–293.

Tüzüntürk, S. (2018). Sosyal Bilimlerde İstatistiksel Araştırmanın Temelleri, Bursa: Aktüel 16.

Tüzüntürk, S. (2020). "The Applications of Two-Sample Hotelling's T^2 Test and One-Way Multivariate Analysis of Variances (MANOVA) Test". In Özer Özçelik (Ed.), Studies on Interdisciplinary Economics and Business Volume III (p. 221–234), Germany, Berlin: Peterlang.

Welch, B. L. (1947). The generalization of Student's problem when several different population variances are involved. Biometrika, 34, 28–35.

Welch, B. L. (1951). On the Comparison of Several Mean Values: An Alternative Approach. Biometrika, 38, 330–336.

Cemalettin Hatipoğlu

E-Commerce: Characteristics and Benefits

1 Introduction

E-marketing is a method that utilizes the Internet to market goods or services. It utilizes a broad variety of technology to connect people to companies. It covers both direct and indirect marketing practices by leveraging a variety of technology to better communicate business with customers. The integrated system improves the productivity of firms' transactions and reduces marketing expenses. Buyers are offered a variety of useful knowledge from the website, so they are less unwilling to buy from a single vendor. It delivers products and services to those that need them. The product/service consists of all procedures and activities intended to attract, identify, gain and maintain the consumer base. The use of websites are subject to online marketing techniques, such as social marketing, search marketing, online advertising, online ads, email marketing, social media, media advertising, video marketing, SMS marketing, mobile marketing and mobile app marketing.

Nowadays, the use of technology is widespread in each and every sector. In this era of globalization, almost all sectors integrate technology in one form or another. There is no hesitation, and it is fairly natural that the business world will efficiently use modern technology to obtain the greatest advantage of technology. The Internet is one of the biggest technology benefits, allowing people from distant areas or counties to interact and communicate easily. The world has become a single village.

Technological development is a non-stop phase. In recent years it has given birth to an information age. Both buyers and sellers now have a lot of power due to the huge use of many advanced tools, as well as the Internet itself. Most of today's companies operate on digital networks worldwide due to e-commerce requirements. The Internet connects people with businesses, and these facilities are enjoyed by most people. In the future, there is a great field of economics and affects community.

2 Definition of E-Commerce

The E-commerce term was used to define the process of Electronic Data Interchange (EDI) and Electronic Fund Transfer (EFT), which began in the 1960s and was formally accepted by the accredited certification committee of industry representatives in the late 1970s (Winter, 2011). E-commerce technology provided commercial transactions with the opportunity, including but not restricted to, to buying and paying for goods, sending purchasing orders, and exchanging money electronically between businesses. Transfer was limited because setting up EDI was expensive; by the 1990s only around one quarter of the businesses in Europe and the US had implemented EDI (Becker,2007).

E-commerce is known by many terms, and the meaning of the term has become a point of conflict. People view e-commerce mainly as the method by which to purchase and sell products and services digitally, while others see it as a more significant market operation. Wan (2002) argues that e-commerce is utilizing the Internet to implement market transformations. Either way, the usage of new technology is involved in the exchange of products and services. Either way, digital purchases are involved instead of the normal direct exchanging of products and services. E-commerce entails market operations carried by digital data sharing as well as those created over the web. E-commerce is also a range of commercial purchases carried out via computer networks such as the internet (Hajli, Sims and Shanmugam, 2014). Elseoud (2014) defined e-commerce as transactions that are carried out between individuals, companies and organizations via internet networks. Abebe (2014) defines e-commerce as the purchase and sale of materials, goods and services via computer networks. Muhannad and Ahmed (2014) defined e-commerce as the activity of individuals exchanging business information and transactions through e-mails and the Internet. According to Muhannad and Ahmed, electronic methods of transacting e-commerce company involve internally and externally computer-connected networks such as the Internet, exchanging of business transactions through electronic data interchange (EDI), the use of telephones and fax machines, and ATMs for transacting business and receiving digital currency. Electronic commerce is the transfer of products and resources through electronic networks (Laudon and Traver, 2013). Although some authors consider e-commerce to be purely a commercial transaction medium, all authors accept e-commerce as a portal to carrying out commercial transactions.

Therefore, the Organization for Economic Cooperation and Development (OECD) and its member countries have implemented two meanings of the term. The general concept of e-commerce includes all purchases and purchasing undertaken via computer controlled platforms (OECD, 2002,89). However, payment and distribution may be done online or offline; likewise e-commerce or online commerce, such as the selling or purchasing of products and services over the Internet, as well as uniform transaction processing for billing and distribution, which may be both on-line and off-line. The trend is to take the large meaning since transactions already exist in electronic media as well. The OECD (2002) provided differentiation in providing a description of e commerce as a commercial operation that takes place over the Internet, including other interactive media, but not specifically the Internet, including the Electronic Data Interchange (EDI). Components of e-commerce are illustrated in Fig. 1 (Qin, et al, 2014)

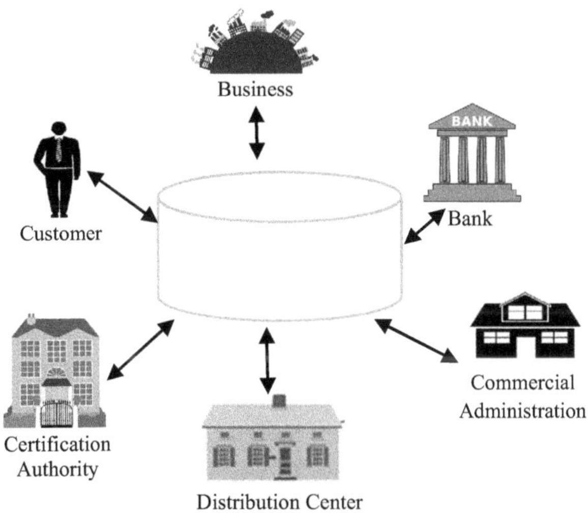

Fig. 1. *Components of e-commerce*
Source: (Qin, et al., 2014)

- Networks: They are internet, intranet and extranet. E-commerce is supported by the Internet, and commercial market knowledge can be found there. The intranet is the system in which businesses perform internal business, and the extranet is the bridge to link enterprises and consumers for commercial transactions.
- E-commerce customer: Both personal and company users are considered. The company customers develop an intranet, extranet and management information system to scientifically control their employees, finances, products, development, delivery and sales. Consumers who have or may have personal internet connections are able to receive details as well as make transactions by utilizing online servers, set-top boxes, PDA's (Personal Digital Assistants), Visual TV and the like.

- Certification Authority: The Certification Authority (CA) is a recognized authority that has legal right to approve and manage digital certificates in order to enable safe online transactions between the parties.
- Distribution Center: It is responsible for delivering products that cannot be distributed online to buyers, and for maintaining control over the movement of goods.
- E-bank: It provides sellers and buyers with real-time applications twenty-four hours a day.
- Commercial Administration: Often made up of industrial, tax, customs, foreign exchange and economic management departments.

Though it is only one aspect of the e-concept, electronic commerce is an instrument for social change and expands opportunities for the future. E-commerce will change anything relevant to the society and laws, because the e-concept can exert a great deal of impact on the world, both in depth and scale.

3 Characteristics of E-Commerce

E-commerce covers a wide range of business practices. It involves using the Internet for purchasing, selling goods or services to a third party online, sharing data among companies, promoting products and transmitting product details through any internet-based telecommunication devices.

In contrast to the traditional marketing form, e-commerce has the following advantages: (Rayport and Jaworski, 2002). First, e-commerce decreases the amount of intermediaries in industry. In the traditional way of doing industry, a multilevel system runs from the manufacturers to the enterprise, to the wholesaler, to dealers and to end consumers. However the e-commerce system removes the need for third party intermediaries and improves the relationship between the seller and the final buyer. Second, the Internet allows companies to do business digitally with consumers everywhere in the world, while the traditional business is restricted by transportation and access to knowledge. Third, e-commerce may be completed at any time online. The requirement for a physical shop is minimized. Fourth, e-commerce offers a more convenient channel to learn consumer preferences and makes for more effective trading procedures. Fifth, e-commerce removes barriers to entry and increases consumers' knowledge regarding vendors. The purchase is done entirely online, and the buyer has the opportunity to search for various vendors. Communication Platforms used by traditional and digital marketing are shown in table 1.

Tab. 1 *Communication Platforms Used by Traditional Marketing and Digital Marketing*

Traditional Marketing	Digital Marketing
• Print ads, online ads, direct mailers and other print material. • Radio ads – such as TV ads. • Direct mail including newspapers, brochures, and letter mailings. • Telemarketing.	• Website • Social network sites • Content marketing • Banner ads • Google ads • Video marketing

Source: Sawrov and Islam, 2018;220

As opposed to traditional trade, e-commerce has modified the dynamical behaviours of purchasing and exchanging practices. In addition, there is a noticeable difference between two types of business. Traditional activity typically operates at physical locations such as malls, retail stores and warehouses. Traditional business occurs in physical spaces such as in shopping centres where consumers come and go (Kalakota and Robinson, 1999). According to the characteristics of e-commerce, e-commerce has modified both physical and conceptual features of contemporary economic activities. If we agree that space is relational, we should recognize that the growth of e-commerce is not just a fundamental shift in socioeconomic practices, but also a transformation for the way space is considered. Compared to traditional business transactions e-commerce is redefining all three dimensions of space, time and multiplicity within the economic relations of development.

E-commerce brings fresh spatiality's into the marketing world. The redefinition of company in e-commerce emerges from its growing technical dependency. Second, the place of an e-commerce company can be any place of the person's choice; e-commerce has expanded the reach of the corporate world. Having the opportunity to function remotely it helps more individuals to enter and engage in business. Second, social, fiscal and cultural obstacles have been eliminated, contributing to greater access to all consumers and buyers. The dynamism of e-business is highly dependent on the complex existence of storage.

E-commerce operations provide a specific challenge to the established temporality of industry. E-commerce reduces the temporal constraint of hours of service and becomes a practice that can be performed every time, (Chaffery, 2007) and often implies a business that is evolving continuously. Additionally, e-commerce eliminates the time taken for procedures such as scheduling trips and scheduling corporate meetings. The sharing of knowledge over the Internet will cause the communication to be transmitted globally in seconds. Because shortfalls in both manufacturing and transaction time may be reduced, the output and business cycle are accelerated (Karavdic and Gregory, 2005). Unless the rate of accumulation of resources rises, the acceleration of time increases, and time is compressed. The latest e-commerce features have a significant influence on the progression of the increasing social network creation.

E-commerce shifts the traditional partnership between company owners and customers. The fewer intermediaries involved in commercial dealings, allows for a more transparent and productive relationship between firms and consumers (Lu et al., 2010). Additionally, since companies will transact business through fibre optics, the current temporality of e-commerce results in the acceleration of capital circulation. The more currency moves widely across the world, the more complex and diverse the world's politics become. The overall result of this is more intense commercial interactions, effective knowledge sharing, complex government and power systems and better resource cycles.

4 Benefits of e-Commerce

The nature and aspects of traditional trade have been modified significantly by electronic commerce. The fundamentals of how companies operate haven't shifted owing to the growth of e-commerce. The aim of all companies is to generate as much revenue as possible while incurring the lowest possible cost. The economic impact of e-commerce will be felt by the world economy once businesses adapt to and use e-commerce.

The most critical economic effect of e-commerce is that it creates an extra a segment in the market that was traditionally unavailable to other market operations. This effect results from the increasing development of information technology. Because e-commerce depends on the increasingly developing technology, its effect on the economy is similar to other commercial sectors. (Yu, and Dong, 2013)

Although there is little difference in terms of free entry and exit to the market, selling space, and online space and services available for product distribution, pricing and marketing between a big chain of shops and an ordinary small-and medium-sized company (SME), there are significant differences during the sales and promotion phases of the commodity (Wymbs, 2000).

E-commerce lowers after-sales services expenses by growing the enterprise's manufacturing inputs, increasing buying, ordering procedures and increasing efficiency standards (Visser and Lanzendorf 2004).

According to Sila, e-commerce will save money by influencing a variety of ‘processes, the nature of the marketplace, customer decisions, the degree of information gaps and the ability to implement (Sila, 2013)

When the e-commerce input supply is transferred from one company to another, financial gains are frequently obtained.The order-processing software in e-commerce expands order processes by reducing the amount of paper, and minimizing costs resulting from the distribution of documents by special courier, since less paper is needed in businesses (Santos, B. 2018).

Through e-commerce, a customer will save on shipping costs as well. In e-commerce, the items are marketed first and then produced, which reduces needless inventory and stock-related costs (Baily and Lawrence 2001)

More spending and other operational costs are faced as the number of consumers, goods and transaction volumes rise. However, such a situation is rarely identified in e-commerce (Malecki, 2002). Research costs, including time, energy and expense, are greatly decreased for e-commerce. The positive effect of e-commerce on research costs, particularly time savings, benefits companies by boosting productivity. Although favourable to both customers and manufacturers, the positive impact of e-commerce on research costs is no less important to one community than the other. E-commerce succeeds with both buying input resources and shipping goods to consumers.

E-commerce reduces the effort and time involved in procedures such as identifying the suppliers, determining the commodity properties and costs, and engaging with these companies(Chaffey,2007). E-commerce is a major help to customers, and it is definitely seen in the costs of products and services (Dignum, 2002).

On the other side, e-commerce has altered the type and emphasis of competition and has facilitated the production of new products and services in the Internet environment. The scope of commerce has developed, and the competitive environment has developed too (Freebain, J. 2001). The fact that companies have reduced costs due to e-commerce and how that affects pricing shows their competitive edge. Due to e-commerce, companies achieve economic advantage because they have the potential to do business on an international scale.

E-commerce helps improve quality and competitiveness in the economy while at the same time consuming less capital and fewer inputs (Freund and Weinhold, 2002). Changes in consumer dynamics and corporate structures surround the transition from the retail market to the electronic market of e-commerce. The accessibility of buying for seven days, twenty-four hours a day, impacts the e-commerce industry in a significant manner. Thus, the general corporate organization of the business is changed (Borenstein and Saloner. 2001).

5 Conclusion

The usage of information and communication technology (ICT) in the last quarter century of manufacturing has contributed to quality and performance improvements in production processes. The great opportunities that have recently emerged, particularly for firms with limited marketing and advertising budgets, are illustrated here. The Internet opens for new prospects and possibilities that companies couldn't achieve before. The economy's most dynamic companies have the ability to make a significant influence to the economy in the future through their commitment to e-commerce and their degree of acceptance of e-commerce applications.

E-commerce has had a significant impact on the structure of economies and enterprises. While the marketplace itself is still relatively broad and virtual, the functions of the marketplace members are also shifting. Consumers have a greater influence on trade market direction than they had in the past. Through e-commerce, the perception of a global market composed of millions of consumers has shifted, and the view that the market is made up of millions of markets has gained support. Every company, whether conducting e-commerce or not, is faced with the requirement of dealing with evolving business conditions and reorganizing their business structure. With the influence of e-commerce, organizations are moved from multi-level hierarchical systems to horizontal and network structures. Supplying utilities such as VOIP, chat and newsgroups lays the foundation for collaboration even though staff are not in the same place. This suggests an increase in efficiency and improvement in the business's internal processes. The most effective marketing technique that e-commerce companies should use is developing an easy-to-use site interface. A variety of steps will include automated scanning functionality specific to the items searched on this page, information about after-sales assistance programs, and an on-line sales agent to advertise products with technological characteristics. In addition, hiring a customer care specialist who is willing to respond to e-mail inquiries will be employed.

With the growth and usage of the Internet, there has been an improvement in protection with better accessibility, and therefore, more opportunity for governments, individuals and enterprises to profit from the internet. As electronic commerce technologies have advanced, economic advantages connected with them have become more evident, and firms who discover these advantages exploit electronic commerce in order to improve their market place, broaden their consumer base and reap various other benefits.

References

Abebe, M. (2014). Electronic commerce adoption, entrepreneurial orientation and smalland medium-sized enterprise (SME) performance. Journal of Small Business and Enterprise Development, 21, 100–116. doi:10.1108/JSBED-10-2013-0145

Baily, M. N. and Lawrence R.Z.(2001) . Do we have a new E-conomy?. American Economic Review 91(2):308-312 .DOI:10.1257/aer.91.2.308Becker, A. (Ed.). (2007). Electronic commerce: Concepts, methodologies, tools, and applications. IGI Global. Retrieved from https://books.google.com.ng/books?hl=enandlr=andid=qAMtUzo00BMCandoi=fndandpg=PR1 andots=-Sn5cKAuN- andsig=D_CzeYvNoePastfyCOBlmdhL dN0andredir_esc=y#v=onepageandqandf=false

Borenstein, S. and Saloner. G. (2001). Economics and Electronic Commerce. Journal o f Economic Perspectives, 15(1): 3–12.

Chaffey, D. (2007). E-business and E-commerce Management: Strategy, Implementation and Practice. Pearson Education

Dignum, F. (2002). E-Commerce in Production: Some Experiences. Integrated Manufacturing Systems, 13(5): 283–294..

Elseoud, M. S. A. (2014). Electronic commerce and economic growth in Saudi Arabia. International Journal of Economics, Commerce and Management, 2(5), 1–16. Retrieved from http://ijecm.co.uk/

Freebain, J.(2001). Some Market Effects of E-Commerce. The Singapore Economic Reviews, 46(1): 49–62.

Freund, C., and Weinhold, D. (2002). The Internet and international trade in services. American Economic Review, 92(2), 236–240.

Hajli, N., Sims, J., and Shanmugam, M. (2014). A practical model for e-commerce adoption in Iran. Journal of Enterprise Information Management, 27, 719–730. doi:10.1108/JEIM-09-2013-0070

Kalakota, R., and Robinson, M. (1999). e-Business. Roadmap for Success. Addison Wesley

Karavdic, M., and Gregory, G. (2005). Integrating e-commerce into existing export marketing theories: A contingency model. Marketing Theory, 5(1), 75–104.

Laudon, K. C., and Traver, C. G. (2007). E-commerce. New York: Pearson/Addison Wesley.

Lu, Y., Zhao, L., and Wang, B. (2010). From virtual community members to C2C e-commerce buyers: Trust in virtual communities and its effect on consumers' purchase intention. Electronic Commerce Research and Applications, 9(4), 346–360.

Malecki, E. J. (2002). The economic geography of the Internet's infrastructure. Economic Geography, 78(4), 399–424.

Muhannad, K., and Ahmed, G. (2014). Customer perceptions of e-commerce in the United Arab Emirate. International Journal of Global Business, 7(1), 95–109. Retrieved from http://www.gsmi-ijgb.com/

OECD. (2002). Resources for the information economy. Measuring the information economy 2002, 9–17. doi.org/10.1787/9789264099012-en

Qin, Z., Chang, Y., Li, S., Li, F.(2014). E-Commerce and E-Commerce Strategy. E-Commerce Strategy. Zhejiang University Press, Hangzhou. Heidelberg: Springer. ISBN 978-3-642-39413-3.

Rayport, J. F., and Jaworski. B. J. (2002). Introduction to e-Commerce. Boston, MA: McGraw-Hill/Irwin series in marketing, https://books.google.com.tr/books?id=BddbAgAACAAJ

Santos, B. (2018). Consumer search on the internet. International Journal of Industrial Organization, 58, 66–105.

Sila, I. (2013). Factors affecting the adoption of B2B e-commerce technologies. Electronic Commerce Research, 13(2), 199–236

Sawrov, M. H. and Islam, M. M. (2018) "Scope of E-Marketing" A Comprehensive Study on E- Marketing in Bangladesh, The International Journal Of Business and Management (ISSN 2321–8916), 6(2).

Visser, E. J., and Lanzendorf, M. (2004). Mobility and accessibility effects of b2c e-commerce: a literature review. Tijdschrift voor Economische en Sociale Geografie, 95, 189–205.

Wan, W. P. (2002). Interview: United parcel service's director of electronic commerce, Alan Amling, on the opportunities and challenges of global electronic commerce. Thunderbird International Business Review, 44(4), 445–454. doi: https://doi.org/10.1002/tie.10030

Winter, S. J. (2011). The rise of cyberinfrastructure and grand challenges for eCommerce. Information Systems and e-Business Management, 10(3), 279–293. doi:10.1007/s10257- 011-0165-5

Wymbs, C. (2000). How e-commerce is transforming and internationalizing service industries. Journal of Services Marketing, 14(6), 463–477.

Yu, C. S., and Dong, X. B. (2013). A conceptual framework for e-commerce innovation in Chinese SMES. Journal of International Technology and Information Management, 22(1), 17–41.

Ahmet Yanık and Hakan Güveli

Assessment of TFRS-16 Leasing Procedures in Terms of Income Tax and VAT Deduction

1 Introduction

TFRS 16 lease standards that replaced TAS 17 lease standards in our country for companies that prepare financial statements according to financial reporting standards entered into force on 1 January 2019, causing material changes to the production of financial statements. The TAS 17, which was executed from the financial year starting after 31 December 2005, did not include any provisions concerning the reflection of assets and obligations from financial leases on financial statements. Enabling a reflection of operating leases on financial statements, published by the International Accounting Standards Board (IASB) as IFRS 16 in January 2016, the standard entered into force as of 1 January 2019 as the TFRS 16 lease standard (TÜRMOB, 2021).

In our country, this standard was published in the Official Gazette dated 16 April 2018, issue number 29826, to be applied in the financial years following 31 December 2018. Presenting financial leases on financial statements using the TFRS 16 lease standard shall affect industries such as retail, transportation, communication, technology-science and production.

Leaving lessee assets and obligations under operating leases outside financial statements caused deficiencies in the measurement of leases. The off-balance obligations in the world during 2014 was $3 trillion (US), while in our country this amount reached about 10 billion lira (TRY) (TURMOB, 2021).

2 Assessment of Lease Contracts

Lease contracts might not be subject to TFRS 16 lease standards. Lease contracts must be in line with article 9 of the standard 'in case the contract transfers against remuneration the right to control use of the defined asset for a period, this contract is a lease contract or it involves a lease procedure' in order to be subject to the standard (KGK, 2021) (Karataş, 2019). According to this article, three important particulars that must be in the contract should be determined. These are (KGK, 2021; Örten, 2020):

- Lease Term: The non-cancellable period when the lessee has the right to use the underlying asset. In case there is a reasonable assurance that the lessee shall use the option to extend lease, the term this option covers, in case there is reasonable assurance that lessee would not use an option giving the right to terminate lease, must be established. In other words, a lease contract that could be voluntarily cancelled or where the option to cancel outweighs other options for the lessee is not a lease but a service contract in this scope.
- Lease Price: In scope of the standard, a lease contract must have a constant price. In the scope of the standard, *constant lease payments can be variable pro forma while in essence they are inevitable payments.* For instance, while lease prices of companies are calculated, it is not possible to assess the contract as a lease contract by making the lease price dependent on revenue or a certain sales amount. Lease prices determined in a foreign currency or indexed to wholesale price index-consumer price index would be assessed as a fixed lease payment.
- Control of Use: Controlling the use of asset by the lessee during period of use expresses the right to control the use of the asset. Controlling is linked to the right to acquire the entire economic benefits that come with use of the asset and the right to manage.

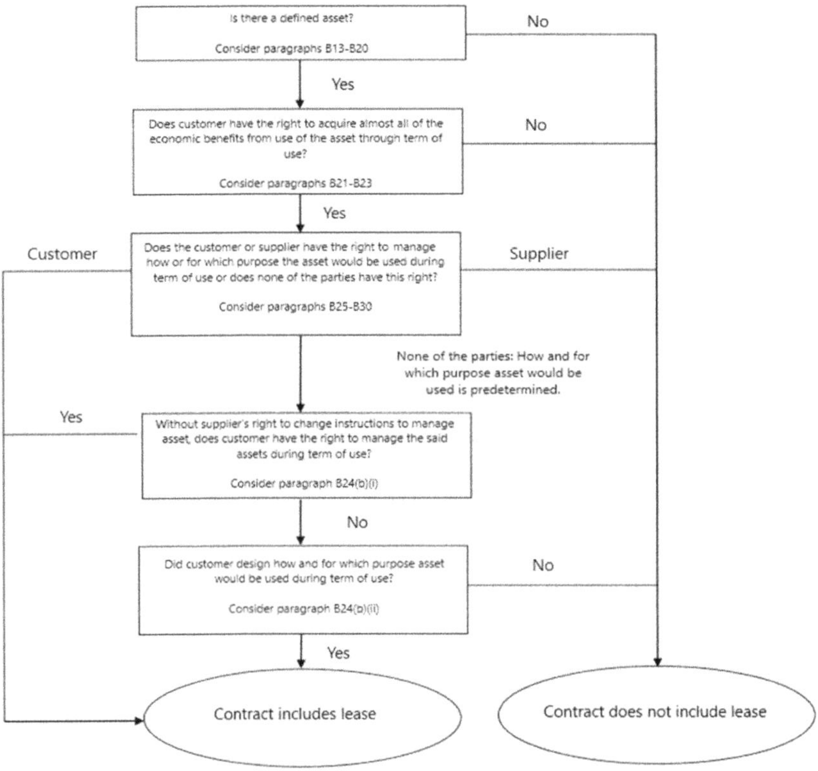

Fig. 1. *Determination of a Lease Contract*
Source: TFRS 16 B31

2.1 Classification of Lease

A lease can take place in various ways. Registering and classifying lease is important for accounting purposes. Classification can take place in the following way (KGK, 2021):

- Operating Lease: A lease where all risks and returns from the underlying asset are not materially assigned.
- In case all risks and returns from ownership of underlying asset are openly demonstrated as not materially assigned, the said lease is classified as an operating lease.

- For instance, this might be possible in case when the ownership of underlying asset is assigned at the end of lease term in return for a variable payment or for variable payments at fair value at the time or in case there is variable lease payments causing the lessor to not materially assign all risks and returns.
- Financial Lease: A lease where all risks and returns from the ownership of underlying asset are materially assigned. There are indicators that might result by itself or in conjunction with others in the classification of a lease as financial lease. These are:

  - Compensation by the lessee of damages to the lessor resulting from termination when lessee can terminate leasing in case lessee can terminate leasing, compensation by lessee of damages to lessor resulting from lease,
  - Meeting by the lessee of gains and losses as a result of changes changes in fair residual value (for instance discount on lease price equal to the major part of amount acquired from sale at the end of lease) and.
  - The lessee having the right to continue the lease for a second period in return for a lease price considerable lower than market price.

- Short Term Leasing: A lease with a lease term of twelve months or less from the date the lease begins. A lease with purchase option is not a short-term lease.
- Sub-lease: A procedure by which the underlying asset is re-leased by the lessee ('lessor under sub-lease') to a third party; the lease between the lessor and the lessee under head lease ('head lease') continues to stay in force.
- Leases when the underlying asset has a low value: Assesses value of underlying asset without regard to the age of the leased asset and its value in its new state. An assessment of whether an underlying asset has a low value or not is conducted on an objective basis. This assessment is not affected by size, quality and the conditions of the lessee. Thus, it is expected that different lessees would arrive at the same conclusion if a certain underlying asset is of low value or not.
- Sell-Re-lease: In case a business (seller-lessee) assigns an asset to another business (buyer-lessor) and re-leases the same asset from the buyer-lessor, the seller-lessor and the buyer-lessor must recognize an assignment contract and lease according to TFRS 16.

A lease is classified as financial lease in case all risks and returns from ownership of underlying asset are materially assigned. A lease whereby all risks and returns from ownership of underlying asset are not materially assigned is classified as operating lease.

Whether a lease is financial lease or an operating lease depends more on the essence of procedure rather than the contract. Examples of situations where a lease is usually classified as a financial lease by itself or in conjunction with each other are as follows (KGK, 2021):

- Where a lease foresees that the ownership of underlying asset is assigned to lessee until the end of the lease term,
- A lessee that has the option to purchase an underlying asset for a price that is expected to be sufficiently lower than fair value on the date option is exercised is reasonably expected to exercise this option on the effective date of lease contract.

Based on the Law on Leasing, Factoring, and Finance Companies Law, number 6361, a lease was defined as a 'Lease procedure based on a lease contract, whereby lessor authorized according to this Law or relevant regulations assigns ownership of an asset at the end of its lease term for financing purposes; giving lessee the right to purchase the asset for a price under market value at the end of the lease term; that meets one of the conditions of lease term covering more than eighty per cent of the asset's economic life or total current values of lease payments made according to lease contract equaling a higher value that ninety per cent of the asset's market price' (Official Gazette, 2021).

While lease is defined in the law, some points are materially defined. These are;

- It must be based on a contract,
- It must be for financing purposes in terms of the lessor,
- It must assign ownership of the asset to lessee at the end of lease term or give the right to purchase for low price,
- The lease term must cover more than eighty per cent of the asset's economic life or total current value of lease payments according to lease contract must be higher than ninety per cent of the asset's market price

Such material conditions are not in the standard. While the law defined participation banks, leasing companies and investment and development banks as able to lease, and that only such institutions could be authorized, according to the standard producers and sellers can also lease.

3 Declaration and Payments of Vat Deduction in Lease Procedures

In Turkey property owners are responsible from payment of property tax (ÇİFTÇİ, T., ORGAN, İ. (2019)), unless the contract states that the lessee is responsible for the payment of property taxes, and that payment should be made by the lessee. Property tax is accepted as a constituent part of lease payments (Karataş, 2019). Regarding assets leased by those that do not have VAT liability; the VAT that accrues on lease payments must be accepted as a part of payment for which the lessee is liable.

Based on article 1/3-f of the Law on Value Added Tax, number 3065, the lease procedures of property and rights are subject to VAT (Information System of Regulations, 2021).

Thus, although leasing the said properties and rights is not a service given within the scope of commercial, industrial, agricultural and self-employment activity, it shall be subject to VAT.

VAT regarding such lease procedures (Information System of Regulations, 2021).

In case the following conditions exist together:

- The lessee not being a VAT payer due to other activities (including those that only pay reverse charge VAT), and
- The lessee being a VAT payer (excluding those that only pay reverse charge VAT),

The lessee shall declare reverse charge VAT.

Also, in the case of the lessee (Information System of Regulations, 2021)

- When taxed as a small business based on Income Tax Law (even if they do not become a VAT payer by renouncing the VAT exception),
- Businesses with activities exempt from VAT such as banks and insurance companies,
- Those that were only required to submit a declaration by establishing VAT obligation when there were only processes subject to the VAT,
- Administrations, institutions, and organizations in schedules attached to Law number 5018.

VAT regarding leases shall be subject to deduction by the said lessees within the scope of this section (Information System of Regulations, 2021).

In case of leases subject to the VAT where the lessor is a VAT payer due to other activities, full deduction is not in question (SAYIŞTAŞ, 2021). For instance, X and Y companies are VAT payers. An invoice issued by these two companies to each other in respect of a lease is subject to VAT and must be declared. Whether company X is the lessor and Y is the lessee, or vice versa, VAT liability would not change. The important point here is that the parties are VAT payers. What the lessor must do here is to declare VAT regarding lease activities together with other activities according to general conditions.

However, in case person A, who is not a VAT payer, leases a venue to company X, company X must declare and pay reverse charge VAT. Parties whose activities fall under VAT Declaration No 2 are not assessed within this scope.

Deduction has a limited application in lease procedures. The reason for this being the exemption from VAT of real estate (building, land and rights registered as real estate) that are not assets of commercial enterprises. Since VAT is not applicable to the leasing of real estate that is not registered as an asset of an enterprises, there will be no obligation.

Application of such deduction is based on two criteria. These are (Maç, 2021):

- If lessor is not a VAT payer,
- If the leased property or right does not fall within the definition of 'real estate', despite being one of the properties and rights that are among properties and rights under article 70 of Income Tax Law (ITL).

For instance, when an office that belongs to a person (and not commercial enterprise) is subject of lease contract, there will be no VAT obligation because it does not belong to a commercial enterprise.

Similarly, leasing a car belonging to a person who is a VAT payer would bring a VAT obligation; i.e. since the car is included in article 70 of ITL and does not qualify as real estate, VAT shall be charged.

4 Assessment of Leasing Procedures in Terms of Withholding with Respect to Income and Corporation Tax

Stopaj, which means withholding in Turkish, comes from 'stoppage' in French meaning pre-deduction (TÜRK DİL KURUMU, 2021). Lease withholding is the deduction made by converting the lease price of an office to gross in case the lease agreement was made at the net price. Lease withholding is a taxation system. Through this procedure lease revenue is taxed before being received by the real estate owner. Thus, the government receives its revenue by taxing the source. The lessee is responsible for payment of lease withholding (Sahibinden.com, 2021).

According to Presidential Proclamation number 2813, issued in the Official Gazette on 31 July 2020, the withholding rate on income and corporate tax applied on some lease payments is predetermined at 10% (Official Gazette, 2021).

According to article 94 of Income Tax Law on payments made in return for leasing of properties and rights under article 70, the withholding tax shall be 10% instead of 20% between, 31 July 2020 and 31 December 2020.

It was declared that the 10% withholding tax would be applied instead of 20% on lease payments regarding the lease of real estate of foundations (excluding fused foundations) and associations between 31 July 2020 and 31 December 2020. In this withholding, it is not important whether the association receiving the lease payment was acting in the public interest or was a foundation given a tax exemption by the Council of Ministers. In other words, except for fused foundations, this deduction must be made on lease prices paid to all association or foundations on a non-discriminatory basis.

In case real estate belonging to associations or foundations are leased to establish a commercial enterprise, no tax deduction would be made over lease revenues because the resulting commercial enterprise would be corporate tax payer (Information System of Regulations, 2021)

A withholding tax of 10% instead of 20% would be applied on lease payments made in return for leasing of properties without diplomatic status that belong to foreign states, foreign public administrations and institutions, and international organizations between 31 July 2020 and 31 December 2020.

Within the scope of article 15 of Corporate Tax Law, it was declared that 10% withholding tax would be applied instead of 20% on lease payments made for leasing immovable property belonging to cooperatives between 31 July 2020 and 31 December 2020. The type of cooperative and its status as a tax payer does not affect the tax cut on the said lease payments (PWC Turkey, 2021).

No changes were made to the withholding rate applied to lease payments made to limited taxpayer institutions, according to article 30 of Corporate Tax Law (PWC Turkey, 2021).

In case a new legal regulation is not made, the rate of 20% shall again be applied on payments in cash or on accounts as of 1 January 2021.

The 10% discount on withholding on office lease procedures was extended until 31 May 2021, published by the Official Gazette, issue number 31343, dated 23 December 2020.

On the other hand, income tax deduction on lease payments made to unions, chambers of commerce, chambers of industry, commodity exchanges, chambers of artisans and their unions, chambers and unions of other vocational organizations, political parties, and retirement and provident funds is required (Information System of Regulations, 2021).

Tax cuts shall not be made on lease payments made in return for leasing immovable property belonging to the state, local governments, municipalities and villages to the said public institutions.

Regarding uses without lease payments, but when the lessor declares revenue based on imputed rental value, withholding would not be possible since there are no payments in cash or on account. There are no regulations for calculating withholding based on imputed rental value (Doğrusöz, 2021).

The ruling, dated 7 March 2017, numbered 19208162-010-10, on this issue mentioned that an income tax deduction would not be made for office owned by your father, as long as you do not pay for the lease in cash or on account and no expenses would be entered into the accounts for an office assigned free of charge, and withholding tax return would not be submitted as long as there are no other payments subject to deduction. There was only mention that the father was only required to make a declaration where the imputed rental value exceeded the exception provided in law (in his annual income tax declaration) (Doğrusöz, 2021).

5 Results and Suggestions

There are only a few companies that do not lease out assets or that do not lease tangible or intangible assets. At enterprises one can see lease procedures as tangible or intangible groups of assets. Leasing procedures take place mostly in retail, transportation and communication industries. Based on a study conducted by International Accounting Standards Board (IASB) on more than 30,000 publicly traded companies, 14,000 companies had off-balance leasing, and that such companies did not report $2.86 trillion (US) in their financial statements (TURMOB, 2021). TFRS 16 will ensure the inclusion of this amount on financial statements.

VAT and withholding tax would accrue based on the status of lessor that companies lease assets from. In leasing procedures, in cases where the lessor and the lessee are tax payers, an invoice including VAT would be issued, thus withholding would not accrue. However, where the other party is not taxpayer, this would change. If the lessor is not a taxpayer, withholding must be calculated and VAT would not accrue. In this case the lessee must issue a note of expenses and get the lessor's signature to declare and pay tax with withholding tax returns.In case a taxpayer lessee leases a car from a lessor, both withholding and VAT would accrue. The lessee must then make a reverse charge discount and and pay VAT and withholding.

References

Doğrusöz, B. (2021). *Kira sözleşmelerinde stopaj ve KDV*. Dünya: https://www.dunya.com/kose-yazisi/kira-sozlesmelerinde-stopaj-ve-kdv/27548 adresinden alındı

Karataş, M. (2019). İSMMMO. *TFRS 16 Kiralamalar: Yenilenen Kiralama Muhasebesi, Açıklama ve örneklerle işletmelere olası etkileri* (s. 33). içinde İstanbul: İSMMMO.

Karataş, M. (2019). İSMMMO. *TFRS 16 Kiralamalar: Yenilenen Kiralama Muhasebesi, Açıklama ve Örneklerle İşletmelere Olası Etkileri* (s. 56). içinde İstanbul: İSMMMO.

KGK. (2021). *TFRS 16.* Kamu Gözetimi Muhasebe ve Denetim Standartları Kurumu: https://kgk.gov.tr/Portalv2Uploads/files/Duyurular/v2/TFRS/TFRS_16_2018.pdf adresinden alındı

Maç, M. (2021, 4 11). *BDO Yayıncılık.* www.denet.com.tr: https://www.denet.com.tr/vergi/dosyalar/kdv6/KDV6-9.pdf adresinden alındı

Mevzuat Bilgi Sistemi. (2021). *Katma Değer Vergisi Kanunu.* T.C. Cumhurnbaşkanlığı Mevzuat Bilgi Sistemi: https://www.mevzuat.gov.tr/MevzuatMetin/1.5.3065.pdf adresinden alındı

Mevzuat Bilgi Sistemi. (2021). *1 Seri Nolu Kurumlar Vergisi Genel Tebliği.* T.C. Cumhurbaşkanlığı Mevzuat Bilgi Sistemi: https://www.mevzuat.gov.tr/anasayfa/MevzuatFihristDetayIframe?MevzuatTur=9andMevzuatNo=11219andMevzuatTertip=5 adresinden alındı

Mevzuat Bilgi Sistemi. (2021). *Katma Değer Vergisi Genel Uygulama Tebliği.* T.C. Cumhurbaşkanlığı Mevzuat Bilgi Sistemi: https://www.mevzuat.gov.tr/anasayfa/MevzuatFihristDetayIframe?MevzuatTur=9andMevzuatNo=19631andMevzuatTertip=5 adresinden alındı.

Mevzuat Bilgi Sistemi. (2021). *T.C. Cumhurbaşkanlığı Mevzuat Bilgi Sistemi.* www.mevzuat.gov.tr:https://www.mevzuat.gov.tr/anasayfa/MevzuatFihristDetayIframe?MevzuatTur=9andMevzuatNo=11219andMevzuatTertip=5 adresinden alındı

Örten, R. K. (2020). *Türkiye Muhasebe – Finansal Raporlama Standartları Uygulama ve Yorumları TMS – TFRS 2020.* Ankara: Gazi Kitabevi.

PWC Türkiye. (2021, 01 25). *İşyeri Kira Ödemelerinde Stopaj Oranı Geçici Bir Süre İçin%10.* Vergi Bülteni 2020/59: https://www.pwc.com.tr/tr/hizmetlerimiz/vergi/bultenler/ 2020/isyeri-kira-odemelerinde-stopaj-orani-gecici-bir-sure-icin-yuzde-10.html#:~:text=Kurumlar%20Vergisi%20Kanunu%27nun%2030,%C3%B6demelerde%20yeniden%20%20%20oran%C4%B1%20uygulanacakt%C4%B1r. adresinden alındı

Resmi Gazete. (2021). *FİNANSAL KİRALAMA, FAKTORİNG VE FİNANSMAN.* Resmi Gazete: https://www.resmigazete.gov.tr/eskiler/2012/12/20121213-1.htm adresindenalındı

Resmi Gazete. (2021). *Cumhurbaşkanı Kararı.* Resmi Gazete: https://www.resmigazete.gov.tr/eskiler/2020/07/20200731-5.pdf adresinden alındı

Sahibinden.com. (2021). *Kira Stopajı Nedir, Nasıl Hesaplanır?* S Emlak 360: https://www.sahibinden.com/emlak360/kira-stopaji-nedir-nasil-hesaplanir adresindenalındı

Sayıştay. (2021). *Temyiz Kurulu Kararları.* Vergi Resmi Harç ve Diğer Gelirlerle İlgili Kararlar: https://www.sayistay.gov.tr/tr/kararlar/tkk/?krr=13397#:~:text=KDV%27ye%20tabi%20olan%20kiralama,genel%20esaslara%20g%C3%B6re%20beyan%20eder. adresinden alındı

Türk Dil Kurumu. (2021). *Genel Türkçe Sözlük.* Türk Dil Kurumu: https://sozluk.gov.tr/adresinden alındı

TÜRMOB. (2021). *TURMOB.* Muhasebe Standartları Daire Başkanlığı: https://www.turmob.org.tr/Arsiv/TurmobGaleri/Dosyalar/8198a91a-3aff-4596-bc3a-2f6f455a79bf/19112018_110858_5a1d8d48-359c-46ba-ae09-28b728dd462f.pdf adresinden alındı

TÜRMOB. (2021). *Muhasebe Standartları Daire Başkanlığı.* www.turmob.org.tr:https://www.turmob.org.tr/Arsiv/TurmobGaleri/Dosyalar/8198a91a-3aff-4596-bc3a-2f6f455a79bf/19112018_110858_5a1d8d48-359c-46ba-ae09-28b728dd462f.pdf adresinden alındı

Yüce, M. (2001). Gayrimenkul Sermaye İratlarının Beyanı ve Vergilemesi. *Mevzuat Dergisi* (37), 1–13.

Mihriban Cindiloğlu Demirer, Ömür Demirer, Leyla Erat and Nadide Aktaş

Green Innovation Applications in the Logistics Sector in the Context of Sustainability

1 Introduction

Modern companies face many environmental challenges and pressures (Song and Yu, 2018: 135). Therefore, there are many sources of motivation pushing companies to green practices. These are environmental regulations, market demands, in-house initiatives, ecological responsibility and technological opportunities (Chavez et al., 2016; Lin et al., 2014; Melander, 2017; Zailani et al., 2015). Company executives have realized that green innovation is an important factor in sustainable development and can provide a competitive advantage (Song and Yu, 2018: 135). The inclination of companies toward green practices not only eliminates negative environmental effects but also contributes to their economic and social performance. Conducted studies demonstrate that these contributions also help companies gain a competitive advantage (El-Kassar and Singh, 2019; Ge et al., 2018; Lee and Min, 2015; Lin et al., 2013, 2014; Qiu et al., 2020; Singh et al., 2020; Zailani et al., 2015).

The World Bank has added a new question to the survey, which is used for the logistics performance index calculations and published regularly since 2012. This question is about measuring how often customers demand environmentally friendly options (level of emissions, route options, vehicles, processes etc.). The results of the survey show that 28% of the participants in the top quintile demand environmentally friendly options from their customers. Twenty-three per cent of all energy-related emissions can be attributed to transportation, and about seven per cent of global CO_2 emissions can be attributed to freight transportation; 3.2 gigatons of CO_2 emission occurred in 2015. This number is expected to increase in the next decade and to grow more in developing economies than in Europe (Arvis et al., 2018: 34).

As a developing country, the logistics sector in Turkey has grown stably, and has gained more importance. Over the past seventeen years it has been stated that the main objective of the 145 billion transportation infrastructure investments and expenditure in US dollars is to enable Turkey to become a logistics base to provide a fast and continuous connection between Asia and Europe. Due to the global crisis, it is observed that the annual growth rates of the transportation and storage sector in the last ten years, excluding 2009, are in line with the growth trend of GDP. Assumptions made about the size of the logistics sector show that the sector share in GDP is between 11–13%. A 50% share of this ratio is directly caused by the activities of logistics service provider companies, and the remaining 50% is due to the logistics activities carried out by the companies trading goods (UTİKAD, 2019).

The 10th and 11th Development Plans put forward important policies regarding the logistics sector. The 10th Development Plan includes goals for the development of logistics and transportation infrastructure, while the 11th Development Plan goals are to provide the continuous high quality and safe energy required by the manufacturing industry at a minimum cost, and focus on freight transportation in railway investments. The 11th Development Plan aims to increase efficiency and competitiveness by developing maritime infrastructures at an appropriate place and scale, expand intermodal transportation and reduce logistics costs (Ministry of Development, 2013; Presidency of Strategy and Budget, 2019).

In line with the aforementioned, the purpose of the study is to demonstrate the significance of green innovation in the logistics sectors, which has become more important in recent years and highlights green innovation practices both in Turkey and the rest of the world. The study describes the green innovation concept and touches on studies conducted in the related literature in terms of this context and green innovation applications in the logistics sector. The importance of the study is evaluating the issue in a holistic framework. There is no conceptual study that deals with green innovation practices in the logistics sector in Turkey and the world from a holistic perspective. Therefore, the study aims to contribute to the literature with this viewpoint.

2 Innovation

The concept of innovation is a key one that has been in the literature for a long time, and it is expressed as *innovation* (Cindiloğlu Demirer, 2020: 170). Innovation is defined as the development of new products and services that provide an economic advantage to the business (Calof, 2018: 31). In addition to this definition, there are other definitions for innovation in the literature, such as innovation is the production, acceptance and implementation of new ideas, processes, products or services (Cindiloğlu Demirer, 2020: 170). Innovation covers a wide range of activities including the creation and implementation of new concepts and products for the organization (Basu and Green, 1997: 477).

Innovation is the development and use of new ideas and behaviours in organizations in terms of services and production methods, such as new administrative structures, markets and products. Managers develop their technologies with innovative ideas and adopt new strategies. As a result, managers improve their consumer/customer base, and they also seek better ways to satisfy them and increase their satisfaction levels with quality products and positive services (Kaya and Altındağ, 2019: 151). Regarding the definitions, innovation is a significant factor in terms of sustainability or sustainable growth not only for an existing manufacturing business, but also for structures such as a service business, a newly established business and a non-profit organization (Allahar, 2019: 195).

The OECD has expanded these definitions of innovation and mentioned the existence of four types of innovation. These types are *product innovation, process innovation, marketing innovation* and *organizational innovation* (OECD, 2018). Product innovation is the most prominent type of innovation and involves significant improvements in existing products and services. *Product innovation* includes significant improvements in technical specifications, components and materials, software in the product, ease of use or other functional features (OECD, 2018). *Process innovation* includes improvements in equipment, technology and software related to production, distribution and the delivery method (OECD, 2018). Also, process innovation includes support activities such as maintenance, repair, purchasing, programming and improvements in production and logistics methods (Yılmaz, 2015: 67). *Marketing innovation* is a new marketing method that includes significant improvements in product design, packaging, product placement, product promotion and pricing. *Organizational innovation* includes improvements in organizational practices (OECD, 2018). Other than these, the types of innovation in the literature are *service innovation, technological innovation, breakthrough innovation, component innovation, architecture/design innovation, business model innovation, revolutionary innovation and radical innovation* (Yılmaz, 2015). Another type of innovation in the literature is green innovation.

The idea that innovation can lead to economic growth and development has been widely accepted by academia and industry. However, it was not until the 1990s that the problem of how to achieve a win-win state result for the economy and the environment through innovation was realized by researchers. The OECD estimates that in 2050 the global population will reach 9.2 billion, with a new population of 2.2 billion. Billions of people's needs will lead to a deterioration of the natural environment and global climate change, and more natural resources will face depletion. Current types of innovation will not fully support global economic development in the coming years. Fortunately, political elites, entrepreneurs, environmentalists and other people are starting to discover this problem, and realize the importance of green product innovation in achieving sustainable development. The most recent literature studies on green innovation, including green products, focus on the impact of this type of innovation on firm's performance. There are theoretical and empirical studies in the literature to solve this problem (Ma et al., 2018: 1). These studies are explained under the title of 'literature review for green innovation studies'.

When green innovation is evaluated in terms of sustainability, it can be defined as the new skills that an enterprise has to develop. Today, green innovation is as important as new product development and improvement. Therefore, it can be stated that 'green innovation' should also be among the innovation types. So, how is green innovation explained and what is its significance for businesses?

3 Green Innovation

The effect of green innovation on competitive advantage is explained in the literature in the context of resource-based theory and ecological modernization theory (Singh et al., 2020: 2; Karia and Asaari, 2013: 459). When the green innovation studies conducted in the literature are evaluated, it is possible to say that there is no single definition of green innovation that aims to develop products, services, processes and applications that contribute to the environment by reducing ineffective resource use. However, in general, to achieve ecologically determined sustainability goals (reducing pollution related to air, water and soil; all kinds of waste-solids; liquids and gas; energy use, noise pollution and increasing activities such as energy-saving; the use of renewable energy; treatment; reuse; recycling and disposal), green innovation is defined as behaviour, process and product practices that contribute to the reduction of environmental impacts (Arfi et al., 2018: 211; Calza et al., 2017: 2–3; Cheng et al., 2014: 81; Park et al., 2017: 1–2; Song and Yu, 2018: 138–9). In the literature terms such as eco-innovation, environmental innovation and sustainable innovation are used for green innovation – there are only small differences in their definitions. They basically have similar concerns and goals. In general, these expressions can be defined as types of innovation that reduce negative environmental impacts (Arfi et al., 2018: 211).

First, Fussler and James (1996) defined eco-innovation as 'products and processes that increase customer and firm value by reducing environmental impacts' (as cited in: Schiederig et al., 2011: 3). Oltra and Saint Jean (2009: 567) explained environmental innovation as a new or modified process, practices, systems and products that contribute to the environment and environmental sustainability. Green innovation is defined as 'hardware or software innovation related to green products or processes, including the innovative technologies that are involved in energy-saving, pollution prevention, waste recycling, green product designs or innovations in technologies involved in corporate environmental management' by Chen et al. (2006: 332). It achieves energy efficiency, reduces companies' dependence on fossil fuels while increasing the use of green and renewable energy sources (Cosimato and Troisi, 2015: 261). In addition to these three terms, which include economic and environmental dimensions, it is stated that sustainable innovation is a wider concept and includes a social dimension (Arfi et al., 2018: 211).

Schiederig et al. (2011: 5) stated that the four concepts mentioned above are interchangeable and that they examine the same subject in terms of content. In their studies, they mention the existence of six important issues in definitions. These are as follows:

1. Innovation object: Product, process, service and method.
2. Market orientation: Meeting the needs / being competitive in the market.
3. Environmental aspect: Reduction of negative impact (optimum = zero impact).
4. Phase: The full life cycle has to be considered (to reduce material flow).
5. Impulse: The determinant for reduction can be economic or ecological.
6. Level: Setting a new green standard for the company.

Green innovation basically contains green product innovation and green process innovation (Tang et al., 2018: 40). However, more detailed distinctions are also found in the literature. Park et al. (2017: 3) categorize green innovation as product innovation, process innovation, marketing innovation, organizational innovation, material flow innovation and social innovation.

The distinction made by Rennings et al. (2006: 47) for green innovation is as in Figure 1. According to the researchers, green product innovation is the production of goods or services whose negative effects on the environment are reduced or eliminated; green process innovation has been specified as the improvement of existing production processes and the use of environmentally friendly technologies (Tang et al., 2018). Green environmental/organizational innovation is the reorganization of processes and responsibilities within the company in order to reduce environmental impacts. End-of-pipe approach technologies can be mentioned as additional measures for environmental requirements. Incinerators (waste disposal), wastewater treatment plants (for reducing water consumption), sound absorbers (noise reduction) and exhaust gas cleaning equipment (air quality control) are examples of end-of-pipe technologies (Rennings et al., 2006: 47). These technologies are implemented at the end of the process. This prevents solid, liquid and gas wastes, generated in the process, from spreading to the environment at the end of the process. Cleaner production methods improve the process; for instance, using less raw materials and energy and all kinds of hazardous or non-hazardous waste, etc. (Cılız et al., 2011: 7).

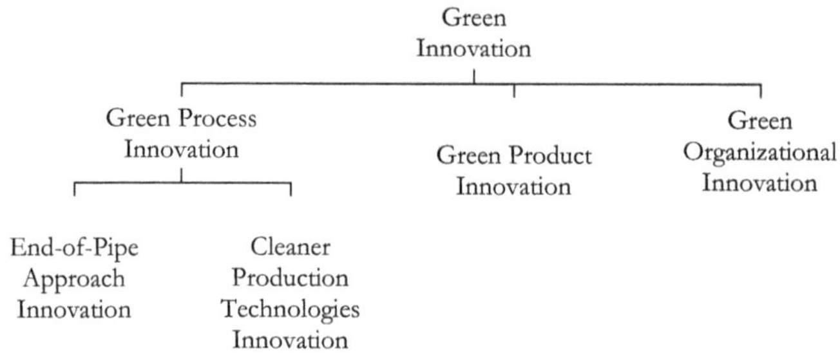

Fig. 1. *Green Innovation Types*
Source: Rennings et al. (2006)

Within the scope of green innovation, states determine strategies and applications with laws and incentives; businesses with the pressure and/or support of individuals and stakeholders. These strategies include many alternatives such as investing in renewable energy, reducing energy consumption and pollution, recycling, reusing, disposal, optimizing production processes and reducing waste amounts by way of technological investments. Additionally, processes such as designing buildings to make more use of daylight, sending all kinds of wastes to recycling facilities,treating the water used so as to reuse them in the production processes and minimizing the damage caused to other living species in the environment are among the activities of companies within the scope of green innovation. Kitchen cabinets (Kungsbacka) which are made of 99.9% recycled wood and plastic bottles by IKEA (Cosmo and Yang, 2017: 40), Toyota hybrid vehicles and organic plastic products called Greenbox (Yıldız, 2016: 328) are examples of these processes. Apart from these examples, the number of environmental innovations patented worldwide every year is demonstrated in Figure 2.

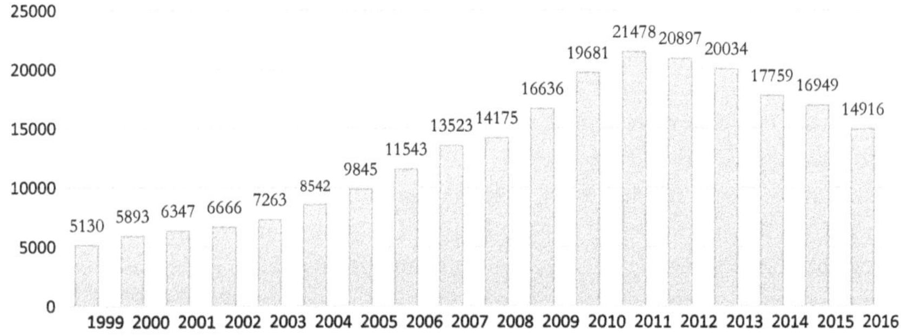

Fig. 2. *Environmental Patents*
Source: (OECD, 2019)

The graph shows an increase in environmental patents until 201,1 and a decrease after 2011. The fact that most patents were received in 2011 may be related to Industry 4.0.

3.1 Literature Review for Green Innovation Studies

Karia and Asaari (2013) argued that the forerunners of green innovation are organizational support and incentives, management skills/quality, human resources, environmental uncertainty, knowledge, environmental policies, legal regulations and government support variables, and that green innovation will create a competitive advantage. Lin et al. (2013) showed that market demand is positively associated with both green product innovation and company performance. Chen and Hung (2014) argued that for green innovation, companies can gain additional competitive advantage by cooperating with the environment, but they need to use their social capital for this. In addition to these, Lin et al. (2014) demonstrated the benefits of environmental performance in helping companies take a leadership role in the market, outperform their competitors by providing low-cost or differentiated strategies, develop a strong green reputation, attract more customers and expand their market shares.

Zailani et al. (2015) concluded that environmental regulations, market demand and in-house initiatives have a positive impact on green innovation initiatives, and green innovation initiatives have a positive impact on sustainable performance (i.e. environmental, social and economic performances). Lee and Min (2015) claim that for companies to manage their environmental and financial performance in the best way, they must adopt a proactive environmental strategy and urgently find unique resources and develop skills for this. Albort-Morant et al. (2016) argued that the forerunners of green innovation performance are the firm's dynamic and ordinary capabilities. Chavez et al. (2016) found that customer pressure has a positive effect on the implementation of a customer-centric green supply chain that allows them to develop multiple operational performances (flexibility, delivery, quality and cost) and stated that this process results in customer satisfaction. Doran and Ryan (2016) showed environmental and legal regulations and customer pressure as viable mechanisms that encourage companies to make eco-innovations.

Buhl et al. (2016) predict that as the environmental performance of firms increases there may be an increase in green human capital. They advocated that companies that encourage employees to share their experiences and participate in eco-innovation activities should clearly communicate their environmental policies and strategic green goals. Melander (2017) argued that the driving forces that cause companies to collaborate in green product innovations are economic factors, legal and environmental regulations, customer demand, competitiveness and firm performance and listed inter-organizational (partner selection, relationship management, information access and agreements) and intra-organizational factors (cross-functional cooperation, capabilities and internal applications). Nanath and Pillai (2017) argued that green information systems are not just an investment, but a factor that contributes to the company's innovation performance and competitive advantage. Ge et al. (2018) demonstrated that with the effective implementation of a green product strategy, the potential value of a product will increase and the company will improve its brand and ethical values, so that the company will gain a competitive advantage. Song and Yu (2018) stated that managers need to develop the sense of green identity of their companies, and that it is important to encourage green creativity as it will improve the sustainable development ability of their companies. El-Kassar and Singh (2019) thought that green innovation practices could help companies gain competitive advantage and increase their corporate and environmental performance. Wang (2019) claimed that unless green innovation is based on an organizational green culture, the ultimate impact of any organizational culture on a firm's green performance will be questionable.

Borsatto and Amui (2019) investigated the development of the relationship between green innovation with environmental regulations and competitiveness, and demonstrated the importance of green innovation in their study of 186 businesses among the top 500 companies by the Financial Times. Zhang et al. (2019) found a positive and significant relationship between green processes and firm's performance in their research on manufacturing companies in China. In this study the content analysis method was conducted by Xie et al. (2019), where it was found that the green innovation processes of businesses had a positive effect on green product innovation and that both green process innovation and green product innovation can improve the financial performance of a company. According to the results of the research conducted by Abbas and Sağsan (2019) on the role of knowledge management in green innovation and corporate sustainable development activities in Pakistan they found that knowledge management has a significant effect on green innovation and corporate sustainable development.

Singh et al. (2020) demonstrated that green human resource management practices mediate the effect of green transformational leadership on green innovation and that green human resources management indirectly affects a firm's environmental performance through green innovation. Qiu et al. (2020) concluded that green product innovation contributes positively to both the firm's green dynamic capabilities while gaining competitive advantage, and stated that corporate reputation positively affects the relationship between green product innovation and resource integration capability.

4 Green Innovation Practices in the Logistics Sector

This study aims to give insight into the definition and importance of green innovationr. This part further discusses green innovation practices both in the logistics sector in Turkey and the rest of the world.

4.1 Green Innovation Practices in the Logistics Sector in the World

There are many examples of green innovation in the logistics industry around the world. In this study, the green innovation practices of the world's largest logistics companies (Eniyi10lar, 2020) are presented as follows.

4.1.1 CEVA Logistics

CEVA Logistics, which was founded in the United Kingdom in 1976, serves more than 1,000 locations in 160 countries with more than 58,000 employees (Ceva Logistics, 2019). The applications of the business within the scope of green innovation can be listed as follows (Lojistürk, 2019):

- CEVA Logistics uses exhaust and engine systems that comply with Euro emission standards in all its vehicles. With Euro 4 and Euro 5 compliant vehicles used in road transport, 2% less fuel is consumed compared to normal motor vehicles.

- The company reuses the materials used as packaging materials and reuses products such as pallets by the reverse logistics method. Also, more than 3.487 million recyclable packaging materials are used worldwide. Within the scope of waste management, plastic, cardboard and electronic wastes are separated and sent to licensed recycling companies. CEVA Logistics brings a different perspective to green innovation by redesigning its packages to carry more products.
- 7,800 tons of paper is saved annually in airline transportation through electronic invoicing with the agreement between CEVA Logistics and IATA (International Air Transport Association).
- The company uses multimodal transport systems to reduce harmful emissions in road transport.

Within the scope of the new green applications in warehouses and management offices, 30% less electricity and water is consumed (Çetin and Sain, 2018: 917–918). Additionally, CEVA Logistics received the award for the best green logistics company at the Asia Freight, Logistics and Supply Chain Awards (AFLAS) in 2014 (Autoparts, 2019).

4.1.2 DB Schenker

DB Schenker, founded in 1872, is a logistics-focused division of German railway operator Deutsche Bahn AG. The company has 76,000 employees. The applications of DB Schenker in the field of green innovation are as follows (DB Schenker, 2019):

- DB Schenker has launched several initiatives and expanded its green areas to reduce CO_2 emissions by 30% in 2020, and it is planning to reduce this to 50% by 2030. It also reduced CO_2 emissions by 20% in air transport and 50% in ocean transport by offering eco-solutions for each mode of transport.
- As a global leader focused on green innovation, the company provides recommendations for optimization by transparently calculating the CO_2 footprint of its customers' supply chains.
- Also, it focuses on reducing its fleets through consolidation, switching to the most environmentally friendly mode of transport, and developing sustainable solutions in green innovation with continuous fleet renewals.

4.1.3 DHL Supply Chain

Deutsche Post DHL, founded in 2005, is an international courier, parcel and express mail service. It is the world's largest logistics company with 380,000 employees in more than 200 countries and regions worldwide, especially in sea and air mail (Logistics DHL, 2019). Believing that its success is based on environmentally friendly business processes, DHL launched a corporate social responsibility program called GoGreen in 2005 to ensure environmental sustainability and became the first global logistics company to set itself a quantitative carbon emission target. The activities of DHL within the scope of green innovation practices are as follows:

- The company identifies that there are many different methods of reducing carbon dioxide emissions and various environmentally damaging factors that occur during the transportation of products. DHL also maximizes this potential with the contribution of customers. (DHL Turkey, 2016).
- DHL plans to increase energy efficiency by 30% in all areas by 2020 (Bi, 2011: 6). In this sense, it has built a wind turbine platform to take advantage of renewable energy.
- To train employees about energy saving, the company implements the 'Switch Off' project in all warehouse and office areas, attaching labels to the side of the faucets in electrical appliances and sinks (Bi, 2011: 7).
- By developing an ISO 14001 compliant environmental management system and minimizing the environmental impact of products and services, it takes environmental issues into account in all its major investments and cares about sustainability (Bi, 2011: 6).
- It offers its customers various alternatives to improve their environmental performance by providing green optimization services.
- In terms of protecting natural resources and reducing waste, DHL offers optimization options to customers in the field of reverse logistics with an environmental solutions service (Kaşık, 2016).
- The company implements green office practices in all units globally. Recycled papers, water-powered calculators and water-powered clocks are utilized in all headquarters offices and warehouses. For energy efficiency in the fleet, hybrid vehicles are preferred and trucks with Euro 4 and Euro 5 standards are used for transportation (Bi, 2011: 8).
- DHL has stated that it will certify its 80% employees by giving GoGreen expert training by 2025 and reduce all emissions related to logistics to zero by 2050. It has also announced that it will include its employees in environmental and climate protection activities (Logistics DHL, 2019).

4.1.4 FedEx

FedEx, founded in 1971, is among the world's most respected companies providing transfer, cargo and logistics services worldwide. It serves its customers in 220 countries and regions around the world with more than 280,000 employees. Sustainability activities carried out by the company within the scope of green innovation practices are as follows (FedEx, 2019):

- With FY05, FedEx aims to improve its vehicle fuel efficiency target by 50% in 2020. It has increased its fleet of electric and hybrid vehicles by 18%. By doing so, 480,000 gallons of fuel have been saved. The company serves London and Paris with zero-emission electric distribution vehicles. In addition, it has added eighty-seven fully electric trucks to its green fleet in a short time.
- The company uses Boeing 777F aircraft, which use 18% less fuel and have a higher payload than MD11 freighters.
- All FedEx branded envelopes are carbon neutral.
- Reduces customers' environmental footprint by reducing the need to print and sign multiple copies of Electronic Trade Documents (ETDs).
- Most FedEx packaging contains both recycleable and recycled materials.
- The company operates solar energy which is capable of generating more than 800,000 kWh of electricity each year. Besides, the energy distribution centre in Antwerp ensures a 40% reduction in energy consumption and a 60% reduction in CO_2 emissions.

4.1.5 Kuehne + Nagel

Kuehne + Nagel, founded in 1890, has grown from a traditional international shipping company to a leading global supplier of innovative and fully integrated supply chain solutions. The Kuehne + Nagel Group has 1,300 offices in more than 100 countries with approximately 82,000 employees. Green innovation applications carried out within the company are as follows (Kn-Portal, 2019):

- Kuehne + Nagel point out to CO_2 reduction in shipping and logistics services around the world with their Net Zero Carbon program. In addition to CO_2 neutrality, the company uses data and predictive analytical methods to bring solutions to reduce the CO_2 footprint of its customers' supply chains and offer new digital platforms that support the choice of transport routes and modes that emit significantly less CO_2.
- According to globally accepted calculation standards, it reduces carbon emissions in the world with state-of-the-art carbon calculators and neutralizes them by using carbon emission compensation services.

- The company enables transporters to gather reliable information about the use of equipment and monitoring systems by incorporating CCWG (Clean Cargo Working Group) methodology and emission factors into carbon calculations and customer emission reports. In this way, optimized routing enables carrier and vessel selection and reduces the carbon footprint caused by unnecessary work movements.
- Kuehne + Nagel provides digitally effective information to the world's largest maritime transport service network with its online maritime transport services platform, thanks to the Sea Explorer (naval navigator) it has developed. Among other features, Sea Explorer offers full visibility into realistic and accurate CO_2 and sulphur emissions across services, which supports routing and planning activities when selecting services with the lowest CO_2 emissions. It also informs shippers about how each ship carrying their goods will comply with the upcoming IMO 2020 regulation.
- In addition, the company sees environmental problems as an integral part of QSHE management systems within the scope of green innovation and has ISO 14001 environmental certificate for more than 200 locations around the world.

4.1.6 Maersk Line

Maersk Line, founded in 1904, is an integrated container logistics company. The company, which has more than 76,000 employees operating in 130 countries, has 100,000 customers around the world (Maersk, 2019). The activities carried out within the scope of green innovation practices are presented as below:

- Maersk Line reduced ship air carbon emissions by over 2,400 tonnes with its Environmental Protection Initiative using a cleaner fuel in its ports on the west coast of North America. It reduces the water-resistance of the ships by painting them with environmentally friendly silicone paints, thus saving 1,200 tons in the annual fuel consumption of the ship.
- It calculates the waste handling performance of each port and requires each port to reach a certain rate (Evren, 2011: 47).
- Technology and technical equipment used in the ships allows 16% larger capacity utilization and reduces 50% CO_2 emission rate per container. Furthermore, small changes have been made to the propeller, breakwater and hull of the ships to travel more effectively on the water surface.
- The floorboard of the company's container units is made of bamboo trees that grow in a short time instead of trees that grow in a long time (Evren, 2011: 48–9).

- The company's 2020 target is to reduce the carbon emission rate by 25%. Moreover, Maersk Line uses one of the world's lowest carbon emission ships called Triple-E (Zengin, 2017: 55).

4.1.7 Nippon Express

Nippon Express, founded in 1937, is a globally renowned logistics company based in Japan. The land transportation of Nippon Express, which started working as a logistics provider more than eighty years ago, dates back to 1872. Nippon Express green innovation applications can be listed as follows (Nippon Express, 2019):

- The company has designed Mitsubishi Fuso Truck and Bus, an initiative to reduce CO_2 emissions at every step from product manufacturing to supply and product transportation as a solution to optimize logistics by putting modal shift expertise to work. Mitsubishi Fuso Truck and Bus provided a reduction of approximately 70% in CO_2 emissions in the luggage line.
- Nippon Express has increased the number of CNG, hybrid and LPG trucks, adding low-emission diesel trucks to its fleet that comply with the new regulations for large-scale vehicles in Japan.
- Also, it determines a route to collect shipments with *a round tour* (milk-run) method to make shipping and delivery times regular and ensure well-planned and efficient procurement logistics. *The round tour* is a system where the same or different loads are taken from various points within a program by a vehicle and delivered to one or more points and after all the deliveries are completed, the empty containers are collected and returned by following the reverse route.
- Thanks to the 3R recycling system, Nippon Express *reduces* the volume of waste, *reuses* materials whenever possible and *recycles* used products as resources.

4.2 Green Innovation Practices in the Logistics Sector in Turkey

In the logistics sector, the practices of green logistics companies in Turkey are presented below.

4.2.1 Arkas Logistics

Arkas Logistics, founded in 1989, has been in the logistics industry for more than a quarter of a century, and today it carries out open freight and project shipments, forwarding and warehouse services, and combined shipments on land, sea, air and rail. The activities carried out within the scope of green innovation practices are as follows (Arkas Logistics, 2019):

- The company minimizes its carbon footprint by focusing on combined transport in rail and maritime transport.
- It reduces greenhouse gas emissions by continuous improvement, constantly monitoring greehouse gas emissions in road transportation.
- As part of the green office project, it saves electricity, water and natural resources.
- Within the scope of the electric crane project, it uses energy efficiently by reducing energy costs.
- It saves twenty tons of fuel per ship by operating its ships at an economical speed.
- Arkas Logistics has built a wastewater treatment facility. In this way, all kinds of waste are made harmless to the environment by recycling or disposal methods. It also delivers waste motor oils to PETDER (Turkish Oil Industry Association).
- Besides, Arkas Logistics is the first port to receive the green/eco port certification and adopt the ISO 14064 greenhouse gas management system in Turkey.

4.2.2 Borusan Logistics

Borusan Logistics, founded in 1973, takes its place in the sector as an integrated logistics service provider with 3,500 employees. Borusan Port has also been awarded a green/eco port certificate Moreover, it is the first leading company that has the ISO 50001 Energy Management System and an ISO 14064 Carbon Footprint Verification at the same time. Green innovation practices implemented by the company can be listed as follows (Borusan Lojistik, 2019):

- With the RTG electricity conversion project, the company improved its CO_2 emissions by 94% and, consequently, saved approximately 6,000 tons of trees from being cut down annually.
- It cares about the environment, with rotor blade adaptors to carry gigantic wind blades.
- Borusan Logistics is one of the leading ports holding waste collection licenses from ships, thus preventing marine pollution.
- By developing a Fast Card System, the firm prevents the use of no. 10 oil in all transportation operations and reduces CO_2 emissions. Borusan Logistics carry out environmentally friendly activities within the scope of green innovation using electric trucks purchased from TESLA (Lojiport, 2019).
- Approximately 90% of the hazardous wastes generated from its facilities and activities are sent to licensed recycling companies under contract, and the unrecoverable wastes are sent to Izaydaş.

- The company reduces its CO_2 emissions by using Euro diesel fuel in construction machinery (Gürgenç, 2011: 33).
- Approximately 50% of its fleets consist of Euro3 and Euro 4 vehicles and new ones are Euro 5. Moreover, as a result of the project regarding the reduction of fuel consumption rates, they are mounted on vehicles with suitable spoilers (Gürgenç, 2011: 34).

4.2.3 Ekol Logistics

Ekol Logistics, founded in 1990, operates in eighty-five locations in thirteen countries, and is one of the leading companies in the logistics sector in Turkey. According to the WWF's results (World Wide Fund for Nature), Ekol was the first logistics company in Turkey to receive a green office diploma. Ekol Logistics handles waste management within the scope of the green office program and disposes of all kinds of waste under appropriate conditions. It also aims to reduce the use of raw materials, energy and other natural resources with appropriate separation. The important green innovation activities of the business are as follows (Ekol, 2019):

- The company saves 365,000 trees every month by providing intermodal transportation with modern Ro-Ro ships and electric block trains.
- With the Virtual Server Project, a 20% saving in electricity consumed was made, and special solutions are provided by determining the paper production rates.
- Ekol Logistics is the ambassador of the Earth Hour, the world's largest environmental movement, organized by the WWF to draw attention to global climate change.
- Ekol renews all the tow trucks in its fleet and makes them compatible with Euro 5 standards. Besides, it serves in countries where it operates with Euro 6 vehicles, with its own facilities in Europe.
- Ekol reduces the use of diesel equipment by using electric lifting equipment in its new warehouses (Lojiport, 2019).

4.2.4 Mars Logistics

Mars Logistics, founded in 1998, is a logistics company that originated in Turkey (Mars Logistics, 2019). Aiming for a better environment for future generations, Mars Logistics plans green innovation applications around this understanding. These practices are as follows (Transmedya, 2019):

- Mars Logistics has managed to reduce its CO_2 emission from 1.19 tons per vehicle to 0.76 tons, despite the increasing number of fleets and voyages as a result of its environmentalist approaches. Furthermore, it contributes to the protection of nature by renewing the vehicles in its fleet with environmentally friendly vehicles every year.
- With the intermodal transportation system, the company reduces the carbon dioxide emission to the lowest level. Thanks to this intermodal method of transportation, 48% emission savings are achieved, and thus more than 2 million trees and 5.9 hectares of forest are saved.
- The company uses Euro 5 motor vehicles that are less harmful to the environment. It reduces fuel consumption by using long-lasting and durable tyres with its tyre fleet system.
- It purchases the electricity consumed in the offices as green energy from the hydroelectric power plant and the natural gas combined cycle power plants from the company Voytron, which produces electricity. Thus, it provides its office needs from renewable energy sources.

4.2.5 Netlog Logistics

Netlog Logistics, founded exactly at the end of 2004, is Turkey's largest domestic logistics company. With fifty-seven warehouses in eighteen provinces and its 390,000 palletized cargo stock capacity, it is one of the leading companies in warehouse stock management and optimization in Turkey. Green innovation practices within the company are as follows (Netlog, 2019):

- The company saves costs by providing double-sided use of 40% of paper used, and by giving it to the enterprises to ensure the recycling of wastepaper. Thus, approximately 10.350 kg of paper is recycled to prevent 130 trees from being cut down and saves 800 m2 of forest land from being destroyed.
- Also, a significant increase of approximately 107% was achieved in the recycling of waste batteries (by training employees on the recycling of used batteries).
- The company has bought 300 trucks with Euro 5 green engines and disposed of old vehicles with Euro 3 engines. Thanks to trucks with Euro 5 engines, 30% less CO_2 is emitted.
- It also delivers the waste motor oil of vehicles to PETDER.
- At Netlog Logistics, end-of-life tyres are recycled in two ways. If possible, the tyres are retreated and reused, and if unusable they are sent to LASDER for recovery.

- Employees are trained to reduce electricity consumption, and helped to raise awareness by writing notes at certain points.

4.2.6 Omsan Logistics

OMSAN Logistics, founded in 1978 as a subsidiary of OYAK, operates in the logistics sector with 2,600 personnel. It is the most prominent business with green innovation practices in Turkey (Omsan, 2019). The company benefits from intermodal transport in international transport services. The company reduces economic and environmental risks by transporting the changing loads with various modes of transport, depending on the nature of the operation. The important green innovation activities of it are as follows:

- Safe and Economic Driving Simulator, developed by OMSAN Logistics engineers, aims to reduce fuel consumption, minimize wear and tear on vehicles and equipment caused by driving errors, minimize damage and accidents and reduce carbon emissions. Besides, the simulator has 6 DOF freedom of movement and features to simulate the load carried in the trailer (Yeşil Lojistikçiler, 2019). Within the scope of this project, OMSAN Logistics has been awarded the 'The Green Era Award', which is regarded as an internationally respected environmental award, and is the first and only Turkish logistics company to receive this award (Lojiport, 2019).
- OMSAN is the only authorized company responsible for the collection, transportation and delivery of waste oils to PETDER within the scope of waste oil control regulation.
- Within the scope of green innovation, it transports customers' vehicles from Istanbul and Ankara to Antalya, Bodrum, Izmir and Dalaman with the My Car is on Vacation application. Thanks to the truck, which has a carrying capacity of eight vehicles, it ensures less pollution of the environment by reducing fuel consumption and emissions (Transmedya, 2019).
- In the logistics sector in Turkey, OMSAN Logistics published the first sustainability report, which was prepared in accordance with GRI-G4 principles.
- In addition, by adding five electric vehicles to its fleet, it helps to create quiet and clean traffic without exhaust fumes and engine noise, and electric vehicles do not emit CO_2 (Yeşil Logistics, 2019).

4.2.7 Reysaş Logistics

Reysaş Logistics, founded in 1989, continues its activities in Turkey and abroad with more than 600 self-owned trucks, headquartered in Ankara. The practices implemented within the scope of green innovation can be listed as follows (Reysaş, 2019):

- The company produces electricity from solar energy on the roofs of its warehouses and turns them into environmentally friendly green warehouses by consuming less energy.
- By choosing natural gas as an alternative fuel in trucks and tractors, it reduces exhaust emissions such as carbon monoxide, nitrous oxide and solid matter.
- Thanks to the new routes and plans developed with the multimodal transportation system, it mainly supports its activities in railway transportation.
- Reysaş Logistics uses its resources efficiently to irrigate green areas, trees and olive groves with the rainwater collection system installed on the roofs of its warehouses. In addition, apart from irrigation, it also uses rainwater for vehicle and environmental cleaning.

5 Conclusion

In the last quarter of the twentieth century, the understanding of sustainability developed rapidly, and it did not take long to realize the size of businesses' effects on sustainability. Businesses, which have environmental and social impacts as well as economic impacts, felt the need to update their processes with green and sustainable activities due to reasons such as legal regulations and the increasing environmental and social awareness of stakeholders, and even social responsibility. As one of the processes that emerged as a result of these update requirements, green innovation is one of the most prominent issues in the literature and in company activity.

About leaving a more sustainable world for the future, all sectors and companies have a responsibility. The logistics sector is more amenable toward green and sustainable activities due to its dependence on globalizing trade, and its rapid growth. It aims to reduce and, if possible, eliminate the negative effects of activities such as order management, packaging, transportation, and storage and stock management on the environment by using environmentally friendly logistics. Digital integration, continuous improvements, and process optimizations may reduce negative environmental impacts. For example, while the use of paper and stationery is reduced thanks to the digitalized order stages, using recyclable or reusable packaging systems in the packaging stage will provide a greener result. In particular, for transportation activities such as reducing fuel consumption, using biofuels and minimizing the distance travelled can be achieved (Cosimato and Troisi, 2015: 258). It can be said that businesses now invest in green innovation or green product innovation. Accordingly, the current study aims to reveal the contributions of green innovation practices to companies that wish to gain competitive advantage, with evidence from the literature and application examples.

Since the environment does not have unlimited resources, environmental sustainability is extremely important. Businesses, institutions, organizations, society, employees, and other stakeholders should take action on sustainability with common awareness. Because the future obliges businesses to enter a green world, the balance point of this world is based on sustainability. In this sense, thanks to sustainability, businesses will likely face fewer constraints in the economy, especially in terms of resources. The concept of green innovation, which succeeded in entering the logistics sector in the late 1980s, provided an awareness of the environmental problems created by logistics systems. With the environmental aspect of logistics coming to the forefront, environmentally friendly practices have started to be seen in the logistics sector. In this context, the damage caused by logistics activities to the environment and sustainability, has started to be examined, and national and international precautions have been taken to minimize this damage. These precautions have brought about the start of a new era in the field of logistics. Due to the pollution the world faces, environmental awareness is now important among customer expectations. At this point, green innovation contributes significantly to enterprises' gaining competitive advantage and sustainability.

Activities carried out within the scope of green innovation practices of logistics companies, both in the world and Turkey, were examined and results, such as the use of environmentally-friendly vehicles, disposal of wastes within the enterprise, taking precautions to reduce the carbon footprint, reducing energy consumption and emission rates, using intermodal transportation systems, the presence of environmental management certification, environmental cooperation and coordination with customers initiating actions, taking precautions for freight transport and storage, and preparing sustainability reports were achieved.

To reduce the environmental damage of traditional methods, logistics businesses that want to achieve a good position in the competitive environment and have a positive impact on their environmental performance need to include green innovation practices in their business policies. In the context of sustainability, this study is thought to contribute to the related literature and logistics businesses. Based on the research, it is suggested that green innovation practices should be carried out in different sectors and the results should be evaluated in a way that allows comparison.

References

Abbas, J. and Sağsan, M. (2019). Impact of Knowledge Management Practices on Green Innovation and Corporate Sustainable Development: A Structural Analysis, Journal of Cleaner Production, 229, 611–620.

Albort-Morant, G., Leal-Millán, A. and Cepeda-Carrión, G. (2016). The Antecedents of Green Innovation Performance: A Model of Learning and Capabilities, Journal of Business Research, 69(11), 4912–4917.

Allahar, H. (2019). Innovation Management and Value Chain Design: Case of a Small Professional Services Firm, International Journal of Innovation, 7(2), 192–209.

Arfi, W. B., Hikkerova, L. and Sahut, J.-M. (2018). External Knowledge Sources, Green Innovation and Performance, Technological Forecasting and Social Change, 129, 210–220.

Arkas Lojistik (2019). Arkas Lojistik, http://www.arkaslojistik.com.tr (05.11.2019).

Arvis, J.-F., Ojala, L., Wiederer, C., Shepherd, B., Raj, A., Dairabayeva, K. and Kiiski, T. (2018). Connecting to Compete 2018: Trade Logistics in The Global Economy. The Logistics Performance Index and Its Indicators. Global Trade and Regional Integration Unit, The World Bank Group, Washington, DC.

Autoparts (2019). Ceva Lojistik, En Yeşil Lojistik Şirketi Seçildi, http://www.autoparts.com.tr/haber-detay/741/ceva-lojistik-en-yesil-lojistik-sirketi-secildi (15.12.2019).

Basu, R. and Green, G. S. (1997). Leader-Member Exchange and Transformational Leadership: An Empirical Examination of Innovative Behaviours in Leader-Member Dyads, Journal of Applied Social Psychology, 27(6), 477–499.

Bi, S. (2011). Yeşil Çevre ve Yeşil Lojistik. Lojistical Dergisi, (9), 6–8, http://cdn.istanbul.edu.tr/statics/ulastirmalojistik.istanbul.edu.tr/wpcontent/uploads/2015/10/Logistical-Say%C4%B1-9.pdf (16.12.2019)

Borsatto, J. M. L. S. and Amui, L. B. L. (2019). Green Innovation: Unfolding The Relation with Environmental Regulations and Competitiveness, Resources, Conservation and Recycling, 149, 445–454.

Borusan Lojistik (2019). Haberler, https://www.borusanlojistik.com/tr/haberler (05.11.2019).

Buhl, A., Blazejewskı, S. and Dittmer, F. (2016). The More, The Merrier: Why and How Employee-Driven Eco-Innovation Enhances Environmental and Competitive Advantage. Sustainability, 8(9), 946.

Calof, J. (2018). Enhancing Innovation Performance in Companies. Foresight and STI Governance, 12(3), 30–33.

Calza, F., Parmentola, A. and Tutore, I. (2017). Types of Green Innovations: Ways of Implementation in a Non-Green Industry. Sustainability, 9(8), 1301, 2–16.

Ceva Logistics (2019). Our history, https://www.cevalogistics.com/about-us/our-history (21.11.2019).

Chavez, R., Yu, W., Feng, M. and Wiengarten, F. (2016). The Effect of Customer-Centric Green Supply Chain Management On Operational Performance and Customer Satisfaction, Business Strategy and the Environment, 25(3), 205–220.

Chen, P.-C. and Hung, S.-W. (2014). Collaborative Green Innovation in Emerging Countries: A Social Capital Perspective. International Journal of Operations and Production Management, 34(3), 347–363.

Chen, Y.-S., Lai, S.-B. and Wen, C.-T. (2006). The Influence of Green Innovation Performance on Corporate Advantage in Taiwan. Journal of Business Ethics, 67(4), 331–339.

Cheng, C.J.C., Yang, C.-L. and Sheu, C. (2014). The Link Between Eco-Innovation and Business Performance: A Taiwanese Industry Context. Journal of Cleaner Production, 64, 81–90.

Cindiloğlu Demirer, M. (2020). Effects of Structural and Psychological Empowerment on Career Satisfaction and Innovative Work Behaviour, Eskisehir Osmangazi University, Journal of Faculty of Economics and Administrative Sciences, 15(1), 165–184.

Cılız, N., Daylan, B. and Baydar, G. (2011). Sürdürülebilir Üretim ve Tüketim Yayınları-II, Temiz Üretim. Ankara: Çevre ve Şehircilik Bakanlığı.

Cosimato, S. and Troisi, O. (2015). Green Supply Chain Management: Practices and Tools for Logistics Competitiveness and Sustainability. The DHL Case Study, The TQM Journal, 27(2), 256–276.

Cosmo, D. E. and Yang, K. (2017). A Further Strategic Move to Sustainability – A Case Study on Ikea. Journal of Strategic Innovation and Sustainability, 12(2), 39–47.

Çetin, O. and Sain, A. D. (2018). Lojistik Sektöründe Sürdürülebilirlik Uygulamaları, IV. International Caucasus-Central Asia Foreign Trade and Logistics Congress (p. 910–921), September 7–8, Didim/AYDIN.

Db Schenker (2019). Environmental, Profile, https://www.dbschenkerarkas.com.tr (10.11.2019).

Dhl Türkiye (2016). Dhl Express Customer Satisfaction, http://dhl.com.tr/content/downloads/tr/express/tr/dhl_express_customer_satisfaction (25.11.2019).

Doran, J. and Ryan, G. (2016). The Importance of the Diverse Drivers and Types of Environmental Innovation for Firm Performance. Business Strategy and the Environment, 25(2), 102–119.

Ekol (2019). Yeşil Lojistik, https://www.ekol.com/tr/lojistik/yesil-lojistik/ (05.11.2019).

El-Kassar, A.-N. and Singh, S. K. (2019). Green Innovation and Organizational Performance: The Influence of Big Data and The Moderating Role of Management Commitment and Hr Practices. Technological Forecasting and Social Change, 144 (December 2017), 483–498.

Eniyi10lar, (2020). Dünya'nın En İyi 10 Lojistik Firması 2019 / Kargo Şirketi, https://eniyi10lar.com/dunyanin-en-iyi-10-lojistik-firmasi-kargo-sirketi/ (22.05.2020).

Evren, M. S. (2011). Maersk Line Çevre Koruma Bilinci. Lojistical Dergisi, (9), 47–49, http://cdn.istanbul.edu.tr/statics/ulastirmalojistik.istanbul.edu.tr/wp-content/uploads/2015/10/Logistical-Say%C4%B1-9.pdf. (26.05.2010)

Fedex (2019). Company Information, Fedex and the Environment, http://www.fedex.com (10.11.2019).

Ge, B., Yang, Y., Jiang, D., Gao, Y., Du, X. and Zhou, T. (2018). An Empirical Study on Green Innovation Strategy and Sustainable Competitive Advantages: Path and Boundary. Sustainability, 10(10), 3631.

Gürgenç, Kaan (2011). Borusan ile Çevre Bilinci. Lojistical Dergisi, (9), 33–35.

Karia, N. and Asaari, M.H.A.H. (2013). Green Innovations in Logistics Industry: Sustainability and Competitive Advantage. In s.k.s. (ed.), Entrepreneurship Vision 2020: Innovation, Development Sustainability, and Economic Growth – Proceedings of the 20th International Business Information Management Association Conference, IBIMA 2013, Vol. 1, Issue January 2013, pp. 456–462.

Kaşık, S. (2016). Yeşil Lojistik: Mevcut Durumu ve Geleceği Üzerine Bir Çalışma, https://www.sametkasik.com.tr/yesil-lojistik-mevcut-durumu-ve-gelecegi-uzerine-bir-calisma.html (26.11.2019).

Kaya, Ç. and Altındağ, E. (2019). Firmaların İnovasyon Yeteneğini Artırmada Örgütsel Öğrenme ve İnsan Kaynakları Yönetiminin Rolü. İçinde: Teknoloji, İnovasyon ve Girişimcilik, İnovasyon Stratejileri ve Endüstri 4.0 (Ed. Sefer Şen), Beta Yayıncılık, İstanbul.

Kn-Portal (2019). About Us, Environment, https://www.kn-portal.com (14.12.2019).

Lee, K.-H. and Min, B. (2015). Green R&D for Eco-Innovation and Its Impact on Carbon Emissions and Firm Performance. Journal of Cleaner Production, 108, 534–542.

Lin, R.-J., Chen, R.-H. and Huang, F.-H. (2014). Green Innovation in The Automobile Industry. Industrial Management and Data Systems, 114(6), 886–903.

Lin, R.-J., Tan, K.-H. and Geng, Y. (2013). Market Demand, Green Product Innovation, and Firm Performance: Evidence from Vietnam Motorcycle Industry. Journal of Cleaner Production, 40, 101–107.

Logistics Dhl (2019). Dhl Logistics Fort He Connected Age, https://www.logistics.dhl/tr-en/home/about-us.html (25.11.2019).

Logistics Dhl (2019). Zero Emissions by 2050: DHL Announces Ambitious New Environmental Protection Target, https://www.logistics.dhl/global-en/home/about-us/delivered-magazine/articles/2017/issue-2-2017/zero-emissions-by-2050.html (25.11.2019).

Lojiport (2019). Borusan Lojistik'ten Tesla'ya Elektrikli Tır Siparişi, https://www.lojiport.com/borusan-lojistikten-teslaya-elektrikli-tir-siparisi101536h.html (05.11.2019).

Lojiport (2019). Mars'ın Enerjisi Yenilebilir Kaynaklardan Geliyor, https://www.lojiport.com/marsin-enerjisi-yenilenebilir-kaynaklardan-geliyor-93935h.html (08.11.2019).

Lojiport (2019). Omsan, Yeşil Lojistiğin Başrolü Olmaya Aday, https://www.lojiport.com/omsan-yesil-lojistigin-basrolu-olmaya-aday-93902h.html (.11.2019).

Lojistürk (2019). Ceva'dan Yeşil Hareket, http://www.lojisturk.net/lojistik/cevadan-yesil-harekat-1341822869h.html (10.11.2019).

Ma Y., Yin, Q., Pan, Y., Cui, W., Xin, B. and Rao, Z. (2018). Green Product Innovation and Firm Performance: Assessing The Moderating Effect of Novelty-Centered and Efficiency-Centered Business Model Design. Sustainability, 10, 1843, 2–13.

Maersk (2019). About, https://www.maersk.com/about (10.12.2019).

Mars Logistics (2019). Hakkımızda, https://www.marslogistics.com/hakkimizda (08.11.2019).

Melander, L. (2017). Achieving Sustainable Development by Collaborating in Green Product Innovation. Business Strategy and the Environment, 26(8), 1095–1109.

Ministry of Development, The Tenth Development Plan 2014-2018. https://policy.asiapacificenergy.org/sites/default/files/The%20Tenth%20Development%20Plan%20%282014-2018%29.pdf

Nanath, K. and Pillai, R. R. (2017). The Influence of Green Is Practices on Competitive Advantage: Mediation Role of Green Innovation Performance. Information Systems Management, 34(1), 3–19.

Netlog (2019). Çevresel Sürdürülebilirliğin Önemi, https://www.netlog.com.tr/surdurulebilirlik/cevresel-surdurulebilirlik/cevresel-surdurulebilirligin-onemi.asp (12.11.2019).

Nippon Express (2019). About Us, Commitment to Environment, https://www.nipponexpress.com/about/ (06.12.2019).

OECD (2018). Defining Innovation, https://www.oecd.org/site/innovationstrategy/defininginnovation.htm (10.04.2020).

OECD (2019). http://www.oecd.org/ (25.12.2019).

Oltra, V. and Saint Jean, M. (2009). Sectoral Systems of Environmental Innovation: An Application to The French Automotive Industry. Technological Forecasting and Social Change, 76(4), 567–583.

Omsan (2019). Tarihçe, http://www.omsan.com/lojistik/hakkimizda/tarihce (17.11.2019).

Park, M. S., Bleischwitz, R., Ki, J. H., Jang, E. K. and Ji, J. H. (2017). Eco-Innovation Indices as Tools for Measuring Eco-Innovation. Sustainability, 9(12), 2206, 2–28.

Presidency of Strategy and Budget. (2019). Eleventh deveopment Plan 2019-2023. https://www.sbb.gov.tr/wp-content/uploads/2020/06/Eleventh_Development_Plan-2019-2023.pdf

Qiu, L., Jie, X., Wang, Y. and Zhao, M. (2020). Green Product Innovation, Green Dynamic Capability, and Competitive Advantage: Evidence from Chinese Manufacturing Enterprises. Corporate Social Responsibility and Environmental Management, 27(1), 146–165.

Rennings, K., Ziegler, A., Ankele, K. and Hoffmann, E. (2006). The Influence of Different Characteristics of the EU Environmental Management and Auditing Scheme on Technical Environmental Innovations and Economic Performance. Ecological Economics. Ecological Economics.

Reysaş (2019). Haberler, http://www.reysas.com/haberler (17.11.2019).

Singh, S. K., Giudice, M. Del, Chierici, R. and Graziano, D. (2020). Green Innovation and Environmental Performance: The Role of Green Transformational Leadership and Green Human Resource Management. Technological Forecasting and Social Change, 150, 1–12.

Song, W. and Yu, H. (2018). Green Innovation Strategy and Green Innovation: The Roles of Green Creativity and Green Organizational Identity. Corporate Social Responsibility and Environmental Management, 25(2), 135–150.

Schiederig, T., Tietze, F. and Herstatt, C. (2011). What is Green Innovation? – A Quantitative Literature Review. Working Papers 63, The XXII ISPIM Conference, June 12–15, Hamburg University of Technology (TUHH), Institute for Technology and Innovation Management. 1–18. Dost: file:///C:/Users/%C4%B0%C4%B0BF/Downloads/SSRN-id1846882%20(1).pdf (17.01.2020).

Tang, M., Walsh, G., Lerner, D., Fitza, M., A. and Li, Q. (2018). Green Innovation, Managerial Concern and Firm Performance: An Empirical Study. Business Strategy and the Environment, 27(1), 39–51.

Transmedya (2019). Mars Logistics'den Yeşil Başarı, http://www.transmedya.com/lojistik/mars-logistics-den-yesil-basarı-h11896.html (08.11.2019).

Transmedya (2019). Omsan Çevreci Hizmete Odaklandı, https://www.transmedya.com/lojistik/omsan-cevreci-hizmete-odaklandi-h10961.html (17.11.2019).

Utikad (2019). Lojistik Sektörü Raporu. https://www.utikad.org.tr/Images/Duyuru/09012020utikadsektorraporu949343.pdf (15.04.2020).

Wang, C.-H. (2019). How Organizational Green Culture Influences Green Performance and Competitive Advantage. Journal of Manufacturing Technology Management, 30(4), 666–683.

Xie, X., Huob J. and Zouc, H. (2019). Green Process Innovation, Green Product Innovation, and Corporate Financial Performance: A Content Analysis Method. Journal of Business Research, 101, 697–706.

Yeşil Lojistikçiler (2019). Omsan İçin Çevre Her Şey, http://www.yesillojistikciler.com/haber/omsan-icin-cevre-her-sey-393.html (17.11.2019).

Yıldız, H. (2016). Sürdürülebilirlik Bağlamında Sağlık Sektöründe İnovatif Uygulamalar: Yeşil Hastaneler. KAUIIBFD, 7(13), 323–340.

Yılmaz, H. (2015). Stratejik İnovasyon Yönetimi, İstanbul, Beta.

Zailani, S., Govindan, K., Iranmanesh, M., Shaharudin, M. R. and Sia Chong, Y. (2015). Green Innovation Adoption in Automotive Supply Chain: The Malaysian Case. Journal of Cleaner Production, 108, 1115–1122.

Zengin, E. (2017). Yeşil Lojistik Göstergeleri ve Türkiye'de Yeşil Lojistik Uygulamaları. Yüksek Lisans Tezi, Gazi Üniversitesi Fen Bilimleri Enstitüsü, Ankara.

Zhang D., Rong Z. and Ji, Q. (2019). Green Innovation and Firm Performance: Evidence from Listed Companies in China, Resources, Conservation and Recycling, 144, 48–55.

Ali Kestane and Niyazi Kurnaz

Determining the Attitude of Accounting Students Regarding Gender Discrimination: Kilis 7 Aralik University Feas Case

1 Introduction

Today, the globalization concept has gained a place in almost every area, from the business world to the social order of countries. It has expanded to all places where human beings exist; social-cultural phenomena, especially in economic, social, legal and political environments, have been affected by it. With the disappearance of economic borders between countries, communication and interaction between people living in different areas has increased. Consequently the values of societies have transformed. Following the increase in differences among people, the concept of discrimination has become eminent. This has led to academic interest in the above-mentioned areas, as well as educational activities. Therefore, it would be beneficial to clarify the concept of discrimination.

Discrimination includes all negative behaviours or attitudes expressed toward a group or members of a group, fed by prejudices. (Göregenli, 2012: 21). Due to the nature of human beings, many separating factors have emerged resulting from their differences. There are many types of discrimination arising from ethnic origin, nationality, legal formations, physical characteristics and likewise (Mathis and Jackson, 2000). Within the scope of this study, the gender discrimination concept (Reed, 1994: 172), which is described as the exposure of two individuals with equal conditions to different treatments because of their gender, is discussed. Gender discrimination means treating the different sexes separately (Türker, 1997: 75) or believing in the superiority of one sex to the other (Altan, 2004: 229). In this age where connecting with people is quicker than ever, the said concept has become a research subject in many fields that exhibit the differences between individuals. Gender discrimination brought about many discussions, especially in education. Hence, the attitudes of students towards gender discrimination has aroused significant interest and resulted in the preparation of this study. In this study, the aim is to determine the attitudes of accounting students towards gender discrimination. Thus, the research on gender discrimination in domestic and foreign literature is investigated and important studies within the framework of the study are expressed below.

In their study regarding gender discrimination in recruitment, Ahmed et al. (2021) found that there was no difference in employer responses in the fifteen selected professions in the male and female-dominated profession groups. Napier et al. (2020) stated in their studies on the rejection of gender discrimination that the rejection of gender discrimination hinges on promoting the argument that the judicial system in the relevant country is fair. McCrackin and Itier (2019), in their study in which they investigated gender discrimination on the basis of emotional, attention and gender, found more positive findings for avoiding gaze rather than direct gaze on the gender discrimination task. Kucharska (2018) investigated the mediating role of self-esteem and emotion regulation on gender discrimination and mental health in women, and discovered that self-esteem is a partial mediator between gender discrimination and its symptoms, stating that emotion suppression is a partial mediator between cumulative trauma and symptoms. Verniers and Vala (2018) inspected the mediating role of motherhood myths in the justification of gender discrimination in the workplace and determined that motherhood myths enlighten the gender perception in countries that support gender equality. Kılavuz (2019) emphasized in the study on the reproduction of gender discrimination in primary schools that the established processes in primary schools create sexist stereotypes in the mind of the students, and gender discrimination begins in primary school. Kılınç (2019) conducted a mobbing research regarding gender discrimination in public institutions and detected that elements such as gender and marital status are significantly effective in the perception of mobbing. Kartal and Çoban (2018) concluded in their study on gender discrimination against women employees that attitudes arising from gender discrimination decrease in the labour market. Demir (2018) established in their study on determining gender discrimination and prejudice in diving tourism that employers are more prone to discrimination in recruitment processes but, still, women can avoid prejudices during the realization of activities.

Regarding the aforementioned studies, it has been determined that the studies in the Turkish literature on gender discrimination in the field of education are insufficient. This study is expected to fill the gap in the relevant field, and shows the importance of conducting research in this field. On the other hand, accounting students who are the accounting profession candidates of the future are critical in determining views on gender discrimination within the profession because, with the help of this study, students' own attitudes towards gender discrimination will be clarified and they will gain awareness.

Depending on the above-mentioned facts, this study consists of two main sections. In the first section, a conceptual framework is created in order to determine the attitudes of accounting students towards gender discrimination, where studies in the existing literature are mentioned. In the second section, application studies are included, and decisions and measures that should be considered for the future are suggested.

2 Research Method

In this section of the study, the purpose and significance of the research, its scope and limitation, the model and hypothesis of the research, and the findings obtained by collecting and analyzing the data are included and explained in detail.

The aim of this study was to determine the attitudes of the accounting students at Kilis 7 Aralık University, Faculty of Economics and Administrative Sciences, towards gender discrimination. In accordance with the purpose of the research, this study is especially important for i) researching the opinions of accounting students to determine their attitudes towards gender discrimination, ii) raising awareness of students concerning the accounting profession in the future, iii) revealing the existing prejudices about gender discrimination in the accounting profession and iv) strengthening the image of the accountancy profession.

However, in order to obtain accurate, consistent and reliable information, and to interpret the findings correctly, students enrolled in the Faculty of Economics and Administrative Sciences in the 2020–2021 academic year were accepted as a significant section in the study.

2.1 Obtaining and Analyzing the Data

In the research, the survey method was adopted to obtain the data. The data was collected electronically from the students because of the pandemic. In the creation of the content of the questionnaires, previously proven studies (Sipe et al., 2009; Brewis, 2010; Zheng, 2016) were used. The questionnaire form consisted of thirty-three statements and three groups. Each statement was coded from 1 to 5, meaning **'Strongly Disagree', 'Disagree', 'Neither Agree nor Disagree', 'Agree' and 'Strongly Agree',** respectively. In the first group of questions, twenty-four statements were used to determine students' attitudes towards gender discrimination. In the second group of questions, there were four open-ended expressions to determine the students' attitudes towards gender discrimination. Finally, in the third group, there were four expressions for detecting the demographic and descriptive characteristics of the participants regarding their grade, age, gender, department and marital status. The data obtained from the questionnaires was collected, organized and coded by reviewing them in line with the purpose and quality of the research. It was determined that 330 students were actively studying at Kilis 7 Aralık University during the research period. In the implementation process of the survey, due to the difficulty in reaching a group of students, 308 questionnaires were able to be distributed and 173 of the 180 questionnaires were considered appropriate for evaluation. The fact that the number of collected questionnaires represents a significant quantity of the accounting students at Kilis 7 Aralık University, Faculty of Economics and Administrative Sciences, evaluated as part of the research, shows the generalizability of this study. The data were encoded in the 'Microsoft Excel 2016' program and transferred to the 'SPSS (Statistical Package for the Social Sciences) 22.0' program. After appropriate analyses, *(reliability analysis, descriptive statistics, frequency distribution, non-parametric variance analysis,* the *Kruskal Wallis H test and* the *Mann-Whitney U test)* the results were evaluated.

It is asserted in various studies that the application of statistical tests depends on providing some assumptions. The most significant of those is considered to be the conformity of the distribution of interest to the normal distribution. In practice, it is generally assumed that the data came from a normally distributed population. In addition, it is seen that the reason for this situation is the effort to adapt nature and human behaviors to a normal distribution in general (Özdamar, 2013: 103). In this context, non-parametric tests can be applied if there is a data set that does not show a normal distribution after the validity tests (Baş, 2019: 96). Regarding applying non-parametric tests, it is deemed sufficient for the data to be collected independently and randomly, to be measured with a sorting or classifying scale, and to not show normal distribution characteristics (Karagöz, 2010: 19). Since the analysis of the data in this study did not show a normal distribution, the non-parametric T-Test (*Mann-Whitney U*) was preferred for the comparison of two groups and non-parametric analysis of variance for more than two groups (*Kruskal Wallis H test*) (Eymen, 2007: 117).

2.2 Findings and Evaluation

In this section of the research, (i) the information on the demographic characteristics of the participants; (ii) the results regarding the mean (standard deviation) values of the expressions of the accounting students to determine their attitudes towards gender discrimination; (iii) frequency analysis results, (iv) the

Kruskal Wallis H test and (v) the *Mann-Whitney U test results* were outlined and evaluated.

Reliability analysis was carried out to detect whether the data obtained by the survey technique in the study was reliable. If the Cronbach's Alpha (reliability coefficient value-∝) obtained as a result of this analysis comes between 0.80–1.00, the data collected from the sample is considered highly reliable (Yıldız and Uzunsakal, 2018: 19). For this study, a reliability analysis was performed for the data concerning all participants, and the ∝value was found to be 0.822. The result obtained indicates that the study is highly reliable.

Tab. 1: *Demographic Characteristics of Students*

Definition		**Number**	**Percentage (%)**	**Definition**		**Number**	**Percentage (%)**
Department	Business	61	35.3	Age	17–19	37	21.4
	Economy	51	29.5		20–22	91	52.6
	Political Science and Public Administration	12	6.3		23–25	36	20.8
	International Trade and Logistics	50	28.9		26 and above	9	5.2
	Total	173	100		Total	60	100
Grade	1	83	48.0	Sex	Male	87	50.3
	2	10	5.2		Female	86	49.7
	3	39	23.1		Total	173	100
	4	41	23.7				
	Total	173	100				
Marital Status	Single	169	97.7				
	Married	4	2.3				
	Total	173	100				

Table 1 states that the students participating in the research are between 20–22 years old (52.6%). While 86 (49.7%) of the students participating in the research were female, 87 (50.3%) of them were male. It was determined that a significant quantity of the students (61 people, 35.3%) studied in the business department, 83 (48.0%) were freshman and 169 (97.7%) were single.

Tab. 2: *Attitudes Of Students Studying Accounting Towards Gender Discrimination*

	Explanations and Expressions	**Number**	**Percentage (%)**	**Number**	**Percentage (%)**
Students' lowest (1) and highest (5) agreement indicators		**1**		**5**	
Expression 1 (A1)	Professional certificates are very important for individuals associated with the accounting profession.	2	1.2%	92	53.2%
Expression 2 (A2)	Those who have a professional certificate are more likely to be promoted.	-	-	66	38.2%
Expression 3 (A3)	Having a professional certificate increases opportunities for career advancement.		-	85	49.5%
Expression 4 (A4)	Having a professional certificate increases wages.	2	1.2%	64	37.0%
Expression 5 (A5)	Having a professional certificate improves professional standings.	3	1.7%	84	48.6%
Expression 6 (A6)	Accounting is a male dominated profession.	71	41.0%	10	5.8%
Expression 7 (A7)	In the field of accounting, women are not as skilled as their male colleagues.	90	%52,0	3	1.7
Expression 8 (A8)	In the field of accounting, women have difficulties in supplying tools.	62	35.8%	7	4.0%
Expression 9 (A9)	In the field of accounting, men are more capable in customer relations than women.	75	43.4%	11	6.4%
Expression 10 (A10)	In the field of accounting, women's presence in the profession can be considered at the secondary labour force level.	59	34.1%	13	7.5%

Tab. 2: *Continued*

	Explanations and Expressions	Number	Percentage (%)	Number	Percentage (%)
Expression 11 (A11)	In the field of accounting, women have problems with their colleagues and professional organizations.	58	33.5%	8	4.6%
Expression 12 (A12)	In the field of accounting, there is a a disparity between the recruitment of men and women.	42	24.3%	12	6.9%
Expression 13 (A13)	In the field of accounting, having individual or family support would not affect my career.	21	12.1%	17	9.8%
Expression 14 (A14)	In the field of accounting, women expect to be offered same promotions and similar opportunities with their men colleagues.	6	3.5%	52	30.1%
Expression 15 (A15)	In the field of accounting, women expect to be appointed to jobs of a similar quality to their male colleagues.	9	5.2%	40	23.1%
Expression 16 (A16)	In the field of accounting, women going into the profession are not welcome.	72	41.6%	8	4.6%
Expression 17 (A17)	In the field of accounting, few women work compared to men.	21	12.1%	18	8.7%
Expression 18 (A18)	In the field of accounting, women are less trusted than men.	51	29.5%	7	4.0%
Expression 19 (A19)	In the field of accounting, women live through more stress than men.	28	16.2%	14	8.1%
Expression 20 (A20)	In the field of accounting, the possibility of being subjected to sexual abuse is higher than in other professions.	49	28.3%	5	2.9%

(continued on next page)

Tab. 2: *Continued*

	Explanations and Expressions	Number	Percentage (%)	Number	Percentage (%)
Expression 21 (A21)	Women in accounting profession experience discrimination based on gender while practicing their profession.	28	16.2%	15	8.7%
Expression 22 (A22)	The educational and cultural level of the customer with whom we deal with can cause discrimination based on gender.	36	20.8%	16	9.2%
Expression 23 (A23)	Women find the uncertainty of working hours difficult.	24	13.9%	19	11.0%
Expression 24 (A24)	In the field of accounting, women earn a lower income than men.	44	25.4%	7	4.0%

* *While 22 (12.7%) of the students are members of professional organizations, 151 (87.3%) of them are not.*

** *Currently 17 (9.8%) students are doing internship and 19 (13.3%) students are actively working while 137 (76.9) students have never worked before.*

When the responders' level of agreement regarding the first twenty-four questionnaire statements was examined, see Table 2, it was noticed that a large majority of them chose 'agree' and 'absolutely agree' options. Open-ended expressions were used to find the students' awareness of the accounting profession and it was detected that twenty-two (12.7%) of the students are members of professional organizations while nineteen (13.3%) of them were active workers in the accounting profession. The professions that students heard most of regarding the field of accounting are specified in Graph 1 and the areas that mostly present students' future plans after graduation are in Graph 2.

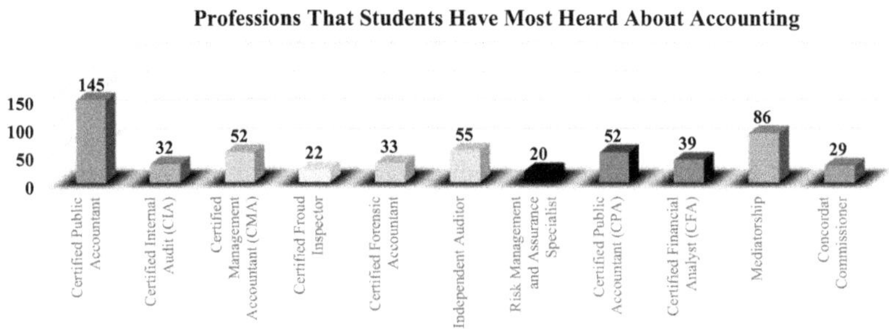

Graphic 1: *Professions That Students Have Heard Most Regarding The Field Of Accounting*

It is pointed out in Chart 1 above that a significant majority (145 people) of the accounting students were determined to be familiar with the certified public accountant profession, whereas they were less interested in the risk management and assurance specialist (twenty people) position. This is consistent with the Certified Public Accountant (CPA) profession being eminent regarding accounting professions in Turkey. On the other hand, it exposes the need for the students to be introduced to new areas of accounting profession.

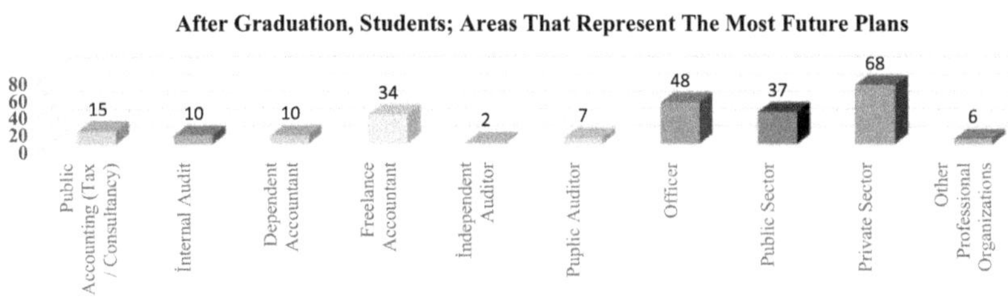

Graphic 2: Areas That Mostly Present Students' Future Plans After Graduation

When the future plans of the students were inspected after the detection of their awareness of the accounting profession, it was found that a significant majority of them aim to practice in the private sector. On the other hand, it can be concluded from Graphic 2 that the number of students who plan practice in the public sector (civil servants) was also considerable. Besides, the entrepreneurial spirit lies behind the plans of students to practice the accounting profession to gain economic independence in the future. That is, the data obtained and the orientation of the profession to the private sector are concordant. Thus, the analysis results of the attitudes accounting students have towards gender discrimination from different perspectives were presented.

Participants in the study; The results of the non-parametric Mann-Whitney U (t-Test) since marital status and gender statuses include two groups, and the non-parametric Kruskal Wallis H (analysis of variance) results because age, class and department statuses include more than two groups are presented below. The results with significant relationships between them are presented in tables.

Tab. 3: *Kruskal Wallis H (Variance Analysis) Results In Relation With The Departments Of The Students*

Kruskal Wallis H **(variance analysis) results in relation with the departments of the students**			
Expression	**Kruskal-Wallis H**	**df**	**p**
A1	8.972	3	.030
A2	7.266	3	.064
A11	6.546	3	.088
A15	14.942	3	.002
A17	11.849	3	.008
A24	7.809	3	.050

Significance value; p<0.05

When Table 3 is examined, it is observed that the students' attitudes towards gender discrimination has a significant difference statistically, as evaluated by the expressions A1, A2, A11, A15, A17 and A24 being less than 'p <0.05'. This reveals that students' attitudes towards those expressions differ according to their age, and the age of the students has a statistically significant effect on their attitude toward gender discrimination. Results show that students' attitude towards i) the importance of professional certifications related to the accounting profession for promotion, ii) the possibility of women encountering problems with their colleagues, iii) women practicing professions of similar quality to their male peers, and iv) having fewer positions in professional activities compared to men and earning a lower income differ in accordance with their departments.

Tab. 4: *Kruskal Wallis H (Variance Analysis) Results In Relation With The Age Of The Students*

Kruskal Wallis H **(variance analysis) results in relation with the age of the students**			
Expression	**Kruskal-Wallis H**	**df**	**p**
A6	6.995	3	.072
A7	10.608	3	.014
A9	10.770	3	.013
A11	6.991	3	.072
A12	9.052	3	.029
A13	6.666	3	.083
A16	6.415	3	.093

Significance value; $p<0.05$

When Table 4 is examined, it is observed that the students' attitudes towards gender discrimination has a significant difference statistically, as evaluated by the expressions A6, A7, A9, A11, A12, A13 and A16 being less than '$p <0.05$'. The aforementioned case reveals that students' attitudes towards gender discrimination differ according to their age and the age of the students has a statistically significant effect on their attitudes towards gender discrimination. These results indicate that students' attitudes regarding i) the accountancy being a male-dominated profession, ii) women being less skilled than their male colleagues, iii) men being more capable in customer relations than women, iv) women encountering problems with their colleagues, v) the recruitment of women and men in accounting vi) the effect of individual and family support on making a career in accounting, and the vii) the absence of welcoming women into the accounting profession alter depending on their age.

Tab. 5: *Kruskal Wallis H (Variance Analysis) Results In Relation With The Grades Of The Students*

***Kruskal Wallis H* (variance analysis) results in relation with the grades of the students**			
Expression	**Kruskal-Wallis H**	**df**	**p**
A3	6.880	3	.076
A8	7.303	3	.063
A12	7.050	3	.070
A15	13.912	3	.003
A16	9.054	3	.029
A21	9.290	3	.026
A24	12.390	3	.006

Significance value; p<0.05

When Table 5 is evaluated, it is discovered that the students' attitudes towards gender discrimination has a significant difference statistically, as evaluated by the expressions A13, A8, A12, A15, A16, A21 and A24 being less than 'p <0.05'. This points out that students' attitudes towards those expressions alter according to their grades, and the students' grade has a statistically important effect on their attitude towards gender discrimination. The findings demonstrate that the students' attitudes concerning issues such as i) having a professional certificate increasing their advancement opportunities, ii) women having difficulties in the field of accounting, in obtaining equipment, iii) the possibility of a difference in the recruitment in the field of accounting between men and women, iv) women's expectations regarding being appointed to professions of similar quality to their male counterparts, v) women not being welcomed to the field of accounting vi) women experiencing discrimination regarding their gender during the exercise of the accountancy profession, and vii) their attitudes towards issues such as lower income compared to males vary according to their grades.

Tab. 6: *Mann-Whitney U (T Test) Results In Relation With The Marital Status Of The Students*

Mann-Whitney U (t Test) results in relation with the marital status of the students			
Expression	**Mann-Whitney U**	**Wilcoxon W**	**p (bilateral)**
A4	155.000	14520.000	.052

Significance value; p<0.05

Table 6 shows that students' attitudes towards gender discrimination is significantly different statistically where the A4 expression is less than 'p <0.05'. This indicates that students' attitudes towards gender discrimination differ according to their marital status and that the marital status of the students has a statistically significant effect on their attitudes towards gender discrimination. This proves that students' attitudes towards having a professional certificate vary concerning their marital status.

Tab. 7: *Mann-Whitney U (T Test) Results In Relation With The Gender Of The Students*

Mann-Whitney U (t Test) results in relation with the gender of the students			
Expression	**Mann-Whitney U**	**Wilcoxon W**	**p (bilateral)**
A4	3098.500	6839.500	.041
A5	3315.500	7056.500	.164
A6	2586.500	6327.500	.000
A7	2353.000	6094.000	.000
A8	3133.000	6874.000	.054
A9	2510.500	6251.500	.000
A11	3059.000	6800.000	.031
A12	2950.000	6691.000	.014
A14	2766.000	6594.000	.002
A15	2723.000	6551.000	.001
A18	3214.000	6955.000	.097
A21	2531.000	6359.000	.000

Significance value; p<0.05

When Table 4 is considered, students' attitudes towards gender discrimination has a significant difference statistically, as evaluated by the expressions A4, A5, A6, A7, A8, A9, A11, A12, A14, A15, A18 and A21 being less than 'p <0.05'. This shows that students' attitudes towards those expressions vary according to their gender, and that the gender of students has a statistically significant effect on their attitudes towards gender discrimination. The findings are evidence that student's attitudes regarding issues such as: i) having a professional certificate increasing salaries and reputation, ii) accounting being a male-dominated profession, iii) women being less capable than men, iv) women encountering problems in procuring equipment compared to men, v) men being more skilled in customer relations, vi) women having conflicts with their colleagues in the field of accounting, vii) the discrimination between women and men when recruiting personnel in the field, viii) the expectation of being offered the same promotions and similar opportunities as men and being appointed to jobs of similar quality to their male colleagues, ix) trust in women being less compared to men in the field of accounting and x) women facing gender-based discrimination when performing their profession differ according to their gender.

5 Conclusion

Humans are alive, thinking and dynamic by nature, and thus are different. With the increase of social, cultural, economic and other differences in almost every field where humans are dominant, discrimination becomes evident. In today's world, the disappearance of borders as a result of the increase in communication and transportation opportunities between different geographies led to the discussion of the relevant concept. The discrimination movement, which manifests itself in almost every field from the ethnic origin of the person to her physical characteristics, from socio-cultural characteristics to education and training processes, is knotted in gender discrimination. Because gender discrimination suspended the natural flow of life of human beings it is critical to produce solutions to solve this significant issue. To provide a solution the problem, starting from the education level, was considered important in terms of bringing a healthy individual into society and laid the groundwork for the preparation of this study. In this study, the aim was to determine the attitudes of accounting students towards gender discrimination. What distinguishes this study from others is the detection of students' perceptions regarding gender discrimination within the accounting profession and then revealing the perceptions of students regarding gender discrimination within themselves. This research is important and unique in the determination, management and prevention of the gap in perception regarding gender discrimination.

It was determined in the research that nineteen (13.3%) of the majority of the students were actively working in the accounting profession and twenty-two (12.7%) were members of professional organizations. The orientation of students to practice accounting in the private sector after graduation overlap with the characteristics of the accounting profession that appeal to extrovert and entrepreneurial individuals. On the other hand, introducing students to new fields in the field of accounting is considered important with respect to raising awareness.

The study concluded that the accounting students' views regarding the gender discrimination in their field are as following: i) accountancy is not a male-dominated profession, ii) women can be as capable as men, iii) women can be trusted in practicing the accounting profession just as men, iv) it is possible for women to be as successful in customer relations as men and v) women would not encounter difficulties in providing equipment compared to men. In addition, whether the attitudes towards gender discrimination vary in line with the demographic characteristics – and it was detected they did – was in part because of their gender. In other words, while the students' views towards the accounting profession did not reveal any gender discrimination, the examination of their own answers determined that students hold gender-discriminating beliefs. This clearly manifests the nature of human beings. That is to say, while the effect of gender on individual attitudes and behaviors is higher, it is clear that this effect will be much lower on attitudes towards issues other than himself. In substance, based on the results obtained within this study, it is suggested that analyzing the studies on gender discrimination by evaluating them from different perspectives in the field of education will enable the discovery of the different sides of human nature.

References

Ahmed, A., Granberg, M. and Khanna, S. (2021). Gender discrimination in hiring: an experimental reexamination of the Swedish case. PLoS One, January, 29, 1–15.

Altan, Ö. Z. (2004). Sosyal Politika Dersleri, 1. Bs., Eskişehir: Anadolu Üniversitesi İktisadi ve İdari Bilimler Yayınları.

Baş, M. (2019). Bağlantılı k örneklem ile parametrik olmayan cochran q testi: BIST 100 uygulaması. Uluslararası Afro-Avrasya Araştırmaları Dergisi, 4(8), 94–107.

Brewis, D. N. (2010). Performing Professional: University Student Perceptions of Gender Discrimination in Their Future Careers. University of Birmingham for the degree, England.

Demir, M. (2018). Dalış Turizmi Sektöründe Cinsiyet Ayrımcılığı ve Cinsiyet Önyargısının Betimlenmesi. Yüksek Lisans Tezi. Muğla Sıtkı Koçman Üniversitesi, Sağlık Bilimleri Enstitüsü, Muğla.

Eymen, U. E. (2007). Spss 15.0 veri analiz yöntemleri. www.istatistikmerkezi.com (E.T.: 25.02.2020)

Göregenli, M. (2012), "Temel Kavramlar: Önyargı, Kalıpyargı ve Ayrımcılık" İçinde Çayır, K. ve Ceyhan, M. A, Ayrımcılık Çok Boyutlu Yaklaşımlar, ss. 17–29, İstanbul: İstanbul Bilgi Üniversitesi Yayınları.

Karagöz, Y. (2010). Nonparametrik tekniklerin güç ve etkinlikleri, Elektronik Sosyal Bilimler Dergisi, 9(33), 18–40.

Kartal, M. and Çoban, O. (2018). Emek piyasasında kadın çalışanlara yönelik cinsiyet ayrımcılığı: Kahramanmaraş tekstil sektörü örneği. Selçuk Üniversitesi Sosyal Bilimler Enstitüsü Dergisi, (39), 67–81.

Kılavuz, T. (2019). İlkokulda Cinsiyet Ayrımcılığının Yeniden Üretimi. Yüksek Lisans Tezi. Mersin Üniversitesi, Eğitim Bilimleri Enstitüsü, Mersin.

Kılınç, N. (2019). Kamu Kurumlarında Cinsiyet Ayrımcılığına Bağlı Mobbing Araştırması: Gümüşhane İli Örneği. Yüksek Lisans Tezi. Gümüşhane Üniversitesi, Sosyal Bilimler Enstitüsü, Gümüşhane.

Kucharska, J. (2018). Cumulative trauma, gender discrimination and mental health in women: mediating role of self-esteem. Journal of Mental Health, 27(5): 416–423

Mathis, L.R. and Jackson, H.J. (2000), Human Resources Management, 9. Bs. USA: South Western College Publishing.

McCrackin, S.D. and Itier, R. J. (2019). Perceived gaze direction differentially affects discrimination of facial emotion, attention, and gender – an erp study. Frontiers in Neuroscience, 13, (517), 1–14.

Napier, J. L., Suppes, A. and Bettinsoli, M. L. (2020). Denial of gender discrimination is associated with better subjective well-being among women: A system justification account. EASP Wiley, 1191–1209. DOI: 10.1002/ejsp.2702

Reed, E. (1994), Kadının Evrimi: Anaerkil Klandan Ataerkil Aileye, Çev: Semsa Yegin. 2. Baskı, İstanbul: Payel Yayınları.

Özdamar, K. (2013). Paket programlar ile istatistiksel veri analizi I. Eskişehir: Nisan Kitabevi.

Sipe, S., Fisher, D. K. and Johnson, C. D. (2009). University students' perceptions of gender discrimination in the workplace: reality versus fiction. Journal of Education for Business, July, 339–349.

Türker, N. (1997). Konaklama İşletmelerinde Cinsel Taciz ve Cinsiyet Ayrımı. Anatolia: Turizm Araştırmaları Dergisi, 8 (2), 74–76.

Yıldız, D. and Uzunsakal, E. (2018). Alan araştırmalarında güvenilirlik testlerinin karşılaştırılması ve tarımsal veriler üzerine bir uygulama. Uygulamalı Sosyal Bilimler Dergisi, 1, 14–28.

Verniers, C. and Vala, J. (2018). Justifying gender discrimination in the workplace: The mediating role of motherhood myths. PLoS One, 13(1), 1–23.

Zheng, Q. (2016). Student Perception on Female Discrimination in Accounting. Bachelor of Science in Business Administration. University of Arkansas, Fayetteville, Arkansas. Fayettevile.

Nihat Onur Aşikoğlu and Belkıs Özkara

SMEs Clusters to Competitive Effects: Sector Analysis of Marble in Afyonkarahisar Turkey*

1 Introduction

In parallel with liberalization trends observed across the world, limits to national economies from competing in the international arena have become an important determinant of trade relations/ In terms of the importance of increasing competition and changing the traditional trade of countries, the approaches applied by many countries have brought about the success of the proven 'clustering approach', has become today's most prominent approach. Of the known and proven benefits of the cluster, supporting innovation activities to facilitate the commercialization of innovation, productivity and boost employment, 'competition and cooperation' provides the greatest opportunity. Specialized clusters of resources, services, information and research institutes, as well as general needs, more effectively provide access to education, business and operations, providing easier coordination, accelerating the spread of best practices and benchmarking the performance of competitors, which improves efficiency and productivity.

Clustering models, only one project is to increase the competitiveness of the regional. One of the reasons it is so popular in recent years, cluster, regional competitive power of each element and creates a platform for them to accelerate the development of infrastructure. A cluster of firms that produce, sell and increase their ability to innovate in the implementation of infrastructure projects enhances capabilities. Porter to create a competitive advantage for an organization and to identify strategies for the maintenance of comprehensive cost advantage, the difference is the focus of market advantage and used a narrow or wide. Clusters affect competition in three main ways: increasing the productivity of the enterprises established in the cluster; creating of new products in the future, which will increase efficiency by directing innovation; and expanding and strengthening the cluster itself by encouraging the emergence of new business areas. In this study, which is the theoretical analysis of the concept of

* This study is derived from the doctoral thesis named 'Tepe Yönetimin Niteliklerinin Kümelenme Stratejisine Etkileri: Afyonkarahisar Mermer Sektörü Örneği'.

clustering, will be presented in total. Porter's diamond model, based on clusters of afyonkarahisar, affecting the competitiveness level of the marble industry is introduced. The study used the survey method. The survey method, except for face-to-face interviews, and observation techniques will apply. The relationship between clustering and competition is introduced in this context.

With the development of industry in the world over the last century, business organizations entered into a growth process. Business growth, the acceleration of communication, expansion and development of logistics network, such factors as increasing competition, businesses need to implement policies revealed different (Aşıkoğlu, 1993: 5). Businesses to present emerging developments that occur locally, then regional, national and international level shows that is active or effective.

2 Cluster Concept and Definition

As long as the date, The most basic level each other businesses legally binding at the highest levels to the level of partnership in action. In the beginning, gentleman's agreement, cartel, types of business associations such as concerts widely uses the highest level of cooperation shown later claimed to have co-partnership level (Karalar, 1995:165).

After having seen that they have benefited mutually by taking part in the cooperation process, business enterprises made significant progress in developing the technology and making joint use of it. Business enterprises, as a result of collaboration, have specialized in production in specific sectors and areas, and have started to develop the necessary components for production, raw materials, manpower and technology together, and to turn them into production. As a result of communal development of the production elements of the business enterprise, the synergy showed that business enterprises taking part in cooperation became more powerful and provided considerable advantages in terms of costs and competition.

At what level of business cooperation will be discussed theoretical work on how it can perform have been made over many years. In the new era of cooperation in business and the name of his working 'cluster' is named by the M. Port the first time and this concept has been provided by the literature by him.

Private infrastructure, labour pool and the services that share; active production processes, communication and dialogue with channels which are interconnected, thus generally exploits beneficial opportunities and risks to overcome that allow geographically bounded related or complementary services (business lines) in the same area is the concentration (Kaygalak, 2011: 68)

The ideas put forward by Marshall in 1929, improved again handled by Weber, local availability of resources is an important factor in reducing the cost, but as demand for low cost of production is also an important factor for businesses, the most important goal is to obtain high profit and This is to ensure that there is continuity of has expressed.

According to Porter cluster, with each other in the same or similar field of relationships based on common technologies and skills that build businesses that are geographically close groups. Institutions and organizations often contact them forming clusters, providing logistics and ease of interaction in the geographical area (Porter, 1998: 158). Clusters are usually in the same area and are sometimes concentrated in a single city.

Clusters are important because Clusters are usually companies that are within their individual situations when they are more productive and creative. Clustering can increase the performance of the company, as clustering within the limits of a certain range of local suppliers, customers, competitors, universities and research centres etc. are based on common working relations and partnership networks. Proximity, networking and specialization has three main features. Due to these properties, Clusters, business-to-important functions in place of co-operation that is organizing (Beyaz Kitap, 2011: 22).

3 Porter's Fıve Competıtıve Interactıon in Cluster Model

Business competition is one of important factors that affects productivity and efficiency improvements. Business, the available resources effectively and efficiently to take to compete at that level will have increased its in. Hence the productivity of enterprises in order to increase competitiveness, local resources must use an effective and efficient way.

Businesses use local resources effectively and efficiently for the development of behaviour models in cooperation with the importance of the perceived necessity.

Porter's five competitive interaction model, which is valid in many industries, has been generally accepted as a model. Competition from industry to industry: according to Porter competition in any industry will result in suppliers bargaining power, substitute product development potential, new competitors entering the market, potential customers bargaining power and the competition between businesses, which will vary depending on the severity of competition. (Hawken, 1993: 139)

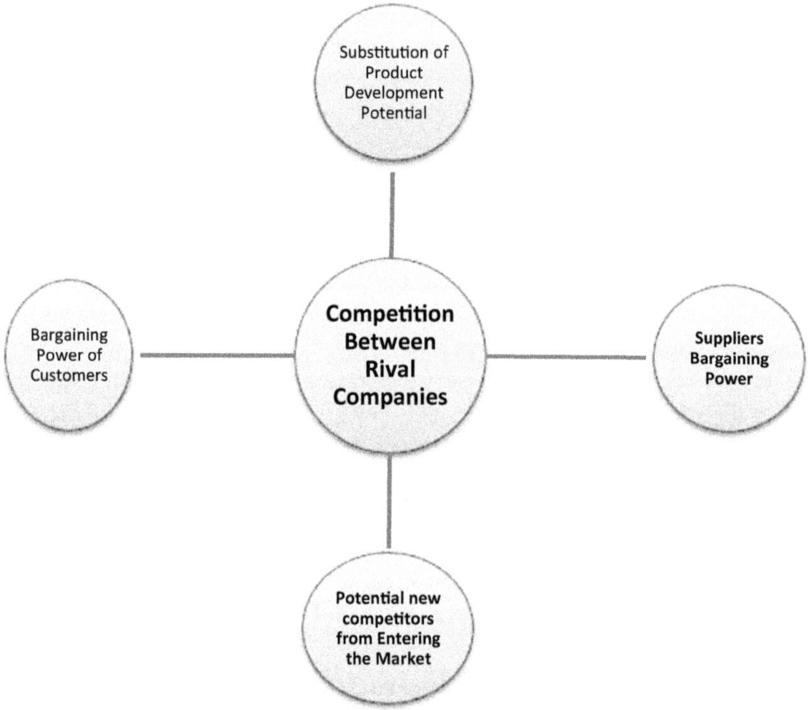

Fig. 1: Porter's Five Competitive Interaction Model (Bakoğlu, 2010: 125)

As shown in Figure 1, to interact with Porter's five model in that they come to look at business opportunities and threats a strategic management position evokes a sense of place in literature has received (Bakoğlu, 2010: 124). Contemporary strategic management approach so that it forces a re-creative to define how and The balance between power, or in what manner any size itself can be changed and a creative way with the internal capacity of the power that you know how to re-shape has become more decisive. Porter's five model interaction with public organizations, local communities, trade unions, special interest groups, and pay owners of various stakeholder groups, as it is necessary to add in (Gladwin, Krause and Kennelly, 2006: 35). Competition rules, the universal system, as a connected relationships, nature science, such as scarce resources, economic as a limited request welcome and by improving your ability to maintain its presence. In this context, competition can be defined in many different purposes with an emphasis on different elements and is a concept with economic, political and social dimensions.

Competition, in the broadest sense, to share something scarce or in order to obtain a reward in the framework of certain rules and restrictions of fundamental freedoms and human rights as guaranteed and no privilege and discrimination in an environment where there is more than one player or a game that is played can be defined as a race (http://www.ekonometrik.com/rekabet-ve-rekabet-gucu-nedir.html).

Cluster formations, to gain a competitive advantage for emerges as an important building (Jacobs and Jong, 1992: 232). Clustering is based on Porter's diamond, who has been working diagram for clustering, expressed as four important element of the policy. These business strategies and the competitive environment, and factor conditions, related and supporting industries and demand conditions as may be received and considered. However, the index is the focal point of suitable areas for investment to promote the availability of between competitors with the creation of regional competition creates (Porter, 2000: 20).

Collaboration is also a set of increasing the competitiveness and international challenges in the face of a common strategic vision, focus, aimed at the strong economic players and interventional a stronger participation. Partnerships and networking, clustering processes, 'the thin communication channels to penetrate', 'horizontality' and 'flexibility', also set the authorization of the local frame to guarantee can bring. (Beyaz Kitap, 2011: 48)

Competitiveness, the country of free market conditions and settled under the real income of the citizens, while trying to increase at the same time their products and services to international markets and to provide successful area. The country's ability to export, production resources, and the efficient use of natural resources in the country and raise living standards, and whether that increase the productivity of a multi-dimensional concept (Çivi, 2001: 4).

Aiginger according to innovation and educated workforce, based on the competitive advantages and capabilities of the countries in the region, it is to determine the competitiveness of enterprises. Long-term competitive advantage can be maintained in the enterprises constantly sought-after features produce high value-added, high wages to their employees and pay high to make a profit, such as that successful businesses are usually endogenous growth or mergers of employment and increase their size could; hence, the long-term success of the businesses that have all of these indicators to the definition of national competitiveness can be imported Aiginger, at the time of the competitiveness of enterprises well-defined profit/loss account for more than that and even business competitiveness to be able to create prosperity can be debated as ability to think.

Hence, innovation, and skilled labour advantage and sustaining their businesses and countries of the competition affects in a positive way (Akal and Kabasakal, 2012: 4).

OECD competitiveness, while providing real income growth in the country; foreign countries, the customers ' tastes and expectations of the ability to produce the product is in the form of definitions (Yalçınkaya et al., 2009: 5).

Clustering of cooperation, countries, markets, and businesses competitive identity, the understanding of international competition, the ability to integrate the power of factors of production, and produced the product and services markets of other countries, spreading rate,the competitiveness of the public authorities for the formation and maintenance of the necessary measures in a short time they will get depends on. Available of resources and policies are important in order to increase their competitive advantages (Çivi, 2001: 15).

In a particular geographic region, similar activities has met, producing similar products businesses in the value chain the other businesses and organizations (public institutions, universities, trade and industry, non-governmental organizations) create together the geographical region where the stack can be defined as. This is the mass in order to increase the competitiveness of enterprises, informed the union is able to create formations is referred to as a cluster. (SME Cooperation and Clustering Project, 2011: 6).

Clusters are located on the basis of trust and cooperation. There are many potential areas of cooperation. It is possible to specify areas of cooperation mainly as follows. (Cooperation and network management for clusters Confidence Building Guide, 2011: 5):

- Innovation and product development
- Sales/imports/exports
- Marketing and brand building
- Education and employment
- Local policies breakthrough

In the same industry with similar production of raw materials or similar uses similar enterprises in cooperation to confront challenges, opportunity or the creation of new opportunities for businesses providing alone much further from their current location to take the position of considerable influence. On the basis of the cluster, although it takes place in cooperation between business clusters together with the basic elements of business support organizations, educational and research institutions are creating.

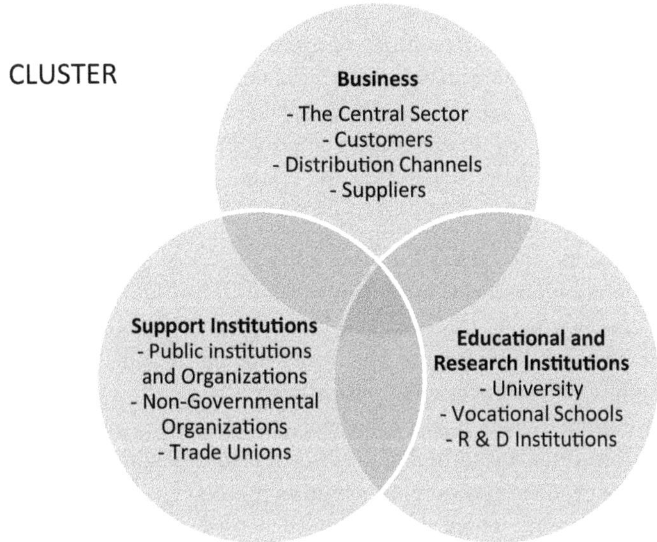

Fig. 2: Key Elements of the cluster (SME Cooperation and Clustering Project, 2011: 6)

As seen in Figure 2, the basic elements of the cluster businesses, support agencies, educational and research institutes constitute. Set in formation of the cluster and in the centre of 'Business'. Business developed by the success of the cooperation strategy of the cluster, it is a key factor affecting the success. Business in the fields of co-operation with customers, suppliers and distribution channels. Business in the fields of co-operation of the power set the power of the puts. The cluster is an important basic elements of the 'Support of Institutions'. Cluster support organizations associated with the cluster as public institutions, Chambers of Commerce and Industry, Professional Associations, OSB Management, NGOs may be considered.

Set an important part of the basic element of the 'Education and Research Institutions'. Educational and Research Institutions, such as Universities and Professional Schools, a set of information and technology needed to be manufactured on the other hand, while the cluster's needs were trained work force plays an important role in the upbringing. Moreover, R&D institutions, enterprises in the cluster needs of the investigation of new technologies plays an important role in the development.

The cluster formation of cluster in the field of businesses, creates a significant contribution. Common problems to overcome, common opportunities with better evaluation of the businesses, R&D and constantly renew themselves and to keep pace with global competition. Clustering processes in the cluster, and the scope of cooperation within enterprises by providing the following benefits as it is possible to order (SME Cooperation and Clustering Project, 2011: 7):

- Cluster management, businesses, recognizing that can analyse, goals and objectives of the enterprises for developing solutions, in developing projects and cooperation networks, and it helps create.
- Cluster management, business products, process development for R&D projects and is able to initiate the work with the product, technology and market to more easily access the information.
- Sets, in developing the final product of the same value chain, operating in cooperation with national and international businesses gradually increase the value of the product may develop common projects.
- The problems of the sector, identifying their solution are to be found in the same sector in other businesses and with industry leaders, together with the related power.
- Located within a cluster of enterprises, markets of targets related to research and education, by taking advantage can improve their export strategy.
- Cluster management by industry and/or business that is held as fair visits, the delegations participating in such events as more and more effectively in a short time.
- A cluster of enterprises in the scope of the international platform increases the visibility of the trust and to enter new markets.

Sets a specific industry, a specific geographic region, the result of the concentration of formations, though, developed and competitive value-generating structure so that they may usually intervention from the outside, and need support with.

Clusters according to their level of development, starting at the level of clusters in developing and mature clusters set to be taken up in three groups incelense also the idea of a set of stages of the stack, with the set of the stage of the transformation process, which is included in the group of five, and on the other hand it may be taken (For clusters, the Internationalization Strategies and Marketing Guide, 2011: 4).

The idea of stage sets, in the same industry, a similar production in the same geographical area in the business community. The stack by the national authorities of regional or clustering were selected for the study. Starting at the level of clusters (a cluster emergence), basic analysis (needs analysis, SWOT and Value Chain) were made, including cluster management and the creation of task definitions have been made, a set of brand identity. Developing cluster / cluster is managed by professional managers, the cluster has been introduced. Advanced analysis was carried out, monitoring and evaluation activities are carried out continuously, the international network creation and development has started. Mature clusters, cluster sustainability has been proven in the international arena industry authority has become and self-financed is able to lobby and competitiveness has had the final goods-producing businesses, suppliers operating in conjunction with joint R&D activities has developed. Static cluster is, in itself, is evaluated in two ways. The first of them, the positive transformation. Positive transformation, the cluster is formed in the expertise of one of the groups has started to develop new sets, developing adaptation to new technologies by providing a basic proficiency in creating change. Static clusters negative transformation, changing conditions in the world, and been unable to adjust to economic conditions, the extreme concentration in the solution of problems posed by the insufficient have been preserved, developing competitiveness with other regions of the lost. (Anderson, 2004: 24).

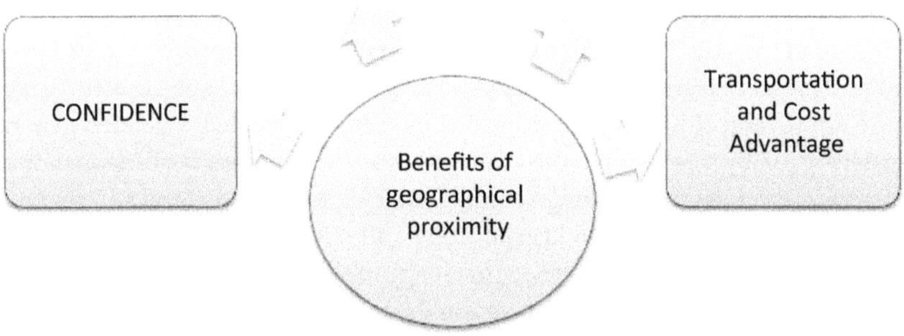

Fig. 3: Benefits Of Geographical Proximity (Lublinski, 2002: 28)

Marshall, operating in the same sector businesses in a specific geographic presence in the region and enterprises on the important benefits that the axiom of choice, and it externalities as stated. This externalities of the labour market and the formation of the pool of the needs of businesses will provide a variety of intermediate goods and services, and transportation will be easier and the dissemination of knowledge, which can be expressed in the form (Cortright, 2008: 8). Marshall, geographical concentration of the information needs of businesses and skills of the workforce in this region will develop, and stated that the focus.

Businesses which need work force in the region, which can be obtained easily in any business, and the power will be able to employment. Also search needs of businesses producing goods and services, this will focus on the geographical region of the businesses they want to quality of the goods and services in more favourable conditions, with the possibility of supply, such as they may have problems with the system that they will encounter. In addition, the geographical area of the nature of the goods and services produced in the new knowledge and ideas will emerge more often by more businesses and between businesses will spread more easily and quickly.

4 Clusterıng Studies in Turkey

In Turkey, it was started in 1999 by the Middle East Competition Center which was constituted under the guidance of Michael Porter and the CAT platform (Competitive Advantage of Turkey), which was established with contributions from the Turkish private sector. The CAT platform took the name 'International Competitive Studies Institution' (ICSN) (Beyaz Kitap, 2011: 34).

In Turkey, creating policy for clustering was given place in the medium-term program of the year 2009. It was indicated that clustering approach is a succesful method for increasing competitive power in the program. It stated that in Turkey there are several clustering constitutions in sectoral level but a defined general clustering policy is needed. In this context it is asserted necessity of supporting of clustering attempts to preparing several clustering maps in sectoral and regional level and using Organized Industrial Zone and similar clustering backgrounds and producing new models. Within this scope in the year 2009 by the ministry of industry and trade it is stated that National Cluster Support Policy will be developed. In the context of measure for increasing competitive power it is stated that notably OIZs collaboration activities like establishing common R&D, design and test analysis centres of enterprises which are active in existing clustering fields will be supported by KOSGEB (DPT 2009 Yılı Programı, p. 133)

By increasing the competitiveness and efficiency of Turkish industry, in order to accelerate to change of an industrial structure which is getting more share from world export, producing predominantly high technology products, has qualified workforce, sensitive to environment and society, clustering which has the potetial of specified competitiveness and maintainability, has the importance in national aspect and predominantly is active in manufacturing industry, 'Clustering Support Program Regulations' was regulated by the Ministry of Science, Industry and Technology (Official Gazette, 15 September 2012, issue : 28412).

In Turkey, the Ministry of Economy by reflecting accumulation of knowledge about clustering to subsidies policy, called 'Notification About Supporting of Developing of International Competitiveness' (UR-GE) subsidy mechanism which is based on clustering understanding, project-based, target market and target sector focused put into action on the date 23 September 2010. Within the frame of this notification it supported 116 projects including the following : KOBİ İşbirliği and Kümelenme Projesi, Ağ Oluşturma and Bölgesel İşbirliği İçin KOBİ'lerin Güçlendirilmesine Yönelik Teknik Yardım, 2013: 3. However another important study which the ministry conducts in order to develop export focused collaboration is 'SME Collaboration and Clustering Project' which includes the February 2011–November 2013 period.

In order to actualize UR-GE project and determine sectoral vision primarily an analysis study must be conducted to members of collaboration institution in the existed field. This analysis study as it will indicate the existence of divided one or more sector structure in the studied filed, it can assert that existence of structure of sector constituted by enterprises focused on specified fields. In both case UR-GE project can be prepared. But having similar requirements enterprises placing in the project, possibility of benefiting from training and consultancy services together, the potential of creating sectoral power together to aimed markets, in other words, the potential of collaboration of enterprises and export target must be asserted (KOBİ İşbirliği ve Kümelenme Projesi, 2011: 20).

Within the scope of UR-GE Project Sivas Natural Stone cluster studies subsidied officially. Because of database related wtih this cluster have not consisted of yet, there is no data to express.

5 Natural Stone and Marble Clustering Studies in Afyonkarahisar

In ancient Rome, marble blocks, which were mined from Afyonkarahisar, were processed and used to build and decorate a lot of religious, social and cultural places in Italy, in Spain and in France.

In lots of works which were built in before christ marble is encountered. Types of marbles used in these works are a great variety as well as, it draws attention that their dimensions are very big. Marble is found in historical ancient temples, statues, palaces, Egyptian pharaoh's tombs, pyramids, ramparts, castles, stadiums and open-air theatres (Arıkan, 2012: 2).

It is possible to express the approximate beginning of production and process of marble thousands of years. Therefore production of marble and processing of natural stone, on the one hand when it generates one of the traditional production sectors of Afyonkarahisar on the other hand nowadays with developed technology and lived globalism process it becomes to be wanted and liked. As of the end of the 2020, production of marble got an important place in the main production branches.

Concerning acting enterprises in production of natural stone and marble informations determining greatness compiled under. These informations were gotten from ATSO, Afyon Marble-Cutter Associations and by meeting administrators and enterpreneurs of major institutions.

As of the year 2020 there are 314 marble and natural stone production plants acting in region as SME. 6436 people works in these plants in total. 15% of the workers works as white-collar.

Total area of usage of enterprises acting in marble and natural stone sector in Afyonkarahisar is about 3,100,000 m2. In about 500.000 m2 closed area marble and natural stone production is realized. (ATSO Dış Ticaret Raporu 2020).

European Commission described clusters in the notification entitled 'Towards world-class clusters in the European Union: Implementing the broad-based innovation strategy' as group of economic actors and institutions related with enterprise which is located near together and reached on a sufficient level in private field to develop specialization, service, fund, supplier and skill.

For accumulation point revealing in marble sector, substructure ready. For this reason, in Afyon; to begin clustering studies, ATSO, Economy Ministry and University applies. The first study in this subject has done in ATSO in 20 November 2013. In this studying, there are subjects and aims at the begining step with details. If managements in our city, work in a cluster with cooperation, they will go into strongly not only Turkey's market but also international market. Managements can't reach individually and can reach with cluster easily to the markets and market enlarges, in Afyonkarahisar exportation prices will increase 700 million dollars to 1.5 million dollars.

6 Conclusion

Because of globalization, companies have to compete in international markets. Competition's basic elements are quality and price. Managements must reduce their input cost to procure a competition environment with submit quality products at a cheaper price in international market. Input costs change with local conditions. Managements who use the local conditions to work with reducing input costs have more advantages. In a process which consist of local conditions production, have to use this process active and productive, in case of make a cluster with local managements where are in the same area.

In last years in the world, Porter's cluster notion and his theorical studies have a great importance and find a execution area. In Turkey, cluster studies have begun under routing of Porter, CAT platform has started in 1999. CAT platform called International Competition Research Foundation (URAK) with switching to institutionalization process.

Studies in clustering, especially in 2010 has increased in Turkey. To consider the number of marble processing plants in Afyonkarahisar, there is a stack in the first step of this subject, marble and natural Stone studies have begun in 2013 in this year, in Afyonkarahisar; marble and natural Stone exportation is $250 million (US), in the end of clusterin studies, there will be a cluster and it procures a competition advantage, and an aim is $1 million (US) in exportation.

References

Akal M., Kabasakal A., Oecd Ülkelerinin Rekabet Gücünü Açıklayıcı Kurumsal Ve Karma Modeller, Business and Economics Research Journal, Volume 3, Issue 1, 2012, pp. 109–130.

Arıkan M., Türkiye'de Mermercilik, 2012.

Aşıkoğlu, R., Globalleşme Sürecinde Uluslararası Finansal Yönelimler, T.C. Dumlupınar Üniversitesi Yay. No: 2, İ.İ.B.F. Yay. Kütahya, 1993.

Bakoğlu R., Çağdaş Stratejik Yönetim, Beta Yayınevi, İstanbul, 2010

Beyaz Kitap, Türkiye İçin Kümelenme Politikasının Geliştirilmesi T.C. Ekonomi Bakanlığı, 2011.

Cortrıght J., Making Sense of Clusters: Regional Competitiveness and Economic Development, 2006, Us.

Çivi, E., 'Rekabet Gücü: Literatür Araştırması', Celal Bayar Üniversitesi, İktisadi Ve İdari Bilimler Fakültesi, Yönetim Ve Ekonomi Dergisi, Cilt: 8, Sayı: 2, Manisa, 2001.

Erkut F., Kümelenme Ve Aydın İlindeki Kümelenme Potansiyeli Olan Alanlar, Adnan Menderes Üniversitesi, Sosyal Bilimler Enstitüsü, Aydın, 2011.

Gladwın T., Kennelly James, Krause Tara-Shelomith, Shıftıng Paradıgms for Sustaınable Development: Implıcatıons for Management Theory and Research, The Academy of Management Review, Volume 20, Issue 4, New York, 1995.

Jong M., Jacobs D., Industrial Clusters and the Competitiveness of the Netherlands 1992, Volume 140, Issue 2,

Karalar R., İşletme Temel Bilgiler İşlevler, Eskişehir, Etam, 1995.

Kaygalak, İ.. "Uşak Geri Dönüşüm Kümesi'nin Yapısal Özellikleri", Ege Coğrafya Dergisi, 20 (1), 2011

Lublınskı A.E, Concepts for Cluster-Identification with an Application to an Alleged Aeronautics Cluster İn Northern Germany, Hamburg, Juni 2002.

Porter M., Location, Competition, And Economic Development: Local Clusters İn A Global Economy, Economic Development Quarterly, 2000.

Porter M., The Adam Smıth Address: Locatıon, Clusters, and the "New" M. of Competıtıon, Business Economics,Volume 33, Issue 1, 1998.

Porter M., On Competition, Boston, MA: Harvard Business School Pub., 2008.

Porter M., The Competitive Advantage of Nations, Free Press, New York, 1998.

Hawken P., The Ecology of Commerce, Harper Collins, 1993.

Atso 2012 Dış Ticaret Raporu, Afyonkarahisar.

Dokuzuncu Beş Yıllık Kalkınma Planı, 2009 Yılı Programı T.C. Başbakanlık Devlet Planlama Teşkilatı Müsteşarlığı, Ankara, 2009.

Kobi İşbirliği Ve Kümelenme Projesi Ağ Oluşturma Ve Bölgesel İşbirliği İçin Kobi'lerin Güçlendirilmesine Yönelik Teknik Yardım, T.C. Ekonomi Bakanlığı, Tr 07r2.02-01.

Kümeler İçin Güven Oluşturma, İşbirliği Ve Ağ Yönetimi Kılavuzu T.C. Ekonomi Bakanlığı, 2011.

Kümeler İçin Uluslararasılaşma Stratejileri Ve Pazarlama Kılavuzu, T.C. Ekonomi Bakanlığı, 2013.

Resmi Gazete, Sayı:28412, 15 Eylül 2012.

Http://Www.Ekonometrik.Com/Rekabet-Ve-Rekabet-Gucu-Nedir.Html (12.14.2013)

Münevver Bayar and Nuran Varışlı

The Impact of Strategic Leadership in the Strategic Management Process

1 Introduction

Leadership, which is the process of strategic management has become an element that is needed day-by-day because it has a very important place in modern management. For this reason, leaders in the management process have an important to achieve success. Strategic leadership, which has an active role in carrying an organization, institution or structure from a certain level to a higher level, as well as the individuals behind it, make a significant contribution to the strategic management process. Strategic leaders have a great impact on assigning other uppe-r and middle-level personnel working in institutions and directing employees towards more creative goals in their establishments. Strategic leadership is the combination of strategic management processes with leadership. Within the definition of strategic leadership, a person who has the qualification of a leader must be able to make a fictional definition of the future; that is, to have a vision. The ability to think strategically when making decisions that are important to the organization or institution should be able to provide advanced and flexible working opportunities. In addition, strategic leaders must be able to transform, manage and fulfill the ethical values of the institution and company policy. In the face of rapidly developing technological developments, today's companies have to make moves to rapidly transform their institutions. The expanding competitive environment has extended to international levels, effecting developed and developing technological environments. Despite these developments, companies should be able to develop their future adaptation policies. As a result, leaders apply strategic moves to manage their development and be open to changing roles within the company management. This is an indication that the leadership formed in the past has changed. The purpose of this study is to determine the position of the leadership concept and strategic leadership within the framework of certain theories, the importance of strategic leadership in strategic management, and the characteristics that a strategic leader should have. In line with these limits, the characteristics of the strategic leader and the strategic leadership must be considered, making use of the different resources available.

2 Strategic Management Process

Businesses are becoming increasingly complex in terms of business volume and organizational structure. The environment, which is a challenge for business, turns towards new production ideas with advances in technology and the convenience of accessing information. It has become very important to seize new opportunities in order to achieve competitive success, to meet the rapidly changing demands of the customers and to ensure sustainability. In order to meet all of these, ensuring efficiency in management and making strategic decisions is paramount for business. For this reason, it is important to develop a strategic plan that takes into account the institutional structure in order to achieve the determined goals, and to effectively manage the strategic management process for the implementation of this plan (Taylor et al., 2008: 370–1). The strategic management process is the process of preparing, putting into practice and auditing the strategic plans suitable for the company in order to gain an advantage that can provide permanence in the ongoing competitive environment, and to provide an income above the average (Eren 2010: 21–4).

The strategic management process has been evaluated in three separate phases:

1- At this stage, the strategic planning of the company's strategy, mission, policy and vision are determined. Internal and external environmental analyses are made for these.
2- At this stage, the general structure of the company (its culture and technical facilities) is examined and the environment necessary for the implementation of the strategies is prepared and put into practice. At this stage, the budget is determined and the implementation process becomes clear.
3- In this last stage, the results of the strategy applied are evaluated. If there are deficiencies in the strategy applied, those deficiencies are found and improvement policies are made.

In this study, a certain classification is made based on the approach of Ülgen and Mirze (2016: 57). In this direction, strategic management consists of two basic phases; these are the preparation and realization phases.

The preparation phase is to take the internal and external environmental analyses required at the moment when strategic planning is made and explain the strategic plan to others in the organization to create a certain awareness. The realization phase is the stage of preparing strategic plans, transferring the plans from theory to practice and checking whether the applied practice has acieved the desired goal. These stages are organized with strategic flexibility, especially after making the necessary control arrangements. Achieving the desired strategic goal is described as corporate performance (Akgemci, 2008: 517).

3 Position and Importance of Strategic Leadership In The Strategic Management Process

For a company to ensure its existence and development in a competitive environment with global dimensions it is necessary to analyse the competitive market and make strategic plans that will develop the company.

In order for these plans to be realized, all the qualities of strategic leadership must be owned. A leader who possesses these qualities will gain a competitive advantage over other institutions.

Without a strategic leader, it is difficult for a business to obtain a result that will satisfy the company insofar as the problems and risks they encounter in the globalized competitive environment are concerned (Ireland and Hitt, 2005: 63). The strategic leader prepares the future strategic plans of the enterprise and reveals the regulations for implementation. One of the most important tasks of the strategic leader is to analyse the business environment correctly and establish an effective team that will achieve the goals of the business. Changes experienced in the business world due to the effect of globalization sometimes bring about difficult processes and opportunities. In these changing conditions the most important factors for businesses are their survival and long-term success. The most effective role in maintaining this success falls to the company executives. Leaders who have the ability to think strategically in order to create and implement success strategies are now one of the most important factors for businesses (Hitt et al., 2010: 438).

Stakeholders, including employees, customers, investors, partners, suppliers, competitors and the community, are increasingly putting pressure on businesses. Responding to the wishes of all these stakeholders, gaining superiority over competitors and creating added value can only be achieved with an innovative perspective. Having this point of view of the leader is of great importance in creating the strategy that will carry the business to the future (Slavik et al., 2015: 1160; Latham, 2014).

One of the characteristics of strategic leadership is that the company can continue its existence in the long-term due to the efficiency of the decisions it takes while ensuring the stability of the financiality that is not long term. It makes its decisions arbitrarily, or without any obligation, in line with the strategic direction of the company. The strategic leader must ensure that the decisions s/he takes in the short-term, creates confidence in every person in the company management. This is another feature that shows that a strategic leader has the influence and persuasive ability s/he should have. It includes not only the short- or long-term decisions made by the strategic leader in conflict with company policy, but also the ability to change decisions taken in the developing process by ensuring the permanence of the company on its basis (Akyüz, 2018: 54).

An effective strategic leader is the primary factor in the most efficient execution of the strategic management process. Leaders who can act strategically play an active role in increasing the strategic competitiveness by rapidly implementing the activities determined in line with the business strategy (Jabbar et al., 2017: 100).

While conveying the position and importance of the strategic leader in the strategic management process, it is necessary to reveal the strategic leadership.In large companies or institutions, those at the top level are strategic, those at the middle level are organizational, and the leaders at the lowest level are concerned with production and operational points. In line with this hierarchy, the initiatives of leaders decrease from the top of the pyramid to the bottom. The difference between leadership and strategic leadership appears in two ways. According to the first difference, strategic leadership is only about people at the top level of the company, while leadership is about people who have a leader status in every part of the company. According to the second difference, while leadership is mainly concerned with the relationships between those who come after it, strategic leadership is not only concerned with relational dimensions but also interested in strategic activities (Finkelstein et al., 2009: 127).

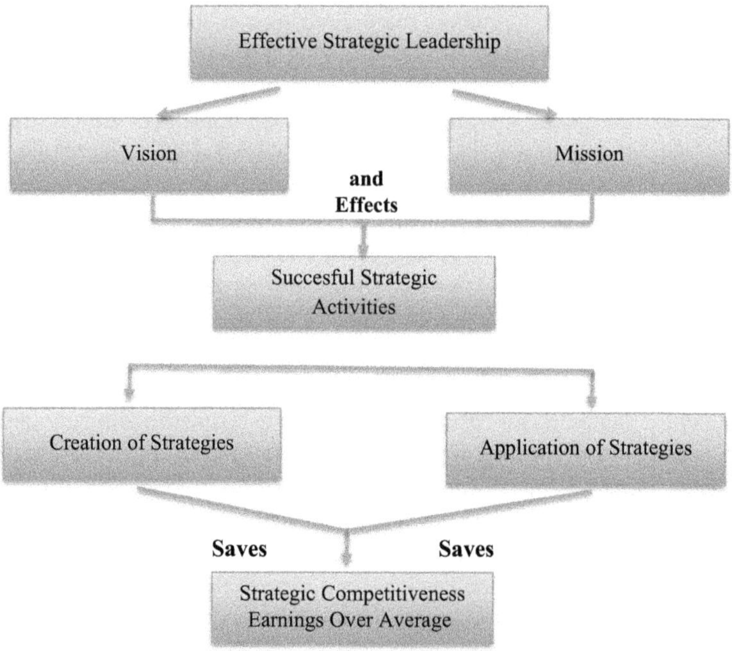

Fig. 1: *Strategic Leadership in the Strategic Management Process.* **Reference:** Hitt, M.A., R.E. Hoskisson and R.D. Ireland, (2007). Management of Strategy (International Student Edition). China: Thomson South-Western

3.1 Features of a Strategic Leader

According to Bolt, three important factors are important in a leader. These are leadership qualities and business and individual competence. According to the traditional understanding, the business element is in first place and significantly affects the forward-looking development of the manager. Individual competence includes an innovative perspective and the ability to manage change in organizations (Bolt, 1996). In most of the studies, it is seen that leadership is considered as a feature that cannot be gained and learned later, and therefore is considered as an overlooked factor (Wong et al., 2003).

In the ongoing researches until today, although the characteristics that strategic leaders should have and what they should do are different, they are views that are close to each other. Strategic leaders must reflect the company they are in, both with their work discipline and ethics. This situation positively affects every person in the company, especially company employees, and guides the company employees on how to work. There are three characteristics of strategic leaders. The first of characteristic feature is to determine the best and highest targets for the company. The way to reach this goal shows how the activities within the company will proceed with the vision determined by the strategic leader. The second feature of the strategic leader is that he is a role model among company employees. The third feature is that the strategic leader should show a successful performance in line with the standards set, and instill a sense of trust in the team members who follow his footsteps while performing their duties (Çoban, 2016: 30).

If we were to create a list the basic characteristics that a strategic leader should have can be summarized as follows:

- Determines a vision for the future and explains the vision.
- Ensures the participation of people at all levels of the company and with different experiences in strategic management processes.
- The moves he makes are for the future.
- The strategic leader should give importance to human values and demonstrate this to their employees first. S/he must communicate effectively with his/her employees.
- S/he should allow their employees the luxury of making mistakes and taking risks.

- Instead of going into detail, strategic leaders rely on the decisions of their employees due to the environment of trust they provide to the company employees.
- S/he should provide the time necessary to progress of the works of his/her employees.
- S/he is a role model for their employees.
- S/he aims to empower their employees to direct problems to solution points.

A strategic leader must realize the following characteristics:

- To determine both the vision and the targets of the company.
- Identifying and advancing the company's core capabilities.
- Developing human resources.
- Creating and advancing an effective company culture.
- Behave ethically and emphasize ethical rules.
- To determine a balanced strategy in an uncertain future (Pajunen, 2006: 344–5).

4 Ensuring Effectiveness In Strategic Management Processes

Regarding the impact of strategic information on organizations, it has been stated that establishing a strategic intelligence unit in an organization creates new challenges for managers, practitioners and consumers. In this context, the factors affecting the success of strategic managers in the strategic management process are listed as follows (Barca, 2005: 18).

a) Resources: Strategic intelligence, when considered in the context of resources, is not an activity that focuses on the needs of expert personnel as a financial output. Therefore, even if activities that require strategic intelligence require reason and time, it is possible to deploy on behalf of appropriate analytical personnel. As a result, the development of employees is achieved through special training.
b) Data need: The strategic use of data depends on institutional requirements. Data on strategic analysis should be collected both within the business and from the external environment of the business. Strategic analysis is unlikely to survive only with data obtained by institutions.
c) Creative thinking: In general, it is stated that strategic research in public institutions has difficulties in terms of quality due to standard movements and approaches focusing on functional thinking. In fact, strategic thinking has a certain capacity but conceptualizes research problems and plans with a conscious understanding to enforce organizational rules.

d) Engagement of practitioners with management: Effectiveness of strategic analysis provides the manager with the ability to establish a close communication link with the IT staff. A cooperation that includes closeness and respect in the organization/customer relationship provides direct benefits for all relevant stakeholders to achieve their goals (Akdemir, 2010: 320).
e) Reliability in decisions and estimates: Strategic intelligence is the assurance of the decision-making power of the relevant personnel in their evaluations about activities, which includes the multiplicity and details of the activities. While this has a long-term impact, it is only directly linked to the responsibility to analyse easily resolvable problems in detail. It seems unlikely that strategic intelligence project results will be more easily measurable in the near future.

By means of strategic leadership, organizations can advance the strategic management process in a way that will bring success. Senior managers with strategic leaders guide the continuation of the vision and mission they have created in their companies. In order to provide an income above the average in a competitive market, strategic leaders determine the appropriate strategy for their companies and carry out activities aimed at the development and sustainability of their companies. As a result of the right moves made by the strategic leaders, they can take the primary roles and progress the necessary stages in order to produce profit in a competitive market (Hitt et al., 2007: 364).

At this point, analytical analysis is not enough to achieve success in companies. In addition to this analysis, it plays a major role in the strategic moves provided by a creative brain. For these reasons, strategic leaders are important in strategic management processes (Daft, 2007: 57).

5 Conclusions

In the face of rapidly developing technological developments, companies have difficulties in adapting to the expanding market and competitive environment, and taking precautions with an uncertain future. In this period, where the uncertainty of the complicated future and the economic fluctuations in the market are intense, it is difficult for the companies under the management of traditional leadership to ensure their presence in the market. Strategic leaders who can prioritize today's technology and vision with strategic leadership qualities and adapt to the market of our age are needed. In line with these needs, almost all of today's companies are led by managers with strategic leadership qualities. Strategic leaders ensure the continuity of their presence in the market by making strategic decisions in the face of the globalizing economic market and by directing the people working within their organization effectively and successfully.

Strategic management involves the realization and implementation of initiatives for the main purpose undertaken by a company's senior management on behalf of the business owners, based on the internal and external environment assessments where resources are valued and the business is in competition. Managers evaluate the developments in their environment in terms of organizational skills within the business. For this reason, it can be seen that administrators make a lot of effort in order to achieve organizational goals.

Strategies are created with the aim of setting direction, defining or clarifying the organization and ensuring coherence or guidance towards the environment. Strategic planning, which has an important place in the concept of strategic management, is analytical and its results directly affect the strategic thinking in the formulation of strategy.

In other words, strategic planning includes strategic thinking and/or strategy formulation. Strategic management generally consists of two main processes. These processes are strategy creation and implementation. Strategic management tools are approaches and methodologies are called methods; these are techniques and models that help managers make strategic decisions. These are the tools that support businesses in order to meet the different demands that appear in the competitive environment, and to provide strategic advantages as against their competitors.

Todays leaders' interest in concepts such as change and globalization must have a deep and methodological meaning. Therefore, leaders need to improve themselves regarding strategic management terminology and duration. Necessary trainings can be prepared for the implementation of the top managers in enterprises, especially in the current and newly developed project studies in their work areas. In private enterprises, project and management services can be closely followed for management applications in the strategic area, thanks to the project and innovation offices that can be established by the managers themselves, instead of receiving external help. This important factor will create advantages for the business.

In addition to the attitudes of strategic leaders in their external relations, their positive behaviour towards their employees within the company, their ability to act flexibly and foresight, and the positive results of their strategic moves towards the solution of any problem that may occur within the company, creates a motivating effect on their employees.

In addition to their managerial skills, strategic leaders also assume the role of trainers in order for their employees to complete their development. It is expected that strategic leaders educate their own people about the leaders of the future. Thanks to this development training provided by strategic leaders, a common vision that develops among company employees makes it possible to adopt the goals and objectives of the company, to feel the positive and negative consequences to be encountered in the company in advance, and to produce quick solutions to the encountered problems. In the face of the correct and positive guidance of the strategic leaders, company employees who are highly motivated can quickly direct the desired job towards the expected goal. As a result, the first goal of strategic leaders is to increase the profits of their own companies in the existing competitive environment and to ensure the continuity of their companies.

In addition, strategic leaders should be able to renew themselves and their companies with their vision that constantly evolves in the changing and developing world market conditions with their reformist attitudes, and make them suitable for innovation in their external activities as well as their reformist attitudes within the company.

References

Akdemir, B. 2010. Stratejik Yol Haritası Uygulamasının Stratejik Yönetim Bilincine Etkisinin Belirlenmesine Yönelik Bir Araştırma. e-Journal of New World Sciences Academy (NWSA) 5 (4), 320–341. Akgemci, T. (2008). “Stratejik Yönetim”, Yenilenmiş 2.b., Gazi Kitabevi, Ankara.

Akyüz, M. 2018. “Stratejik Liderlik”, Stratejik Yönetim Araştırmaları Dergisi, 1/ 1, 45–66.

Barca, M. 2005. “Stratejik Yönetim Düşüncesinin Evrimi: Bilimsel Bir Disiplinin Oluşum Hikâyesi”. Yönetim Araştırmaları Dergisi, 5 (1), 7–38.

Bilincine Etkisinin Belirlenmesine Yönelik Bir Araştırma. e-Journal of New World Sciences Academy (NWSA) 5 (4), 320–341.

Bolt, J.F. (1996) “New Skills for New Leadership Roles,” in Frances Hesselbein, Marshall Goldsmith, and Richard Beckhard, eds., The Leader of the Future: New Visions, Strategies, and Practices for the Next Era, San Francisco: Jossey-Bass, pp. 161–173.

Çoban, Ö. (2016). “Millî Eğitim Bakanlığı Merkez Teşkilatı Yöneticilerinin Örgütsel Değişimi Yönetme Yeterlilikleri ile Stratejik Liderlik Davranışları Arasındaki İlişkinin İncelenmesi”, Doktora Tezi, Gazi Üniversitesi, Eğitim Bilimleri Enstitüsü, Ankara.

Daft, R. L. (2007). Organization Theory and Design, Ninth Edition, South-Western, Thomson Learning Academic Resource Center, ABD,

Eren, E. (2010). Stratejik Yönetim ve İşletme Politikası. İstanbul: Beta Yayıncılık.

Finkelstein, S., Hambrick, D.C. and Cannella, A.A. (2009) Strategic Leadership; Theory and Research on Executives, Top Management Teams and Boards. Oxford University Press, Oxford, 1–451.

Hitt, M.A., Haynes, K. T. and Serpa, R. (2010). Strategic Leadership for the 21st Century, Business Horizons, 53, 437–444.

Hitt, M.A., Hoskisson, R.E. ve Ireland, R.D. (2007). Management of Strategy (International Student Edition). Thomson South-Western, China.

Ireland, R.D. and Hitt, M.A. 2005. "Achieving and Maintaining Strategic Competitiveness in the 21st. Century: The Role of Strategic Leadership", Academy of Management Executive, 19(4), 63–77.

Jabbar, A. A., and Hussien, A. M. 2017."The Role of Leadership in Strategic Management.", International Journal of Research- Cnanthaalayah, vol. 5, No. 5, 99–106.

Latham, John R. 2014."Leadership for Quality and Innovation: Challenges, Theories, and a Framework for Future Research." Quality Management Journal [online]. 21 (1), 11–15. https://drjohnlatham.com/wpcontent/uploads/2014/01/2014_QMJ_Leadership. pdf (01.04.2021).

Pajunen, K. 2006. "The More Change, the More They Remain the Same? Evaluating Strategic Leadership in Organizational Transformations.", Leadership, 2, ss.344–345.

Slavik, J., Putnova, A., Cebakova, A. 2015."Leadership as a tool of strategic management, 4th World Conference on Business, Economics and Management, WCBEM", Procedia Economics and Finance 26, 1159–1163.

Taylor, J. S., Machado, M. D. L., and Peterson, M. W. 2008. "Leadership and strategic management: Keys to institutional priorities and planning." European Journal of Education, 43(3), 369–386.

Ülgen, H. and Mirze, K. (2004). "İşletmelerde Stratejik Yönetim", Literatür Yayıncılık, s.175, İstanbul.

Wong, l., Gerras, S., Kidd, W., Pricone, R. and Swengros, R. (2003). Strategic Leadership Competencies, Strategic Studies Institute, US Army War College, https://www.jstor.org/stable/pdf/resrep11719.pdf (10.04.2021)

Zehra Yeni and Emre Sezici

Talent Management

1 Introduction

In studies it is stated that talent management is a rapidly growing field (Collings and Mellahi, 2009), although it is new (Komar, 2008) and still in its infancy (Tansley, 2011). Some researchers have stressed that there is no complete definition of talent management yet (Lewis and Heckman, 2006), while others have stressed that more research on talent and talent management is needed (D'Annunzio-Green, 2008). In this study, the concept of talent management will be explained, and the research and approaches that help explain talent management will be reviewed.

2 The Concept of Talent Management, Scope and Development

Talent management is defined as workforce planning, talent analysis, the hiring process, training and development and coordinating the retention activities (McCauley and Wakefield, 2006), finding the talent it needs of organizations, the selection of talented individuals from among the applicants (Grobler and Diedericks, 2009). In another study talent management was expressed as determining the key positions to ensure continuity, to provide a competitive advantage for organizations looking to create a high performing talent pool of potential employees to work in these positions (Collings and Mellahi, 2009), as well as providing continuity of leadership and personal development opportunities created to open the way for a systematic process (Rothwell, 2010).

Based on definitions in the literature, we can express talent management as the whole of strategies for attracting talented employees to the organization, including training-development and career opportunities, in order to meet the talent needs of the organization in key positions that exist or are likely to arise in the future in order to ensure a sustainable competitive advantage.

Studies have been conducted on what talent management refers to and what is covered (Lewis and Heckman, 2006; Collings and Mellahi, 2009), and different groupings have emerged. However, there has been no clarity between practitioners and academics about what talent management is. For this gap to not be completed and to bridge the gap between practitioners and academic writing, Sweem (2009) made definitions of the scope of talent management and then developed a perspective on the scope of talent management. The explanations made about the scope of talent management in Sweem's work (2009, pp.20–21) are as follows;

→ **Talent management equals human resource management:** Talent management is a collection of talent management typical of HR department practices (recruiting, selection, development and career/succession management) and replaces the term HR with talent management
→ **Talent management equals talent pool:** Talent management refers to a process designed to provide the appropriate workflow to ensure that all employees working in the organization are in the right places. Talent management is concerned with HR planning and focuses on succession planning and workforce planning.
→ **Talent management equals inclusive talent management:** Talent management focuses on performance, not just specific positions and limited practices, and focuses on managing performance. It emphasizes that demographic factors and business impacts are critical to achieving the highest performance of all employees. This view states that managers at all levels in the organization should cooperate and communicate. Thus, the organization's development needs and the needs of leaders are met, and the organization achieves its goals through succession planning.
→ **Talent management equals holistic talent management:** Talent management integrates HR strategies and organizational strategies as a strategic concept. It is applied in all departments in the organization. It aims to benefit all stakeholders of the organization. It integrates talent with business strategies. It emphasizes sustainability and is proactive as regards the future. It tries to improve regulated processes to manage and improve capabilities. It aims to create loyalty among employees. This perspective expresses Sweem's view of talent management.

Explanations for the scope of talent management are listed into four main groups. The first emphasizes that talent management is the same as human resource management (HRM), and the second focuses on the systematic and continuous process of HR planning and the employment of the right person in the right place. The third states that talent management is focused on performance management, and all levels are involved in this process. The last emphasizes that talent management plays a strategic role and that organization strategy should be integrated with talent management strategies to establish and operate a system aimed at the future, not the present.

When the studies conducted before and after human resources management are examined, it will be seen that talent management does not date back to very old times. The first traces of HRM were found in England and America in the 1890s. The area of human resources developed in the UK and America until the 1960s and included routine personnel processes such as wages, absenteeism and personal records. After the 1960s, HRM took a managerial role as being the primary supporter of the management function.

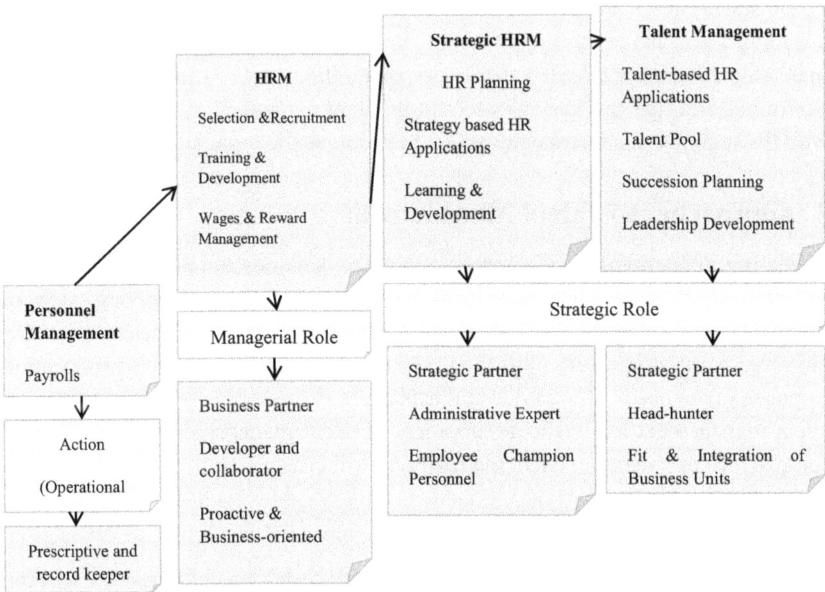

Fig. 1: *Development of HR Management and Changing Roles*
Source: Adapted from Alayoğlu (2010: 75).

By the 1980s, personnel management had been replaced by HRM, and HR departments were of strategic importance. After the 1980s, elements such as the importance of the human element in organizations, globalization, increasing competition and changing management models made it necessary to act strategically for organizations. At the same time, studies on strategic HRM began at Michigan and Harvard Universities. Studies indicated that a functioning HR department integrated with its structure was needed, which placed a strategic role on human resources (Budak, 2008). HRM changed from a 'personnel' function to 'human relations', then to 'business relations', then to 'industrial relations' and finally to strategic HRM (Deadrick and Stone, 2014).

In the above figure (Figure 1), HRM has experienced a change that began with personnel management and reached the present day with strategic HRM. According to the explanations, we can say that this process carried HRM to a context of strategic importance for organizations. On the other hand, talent management has common characteristics with strategic HRM, but we can say that some aspects diverge.

In this context, we can say that talent management aims to benefit all organization stakeholders and is a system that creates strategies to achieve competitive advantages and make them continuous. Besides, we can say that talent management aims to manage talented employees, retain them and create loyalty among all personnel, and that the strategies set out in talent management should be aligned with the organizational strategies applied to achieve the organization's goals.

3 Approaches to Talent Management

Increasing competition, society's expectations, the demands and needs of employees, the increase in intellectual level and the awareness of what employees expect from themselves, and changing conditions, have made the concept of talent a business life. However, some studies, changed the understanding of talent. Models produced in response to the needs of work-life and explanations made by researchers to explain talent management led to the development of talent management. In this section, some of the approaches to talent management will be explained.

3.1 McKinsey Studies

Talent management began to be mentioned in the literature as 'talent wars' in the late 1990s due to research consisting of two parts of the US consulting company, McKinsey. The first part of the study was conducted in 1997 with 6,900 upper and middle-level management from fifty-six organizations in the US. Managers who participated in the study said that the most difficult tasks were attracting talented employees (89%) and retaining them (90%). They had problems finding talented employees in the 35–44 age range (Axelrod, Handfield-Jones and Welsh, 2001).

The second part of the research was conducted in 2000 with 13,000 middle and senior managers from 112 US organizations and focused on identifying intangible aspects of talent. As a result of the research, it was found that the most important element that distinguishes organizations with high performance from others is the talented employees they have, and organizations with talented employees are 22% more profitable. The study stated that the assets of organizations consist of intellectual capital, brands and innovative ideas. It is explained that they do not exist in the organization and are the organization's spiritual ability (Axelrod, Helen and Timothy, 2001).

Several studies support the proposition that talent management has increased because of the McKinsey Research (e.g. Ruppe, 2006; Chugh and Bhatnagar, 2006; Lewis and Heckman, 2006; Cappelli, 2008; Collings and Mellah, 2009). Besides, different names are used for talent management in different countries, including the US, the UK, Australia, Japan, China, India and various countries in Asia, such as talent wars, talent strategy, talent flow, talent retention and scarcity raid, and it is stated that these perspectives have been changing for new and talented employees (Bhatnagar, 2007).

Besides, the McKinsey research also stated that the point of view regarding employees is changing. The research focused on the fact that organizations need talented employees rather than employees who need a job. This research proved the importance of employing talented employees as a competition tool and the difficulty in finding and retaining talented employees, and there is a need for new research to be done (Michaels, Handield-Jones and Axelrod, 2001).

3.2 Conception of Talent

It has been rephrased as: "Talent concept has been considered as important by organizations (McCartney and Garrow, 2006) that all organization employees can develop (Ashton and Lynne, 2005).

According to work done by McCartney and Garrow (2006), understanding talent consists of seven elements. These elements are: appropriate development opportunities; motivating factors; elimination of motivating barriers; employer brand; meaningful roles given to employees and organizations; ideal managment and organizational support. The understanding of talent gains meaning and is formed by combining these elements. Organizations need these elements, and demand by employees has pushed organizations to implement change, which has led to the emergence of talent management.

3.3 Resource-based Approach

The resource-based approach to literature by Wernerfelt (1984) is one of the approaches to talent management. This approach is known as the theory of competitive advantage in strategic management, and it assumes that the desired degree of managerial effort gives the organization a sustainable competitive advantage (Koçak, Özer and Gürel, 2005). Organizational efforts are the assets and capabilities of the organization (Makhija, 2003).

Organizations may have a sustainable competitive advantage as long as their competitors develop strategies that cannot be replicated. Organizations can develop strategies that are different from their competitors while having different resources. Studies show that organizations with unique and irreplaceable resources have higher returns than others (Peteraf, 1993). The key element here is that the competitive advantage will continue as long as the organization has an irreplaceable resource that gives it a competitive advantage, and it will not last forever (Barney, Wright and Ketchen Jr., 1991).

To ensure a competitive advantage continuously, resources must have characteristics such as rarity, non-substitution, uniqueness and non-imitation (Cadogan et al., 2002). For organizations, we can say that this resource is currently talented employees. To achieve sustainable competitive advantage, organizations should consider talented employees to be the most unique, most non-imitated and most irreplaceable resources; attracting and retaining them is vital. Talent management is an important strategy for employing, training and retaining this unique resource to the organization.

3.4 Systems Approach

Traditional talent management consists of four stages. These are acquiring talent, placing talent, developing talent and retaining it. Traditional talent management focuses on acquiring and retaining talent (Akar, 2015). According to Philips and Edward (2008), talent management refers to a process in the form of workforce planning – workforce acquisition – workforce placement – workforce management – workforce retention, and every element in this process is a subsystem, and talent management is based on the integration of these systems.

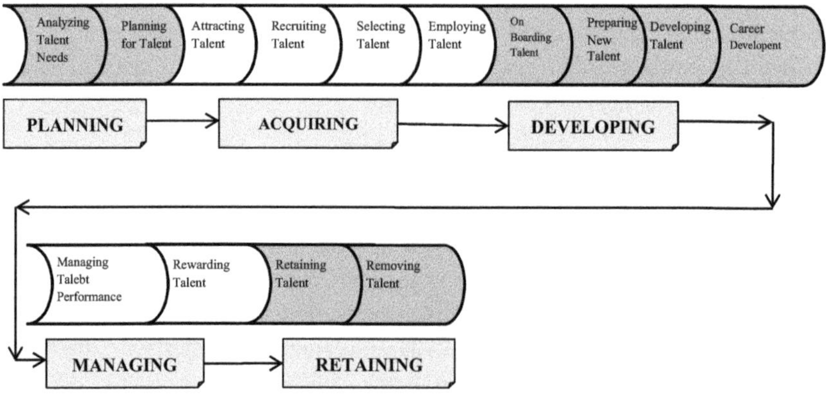

Fig. 2: *Talent Management System*

Source: Phillips and Edwards, 2008: 10. (Deloitte Research'dan akt.)

Talent management consists of analyzing the talent needs of the organization and incorporating the talent into the planning phase; the acquisition of the talent to the organization, recruitment and selection of talent in the acquisition phase; the entry of the talent to the organization; the preparation of the organization for the new talent and career development as part of the talent development phase; retention of the talent and taking precautions for the talent to leave the organization are all subsystems of the talent management. Talent management consists of several processes, and the fact that these processes are the output/input of each other makes it explainable as a system.

3.5 Talent Factory Model

Akar (2015) likened organizations to a mechanism whose production is talent and talent management to a supply chain that provides talent. Fang Li and Devos (2008) stated that all organizations could be talent factories in the talent factory model. As follows, talent management consists of four parts: hiring-development-placement-job retention. Hiring performs the function of identifying the talent that needs to be identified by the organization to discover talented employees and ensure talented employees' recruitment. Development is the production department of the organization, where there are hidden talents. The strategies used by the organization for the realization of this production include becoming a learning organization, placing different cultures within the organization and managing these abilities, and creating communication channels within the organization and e-learning.

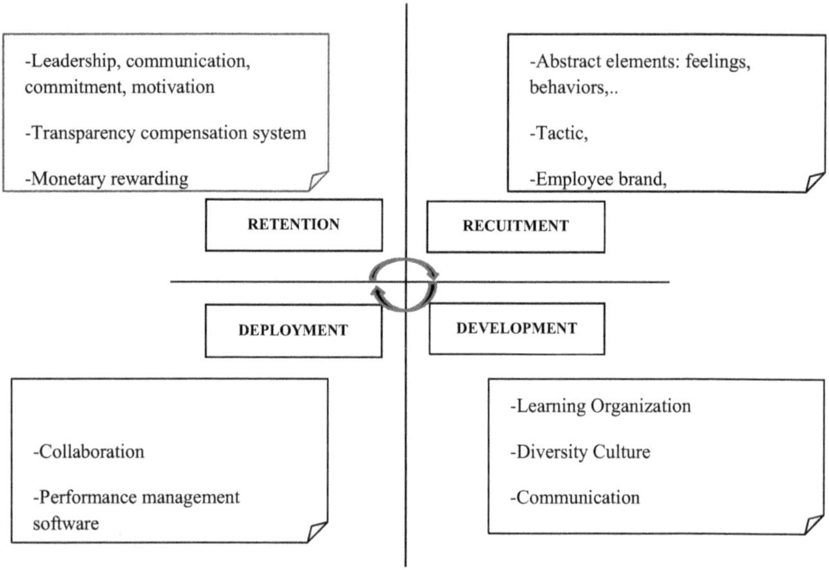

Fig. 3: *Talent Factory Model*
Source: Fang Li and Devos, 2008: 85.

Placement is expressed as employing employees in the right places according to their abilities. In this regard, performance evaluation methods are used to determine how much of the employees' abilities turn into performance so as to ensure that talented employees work in the right positions through training development, promotions and transfers. On the other hand, retention is the part where the work is carried out to protect talented employees from dismissals (Akar, 2015). This model explains what the talent management process consists of, what it refers to, how it feeds each other, and explains that talent management is a factory that produces the talent that the organization needs, and can supply it when necessary (Akar, 2015).

4 Conclusion

In this study the definition of the concept of talent management, the scope of the concept and the literature on talent management have been covered. The importance of talent management has been explained within McKinsey's framework, and the perspectives of the employees on the talent management issues have been explained. It has been stated that with a resource-based approach, organizations will provide a competitive advantage through skilled employees as their unique resource. It has been stated that talent management consists of a process with a systems approach and that this process is considered as a whole consisting of subsystems. Finally, the talent factory model tried to explain talent management by stating that each organization can be a factory that produces talent.

This study provides researchers with limited knowledge about talent management. There is a need to conduct more research on the application stages, examples and advantages of talent management. Investigating different aspects of talent management in terms of conceptual and practical dimensions may be proposed for the future research. A contribution can be made by comparing theoretical and practical applications.

References

Akar, F. (2015). Talent Management. İmge Bookstore.

Alayoğlu, N. (2010). The New Era in Human Resource Management: Talent Management. Journal of Commerce and Tourism Education Faculty, 1: 68–97.

Ashton, C. and Lynne, M. (2005). Managing Talent For Competitive Advantage: Taking A Systemic Approach to Talent Management. Strategic HR Review, 4(5): 28–31.

Axelrod, E. L., Handfield-Jones, H. and Welsh, T. A. (2001). War For Talent, Part Two. The McKinsey Quarterly, 2: 9–12.

Barney, J., Wright, M. and Ketchen Jr, D. J. (2001). The Resource-Based View of the Firm: Ten Years After 1991. Journal of Management, 27(6): 625–641.

Bayraktaroğlu, S. (2015). Human Resources Management, Sakarya Publishing.

Bhatnagar, J. (2007). Talent Management Strategy of Employee Engagement in Indian ITES Employees: Key to Retention. Employee Relations, 2(6): 640–663.

Budak, G. (2008). Competency Based Human Resources Management, Barış Publications.

Cadogan, J.W., ed. (2002). Measuring Marketing Capabilities: A Cross-National Study. Joint ANZMAC/EMACSymposium Marketing Networks in a Global Marketplace, Australia.1–8.

Cappelli, P. (2008). Talent Management for the 21st Century. Harvard Business Review, 86(3), 74–82.

Chugh, S. and Bhatnagar, J. (2006). Talent Management as High-Performance Work Practice: Emerging Strategic HRM Dimension. Management and Labour Studies, 31(3), 228–253.

Collings, D. G. and Mellahi, K. (2009). Strategic Talent Management: A Review and Research Agenda. HRM Review, 19(4), 304–313.

D'annunzio-Green, N. (2008). Managing The Talent Management Pipeline Towards a Greater Understanding of Senior Managers' Perspectives in the Hospitality and Tourism Sector. International Journal of Contemporary Hospitality Management, 20(7), 807–819.

Deadrick, D. L. and Stone, D. L. (2014). Human Resource Management: Past, Present, and Future, Human Resource Management Review, 3(24), 193–195.

FangLi, F. and Devos, P.(2008). Talent Management: Art or Science: The Invisible Mechanism Between Talent and Talent Factory. (Unpublished Master's Thesis) The University of Kalmar.

Grobler, P.A. and Diedericks, H. (2009). Talent Management: An Empirical Study of Selected South African Hotel Groups.Southern African Business Review, 13(3), 1–27.

Koçak, A., Özer, Ö. and Gürel, E. (2005). Dimensions of Marketing Capability: Resource-Based View. Hacettepe Uni. Journal of Economics and Administrative Sciences, 23(1), 179–201.

Komar, E. (2008). Talent Management at Deutsche Telekom, PPT Sunum, Wide Executive Development System: Germany. (Date of Access: 23.10.2019).

Lewis, R. E. and Heckman, R. J. (2006). Talent Management: A Critical Review, Human Resource Management Review, 16(2), 139–154.

Makhija, M. (2003). Comparing the Resource-Based and Market-Based Views of the Firm: Empirical Evidence from Czech Privatization. Strategic Management Journal, 24(5), 433–451.

McCauley, C. and Wakefield, M. (2006). Talent Management in The 21st Century: Help Your Company Find, Develop, and Keep İts Strongest Workers. The Journal for Quality and Participation, 29(4), 4–7.

Michaels, E., Handfield-J., H. and Axelrod, B. (2001). The War for Talent. Harvard Business Press.

Peteraf, M. A. (1993). The Cornerstones of Competitive Advantage: A Resource-Based View. Strategic Management Journal, 14(3), 179–191.

Phillips, J. J. and Edwards, L. (2008). Managing Talent Retention: An ROI Approach. John Wiley and Sons.

Rothwell, W.J. (2010). Effective Succession Planning: Ensuring Leadership Continuity and Building Talent From Within, American Management Association, New York.

Ruppe, L. (2006). Tools and Dialogue Set The Stage for Talent Management at Johns Manville. Journal of Organizational Excellence, 25(3), 37–48.

Sweem, S. L. (2009). Leveraging Employee Engagement Through a Talent Management Strategy: Optimizing Human Capital Through Human Resources and Organization Development Strategy in a Field Study. (Unpublished Doctoral Thesis) Benedictine Uni.

Tansley, C. (2011). What Do We Mean by The Term "Talent" in Talent Management? Industrial and Commercial Training, (43)5, 266–274.

Wernerfelt, B. (1984). A Resource-based View of the Firm. Strategic Management Journal, 5(2), 171–180.

Gülaçtı Şen

Risk-Taking Behaviour in Entrepreneurship

1 Introduction

Entrepreneurship can be defined as assessing opportunities and taking risks with resources at hand and producing existing or new products or services to be presented to the market. Entrepreneurs look after society's needs and continue their efforts by taking risks towards set targets. Their basic characteristic is assuming risks and gaining profits. The decision by entrepreneurs to take risks is important for the establishment of a new company or to improve an existing company and its success (Antoncic et. al., 2018: 2). Entrepreneurs assume responsibilities and risks while creating a new enterprise or improving an existing one (Hisrich et. al., 2010). People that have a different personality structure have the ability to tolerate risk and uncertainty (Bozkurt and Baştürk, 2009: 45). Many people think that taking risks is over risky, but entrepreneurs move with the intention of taking medium and rational risks towards targets they determine. Because while results might be disastrous, taking risks is necessary to achieve success (Kwond et al., 2013: 3).

Risk-taking behaviour is a significant factor in the success of an entrepreneur's makeup and a significant portion of the literature on entrepreneurship (Kreiser et. al., 2001: 3). The personal characteristics of entrepreneurs together with particulars of the environment and the problem itself are important factors effecting risk-taking behaviour. According to Hisrich, Peters and Shepherd, the process of starting a new initiative involves new risks and is an important factor in the success of entrepreneurship (Hirsch et. al., 2010). In addition, the risks entrepreneurs are faced with and their reactions to risks are significant factors effecting the process of entrepreneurship. This study constitutes part of the literature of risk-taking in entrepreneurship as one of the most important concepts influencing the process of entrepreneurship.

Entrepreneurship that is conventionally accepted as a risk-taking action is mostly discussed with the concept of risk. Regardless of its conclusion as winning or losing, it is highly important for entrepreneurs with its impact on presenting many creative ideas, new processes, new products or services. As one of the important features of entrepreneurs, risk-taking enables creation of new opportunities and realization of ideas. The concept of risk-taking behaviour in literature is an important factor ensuring entrepreneurs are successful. In this study, the difference of entrepreneurs from non-entrepreneurs are explained through risk-taking behaviour and risk reactions given to entrepreneurship risks are suggested. In the study where risk-taking behaviour in entrepreneurship is theoretically assessed, risks taken by entrepreneurs are studied and examined under entrepreneurship risks.

2 Entrepreneurship

While there are many studies to understand and explain entrepreneurship, the concept has been defined in diverse ways and came together in different disciplines from the past to today (Koh, 1996: 13). Entrepreneur comes from 'entreprendre' in French meaning 'doing, undertaking something' and in the past was used as the person doing business (Hayes and Drury, 2020). With its meaning in the past, entrepreneurship means doing work in short. Nowadays, entrepreneurship is one of the most striking issues of business and economics literature; however, the concept was mostly approached from general economic meaning. In the 1730's French economist Richard Cantillon was the first person to define entrepreneur as 'the person that does business in uncertainty'. Cantillon drew attention to the risk-taking dimension of entrepreneurship and defined earning income and managing uncertainty in economic parameters as entrepreneurship (Culhane, 2003: 19).

The concept of entrepreneurship is a quite vague concept in scientific literature. Various authors defined the concept by emphasizing its diverse dimensions. The concept entered British literature with published works of John Stuart Mill, but did not capture attention until the end of the nineteenth Century (Döm, 2006: 4). The concept that started to take place in economic literature in this period started to become visible in other disciplines in the twentieth century. It started to be cited in economics, sociology, psychology and anthropology disciplines, and was defined as a person that makes renovations by taking risks (Ağca and Baş, 2013: 300).

Joseph A. Schumpeter (1961) was the first to find Cantillon's definition insufficient to improve the concept of entrepreneurship. According to him, the concept of innovation lies at the heart of entrepreneurship (Döm, 2006: 5). Schumpeter divided entrepreneurship to five types in the historic process of structural changes directed by innovation. These are new industrial structures such as (Śledzik, 2013: 90);

1. Releasing a new product or a new type of an existing product to the market,
2. Exercising new production or sales methods of a product (unproven in the sector),

3. The opening of a new market (market where a branch of the sector is not yet represented),
4. Purchasing new raw materials or semi-finished sources,
5. Forming or destroying a monopoly status.

The definitions of different authors have been effective in giving the concept of entrepreneurship its final state. The concept owes its current state to J. Babtiste. According to him, an entrepreneur is the person that brings all production factors in organization together, coordinating them and producing products/services by taking all risks (Grebel, 2004: 6). While Krueger defined entrepreneurship as a conglomeration of planned actions and thoughts that bring about opportunities (Krueger, 2000: 411), Morris expressed it as the process of bringing resources together to detect and capture opportunities and turn them into data for success (Morris and Davis, 1994: 65).

According to Hirsch and Peters, who made significant contributions to the theory of entrepreneurship, it is accepted as the process of creating a new value. Using sufficient resources under existing conditions at the enterprise and taking risks to use opportunities puts holding personal satisfaction and independence at the forefront (Aytaç, 2006: 141). Kuratko and Hodgetts defined entrepreneurship as the process of creating a dynamic vision and change. Entrepreneurship, according to the authors, requires energy and passion towards the creation and application of new ideas and creative solutions (Kuratko, 2004: 3). The common point of the concept that diverse authors try to explain is using opportunities with risk-taking behaviour. In order to do that, all resources must be mobilized and persons must motivate themselves to manage processes.

McClelland (1960) puts forward that 'practically all theoreticians agree on taking such a risk as is due to definition of entrepreneurship'. Begley and Boyd (1987) discovered that taking risks is in a curvilinear relationship with performance in entrepreneur companies (Kreiser et. al., 2001: 5).

In studies on entrepreneurship and risk-taking behaviour, it was presented that entrepreneurs take risks. Based on the definition of entrepreneurship and daily observations the actions of entrepreneurs are perceived as riskier than those of other people. However, it can be argued that various research on whether or not entrepreneurs are more prone to risk than other people gives unclear results (Macko and Tyszka, 2009: 469). Laboratory research conducted by Macko and Tyszka concluded that, insofar risk attitudes are concerned, entrepreneurs are not very different from other people. Researchers do not deny that entrepreneurs take risks in their attempts outside the laboratory, and even explain that this is the result of a certain motivation and/or a definite risk perception. However, they concluded that the majority of subjects in both groups preferred the risky option.

Marshall emphasized that an entrepreneur must be willing to take risks, but that this was a more general characteristic compared to those that an entrepreneur needs to achieve economic success. Kirzner (1981), accepted that risk exists in the process of development, while he suggested that risk-taking is an inevitable subfactor that comes with unclear profits (Güney, 2008: 55–9).

3 Risk-Taking Behaviour

The word 'risk' has Latin roots and comes from the French word 'risqué' (Çakır, 2013: 44). Later, the English word 'risk' found its place in terminology. According to Covin and Slevin (1991), the concept that involves taking decisions without knowing what consequences it would entail in an unchartered territory or under unknown circumstances (Wakkee et. al., 2010: 4), generally represents the possibility of financial loss or loss of life. Nowadays risk is a popular concept in both academia and media and is used in various ways. Risk can be discussed in terms of the danger of terrorist activities, failure of complicated technologies such as nuclear energy, financial wins or losses, natural disasters such as tsunami and earthquakes and sports such as bungee jumping. Also there are risks concerning the qualifications and reliability of those that manage these different risks (Aven and Renn, 2010: 159). In its simplest form, risk-taking is defined as the situation including actions taken when the results or possibilities are unknown or only partially known (Kwong, 2013: 3). Risk-taking behaviour that takes place in the social sciences is defined differently in entrepreneurship. According to Lumpkin and Dess (1996) and Baird and Thomas (1985), risk-taking behaviour can be interpreted this way (Üstün and Kılıç, 2017: 230);

- Attempting in the face of unpredictable situations,
- Losing as a result of risks taken,
- Feeling uncertainty,
- Feeling pressure concerning resources of enterprise.

Connecting risk with a simple definition is quite difficult. Different situations and outlooks lead to different definitions of risk-taking. Also it is seen that different personal values of researchers impact the definition of risk-taking they use. Vlek and Stallen (1980) reviewed a series of studies and listed six common risk definitions (Trimpop, 1994: 5);

- The probability of loss
- The size of credible loss

- The expected loss
- The variance of the probability distribution over the probability of all possible consequences
- The semi-variance of the utility distribution
- A linear function of the expected value and the variance of the distribution of consequences.

Risk can be expressed as the total resources entrepreneurs shall lose as a result of all attempts they will make to gain competitive advantage (Alpkan et. al., 2005: 177). Risk-taking behaviour might result in some danger and potential of loss while, at the same time, creating some opportunities to gain (Man et. al., 2021). Risks in entrepreneurship are in the shape of chances or uncertainty. When an attempt carries high risk, that means its returns are unclear. In other words, in every attempt there is the probability of success as well as failure. This situation appears as uncertainty.

The measurement of the probability that arises as gain or loss at the end of every option can be expressed as risk. In other words, risk can be defined as a measurable uncertainty. However, the concepts of risk and uncertainty are very different from each other. Risk is the probability of some negative effects of a danger (Short, 1984: 711). Uncertainty expresses the situation that cannot be fully configured or categorized due to not having sufficient data at hand. Uncertainty that could be perceived as threat by some entrepreneurs at an organization might be perceived to be desirable by others (Tabak, Erkuş and Meydan, 2010: 162).

3.1 Factors Impacting Risk-taking in Entrepreneurship

The tendency of risk-taking, in other words, risk-taking behaviour, can be described as a person's tendency to take risks (Antoncic et. al., 2018: 4). How risk-taking behaviour is shaped and what attitudes and precautions individuals shall take in the presence of risks is quite diverse. Yates and Stone (1992) emphasize that lack of a consensus on risk factors is linked to several factors. These are;

- Confusing many different factors with the risk structure as a whole,
- The fact that risk displays different features in different situations,
- Based on difference among individuals concerning its perception, risk being subjective in essence.

The characteristics of entrepreneurs effect the process of entrepreneurship, thus effecting the risk-taking behaviour of employees as a subfactor of entrepreneurship. In addition, features of the environment together with features of the problem are other factors that influence risk-taking behaviour. Work environment: how employees perceive the problem in a work environment is effective on risk-taking behaviour.

3.1.1 Personal Characteristics

The characteristic of having the courage that entrepreneurs have impacts risk-taking behaviour. Using opportunities on time, making fast decisions and taking action and venturing the possibility of losing in the end requires courage. However, general characteristics of entrepreneurs include motivation to succeed, risk-taking behaviour, self-confidence and avoiding uncertainty (Özdemir et. al., 2016: 125). Among personal characteristics of entrepreneurs, when studies in the literature are reviewed, persons with high self-sufficiency draw attention. It was put forward that persons with high self-sufficiency are more inclined to take risks than persons with low self-sufficiency (Basım, Korkmazyürek and Tokat, 2008: 124).

3.1.2 Specialties of the Environment

The work environment of entrepreneurs effects risk-taking behaviour, in addition to their personal characteristics. A positive versus a negative work environment, attitudes and actions of senior management and relations and communication among employees carry weight in the decisions employees take. If the unemployment rate is high in the country, workers will be worried about finding new jobs. In addition, if the wages received cannot maintain social life well, individuals will be hesitant to take risks. The factors that initially impact the work environment are economic, socio-political, cultural etc., attitudes that the country is in. Particulars of the sector and changes in the work environment according to sectors must be considered.

3.1.3 Specialties of the Problem Itself

Another approach influencing the risk-taking behaviour of entrepreneurs is the problem itself and its personal characteristics. Presentation of the problem and its description using positive and negative expressions are important concerning the decisions entrepreneurs take. According to Prospect Theory, developed by Kahneman and Tversky (1979), presentation of the problem is very important in risk-taking behaviour. According to this theory, in positive circumstances persons are inclined to avoid risks because employees do not dare to suffer major losses. On the other hand, persons that do not have much to lose or at risk of facing major losses do not hesitate to take risks under unfavourable conditions (Tversky and Kahneman, 1981: 453).

4 Risk-taking Behaviour in Entrepreneurship

Entrepreneurship, taking risks with innovative and creative ideas and mobilizing resources with new ideas is a necessary process to ensure that newly established or existing organizations can have successful sustainability. Discovering opportunities, presenting a new product with a risk assessment or presenting products that benefit the society are possible through entrepreneurship (AmanAllah and Nakhaei, 2011: 77). Entrepreneurs agree to different types of risks (psychological, social and financial) when they establish new companies (Antoncic et. al., 2018: 4). In addition, they are also faced with risks in the process of improving the existing business. Generally, entrepreneurs take four types of risks. These are financial risks, career risks, social risks and psychological risks. Kuratko and Hodgetts defined entrepreneurship risks with reference to these four risks and argued that economic risks are only one dimension for entrepreneurs and they mostly exist together with career risks, social risks and psychological risks in an unclear environment. AmanAllah and Nakhaei defined entrepreneurship risks as financial risks, business risks and social and family risks. Entrepreneurship risks in the literature are presented in Table 1 with explanations:

Tab. 1: *Risks of Entrepreneurship*

Financial Risk	Most entrepreneurs finance their businesses with their personal savings. If they fail, they lose. This is named financial risk. Entrepreneurs might not be very successful and risk losing their personal savings.
Business Risk	If an entrepreneur fails, there is the risk of not being able to take up previous employment in addition to suffering financial losses. This risk that can be labelled business risk is the most major concern of entrepreneurs. For this reason, entrepreneurs consider rational and certain risks.
Social and Family Risk	Starting entrepreneurship takes time and requires high energy. There is the risk of social and family problems that affect the entrepreneur. This risk effects energy of the entrepreneur and the process of entrepreneurship.
Mental Risk	The most major risk taken by an entrepreneur can be defined as a mental health risk. The risk of problems with money, house, spouse, children and friends could be managed, but mental tensions, stress, anxiety and other mental factors have many disruptive effects due to start and continuation of entrepreneurship activities.

(*continued on next page*)

Tab. 1: *Continued*

Career Risk	The fact that individuals continue their entrepreneurship careers demonstrate that they take career risks. There is the question of whether entrepreneurs will succeed or not and whether they can take up their previous employment in case of failure. This risk is seen especially at corporations with highly-paid employees.
Psychological Risk	Entrepreneurs that embark upon business in the beginning of the entrepreneurship process with a strong will and mental balance might face problems in their mental and physical health due to overworking, long work hours, lack of sleep, coping with challenges and problems with managing people. This situation is labelled psychological risk. As a result of psychological risk, entrepreneurs might lose self-esteem or respect.

Source: Donald, F.K. and M.H. Richard, (2001). *Entrepreneurship: A Contemporary Approach.* Harcourt, USA, p.105. Aman, A.M. and H. Nakhaie (2011). Entrepreneurship and Risk-taking, *International Conference on E-business, Management and Economics,* IPEDR Vol. 25, Singapore, pp.78–9.

Risk emerges in various disciplines in a changeable structure. For this reason, it is possible to classify risks. The main purpose here is defining risks better to measure and assess them. In other words, the purpose is to take risks under control (Çakır, 2013: 49). Entrepreneurship risks define risks that might arise in the process of entrepreneurship. Entrepreneurship activities in a business require financial and non-financial investments and a risk of failure that might bring serious damage to entrepreneur. At this point, entrepreneurship risks must be known and accepted by entrepreneurs.

4.2 Risk Reactions

Risk-taking behaviour is defined as the responsibility of actions related to possibility of what will happen as a result of the events (Yılmaz, Şen and Demirkaya, 2014: 142). According to Vertzberger, risk is the condition between consequences of individual behaviours and the realization of their purposes in any environment. This condition is judged in three dimensions. These are defined as (Vertzberger, 1998);

- Wanting or not wanting the consequence,
- Possibilities related to consequences,
- The level of consistency between consequences and possibilities.

Entrepreneurs assess the consequence of risk-taking behaviour. While they take risks, entrepreneurs can calculate and measure the consequences. One of the best ways of avoiding risk is to never take risks. However, businesses that produce products or services, create advantages and want to achieve financial and moral gains have to be innovative and creative and take risks to create social and economic advantages for society. Taking major risks might be necessary to retain existing customers or to remain at the top of the market. Entrepreneurs might be protected from risks they perceive in the decisions they make.

There are some precautions that entrepreneurs might take against risks and these precautions are generally defined as risk reactions. Some risk reactions can be listed as such (Haftacı, 2015: 7):

- Decreasing possibility of risk,
- Decreasing possibility of loss,
- Assuming risks,
- Transferring risks to others,
- Predicting risks.

At another study, risk reactions that entrepreneurs can apply are studied in four categories. There are as follows (Kip, 2014: 12–15):

Avoiding Risk: This stands for avoiding activities that increase risk. Removing a product from market, remaining in the existing market and not entering in new markets or selling a part of the business can be examples of decisions taken to avoid risk.

Lowering Risk: Expresses the decreasing possibility of risk. Entrepreneurial businesses can progress according to set targets and take decisions to lower risks. Losses could be prevented, opportunities could be delayed for a while and controls could be increased to manage the process with some rules. The situation here is that entrepreneur knowingly decreases impact of risk.

Sharing Risk: This concept defines sharing the effect of the risk. It ensures losses are transferred from persons to groups or from one unit to another in order to manage the situation with the lowest possibility of the risk taken.

Accepting Risk: Not taking any precautions against risks that emerge and even taking no action can be defined as accepting risks. Accepting is acknowledging risk as the possibility of loss. Considering that taking risks means rapidly assessing the opportunities entrepreneurs face, and acting courageously, accepting can be seen as the unwanted precaution among risk precautions.

It was discovered that the distinction between taking and avoiding risk preferences is related to individual characteristics such as control focus, success motivation, uncertainty or sensation seeking. In the first case, risk serves as a tool to reach a certain economic target in the future and in the second it is accepted as a source of strong and momentary emotional thrill (Zalaskiewicz, 2001: 106). Considering the characteristics of entrepreneurs, they will determine risk reactions according to their level of success and motivation.

Entrepreneurs can determine how much risk they can take based on two criteria. The first one is being able to measure targets and the second is the rate of possibility of success (Çakır, 2013: 54). At an assessment of entrepreneurship measuring targets and the possibility of achieving success must be continuously followed. With predetermined plans on how to manage risks, the impact of a risk can be minimized. Especially some part of risks based on taking decisions could be personally prevented by entrepreneurs. The precautions below can be taken for this purpose (Haftacı, 2015: 7);

- Doing research,
- Dividing risks into units,
- Making trade deals,
- Sharing risks.

5 Conclusion

The concept of entrepreneurship has been defined in various ways from the past to the present and the concept of risk has been present in most of such definitions. Emphasized as one of the important characteristics of entrepreneurs, risk-taking can be discussed as the key to achieving competitive advantage and success. Thus, factors impacting risk-taking behaviour of entrepreneur, various risks that entrepreneurs shall be faced with, and their reactions to risks gain importance.

When studies in the literature on the relationship between entrepreneurship and risk-taking are reviewed, it can be seen that entrepreneurs are faced with different risk options under different circumstances. Economic resources such as money, income and fortune, together with financial risks that impact decisions; social and family risk related to social and mostly familial relations and the consequences of relations individuals have with their social environments; and business risks concerning taking up previous employment in case the entrepreneurship fails are entrepreneurship risks. Also, there could be a career risk for individuals that are currently engaged in entrepreneurship activities who take risk and take up a new initiative; psychological risks involving mental and other physical problems related to overworking, long work hours, lack of sleep, coping with challenges and problems managing people; or mental risks, including mental tension, stress, anxiety and other mental factors. It is possible to find different entrepreneurship risks in studies projecting the future.

Mostly it is not possible for entrepreneurs to completely remove the entrepreneurship risks they come across. It is required to consider the risks in the decisions that shall be taken. Entrepreneurs have displayed different risk reactions in decisions taken this way. Risk reactions such as lowering risk, avoiding risk, assuming risk, sharing risk etc. appear and influence the process of entrepreneurship. Risk reaction entrepreneurs display in their decisions risk-taking behaviour. In this process the personal characteristics of entrepreneurs, the environments and particulars of the problem impact the risk-taking behaviour of an entrepreneur.

References

Ağca, H. and Baş, Ü. (2013). İç Girişimcilik. Girişimcilik Editör: Doç. Dr. Himmet Karadal, Beta Yayınları, 2.Baskı, Türkiye.

Alpkan, L., Ergün, E., Bulut, Ç. and Yılmaz, C. (2005). Şirket Girişimciliğinin Şirket Performansına Etkileri. Doğuş Üniversitesi Dergisi, 6 (2) 175–189.

Aman, A. M. and Nakhaie H. (2011). Entrepreneurship and Risk – Taking., International Conference on E-business, Management and Economics, IPEDR Vol. 25, Singapore.

Aven, T. and Renn, O. (2010). Risk Management and Govarnance: Concepts, Guidelines and Applications., Springer-Verlag, Berlin, Doi: 10.1007/978-3-642-13926-0.

Aytaç, Ö. (2006). Girişimcilik: Sosyo-Kültürel Bir Perspektif. Dumlupınar Üniversitesi Sosyal Bilimler Dergisi, Sayı:15, Ağustos, 2006.

Antoncic, J.A., Antoncic, B., Gantar, M., Hisrich, R., Marks, L.J., Bachkirov, A., Li, Z., Polzin, P., Borges, J.L., Coelho, A. and Kakkonen, M.L. (2018). Risk-Taking Propensity and Entrepreneurship: The Role of Power Distance. Journal of Enterprising Culture, Vol. 26, No. 1, 1–26. DOI: 10.1142/S0218495818500012.

Basım, H. N., Korkmazyürek, H. and Tokat, A.O. (2008). Çalışanların Öz Yeterlilik Algılamasının Yenilikçilik ve Risk Alma Üzerine Etkisi: Kamu Sektöründe Bir Araştırma. Selçuk Üniversitesi Sosyal Bilimler Enstitüsü Dergisi, 121,130, 2008.

Bozkurt, V. and Baştürk, Ş. (2009) Kobi Girişimcilerinde Risk ve Belirsizlik Algıları: Bursa Örneği. Anka Üniversitesi SBF Dergisi, Cilt 64, Sayı 2, 43-74.

Çakır, S. (2013). Girişimcilerin Yeni Bir Girişim Yapma Niyetlerinin Risk Alma Eğilimi İle İlişkisi. (Yüksek Lisans Tezi)., Atatürk Üniversitesi Sosyal Bilimler Enstitüsü, Erzurum.

Culhane, J.M. (2003). The Entrepreneurial Orientation Performance Linkage in High Technology Firms: An International Comparative Study, Thesis for The Degree of Doctor of Philosopy, Graduate School of the University of Massachusetts, Amherst.

Döm, S. (2006). Girişimcilik ve Küçük İşletme Yöneticiliği. Detay Yayıncılık, 1.Baskı, Ankara.

Donald F. K. and Richard M. H. (2001). Entrepreneurship: A Contemporary Approach. Harcourt, p. 105.

Grebel, T. (2004). Entrepreneurship A New Perspective. First published 2004 by Routledge 11 New Fetter Lane, London EC4P 4EE, Routledge is an imprint of the Taylor and Francis Group.

Güney, S. (2008). Girişimcilik Temel Kavramlar ve Bazı Güncel Konular. Siyasal Kitabevi, Genişletilmiş 3.Baskı, Ankara.

Haftacı, V. (2015). Kobi'ler ve Girişimcilik., Umuttepe Yayınları, 1.Basım, Kocaeli, ISBN:978-605-5100-58-2.

Hayes, A. and Drury, A. (2020). https://www.investopedia.com/terms/e/entrepreneur.asp (Date of Access: 16.02.2021).

Hisrich, R.D., Peters, M.P., and Shepherd, D.A. (2010). Entrepreneurship with Business Plan Pro CD-ROM (Laureate Custom ed.). New York: McGraw-Hill Irwin.

Kip, H. (2014). Burdur'da Faaliyet Gösteren Girişimcilerin Risk Alma Becerilerini Etkileyen Faktörlerin Belirlenmesi. (Yüksek Lisabs Tezi)., Afyon Kocatepe Üniversitesi Fen Bilimleri Enstitüsü, Afyon.

Koh, H. C. (1996). Testing Hypotheses of Entrepreneurial Characteristics A Study of Hong Kong MBA Students. Journal of Managerial Psychology, 11(3): 12–25.

Kreiser, P., Marino, L. and Weaver, K.M. (2001). Correlates of Entrepreneurship: The Impact of National Culture on Risk-Taking and Proactiveness in SMEs. University of Alabama Department of Management and Marketing Tuscaloosa, AL.

Krueger, N. F. (2000). Competing Models of Entrepreneurial Intentions., Journal of Business Venturing, 411.

Kuratko, D. F. (2004). Entrepreneurship Education in the 21st Century: From Legitimization to Leadership. A Coleman Foundation White Paper USASBE National Conference January 16.

Kwong, K.K., Prabhu, V.P., Shen, M., McGuire, S. and Tang, R. (2013). Entrepreneurial Risk-taking: Influences of Culture, Education and Personality with Evidence from a Multi-Country Study. 12th Annual International DSI Meeting, Bali, 1–20.

Macko, A. and Tyszka, T. (2009). Entrepreneurship and Risk-taking. Applied Psychology: An International Review. 58(3), 469–487. Doi: 10.1111/j.1464-0597.2009.00402.x.

Man, S.S., Chan A., Alabdulkarim, S. and Zhang, T. (2021). The Effect of Personal and Organizational Factors on the Risk-Taking Behavior of Hong Kong Construction Workers. Safety Science 136, 105155. Doi: 10.1016/j.ssci.2020.105155.

Morris, M. and Davis, D. (1994). Fostering Corporate Entrepreneurship: Cross-Cultural Comparisons of the Importance of Induvidulism Versus Collectivizm. Journal of International Business Studies, s. 65.

Özdemir, A., Saygılı, M. and Yıldırım, K. (2016). Risk Alma Eğilimi Ve Başarma İhtiyacının Girişimcilik Potansiyeline Etkisi: Üniversite Öğrencileri Üzerine Bir Araştırma. İşletme Bilimi Dergisi (JOBS), 2016; 4(2): 121–140. Doi: 10.22139/jobs.287249.

Short, J.F. (1984). The Social Fabric of Risk: Toward The Social Transformation of Risk. American Sociological Review, ss. 711-725.

Śledzik, K. (2013). Schumpeter's View on Innovation and Entrepreneurship. Management Trends in Theory and Practice, (ed.) Stefan Hittmar, Faculty of Management Science and Informatics, University of Zilina and Institute of Management by University of Zilina, ISBN 978-80-554-0736-4, 2013.

Tabak, A., Erkuş, A. and Meydan, C. H. (2010). Denetim Odağı ve Yenilikçi Birey Davranışları Arasındaki İlişkiler: Belirsizliğe Tolerans ve Risk Almanın Aracılık Etkisi. Anadolu Üniversitesi Sosyal Bilimler Dergisi, Cilt/Vol.:10-Sayı/No:1, 159–176, Eskişehir.

Trimpop, R.M. (1994). The Psychology of Risk-taking Behaviour. Elsevier Science B.V. ISBN: 0444899618. Amsterdam, The Netherlands.

Tversky, A. and Kahneman, D. (1981). The Framing of Decisions and the Psychology of Choice. Science, 211(4481): 453–458. DOI: 10.1126/science.7455683.

Üstün, F. and Kılıç, K.C. (2017). Örgüte Duyulan Güvenin Örgütsel Yenilik Yönelimi ve Risk Alma Davranışı Üzerine Etkisi., Ömer Halisdemir Üniversitesi İktisadi ve İdari Bilimler Fakültesi Dergisi, 10(2).

Vertzberger, Y. I. (1998). Risk Taking and Decision Making: Foreign Military Intervention Decisions., The American Political Sicence Review, Vol 33, Issue 1, 985-986.

Wakkee, I., Elfring, T., and Monaghan, S. (2010). Creating Entrepreneurial Employees in Traditional Service Sectors the Role of Coaching and Self Efficacy. International Entrepreneurship Management, Doi: 10.1007/s11365-008-0078-z. 6: 1–21.

Yılmaz, F. T., Şen, H. T. and Demirkaya, F. (2014). Başhemşirelerin Yenilikçilik ve Risk Alma Davranışlarının Belirlenmesi. Balıkesir Sağlık Bilimleri Dergisi, Balıkesir, 2014.

Emre Ünver

Presenteeism in Organizations

1 Introduction

The developments in today's modern organizational management make it clear that employees should be valued more if human resources are to be managed efficiently. Finalizing tasks on time in line with the plans made to reach certain goals provide organizations with a competitive advantage. It should be specifically noted that this can only be achieved by employing physically and mentally healthy individuals.

Employees showing up to work despite having health-related problems is one of the common problems encountered lately, which leads to a decrease in performance, harming organizations and the national economy at the macro level. Employees who physically come to work despite having health-related problems are unable to devote themselves to their tasks. Accordingly, considering the problems caused by presenteeism, organizations should focus more on this concept. Presenteeism hinders employees from completing their tasks on time, forcing additional costs on organizations.

Healthy and happy employees in their working lives internalize their work to a greater extent, contribute more to their organizations and are more satisfied with their jobs. Presenteeism, portraying the employees who (have to) show up to work despite being sick, on the other hand, interrupts this mindset.

2 The Concept and Scope of Presenteeism

Presenteeism, a word in English, means the concept of not being present at work. Considering its origin, the word 'presenteeism' was lexicalized from the word 'presence' meaning 'existence, availability, being present, and appearance.' From a lexical point of view, the concept of presenteeism means being physically or visibly present (Çiftçi, 2010: 155).

The concept was first discussed in the literature in 1970s, as an antonym of absenteeism (Johns, 2010: 520). Being an age-old organizational problem, presenteeism was observed to be discussed widely in literature, especially after 2004 (Çoban and Harman, 2012: 162). The definition of the term was first vocalized by Cary Cooper (1998), Organizational Psychologist.

According to Cooper (1998: 314), a fewer number of employees are now present in the work environment with greater amount of work to do, and they feel more at risk of being fired. He also suggests that emerging technologies increase knowledge and, therefore, accelerate the work, while employees are expected to work more. The study further addresses employees' thoughts about being fired and unemployment, and points out that they find themselves in a setting where they compete to be present just to show their commitment to their organization.

In today's organizations, showing up to work when sick is becoming more common than absenteeism, which indicates that organizations need to review their approaches about keeping on working regularly (Gosselin, Lemyre and Corneil, 2013: 75).

The concept of presenteeism refers to showing up to work despite having health problems, as well as relevant productivity losses. The number of studies on presenteeism is limited in Turkey. There are two main opinions about the definition of the concept of presenteeism. According to the first opinion, what defines presenteeism is the feeling of pressure, due to which employees spend long hours at work or at least be present at workplace, while the second opinion argues that showing up to work despite having an incapacitating sickness or health problem is presenteeism. Having said that the main causes of presenteeism is the fear of losing one's job, and the low productivity associated with that fear (Çoban and Harman, 2012: 157).

An in-depth analysis of the concept of presenteeism reveals that this problem is not only associated with physiological disorders. Accordingly, employees may also experience presenteeism due to organizational issues or psychological problems. From this point of view, it can be argued that presenteeism does not only refer to not being present at the workplace due to sickness, but it covers situations in which employees physically show up to work but fail to focus on their tasks due to some reason (Baysal et al., 2014: 136).

3 Definitions of Presenteeism

As a new concept in business life, presenteeism means showing up to work despite being in poor health and performing below average. Critical to revealing the potential for employers, presenteeism has been associated with a range of psychosocial outcome measurements such as poor mental health and employee wellbeing (Brown et al., 2011: 249).

Most employers are not aware that health-related loss of productivity may cost organizations a lot more when compared to other health-related expenses. This is called presenteeism, a hidden cost for organizations (Hemp, 2004: 53). Showing up to work despite having incapacitating health problems is defined as presenteeism (Meerding et al., 2005: 517).

Referring to occasions where employees show up to work despite being sick, presenteeism is a structure that points out the impact of health problems on productivity (Sanderson et al., 2007: 72).

Presenteeism is defined as the decision to go to work despite feeling sick (Hansen and Andersen, 2008: 956). Dew, Keefe and Small (2005: 2273) defined presenteeism as carrying on with the work even when sick or injured.

Presenteeism is defined as loss of productivity associated with showing up to work despite being sick, and therefore performing below average. Costs related to absenteeism have been under investigation for many years, while financial losses associated with presenteeism is a new topic to be studied (Epstein, 2005).

Since serious health problems usually force employees to stay at home, most of the illnesses that result in presenteeism are relatively harmless in nature. Studies on presenteeism focus on chronic or episodic diseases such as seasonal allergies, asthma, migraines and other types of headaches, backache and depression (Hemp, 2004: 51).

4 Causes and Consequences of Presenteeism

Basically, the causes of presenteeism are listed under two categories: health-related problems and work-related problems. Health-related problems cover both physical and mental health, including health-related risk factors and problems associated with an aging labour force. Work-related problems involve perceived work pressure and the fear of losing income or employment. Furthermore, the impact of stress on health, work life, family life and productivity is also under discussion (Lack, 2011: 80).

On some occasions organizations may decide to downsize or merge with other organizations and fire employees in the process, creating a feeling of pressure on others who want to keep their jobs, which is one of the leading factors of presenteeism. On the other hand, the causes of presenteeism can also be addressed under two groups of factors: work-related factors and personal factors. Productivity loss is one of the main organizational problems caused by presenteeism. From the viewpoint of organizations, other significant and high-risk problems include the possibility of the progression of the disease and the relevant contamination risk (Çoban and Harman, 2012: 171).

Taking the causes of presenteeism into consideration, it is clear that both physical and psychological wellbeing have an impact on the productivity of employees. It is also evident that the problems, i.e. causes of presenteeism, affect each other. Therefore, a holistic approach should be adopted to address this issue. Medical problems are not the sole reason of presenteeism. Accordingly, both directly health-related problems and other causes with organizational and environmental roots that have an adverse impact on health may cause this problem. Theoretical causes of presenteeism include working conditions, the fear of being fired, directly related health-related problems, conflicts in business and private life as well as workaholism (Çiftçi, 2010: 157).

Presenteeism is also investigated for its consequences. In their study Abasilim, Salau and Falola (2015: 82) pointed out the following consequences of presenteeism:

- Additional time needed to complete a task,
- Reduced quantity and quality of work,
- Reduced maximum performance capacity,
- Reduced motivation,
- Malfunctioning executive functions,
- Poor relationships with other employees.

Table 1 below presents basic causes and consequences of presenteeism.

Tab. 1: *Causes and Consequences of Presenteeism*

Causes		**Consequences**
- The way the work environment is viewed - Conditions of the workplace - Pressure created by managers and co-workers and poor relations - The possibility of promotion being under risk - The idea of sick leave would risk the possibility of promotion - Job insecurity - The feeling that they, i.e. employees, are not sick enough to stay at home - Diabetes, stress, depression, blood pressure problems, migraine, allergy, asthma and heart diseases - Family problems - High work load - Problems about substituting the employee - Sharing work load with co-workers - Workplace competitiveness	→ Not Being Present At Work (Presenteeism)	- Decreased performance - ecreased collective performance - Deteriorating relationship with co-workers - Decreased motivation - Being in need of additional time to meet the deadline - Increased accidents and risks

Source: Akdoğan, Harmancı and Bayram, 2018: 203.

Employees should balance business and private life in order to be able to avoid problems associated with presenteeism. Other measures include defining working hours, making daily plans, understanding low-energy hours and arranging working hours accordingly, paying attention to not taking work out of the office, having a regular sleep pattern, following a balanced and proper diet and exercising regularly (Çoban and Harman, 2012: 172).

In their study Gosselin, Lemyre and Corneil (2013) addressed the recommendations in the literature and tried to define basic behavioural relationships of presenteeism and absenteeism at work. In the study, that makes a comparative analysis of data obtained from a representative sample of managers from the Canadian Public Service, a presenteeism and absenteeism perspective is presented, which is authentic from the viewpoint of not only the effects of health-related problems but also demographic, organizational and personal factors. The results indicate that the similarities and differences between these concepts should be understood better, and that new organizational measures should be designed to manage absenteeism without causing presenteeism in organizations.

5 Conclusion

It is very significant for today's organizations to employ healthy and highly-productive individuals. The organizations that seek maximum productivity need to make sure that their employees are present at work, both physically and mentally.

Even though presenteeism, i.e. physically showing up to work but being occupied with other things mentally, is generally associated with employees having health-related problems, it actually affects healthy employees who are not mentally present at work as well (Baysal et al., 2014: 135). For each day an employee does not show up at work their whole productivity is lost, which means that organizations are able to calculate the cost of absenteeism. However, presenteeism causes a hidden cost for organizations because the employee in question shows up to work but works at a lower productivity rate (Epstein, 2005).

Both national and international studies draw attention to the decreased productivity of employees associated with presenteeism. Accordingly, by investigating the problems associated with presenteeism, together with the causes and consequences thereof, organizational losses can be avoided. By solving the problems associated with presenteeism, organizations will be able to use human resources in a more efficient and productive manner, which will contribute to their organizational success.

Finally, organizations should take measures to avoid presenteeism. Such measures may involve offering periodical check-ups, applying stress tests, funding health expenses and creating a flexible working environment. Similarly, employees should also take measures to avoid presenteeism and pay attention to stay healthy.

References

Abasilim, U. D., Salau, O. P., and Falola, H. O. (2015). Toward an Understanding of Presenteeism and its Effects in the Workplace. LASU Journal of Public Administration and Management, 1(1), 74–85.

Akdoğan, A. A., Harmancı, Y. K., and Bayram, A. (2018). Algılanan Örgütsel Adalet Ve İşte Var Olamama (Presenteeısm) İlişkisinde Stresin Aracı Rolü. MANAS Sosyal Araştırmalar Dergisi, 7(2), 197–211.

Baysal, İ. A., Baysal, G., Aksu, G. and Aksu, N. (2014). Presenteeism (İşte Varolmama Sorunu) İle Örgütsel Bağlılık Arasındaki İlişki: Adnan Menderes Üniversitesi Akademik Personeli Üzerinde Bir Uygulama. Ejovoc (Electronic Journal of Vocational Colleges), 4(3), 134–152.

Brown, H. E., Gilson, N. D., Burton, N. W., and Brown, W. J. (2011). Does Physical Activity Impact on Presenteeism and Other Indicators of Workplace Well-Being?. Sports Medicine, 41(3), 249–262.

Cooper, C. L. (1998). The Changing Nature of Work, Community Work and Family, 1(3), 313–317.

Çiftçi, B. (2010). İşte Var Ol(ama)ma Sorunu ve İşletmelerin Uygulayabileceği Çözüm Önerileri. Çalışma ve Toplum Dergisi, 1(1), 153–174.

Çoban, Ö., and Harman, S. (2012). Presenteeısm: Nedenleri, Yarattığı Örgütsel Sorunlar ve Çözüm Önerileri Üzerine Bir Alanyazın Taraması. Sosyal ve Ekonomik Araştırmalar Dergisi, 12(23), 157–178.

Dew, K., Keefe, V., and Small, K. (2005). 'Choosing' to Work When Sick: Workplace Presenteeism. Social Science and Medicine, 60(10), 2273–2282.

Epstein, J. L. (2005). Presenteeism and Paid Sick Days. Center For Law and Social Policy (CLASP), February 28.

Gosselin, E., Lemyre, L., and Corneil, W. (2013). Presenteeism and Absenteeism: Differentiated Understanding of Related Phenomena. Journal of Occupational Health Psychology, 18(1), 75–86.

Hansen, C. D., and Andersen, J. H. (2008). Going ill to Work–What Personal Circumstances, Attitudes and Work-Related Factors Are Associated with Sickness Presenteeism? Social Science and Medicine, 67(6), 956–964.

Hemp, P. (2004). Presenteeism: At Work-But Out of It. Harvard Business Review, 82(10), 49–58.

Johns, G. (2010). Presenteeism in the Workplace: A Review and Research Agenda. Journal of Organizational Behaviour, 31(4), 519–542.

Lack, D. M. (2011). Presenteeism Revisited: A Comprehensive Review. American Association of Occupational Health Nurses (Aaohn) Journal, 59(2), 77–91.

Meerding, W. J., Ijzelenberg, W., Koopmanschap, M. A., Severens, J. L., and Burdorf, A. (2005). Health Problems Lead to Considerable Productivity Loss at Work Among Workers with High Physical Load Jobs. Journal of Clinical Epidemiology, 58(5), 517–523.

Sanderson, K., Tilse, E., Nicholson, J., Oldenburg, B., and Graves, N. (2007). Which Presenteeism Measures are More Sensitive to Depression and Anxiety? Journal of Affective Disorders, 101(1–3), 65–74.

Selçuk Yeke

From Individual Ambidexterity to Organizational Ambidexterity: Examples of Companies

1 Introduction

Companies try to survive and grow, which is their main purpose, by adapting to changes in the internal and external environment or by changing the environment. The kinds of information and resources that companies need to fulfill their basic activities are available in the internal and external environment. It is critical for companies to access this information and resources in order to survive. Companies are expected to develop different strategies and collaborate with other companies to access information and resources in the external environment. One of the biggest resources in the internal environment of companies is their employees. It becomes relatively easier for companies with qualified and creative employees to implement the strategies designed to reach resources in the external environment. At the same time, it is an important advantage that employees are open to learning and have a high level of awareness in order to adapt to change in the general and near environment. Particularly in present conditions, the environment that companies are in is continually changing and it is becoming very difficult to follow this change. Changes in customer requests and demands, innovative expectations, resource scarcity and sustainability efforts, digital transformation activities, instability in supplier relations and changing strategies of competitors can direct companies to be flexible and implement different plans and strategies at the same time. In order to have this kind of organizational talent, companies need to retain 'ambidexter' employees and also attract these employees in the environment. These employees are expected to be open to learning and improvement, questioning the current reality and having a high awareness, creative and visionary. It should be noted that organizational learning can be possible with individual learning, therefore the ability of companies to apply different strategies at the same time – that is, organizational ambidexterity – can be assisted by individual ambidexterity. In this chapter, the concept of individual ambidexterity and the process of transition from individual ambidexterity to organizational ambidexterity, and some company examples, are included.

2 Individual Ambidexterity

According to the Turkish Language Institution, the concept of ambidexterity is explained as 'skillfulness and/or resourcefulness, handcraft, dexterity' (www.tdk.gov.tr). Therefore, when the word's meaning is looked at, it can be said that the concept of ambidexterity indicates the ability to use several abilities together at the same time (Çiftçi, 2017: 189). The concept of ambidexterity, which is used to describe people who are equally capable of using both hands (Birkinshaw and Gupta, 2013: 287), is considered a metaphor to describe organizations (Simsek et al., 2006: 647). Ambidexterity can also refer to a special level of competence. For example, a 'ambidexter' craftsman has not dominated over pottery or weaving. However, the skill of the craftsman always ensures that the best potteries or fabrics comes out of the workshop. Likewise, individual ambidexterity should bring to mind a special level of competence in every aspect of life, whether personal or professional (Senge, 1993: 158). Individual ambidexterity requires the ability to take on different and opposite roles together, such as conducting both routine and non-routine activities (Adler et al., 1999: 45). They can quickly switch between different behaviours and roles depending on the situation they are in (Birkinshaw and Gibson, 2004: 49–50). This situation shows cognitive skill of people. In other words, as situations change, skill of understanding develops depending on the transitions between different types of cognition (Lee and Lee, 2016: 25). There are various common basic characteristics in people with high levels of ambidexterity. There is a special sense of purpose behind the vision and their goals. For such a person, the vision holds qualification of call than just a good idea (Senge, 1993: 158). Developing of individual vision is the foundation of shared vision. A truly shared vision is realized only when the individuals' desires to improve themselves are supported by the organization (Ensari, 1998: 101). They see the 'present' reality as an ally, not an enemy. Instead of resisting change, they learn to work together by absorbing it. They are deeply questioning and constantly strive to see reality more accurately. They see themselves as part of a big creative process that they can influence but not unilaterally control. People with a high level of individual ambidexterity live in a state of constant learning. Therefore individual ambidexterity is a lifelong discipline (Senge, 1993: 158–159). They have the ability and motivation to participate in various learning techniques such as confidence building and learning-enhancing activities to both improve and update their skills and knowledge (Floyd and Lane, 2000: 156). These individuals develop and maintain very large and deep personal networks to share the knowledge and skills they have learned (Sheremata, 2000: 398–9).

3 Transition From Individual Ambidexterity To Organizational Ambidexterity on the Basis of Learning

The concept of ambidexterity is associated with performing successful practices. Ability and experience are needed to be successful. The concept of organizational ambidexterity is also built on the applicability of existing resources and skills in all kinds of strategies. In other words, organizational ambidexterity is based on the view that companies can apply these strategies together instead of choosing only one of the different strategic applications. The assumption that the different strategic applications mentioned in organizational ambidexterity can be applied together successfully is also based on the necessity of skill and experience. Therefore, in order for the ambidexterity to affect the entire organizational structure and functioning, employees must firstly become ambidexter in their skills and abilities (Fettahlıoğlu et al., 2016: 401). Ambidexter organizations always need work teams and managers who can understand the needs for many different types of jobs and are sensitive to these needs. Managers with the potential to reduce costs and think freely are rare and a necessity for the organization (O'Reilly and Tushman, 2004: 80–1). Managers' ability to correctly perceive the changes in the environment such as technology, competition, customers and legal regulations, and to seize opportunities and eliminate threats by restructuring the tangible and intangible assets in order to overcome the difficulties, contributes significantly to the formation of organizational ambidexterity (Teece, 2007: 1322–31). However, considering that working teams have intrinsic sources of motivation to work harder in negative situations and focus on challenging goals, the ambidexter employees in these teams contribute to the development of the team's ambidexterity ability (Vallina et al., 2020: 2). The fact that work teams have a clear and persuasive vision and share their vision with other members of the organization also play an important role in shaping organizational ambidexterity. This passion in employees allows exploitation and exploration to coexist in the organization (O'Reilly and Tushman, 2004: 81). In order for the organization to benefit from exploitation and exploration at the same time, employees should be open to learning individually. As individuals learn, the organization will learn and it will be possible to implement different strategies at the same time (Mom et al., 2007: 925: Mom et al., 2015: 133–5). Learning is an abstract and dynamic concept. It enables problem solving and the integration of attitudes and thoughts by unifying the skills, knowledge or behaviours at different levels, such as individuals, groups and organizations (Öneren, 2008: 164). Organizational learning occurs when this function of learning takes place at the institutional level. In this context, organizational learning is evaluated as a process that takes place in the effectiveness of organizational memory and affects organizational action through the acquisition and evaluation of knowledge (Kalkan, 2006: 25). In order for exploitation and exploration activities within the scope of organizational ambidexterity to occur, organizations must renew their knowledge and continue to learn continuously (March, 1991: 73: Wei et al., 2014: 834).

It is important that organizations increase their ability to adapt to the environment to become an open system. The success of organizations as open systems is also closely related to the regulation of information flow. Organizations can reduce uncertainties that may arise by keeping information about the environment (Koçel, 2011: 262–4). The collection and processing of this information, which is critical to organizations, is carried out by ambidexter employees. It should be said that ambidexter employees have the ability to search, find, process, store and update information. Thanks to this ability, it will be possible to improve existing knowledge and reveal new information (Lee and Lee, 2016: 25). It would not be wrong to say that as the employees acquire and develop new knowledge learning behaviour will deepen, the existing reality will be questioned and a suitable environment will emerge for the development of new ideas. It can be said that the culture of learning will emerge throughout the organization through employees who have individual talents and an eagerness to learn, and that the organization will have the necessary coordination and skills to implement different strategies together in order to continue its life.

Organizational ambidexterity refers to the ability to simultaneously pursue radical and ongoing innovations and changes arising from structures, cultures and processes that are in conflict with each other within the same organization (Tushman and O'Reilly III, 1996: 24). That is, it can be considered to be the ability to simultaneously use existing skills and take advantage of new opportunities (Cingöz ve Akdoğan, 2015: 62). Ambidexterity is involved in organizational processes or coordination, learning and transformation processes and enables the organization to perceive opportunities in the environment by using existing skills as well as developing new skills, and to seize these opportunities by successfully allocating resources (O'Reilly III and Tushman, 2011: 6). Organizations with organizational ambidexterity should be able to manage exploitation and exploration strategies simultaneously with the same working teams within the same structure (Parmentier and Picq, 2016: 18). The exploitation strategy involves the use of explicit information and readjustment, preference, productivity, selection, practice and execution (March, 1991: 71). The main purpose of implementing this strategy is to respond to environmental conditions by adapting existing technologies and meeting the needs of existing customers (Teece, 2007: 1319–20). The exploration strategy includes the use of implicit knowledge, the development of new technologies and marketing techniques, research, diversity, risk-taking, flexibility and innovation (March, 1991: 71). Therefore, by creating new capabilities through search, discovery, experimentation and autonomy, new courses of action and the development of innovation are concepts that can be addressed within the scope of this strategy (Cheng and Van de Hen, 1996: 595). The level of creativity of individuals and organizations is important to the process of realizing this strategy. With the increase of creativity, exploitation and exploratory strategies are used more widely (Brion and Mothe, 2016: 15). In organizations with creative employees, it is easier to develop existing products and to reveal new products and services, as well as improve organizational performance and social relations (Parmentier and Picq, 2016: 18–19).

4 Examples of Companies

4.1 Hewlett-Packard, Johnson & Johnson and ABB (Asea Brown Boveri)

Hewlett-Packard (HP), Johnson & Johnson (J&J) and ABB provide good examples of applying different activities and strategies in a balanced way. These companies compete in mature markets and have developed through incremental and periodic innovation, achieving success by going through change processes. They were very different at the first stage. HP was competing in the tool-equipment, network and computer market. J&J was sold transportation systems, electrical transmission equipment, power plants and environmental control products. Over time, these companies renewed themselves and entered the innovation process. HP evolved from a tool-equipment company to a personal computer, mini-computer and network organization. J&J switched from consumer products to the pharmaceutical industry. ABB transformed itself from being a heavy engineering company based predominantly in Sweden and Switzerland into an aggressive global competitor with large investments in Eastern Europe and the Far East. Although the sectors in which these companies operate are different, they transformed into ambidexter organizations in the same way. One of the factors that enabled companies to transform a ambidexter organization has been ambidexter managers. In addition to managers, delayering in the organization, the creation of autonomous business groups and the presence of a multifaceted cultural understanding has also contributed to the transformation of these companies into ambidexter organizations. Employees have been provided with a greater sense of ownership and responsibility by delayering and creating autonomous work groups.

Sharing a corporate culture based on innovative ideas such as autonomy, initiative, risk-taking and openness to change has increased the financial performance of companies by enabling the development of different products and services. Managing units that follow different strategies and have a varying structure and culture is not an easy process for managers. The role played by managers is defined as persuasion and preaching at ABB. Managers at HP consist of modest team players who have learned how to manage different strategies. At J&J, managers encourage other people to work together. They also help lower level employees to learn from their failures and find solutions. Another characteristic of ambidexter managers working in companies is their seniority. Senior and experienced managers strengthen core values such as innovation, initiative, accountability, teamwork and autonomy within the organization (Tushman ve O'Reilly III, 1996: 24–7).

As it can be understood from the examples of HP, ABB and J&J, the existence of managers and employees who have achieved personal ambidexterity is the primary requirement for an ambidexterity organization. These people are able to encourage other employees to achieve their goals and objectives by giving importance to the learning process. In addition, placing factors such as creativity, innovation, openness to change, responsibility and initiative at the foundation of the corporate culture will contribute to the development of the organization's existing products and services, as well as to the creation of new products and services.

4.2 International Safety Research Inc.

The company consists of licensed security controllers and software developers who can efficiently switch between recertification activities for existing customers and new product development efforts associated with simulation products and other innovations. In order to balance activities for existing customers with new product development efforts, employees had to move from customer support to new product development activities. The ability of employees to switch from existing activities to new product development activities has provided benefits for the company. An efficient system was established to ensure that the lessons learned as a result of customer support activities were used in the process of improving upcoming products. Company leaders had to shift their focus from customer service to product development processes, along with other employees. The ambidexterity of the company leaders has been instrumental in other employees to have such mastery (Schreuders and Legesse, 2012: 18–19).

4.3 Apple

Over the past fifteen years, Apple has revolutionized the personal electronics, telecom, media and computer industries through a range of blockbuster products that present 'designer unique' integrated customer experiences. In the process, Apple has helped to accelerate the blurring of industry boundaries and has positioned itself to exert remarkable bargaining power on both customers and industry players with exceptional performance outcomes. Apple was the most valuable company traded on the stock exchange with a marketing value of $600 billion (US) in mid-October 2012, and consistently achieved net margins of over 20 per cent in industries where most competitors reached single-digit margins. Steve Jobs was the chief architect of the business model and the value system that led to this extraordinary performance. Apple's strategy is open to institutionalization and consistency, and it is not possible for its competetors to imitate it because it is rare and difficult. The critical aspect of Apple's strategy is its ability to balance intense efficiency in operations with extraordinary serial innovation and addictive product design. Both activities drive top-notch pricing and redefine the markets. This aggregation challenges the traditional notion that if a company's competitive advantage is based on immense efficiency and value, it will not need to invest more in innovation, service or design than necessary, and will actually try to reduce costs everywhere along the value chain. Apple has become more efficient than traditional cost leader, Dell, achieving serial innovation and extraordinary design in the products that it offers and in the business models that it creates. Apple achieved the lowest costs in the industry with simultaneous intensive efficiency levels, differentiating through innovation (in various dimensions including strategic, serial and incremental innovation). Apple's differentiation approach is exemplary. Apple's design prowess and capability to attract the best people while seamlessly integrating hardware and software is widely admitted. The company focuses on developing innovation capability by attracting the best employees and utilizing their creativity. Innovation has become a part of corporate culture. In addition to this capability, it is necessary to include deep collaboration, which enables innovation to be centralized in a single physical space. It has developed its presence in the market with branding promoted by radically developing new products, and has created a fashion trend for its followers (Heracleous, 2013: 92–5).

4.4 Otosan[1]

With the emergence of the pandemic, the digital transformation process in the automotive industry has accelerated. Digital platform and mobile applications started to be used in every field as people's physical contact was minimized. Ford Otosan started these digital transformation efforts before the pandemic. The 24/7 accessible HR application FObot, while answering questions about payroll and accrual information, administrative affairs, personal rights, operational affairs, occupational health and safety, training and development areas, it also provided great convenience to employees in respect of many issues such as short-time working and, operational processes during the pandemic period, and facilitated daily routines in employees working lives. Its digital infrastructure enabled them to respond instantly to changing customer expectations. It was able to quickly offer applications and solutions such as the 'Pick-Up, Delivery-to-Door' service to the Ford Digital Studio, Webchat and service customers. Looking back, it is seen that a successful working practice was implemented. The key factor in this success were the different working methodologies carried out within the company and the development of the infrastructure thanks to the ongoing digitalization efforts. In addition, by foreseeing change in digital transformation and customer expectations, intrapreneurship and innovation were opened in such a way so as to reach employees at all levels of the company and get their ideas. Intrapreneurship was supported by collecting spontaneous ideas within the scope of Industry 4.0 and digitalization. With the benefits of digitalization, customers expect to reach information in the fastest and most reliably way. In order to present this information quickly, an agile working system was formed within the company. In this context, problems were sought for solutions by engaging employees, and strong teams became better integrated with each other. The removal of hierarchy and bureaucratic insight revealed the potential of employees. The agile transformation team was formed and everyone started to work in small teams where they could demonstrate their potential within their fields of expertise. These teams are autonomous structures capable of making their own decisions and constantly improve themselves. With agile work, it has become easier for units and teams to transparently communicate with each other. Accordingly, employees make greater efforts to contribute more.

1 Content of the Otosan example has been compiled from the Ford website and blog.

5 Conclusion

The purpose of this book chapter is to demonstrate that individual ambidexterity takes on an important function on the road to organizational ambidexterity. As it is understood from the theoretical background and company examples, it is seen that individual ambidexterity plays an important role in the process of achieving organizational ambidexterity. Personal skills, ideas and strategies at the level of ambidexterity are required for developing the careers of employees, as well as the organization's ability to survive, compete and grow, especially in a dynamic and complex environment. As employees learn, develop and share new knowledge they are likely to have important and various skills. Thanks to these skills, it is expected that they will present new ideas, strategies and solutions within the scope of business functions. As these functions acquire new skills decisions can be made to implement more than one strategic decision at the same time by the organization's senior managers. In this regard, the importance of learning emerges. It can be said that learning starts from the individual and spreads throughout the organization. First, employees develop new skills by learning. Then, the business functions in which the employees work run the learning mechanism for the business and processes. Finally, together with the business functions, senior management gets involved in the learning process by following developments in the external environment, acquiring critical information and learning from its mistakes. However, the importance of an autonomous work environment, an organizational structure based on learning, an openness culture and management support means that employees can use the skills they have acquired through learning. If the individual cannot learn, the organization cannot learn.

It should be emphasized once again that organizational ambidexterity is the ability to implement different strategies at the same time. For example, when a cost leadership strategy for a certain product group or a differentiation strategy for another product group is required, there is a need for structure, culture and qualified employees who can both reduce costs in activities and add value to activities. The construction of structure and culture in a way that is open to innovation and learning, and employees' knowledge, experience, creative thinking and innovative behaviour that provides efficiency and value in processes make it possible to apply different strategies concurrently. Since the general environment and business environment are constantly changing, it is not possible for organizations to survive with a single strategy. Strategies may vary according to different periods and mixed strategies will need to be used together in the same period. In this respect, it is critical for organizations to have employees with different abilities, creative ideas and teamwork and learning skills, together with a flexible organizational structure and an innovative culture.

References

Adler, P. S., Goldoftas, B and Levine, D. I. (1999). Flexibility Versus Efficiency? A Case Study of Model Changeovers in the Toyota Production System, Organization Science, 10(1), 43–68.

Birkinshaw, J. and Gibson, C. (2004). Building Ambidexterity Into an Organization, MIT Sloan Management Review, Summer, 47–55.

Birkinshaw, J. and Gupta, K. (2013). Clarifying The Distinctive Contribution of Ambidexterity to the Field of Organization Studie, Academy of Management Perspectives, 27(4), 287–298.

Brion, S. and Mothe, C. (2016). Organizational Context and Innovation Ambidexterity: Is Creativity the Missing Link? XXVe conférence de l'AIMS, Tunis, Tunisia, 1–21.

Cheng, Y. T. and Van de Hen, A. H. (1996). Learning the Innovation Journey: Order out of Chaos? Organization Science, 7(6), 593–614.

Cingöz, A. and Akdoğan, A. (2015). Örgütsel Ustalık (Organizational Ambidexterity): Örgütsel Ustalık Düzeyini Belirlemede Araştırıcı ve Yararlanıcı Stratejilerin Etkileşimsel Rolü, Aksaray Üniversitesi İktisadi ve İdari Bilimler Fakültesi Dergisi, 7(1), 59–67.

Çiftçi, G. E. (2017). Örgütsel Ustalık Çalışmalarının Personel Güçlendirme Üzerinde Etkisi, International Journal of Academic Value Studies, 3(10), 188–202.

Ensari, H. (1998). Öğrenen Organizasyon Olarak Okul, M.Ü. Atatürk Eğitim Fakültesi Eğitim Bilimleri Dergisi, Number 10, 97–111.

Fettahlıoğlu, Ö. O., Fettahlıoğlu, H. S. and Birin, C. (2016). Pazarlama Sektöründe Örgütsel Ustalığa Ulaşabilme Yolunda Otantik Liderlik Davranışlarının Rolü, 3rd International Congress on Social Sciences, Antalya, 400–412.

Floyd, S. W. and Lane, P. J. (2000). Strategizing Throughout the Organization: Managing Role Conflict in Strategic Renewal, Academy of Management Review, 25(1), 154–177.

Heracleous, L. (2013). Quantum Strategy at Apple Inc., Organizational Dynamics, 42, 92–99.

http://www.tdk.gov.tr (02.03.2021).

Kalkan, V. D. (2006). Örgütsel Öğrenme ve Bilgi Yönetimi: Kesişim ve Ayrışma Noktaları, Elektronik Sosyal Bilimler Dergisi, 5(16), 22–36.

Koçel, T. (2011). İşletme Yöneticiliği, Beta Yayınevi, 3–729.

Lee, Y. J. and Lee, J. H. (2016). Knowledge Workers' Ambidexterity: Conceptual Separation of Competencies and Behavioural Dispositions, Asian Journal of Technology Innovation, 24(1), 22–40.

March, J. G. (1991). Exploration and Exploitation In Organizational Learning, Organization Science, 2(1), 71–87.

Mom, T. J. M., Van Den Bosch, F. A. J., and Volberda, H. W. (2007). Investigating Managers' Exploration and Exploitation Activities: The Influence of Top-Down, Bottom-Up, and Horizontal Knowledge Inflows, Journal of Management Studies, 44(6), 910–931.

Mom, T. J. M., Fourne, S. P. L and Jansen, J. J. P. (2015). Managers' Work Experience, Ambidexterity, and Performance: The Contingency Role of The Work Context, Human Resource Management, 54(1), 133–153.

O'Reilly, C. A and Tushman, M. L. (2004). The Ambidextrous Organization, Harvard Business Review, April, 74–81.

O'Reilly, C. A. and Tushman, M. L. (2011). Organizational Ambidexterity in Action: How Managers Explore and Exploit, California Management Review, 53(4), 5–22.

Öneren, M. (2008). İşletmelerde Öğrenen Örgütler Yaklaşımı, ZKÜ Sosyal Bilimler Dergisi, 4(7), 163–178.

Parmentier, G. and Picq, T. (2016). Managing Creative Teams in Small Ambidextrous Organizations: The Case of Videogames, International Journal of Arts Management, 19(1), 16–30.

Schreuders, J. and Legesse, A. (2012). Organizational Ambidexterity: How Small Technology Firms Balance Innovation and Support, Technology Innovation Management Review, February, 17–21.

Senge, P. (1993). Beşinci Displin, İldeniz, A and Doğukan, A (Trans.), Yapı Kredi Yayınları, İstanbul.

Sheremata, W. A. (2000). Centrifugal and Centripetal Forces In Radical New Product Development Under Time Pressure, Academy of Management Review, 25(2), 389–408.

Simsek, Z., Ling, Y. and Veiga, J. F. (2006). Ambidexterity and Performance in Small-to Medium-Sized Firms: The Pivotal Role of Top Management Team Behavioural Integration, Journal of Management, 32(5), 646–672.

Teece, D. J. (2007). Explicating Dynamic Capabilities: The Nature and Microfoundations of (Sustainable) Enterprise Performance, Strategic Management Journal, 28, 1319–1350.

Tushman, M. L. and O'Reilly III, C. A. (1996). Ambidextrous Organizations: Managing Evolutionary and Revolutionary Change, California Management Review, 38(4), 8–30.

Vallina, A. S., Luzón, M. D. M and Marqués, M. G. (2020). From Individual to Team Ambidexterity: The Moderating Role of Collaborative Behaviour and International Experience, Knowledge Management Research and Practice, 1–15.

Wei, Z., Yi, Y. and Guo, H. (2014). Organizational Learning Ambidexterity, Strategic Flexibility, and New Product Development, Journal of Product Innovation Management, 31(4), 832–847.

Resül Yazıcı and Serkan Varsak

The Place and Importance of the Turkish Insurance Sector in the Risk Management of Businesses

1 Introduction

While global financialization and widespread global trade offer new opportunities to businesses, they may also leave businesses face-to-face with both local and global threats. Global commercial and financial threats make business management processes more difficult and lead companies to seek solutions in this context. Businesses that have completed the institutionalization process achieve better results against global financial and commercial risks than businesses that have not completed the institutionalization process. It is an undeniable fact that business myopia and measures taken to eliminate this problem will play an active role in the completion of the institutionalization processes of companies in terms of risk management regarding the adaptation of the insurance sector to this process, and minimizing the risk as well as active and public support for internal and external audit processes.

Permanent financial stability, which has a significant impact on macroeconomic balance, requires the definition of new processes against risk in business management in the global financial system. This process begins with the formation of risk management awareness and continues with the construction of the infrastructure institutionalization process in risk management. The process is completed by creating an awareness of insurance and of being insured by corporate infrastructure companies in risk management. In this regard, risk management awareness and the basic elements and principles that constitute the infrastructure of this awareness are summarized in Table 1 (COSO, 2020).

Tab. 1: *COSO Corporate Risk Management, Five Elements Related to Someone and 20 Principles Related to Them*

Governance and Culture	**Strategy and Goal Setting**	**Performance**	**Review and Correction**	**Information, Communication and Reporting**
1. Board of Directors Implements Risk Oversight	6. Analyses the Business Environment	10. Defines the risk	15. Evaluates Major Changes	18. Makes Uses of Information and Technology Advantages
2. Creates Operational Structures	7.Determines the Risk Appetite	11. Evaluates the Severity of Risks	16. Reviews Risks and Performance	19.Communicates Risk Information
3.Defines the Desired Culture	8. Evaluates Alternative Strategies	12. Prioritizes Risks	17. Monitors Developments in Corporate Risk Management	20. Reports on Risk, Culture and Performance
4. Committed to Fundamental Values	9.Formulate Business Objectives	13. Applies Reactions to Risks		
5. Attracts, Develops and Retains Talented Personnel		14. Enhances Portfolio Perspective		

The COSO (The Committee of Sponsoring Organizations of the Treadway Commission) corporate risk management system offers suggestions that enable companies to complete the necessary infrastructure in risk management, and develop internal control processes.

In order to complete the risk management infrastructure, the process must be approached as a whole and the process related to the company's eigenvalues must be compatible. The success of the process is directly proportional to the internalization of risk management and its applicability with the decisions taken. However, the corporate risk management process and its success cannot be completed solely through internal dynamics. The completion of the process will be achieved after close contact with established and external stakeholders, as well as internal stakeholders. In this regard, the insurance sector is the most prominent complement to corporate risk management.

2 Importance of the Insurance Sector in Risk Management and Future Trends

The insurance sector is an important branch of the financial sector which assesses risks and conditions, such as social, political and technological conditions, natural environment and business environment will create on individual or institutional structures on a large or small scale and buys those risks for a certain premium. Tuncay (2009: 119) summarizes the difference of the insurance sector with the banking sector as follows: In case of any loan, the balance sheet is followed, be collateralized and information about the asset project is obtained. When the likely situation changes course, the risk changes bi-directionally. Although it is not known in advance when the risk will occur, there is also the withdrawal of the loan whose collateral structure dropped and whose nature has changed and there is the strengthening of control mechanisms. However, the risk management of both the sector and its customers will be even more difficult due to the increasing recent risks in the insurance sector.

2.1 The Main Impact Areas of Changing Conditions in the Insurance Sector

Most of the risks classified in Table 3, according to SONAR (2020) and 'Insurance Sector Supports and Products' in the last column of Table 2, are due to unprecedented innovations or new developments in the society and/or insurance framework conditions. These risks have a very high potential to emerge at any time, causing significant damage. Climate change is an example. This risk was noted years ago by Swiss Re (The Swiss Re Group, one of the largest reinsurance companies). The risk arose at that moment, but the associated (and challenging) uncertainties still remain. The impact of climate change and pandemics such as the recent outbreak of the coronavirus on life and health insurance are an example of this.

Tab. 2: *Support and Products that the Insurance Sector Can Provide in the Management of Risks Faced by Businesses*

Risks	**Suggestions**
Systemic Risks	**Insurance Sector Support and Products**
Economic Structure Risks Inflation Risk Regulatory Risks Financial System Risks Interest Rate risk Currency Risk Credit Contraction Problem	Liability Insurances Surety Insurance (Alternative to Letters of Guarantee) Credit Insurance
Market Risks Market and Market Risk Business-Specific Risks Problems in Debt Collection Few Customer Dependence Change in Customer Preferences and Competition Risks Business Interruption Risk for Various Reasons Bankruptcy / Concordat Risk Political Risk	Liability Insurances Credit Insurance Workplace Package Insurance Business Interruption Insurance
Non-Systemic Risks	
Operational Risk Workflow Risks Management Risk	Various Insurances Required by Operational Activities (Workplace / Machinery Breakdown / Electronic Equipment Insurance etc.)
Mistakes in Investment Strategy Capital Insufficiency Risk	Insurance Awareness, Financial Literacy Should Be Created Through Incentives

Swiss Re identified twenty-three macro trends as the risks of today and tomorrow as shown in Table 1. According to SONAR (2020), the management of these risks, which are detailed in the table under four main groups and are related to each other, is very important for the insurance sector and all parties exposed to them.

2.1.1. The Impact of Changes in the Social Environment

Those who flee poverty and war, countries receiving migration constitute important risks for cities that need to be managed. The United Nations Department of Economic and Social Affairs estimates that around 2.5 billion people living in urban environments worldwide will reach 5 billion in 2030. In addition to the social and/or ultranationalist conflicts caused by migration to cities, urbanization and increasing populations, disasters, especially natural disasters, have the potential to cause great financial loss to the business world. It might deepen the unemployment, restlessness and social inequality caused by the inability to provide the training that is appropriate for the work. With the support of social media, the transformation of anger movements into masses increases social unrest (SONAR, 2020: 8).

Tab. 3: *Opportunities and Risks to be Managed by the Global and Local Scale Insurance Sector*

Social Environmentx	**Political Environment**	**Technology and Natural Environment**	**Competitive Environment in the Insurance Sector**
Increase in migration and urbanization risk	Public Sector Risk Passes to Private Sector	Climate Change and Resource Scarcity	Reinsurance / Insurance Supply Chain Divergence
Longevity and Radical Medical Innovation	Protectionism and Partial Editing	Structural Change in Energy Production, Distribution and Consumption	The Rise of Reinsurance
Connected and Collaborative Community	Increasing Nationalism Movements	Increasing Digital and Cyber Risk	Strategic Partnerships with Non-Insurance Companies and Institutions
Mass Migration and Urbanization	Instability of Geopolitical and Economic Systems	The Importance and Protection of Data as an Asset	The Globalization of Regional Champions
Lack of Training for the Job	Low Yield Environment and Inflation Risk	Technology Applications as a Productivity Tool	Increasing Digital Customer Relations
Rising Social Inequality and Unrest		Disruptive Digital Technologies	
		Robotic and Autonomous Systems	

Source: SONAR (2020)

2.1.2. The Effect of Changes in the Political Environment

The benefits of the globalization movement have slowed down over the past ten years. The share of international investment, trade, bank loans and supply chains in world GDP is shrinking and stagnating. Multilateralism, the globalization of trade created by the World Trade Organization, are at risk. Regulations on a global scale (rules on privacy, data and espionage) are being broken down. The practices of regulating tax systems in order for companies to return to their homeland have begun to be predominant on a global scale. Growth on a global scale has slowed while central banks' maneuvering space has become increasingly limited, leading to inflation risks. The fact that central banks can be deprived of the tools and the independence to overcome inflation, and that fiscal policy is dominant, may also run against globalization. Likewise, aging populations in the richer countries mean that pension and health systems will keep pressure on public finances (SONAR, 2020: 9).

2.1.3 The Impact of Changes in Technology and the Natural Environment

The Fourth Industrial Revolution achieved rapid progress with digital analytical technologies that can quickly analyse large amounts of structured and unstructured data (Big Data), the Internet of Things (IOT), applications and process automation. Data obtained through technological advances has been and continues to be a key differentiator in the business world, including the insurance sector, because technologies such as big data and cloud computing can greatly increase data collection, storage and information processing efficiency. In the insurance sector, for example, thanks to a combination of more data and better analytics, it may be easier to better insure products that were previously difficult to price, and to detect fraud.

While technological developments give those who have various data the advantage of using them, they also keep them under pressure in terms of the privacy of data and protecting and preventing data from passing into others' hands. This will increase the pressure of regulatory structures. Because the risks arising from cyber attacks will affect all parties, their frequency and severity are expected to increase significantly. Recent examples show the extent to which unprepared companies and government agencies are threatened by such attacks. Therefore, cyber risk can offer one of the biggest opportunities for the insurance sector, but also constitutes one of the biggest challenges. However, it will be a great success to keep pace with changes in the field of cyber and technology, and to develop solutions to meet the constantly evolving risks that arise. This success of the insurance sector should also be reflected in businesses (SONAR, 2020: 10).

2.1.4 The Effect of Increasing Competition on the Insurance Sector

Traditional insurance companies are working to reshape their systems and processes to serve their consumer base with next-generation insurance solutions. Reinsurers and intermediaries try to access distribution channels and risks outside the traditional value chain. When international reinsurers and insurance companies face further restrictions on data privacy and operational issues regarding legacy systems, innovative business models and digital ecosystems are likely to emerge, starting with fast-growing markets. These might significantly affect the global reinsurer and insurance supply chain. Digital ecosystems will be able to provide good opportunities for insurance companies to interact with potential customers. Strategic partnerships in many sectors appear to be a key element in the development of innovative insurance solutions. Investments in digital platforms by technology giants and insurtech (Insurance Technologies) startups have been steadily increasing since 2014 (SONAR, 2020: 11).

2.2 Development of Insurance Awareness in Risk Management and the Importance of Insurance Products

While the skill of managers is an important factor in the management of the risks that businesses will face, an insurance awareness must be formed in the sense of selling the systemic risks to people. However, this awareness has not been formed for various reasons. According to Özüdoğru and Çetin (2017: 61), Turkish people become more sensitive to and choose to take measures against a future event only after it has happened.

Therefore, these issues should be included in financial literacy training programs. In addition to the inadequacy in risk predictions and management, the risks listed in Table 2, whose effects are increasing day by day, adversely affect and will affect the continuity of businesses. Businesses should immediately analyse these risks, take out the necessary insurances and coverages and transfer the systemic or non-systemic risks they may face to insurance companies. Below are the risks that may arise and certain types of insurance policies that can be taken out against them.

2.2.1 Importance of Credit Insurance: State Supported Commercial Receivable Insurance for SMEs

Trade Receivables Insurance is a system that guarantees the receivables of businesses. Through the intelligence networks in the possession of insurance companies, the risk management of receivables can be facilitated by monitoring the financial status of the customers of businesses that purchase credit insurance. In addition to compensating for losses that may arise due to non-payment of a trade receivable, this product can also pay compensation in cases of bankruptcy or defaults.

For the purpose of the system of government-supported trade receivable insurance for small and medium sized enterprises (SMEs), ensuring that it is structured and operated in a way that will serve all businesses within the scope can serve many of the following purposes:

- Creating insurance awareness in businesses
- It will be possible to create rating notes for the businesses in the system as the awareness of credit insurance becomes more widespread.
- These rating notes can help solve the problems arising from asymmetric information and help prevent businesses from undergoing processes such as bankruptcy and arrangements for bankruptcy due to receivables risk.
- As the term sales opportunities without credit insurance will be narrowed, the informal economy will shrink and thus tax revenues will increase. Thus, the borrowing demand of the Republic of Turkey Ministry of Treasury and Finance from the financial system due to budget deficits may decrease. This way, thanks to lower interest rates in the banking sector, crowding out the private sector and the increase in the financing costs of businesses can be prevented. Ultimately, it may enable the management of the risk of financial failure of businesses thanks to the reduction of systemic risk in the financial system.

The last benefit is an example of the fact that the insurance sector can indirectly support the banking sector, because the strengthening of the insurance sector together with the banking sector may serve to provide an increase of depth in the financial system and to reduce the dependence of businesses on banks. In this regard, it would be a good development to create an alternative to letters of guarantee given by banks, which are considered non-cash loans, in the form of surety insurance. Such competition between the two sectors may prevent the non-cash loan limits of businesses from being blocked and may allow commission fees to be reduced.

2.2.2 *The Importance of the Insurance Sector in Financial Losses Caused by Climate Change and Epidemics*

In terms of systemic risk, the impact of climate change as a result of global warming and pandemics such as coronavirus has been severe. The importance of the insurance sector has increased and may further increase in compensating for financial losses that may arise due to the recent increase in the number and severity of these events. Although climate change and the coronavirus pandemic will affect many branches of the insurance sector, property insurance will cover most out of this effect. It is anticipated that this effect will be felt more clearly in coastal regions with dense settlements as a result of rising water levels, floods and storms. Global warming and the coronavirus pandemic have also begun to affect the health branch closely. The increase in forest fires, the negative effects of floods and droughts on harvests and the decrease in production capacity also directly affect agricultural insurance. Also, considering the statistical increase in accident rates due to the climate change, it is predicted that climate change will also affect motor vehicle insurance (Temelli, 2016: 9).

2.2.3 The Importance of Business Interruption and Profit Loss Insurances

The increase in compensation amounts regarding business interruption insurance, which has occurred in recent years due to the damage caused, in particular, by natural disasters or crises, highlights the importance of this type of insurance. According to Kulan (2018: 4), Business interruption insurance is intended to eliminate the financial loss that reduces profits or causes loss due to interruption of a company's operation as a result of an event covered by insurance.

2.2.4 The Importance of Loss of Profit Insurances Due to Delays of Work

Since businesses use loans by pledging as collateral the assets of their projects undertaken in the form of privatization and 'build-operate-transfer', committing to repay their loan debts with the proceeds from the projects leads them to take important risks. For example: 'Strict provisions regarding delays in the work program have begun to be added to contracts between project owners and financiers and hence project owners and contractors. The fact that project owners and contractors face serious financial risks for said reasons has led to a significant increase in the demand for "Advance Loss of Profit Insurance (ALOP)"'. (Reasürör, 2017: 3). Today, the demand for this coverage is increasing day by day for reasons such as the increase in large and complex projects, private sector investments, new technologies used and increased awareness among the insured' (Temelli, 2017: 25).

2.2.5 The Importance of Cyber Risk Insurance

While technological possibilities have been developing at a dizzying pace in recent years, the fact that companies face cyber threats may increase the demand for insurance products in this area. Because globalization, diversification of channels in access to the market and the dependence of these areas on information technologies leave companies open to digital threats. 'The capabilities of pirates/hackers increase over time, and attacks and fraudulent acts become more sophisticated and widespread. In addition, since cyber-attacks pose a risk both in terms of economy and the national security of countries, constant new legislation and administrative measures impose additional legal obligations on companies/organizations, which creates a need for new insurance coverages' (Ünal, 2017: 4).

According to the Zurich Insurance Group (2015: 19–20), the ones who are most concerned about cyber attacks are businesses located in Malaysia, which ranks this risk at fifth in the threat lists, and Turkey and the United States, which rank this risk at sixth. In this research, stealing money and savings in Turkey, Austria and the United States is considered among the top three cyber risks. Therefore, it is necessary to establish the necessary insurance and coverage limits for businesses exposed to this systemic risk.

With recent events, cyber risk insurance has become a globally important insurance product. As the number of organizations taking out cyber risk policies increases in Turkey, and because insurance companies see an increase in the number of cyber incidents, trust in insurance coverage is expected to be positively affected (Marsh and TÜSİAD, 2020: 15).

2.2.6 The Importance of Public Liability Insurance

In general, public liability insurance covers the indemnity claims payable to third parties by employers due to accidents that may occur in the workplace; by manufacturers due to misuse of the produced goods and services by consumers; and by the self-employed due to mistakes in their professional practices.

According to Ünal (2019: 19), the status of liability insurances is different when it comes to risk management. Classical damage modeling approaches are less useful in this area. Many factors such as economic growth and technological developments, legislative changes, increased awareness of seeking one's rights, globalization and the emergence of the social media reveal new obligation risks and cause current risks to change rapidly and unpredictably.

2.2.7 The Importance of Insurances Against Terrorism Risks

Risks from terrorist activity have become a global threat as it became an international phenomenon due to the rapid development of means of transportation and communication, the increase in technological opportunities that enable development of new weapons and equipment, and organic ties and cooperation between terrorist organizations regarding intelligence, training, logistics, financing and action methods, which became increasingly stronger. Especially, recent developments show that terrorist acts can bypass even the most robust security systems of the most powerful states, and have become a cross-border phenomenon that cannot be prevented merely through military measures, and no country is exempt from this threat, whether it carries geopolitical risk or not (Karakoyunlu, 2017: 10).

3 Conclusion

The financial transformations in the global system, the increasing volume of global trade and the opportunities and threats encountered in this context have brought to the agenda the requirement for businesses to create an institutional risk management infrastructure in order protect themselves. Business risk management processes bring about the requirement to consider not only internal stakeholders and the internal dynamics of companies, but also their external stakeholders and external dynamics outside the control of the businesses. In this regard, the insurance sector plays a complementary role in the risk management processes of companies with its new products and methods.

Among these products mentioned in the last part of the study, credit insurance and government-supported trade receivable insurance for SMEs, which entered into force in 2018, are considered to be very important. If this product can become popular, that is, as the term sales opportunities without receivables insurance will be narrowed, the informal economy will shrink and thus it will be possible to increase the tax revenues of the public. Thus, the borrowing demand of the Republic of Turkey Ministry of Treasury and Finance from the financial system due to budget deficits may decrease. This way, thanks to lower interest rates from the banking sector, crowding out the private sector and an increase in the financing costs of businesses can be prevented. Ultimately, businesses may be more successful in managing the risk of financial failure thanks to the reduction of systemic risks in the financial system.

These indirect supports that the insurance sector can give to the banking sector are important. Because the strengthening of the insurance sector together with the banking sector may serve to provide more depth in the financial system and reduce the dependence of businesses on banks. In this regard, it is good that insurance companies have created an alternative to letters of guarantee given by banks, which are considered non-cash loans, with products in the form of surety insurance. Such competition between the two sectors may prevent the non-cash loan limits of businesses from being blocked and may allow a reduction of commission fees to be incurred.

References

COSO (2019). Enterprise Risk Management Integrating with Strategy and Performance Executive Summary, 29 Kasım 2020 tarihinde https://www.coso.org/Documents/2017-COSO-ERM-Integrating-with-Strategy-and-Performance-ExecutiveSummary.pdf adresinden erişildi.

Karakoyunlu, G. (2017). Terör Riskine Yönelik Ulusal Ölçekte Uygulamalar, Reasürör Dergisi, Ocak 2017, 25 Aralık 2020 tarihinde http://www.millire.com/dergi/SAYI_103.pdf adresinden erişildi.

Kulan, N.E. (2018). İş Durması Riski ve Modellemesi, Reasürör Dergisi, Nisan 2018, 25 Aralık 2020 tarihinde http://www.millire.com/dergi/SAYI_108.pdf adresinden erişildi.

Marsh and TÜSİAD. (2020). 2020 Türkiye Siber Risk Algı Araştırması. 25 Aralık 2020 tarihinde file:///C:/Users/9480/Desktop/Sigorta/2020_siber_risk_algi_arastirmasi.pdf adresinden erişildi.

Özüdoğru, H. Ve Çetin, Ç. (2017). Türkiye de Sigortacılıkta Güncel Sorunlar, 3.Sektör Sosyal Ekonomi Dergisi, Cilt:52, Sayı:2, 57–70.

Reasürör, (2017). Reasürör Gözüyle, 27Aralık 2020 tarihinde http://www.millire.com/dergi/SAYI_106.pdf adresinden erişildi.

SONAR (2019). New Emerging Risk Insights, May 2019, Swiss Re SONAR,, 27Aralık 2020 tarihinde https://www.swissre.com/dam/jcr:5916802c-cf6b-4c67-9d4239cf80c4b00d/ SONAR%20Publication%202019_WEB_quality.pdf adresinden erişildi.

Temelli, A. (2016). İklim Değişikliğinin Dünya, Türkiye ve Sigorta Sektörü Üzerindeki Etkileri, Reasürör Dergisi, Ocak 2016, 1 Aralık 2020 tarihinde http://www.millire.com/ dergi/SAYI_99.pdf adresinden erişildi.

Temelli, A. (2017). İşin Gecikmesinden Kaynaklı Kâr Kaybı Sigortası ve Uygulamada Karşılaşılan Sorunlar, Reasürör Dergisi, Ekim 2017, 27Aralık 2020 tarihinde http://www.millire.com/dergi/SAYI_106.pdf adresinden erişildi.

Tuncay, E. (2009). Türk Finans ve Bankacılık Sisteminde Küresel Dalgalanma Karşısında Risklerin Yönetimi, Yeni Yüzyılda Bankacılık Küresel Riskler ve Bankalarda Sermaye Yönetiminde Yeni Arayışlar (Yayına Hazırlayanlar: Targan Ünal, Kadir Tuna, Çiğdem Börke Tunalı), Derin Yayınları, İstanbul.

Ünal, S. (2017). Siber Risk Sigortalarının Önemi Hızla Artıyor, Reasürör Dergisi, Temmuz 2017, 20 Ocak 2021 tarihinde, http://www.millire.com/dergi/SAYI_105.pdf adresinden erişildi.

Ünal, S. (2019) Sorumluluk Sigortalarında Risk Yönetimi Üzerine Bir Değerlendirme Reasürör Dergisi, Ekim 2019, 20 Ocak 2021 tarihinde http://www.millire.com/dergi/SAYI_114.pdf adresinden erişildi.

Zurich Insurance Group (2015). Küçük ve Orta Ölçekli İşletmelerin Siber Güvenlik Kaygıları İki Kat Arttı, (Reactions Aralık 2015 Çeviren: Selçuk Ünal, Reasürör Dergisi, Ocak 2016, 20 Ocak 2021 tarihinde http://www.millire.com/dergi/SAYI_99.pdf adresinden erişildi.

www.ingramcontent.com/pod-product-compliance
Ingram Content Group UK Ltd.
Pitfield, Milton Keynes, MK11 3LW, UK
UKHW021240300926
15471UKWH00014B/863

9 783631 849330